Best Food
for Your
Baby & Toddler

From First Foods to Meals
Your Child Will Love

D0055113

Jeannette L. Bessinger, CHHC with
Tracee Yablon-Brenner, RD, CHHC

STERLING

New York / London
www.sterlingpublishing.com

This book and the information contained in this book are for general educational and informational uses only. Nothing contained in this book should be construed as or intended to be used for medical diagnosis or treatment. Users are encouraged to confirm the information contained herein with other sources and review the information carefully with their physicians or qualified health-care providers. The information is not intended to replace medical advice offered by physicians or health-care providers. Should you have any health-care-related questions, please call or see your physician or other qualified health-care provider before embarking on a new treatment, diet, or fitness program. The authors and publisher will not be liable for any direct, indirect, consequential, special, exemplary, or other damages arising therefrom.

Grateful acknowledgment is made to *Great Expectations: The Essential Guide to Breastfeeding* by Marianne Niefert, MD, for the medications and breastfeeding information on pp. 74-76. Used by permission.

STERLING and the distinctive Sterling logo are registered trademarks of Sterling Publishing Co., Inc.

10 9 8 7 6 5 4 3 2 1

Published by Sterling Publishing Co., Inc.
387 Park Avenue South, New York, NY 10016
Text © 2010 by Jeannette Bessinger and Tracee Yablon-Brenner
Illustrations © 2009 by Laura Hartman-Maestro
Nutrition label © 2010 by Sterling Publishing
Distributed in Canada by Sterling Publishing
c/o Canadian Manda Group, 165 Dufferin Street
Toronto, Ontario, Canada M6K 3H6
Distributed in the United Kingdom by GMC Distribution Services
Castle Place, 166 High Street, Lewes, East Sussex, England BN7 1XU
Distributed in Australia by Capricorn Link (Australia) Pty. Ltd.
P.O. Box 704, Windsor, NSW 2756, Australia

Sterling ISBN 978-1-4027-3618-6

For information about custom editions, special sales, premium and corporate purchases, please contact Sterling Special Sales Department at 800-805-5489 or specialsales@sterlingpub.com.

Dedication and Acknowledgments

This book is dedicated to all parents trying to nourish their children well.

Special dedication from Jeannette with great love to Frank, Karen, Micah and Ellen Knapp, extraordinary brothers, sisters-in-law, and parents.

Special dedication from Tracee to her sister and brother-in-law, Jodee and Brian Chizever, who are raising an infant and toddler of their own.

The authors would like to thank our phenomenal and hard-working agents, Marilyn Allen and Coleen O'Shea; Sterling's amazing team, and especially our miracle-working editors Jennifer Williams and Melanie Gold. We would also like to thank Dr. Larry Rosen for his support, and Stacey Antine, for all of her tremendous suggestions and writing the fabulous Foreword.

Jeannette's Acknowledgments
Special thanks to our experts Barbara Robinson, RD, certified pediatric nutrition specialist; Eileen Teixeira, RN, obstetrics, lactation specialist; Susan Mudd, MS, CNS, nutritional consultant and research; and Suzanne Copp, MS, clinical nutritionist, researcher, and editor; and Dr. Jonny Bowden, nutrition and laughter guru; my core parents team, especially super-mom Jodi Bass, Ruth, Sam, Allison, and Kevin Jernigan, Jessica Curtis, the Kerr crew (as always!), and the NJ tasters team!

Tracee's Acknowledgments
Special thanks to Leah Rinaldi, Jessica Scanlon, Kevin Bernhardt, D' Amico's Farm; my tasting team Lesley and Ava Carboneri, Leo and Isabel Carvajal, Gideon and Serafina Chizever, the Shea family, Emily, Alana, the neighborhood gang; and Barbara Hayes and her students, who have wonderful taste!

Contents

Foreword

By the time they're 3 years old, most kids have already begun to establish strong preferences for food, which can be a blessing or a challenge! *Great Expectations: Best Food for Your Baby & Toddler* is a comprehensive, must-read feeding guide for every parent.

Most parents learn about food and cooking from their parents, but a lot has changed since we grew up. Nearly everyone is living in an artificial environment that is literally making them sick—the rates of obesity and chronic disease are staggering. If you are committed to raising healthy children, it's time to change the channel and tune into the natural world. *Great Expectations: Best Food for Your Baby & Toddler* offers real-world tips to help you along the journey to raising a strong, healthy child.

- **Be a role model.** Many moms tell me that they don't like vegetables or that their husbands won't eat veggies at the dinner table. At the same time, they want their kids to eat all of their veggies. This wish simply won't come true if parents don't model the desired behaviors. Need some motivation? Carefully read Part I, *They Are What They Eat*, because the facts are powerful: Prevention is definitely the right way to go to ensure your baby's long-term health and wellness.
- **Go natural!** At HealthBarn USA we explore the natural world by learning about food and nutrition through planting, harvesting, and cooking with fresh seasonal foods. Simply stated, natural foods, whether plant or animal, are the best foods for your baby and toddler. Jeannette and Tracee embrace this concept and make it super easy for you to go natural, beginning with your baby's first bite! Part II, *Feeding Your Child*, walks you through the recommended, safe, and nutritious foods for each age group, and includes simple, homemade recipes for serving and storing delicious, nutrient-packed foods. If you need to take baby steps, the Resources section makes excellent recommendations for choosing and buying nutritious prepared baby foods, and "Decoding Food Labels" in Chapter 3 shows you how to identify and keep artificial ingredients and foods off the kitchen table.
- **Involve your children.** Kids love to cook. As soon as they are able, involve them in mixing, stirring, and tasting! This is great for their gross motor skill development, too. The Baked Apple and Soft Oatmeal Cookies in Chapter 10 are delicious and a good starting point to get your little ones excited about helping and tasting.
- **Try it, you'll like it.** We're all about trying fresh, natural foods at HealthBarn USA. The section titled "Healthy Strategies for Raising a Natural Eater" (6 to 9 months) includes great tips to help your child enjoy a wide range of foods for balanced nutrition.
- **Be persistent.** Introducing a new food to your baby or toddler can be challenging, but keep at

it, because sometimes it takes *fifteen tries* before your little one will gobble it up!

- **Go light on sweet beverages.** Beverages are a quick way to fill up on empty calories. Skip the soda and juice and give your young ones milk or water instead.
- **Choose playdates wisely.** Many moms tell me how healthy their children's eating habits are—until they head out to a playdate, where they get super charged on highly processed foods and drinks loaded with sugar! Depending on where you live, it may be easy or challenging to find other parents who share your views on parenting and food, but it's definitely worth the effort.
- **Cooking is cool.** Cooking is simple and doesn't require the time or effort Julia Child poured into it. Start slowly, and as you build up confidence and successes in the kitchen, you will expand your repertoire. For example, Jeannette and Tracee show you how easy it is to blanch, rather than boil, fresh produce to make veggies the way kids love them—crunchy, not mushy. To get started, check out the great recipes in Part III!
- **Be patient.** Food is fundamental to nurturing yourself and your children, so be patient with the process and take deep breaths when things don't go exactly as planned.
- **Make family mealtime, family fun time.** Turn off the TV, BlackBerry, and other electronic devices and sit down at the table to share a family meal every day, if possible. The family meal is disappearing, but it is one of the

most important things you can do for your children's health. Research supporting the family meal is compelling, especially in the teen years, where it has been shown to reduce pregnancy and alcohol and drug abuse, as well as enhance school performance. Good communication and getting the whole family excited about sharing a meal is the key to a happy, healthy experience. That's why Chapter 11 is so great—the whole family can enjoy all the recipes! Check out Spinach Lasagna, Veggie Pancakes, Simple Fried Rice and Pesto Sauce (yes, kids love the stuff).

Great Expectations: Best Food for Your Baby & Toddler will definitely become your family's go-to guide for feeding your baby and toddler, but it offers so much more than meal plans and recipes. The sections on breastfeeding are extremely supportive. Chapter 5 offers delicious and nutritious snack suggestions for nursing moms, and Chapter 3 goes into the scientific aspects of your baby's nutritional needs. And, if you are concerned about food allergies, there are allergen alert write-ups throughout the book so you know what to look for at different stages of your child's development. I'm sure you will use this comprehensive resource often, so keep it within reach in the kitchen or at your bedside for inspirational browsing.

—Stacey Antine, MS, RD, Founder and CEO, HealthBarn USA, Inc., a proven leader in healthy lifestyle education for children and families. www.healthbarnusa.com.

Introduction

Welcome, welcome to the new baby in your life! You are embarking on a very special journey in which you and your little one will change and grow beyond what you ever thought possible. The work of raising your small child is demanding, at times exhausting, and will be filled with some of the most rewarding moments of your life. You want to give your baby the best of everything, and that giving often begins with her first mouthful of food.

As adults we tend to take food and eating for granted. After all, you've been eating several times a day since the moment *you* were born, right? But food is a vital, essential part of life. It's not only your child's main fuel, but it has the power to help her double in size in the first 6 months of her life, and to energize her developing limbs as she learns to walk. Healthy food can have more protective power than medicines to strengthen her young immune system. One of the most important things you can do for the health of your new child is to support her tiny growing body with the thoughtful, loving introduction of healthy foods and drinks.

The way you nurse your child and the types of foods you give her in her first years can impact her eating preferences and habits for a lifetime. While it is vital for you to understand a growing baby's nutritional needs, and to be aware of some important dos and don'ts of feeding in these early years, she will be your partner and teacher in the process, her body and behaviors helping you to understand what she needs at each stage of her development.

On a more somber note, you may be aware of the growing health challenges many of our older children are struggling with today. We are facing an epidemic of childhood obesity and other related health issues. As a lead investigator and strategist on a citywide obesity intervention plan, I worked in depth with state health department officials, pediatricians, nursing consultants, and, of course, lots of busy parents and their families. I learned first hand how much harder it is to fix an existing problem than to prevent it from occurring in the first place.

It turns out that the best evidence-based strategies for preventing childhood obesity are the same practices we encourage for building a young child's nutritional health from the start: breastfeeding when possible, respecting and supporting a baby's hunger and satiety (satisfaction) cues, and training a young toddler's tongue to enjoy the tastes and textures of natural healthy foods.

Today's American kids eat a lot of commercially prepared, prepackaged meals and treats. They also eat out regularly, especially at "family style" chains and fast-food restaurants. The extra-large portions, low nutrient density, and high concentration of poor-quality fats, salts, and sugars of these types of foods are a big part of the reason the number of overweight and obese children in this country has *quadrupled* in the last 25 years.

Chances are that when your baby is ready to start on solids, you will be bombarded with advertising promising the speed, ease, and "balanced nutrition" of commercially prepared baby foods. But we will show you in this book how and why preparing most of your baby's food in your own kitchen is a truly superior choice. Best of all, we'll teach you how to make the bulk of your baby's cereals and purees in about an hour a week.

In Part I of *Best Food for Your Baby & Toddler*, we offer you sound nutritional guidance based on the most up-to-date information from respected agencies like the American Dietetic Association (ADA) and the American Academy of Pediatrics (AAP), plus a clear understanding of the natural needs of your child's developing body and digestive system.

In Part II, we guide you through a series of easy-to-understand nutritional recommendations, tips, tricks, and warnings for each important stage of your child's development from birth through 3 years.

In Part III, we set you up with everything you need to prepare simple, healthy food for your baby and toddler. We provide advice for setting up a great pantry, and a guide to key kitchen equipment that will make cooking for baby much easier. The key techniques for making high-quality baby food are broken down into easy-to-follow steps, including a guide for the three P's of Planning, Purchasing, and Preparing. The heart of this section contains more than 150 kid-tested recipes and snack ideas, many of which your whole family will be able to enjoy. Each recipe offers special tips, and lists nutrient, purchase, and preparation information about the ingredients or the dish. Many are designed for multiple ingredient substitutions for preparation ease or special dietetic needs.

In the closing sections, we'll provide you with additional Web resources for topics such as breastfeeding and food allergies. We'll give you a comprehensive list of whole foods companies and products that make healthy eating faster and easier—particularly useful on those days when you just don't have the time or energy to make it fresh.

As you read this book, keep a few things in mind. First of all, you don't have to do everything we suggest. These offerings are guidelines only—every child and every parent is unique. If making fresh whole foods from scratch is new to you, plan to start slowly and let yourself be a beginner. There will be some trial and error along the way, and that is as it should be. It's all part of the fun of discovery.

We applaud you for taking the time and making the effort to feed your baby well. By nourishing him well, you are helping to create a rich and vibrant future for everyone.

Congratulations!

Warmly,
Jeannette Bessinger
with Tracee Yablon-Brenner

They Are What They Eat

1

American Children's Health Crisis: The Baby Connection

Obesity Epidemic

If you've been reading the newspaper or watching the news at all over the last few years, it's likely that you've heard something about the rapidly increasing number of overweight and obese children in this country. You may not understand why this is such a big deal—a hefty toddler is a healthy toddler, right? Wrong.

Warning

A child who is overweight at the age of 3 is 8 times more likely to become an overweight young adult than a 3-year-old without excess weight.

Overweight children are at a much higher risk of becoming obese adults than their average-weight peers. And if they become overweight at a very young age, their adult obesity is likely to be more extreme. Being obese can lead to type 2 **diabetes, high blood pressure**, or dyslipidemia/ **high cholesterol** (all of which can lead to **childhood cardiovascular disease**), as well as **asthma, sleep apnea**, fatty liver, and even some forms of **childhood cancer**. Childhood weight problems can also lead to some less serious, but still bothersome, repercussions such as joint problems, body discomfort, menstrual problems, and even an increase in acne during puberty. Overweight children are also more likely to be teased by other kids, which can lead to lower self-esteem and even depression—tough for any kid to bear.

Over the past 30 years, the number of overweight and obese Americans has increased so rapidly that we are currently in the midst of an epidemic. The U.S. Surgeon General has predicted that the number of preventable illnesses and deaths connected with obesity will soon likely outnumber those from smoking.

Warning

According to the Centers for Disease Control and Prevention (CDC), 5 of the 6 leading causes of death in this country in 2002 were from chronic disease. Chronic, or long-term, diseases can lead to significant disabilities and negatively impact our overall quality of life.

The problem is real, and it's putting our children at risk for numerous medical problems, including long-term disease. Some researchers believe that this generation of children will be the first in modern history to have a shorter lifespan than their parents.

Flash Fact

Between 1980 and 2000, the number of children and adolescents who were overweight nearly doubled.

EARLY PREVENTION

There is hope, because you, as a parent of a newborn, have the opportunity right now to prevent your child from ever falling into the trap of lifelong overweight and obesity. The good news is that obesity and all of its related diseases, even early death, are largely preventable with simple improvements to our nutrition and eating habits, along with a modest increase in physical activity.

BREASTFEEDING AND CHILDHOOD WEIGHT PROBLEMS

Good nutrition begins from birth. We know that **breastfeeding** is one of the most effective ways to begin protecting your child right from the start. We understand that the decision of whether or not to breastfeed is a personal choice and can be a very emotional one for parents. And we know that, for various reasons, some moms who would like to breastfeed their babies are not able to do so. While this book emphasizes the benefits of breastfeeding, it also provides plenty of information and tips for parents who feed their baby with **formula**, supplementally or exclusively. Our goal is to provide you with the best knowledge available to raise strong, healthy babies. The strongest benefits occur when a baby is fed exclusively **breastmilk** for at least 3 months with no formula supplementation or the introduction of any **solid foods**. Experts at the Centers for Disease Control and Prevention believe that breastfeeding for more than 3 months could prevent 15 to 20 percent of all obesity.

It is unclear exactly why breastfeeding increases children's chances of maintaining a healthy weight, but researchers have made some educated guesses. Milk is released more slowly from the breast than from most bottles, and little mouths have to work harder initially to trigger the milk "drop" and get it to flow. Also, moms can't see how much milk a baby is consuming at the breast, so she has to watch the baby's behavior for cues about his satisfaction or "fullness." With bottle feeding, you can see how much milk the baby is drinking. We have a natural tendency to assume that the baby is done or has had enough when the bottle is empty, as opposed to taking our cues from the baby himself, so we may inadvertently overfeed him with the bottle.

> **TIP**
>
> The American Academy of Pediatrics recommends that you breastfeed your baby exclusively for the first 6 months. At 6 months you can begin to introduce solid foods, but also continue to breastfeed until your child is at least 1 year old.

Breastfed children may be more willing to try new flavors and foods than formula-fed kids. (More on how that helps with obesity prevention in the next section.) The taste of breastmilk is affected by the different foods eaten by Mom— it's never exactly the same flavor twice. Formula, however, always tastes the same and may reinforce the tendency of young infant taste buds to reject the unfamiliar. And finally, breastfeeding appears to have a better effect on a baby's hormonal balance and metabolism than formula. It's possible that her body's sugar-balancing and fat-storage systems may work better if she is breastfed.

OTHER BENEFITS OF BREASTFEEDING

We are mammals, and as mammals, a mother's milk is uniquely designed for the optimum health and steady growth of her young. Breastmilk contains the perfect balance of nutrients for your baby, which is impossible to mimic exactly in a formula. These nutrients change from day to day in direct response to the needs of your growing child. It even contains immune factors that protect your baby from allergens and illnesses specific to your environment.

The benefits of breastfeeding abound—not just for your baby, but also for you and even for the environment. Breastfed children are healthier than their formula-fed peers, and when they do get sick, they generally have fewer symptoms. When they are older, they tend to score better on IQ and vision tests. They are also not troubled as often by digestive disorders, such as diarrhea and **colic**. Their teeth are healthier, too, with fewer cavities and less need for braces when they're older. They also develop fewer ear infections. There is evidence that babies with a family history of **diabetes (juvenile onset or type 1)** who are fed on the breast exclusively for at least 4 months have a reduced risk of developing the disease. In addition, babies at risk for developing allergies who are breastfed for at least 4 months are less likely to develop asthma or eczema.

And what about you? Breastfeeding mothers recover

from birth faster, with less postpartum bleeding. You're also more likely to lose all your pregnancy weight. Breastfeeding reduces your risk of osteoporosis, and makes you less likely to develop ovarian cancer or pre-menopausal breast cancer. The longer you breastfeed, the greater your protection. Breastfeeding moms tend to be less anxious and feel more confident than bottle-feeding moms. There's a financial benefit, too: Breastfeeding costs about four times less than bottle feeding. In terms of germs, it's safer and cleaner, and it requires no fuel consumption or product packaging to tax the environment.

TRAINING THE TASTE BUDS

While the foundation for a healthy weight can be established with at least 3 months of exclusive breastfeeding, there are several additional practices you can adopt to support a solid beginning. The entire first 3 years of a child's life are crucial in determining his future food preferences and eating patterns. While it begins with breast or formula feeding, a lot of this learning takes place when a baby transitions from an all-milk diet to one that is rich in a wide variety of foods.

Young children are genetically programmed to have a preference for certain tastes and a dislike for others. From the first days they are attracted to sweet, which helps motivate them to drink breastmilk, a naturally sweet food. They also like salty tastes, but tend to dislike the sour and bitter. Toddlers are also innately predisposed to dislike the unfamiliar at first taste.

These are natural animal responses that would have helped us survive in the wild. As hunter-gatherers, it would have been crucial for a young child to be able to make safe food choices in the wild. Since most poisonous or toxic plants have a sour or bitter taste, it makes sense that the young would be programmed to avoid those flavors. Preferring familiar tastes over new tastes would also have helped prevent children from eating something potentially unsafe.

What we have learned from research on taste preferences, however, is that despite the fact that children have initial built-in taste preferences for sweet and salty, the way we acquire our learned preferences is through repetition. Simply put, children learn to prefer the flavors of foods that are the most familiar, regardless of the taste, especially if they feel good after eating it. (If they have an uncomfortable digestive response after eating something, they will be more likely to reject that food the next time it's offered.) It can take eight to fifteen tries before a child is familiar with a food and likes it. If you want to help your children develop a taste for the most nourishing types of foods, then that's what you should offer them nearly all of the time.

American children eat too much **junk food** high in salt and sugar. If you give them the option of choosing a very sweet snack, like candy, or a gently sweet snack, like a piece of fruit, many children, though not all, will automatically choose the candy over the apple. So if you're trying to encourage your young child to make healthy choices, super-sweet or super-salty snack foods and drinks (such as potato chips and soda) should not be available to them as an option. If you want your children to learn to prefer the taste of whole natural foods like whole grains, legumes, dairy, lean meats, fruits and vegetables, then regularly serve those foods in simple forms, without adding any extra salt or sugar.

EATING BEHAVIORS

It's not just the types of food we offer that can help our children become healthy eaters. We can also consciously help them develop great eating *habits*, now and for the future. Eating is not just for our bodies; it is also a social event. Eating represents the child's very first interaction with others. Children's early eating cues are learned in a social environment with their families and caretakers. We know, for instance, that if a young child is among peers who are eating a food that's unfamiliar to him, he will usually eat it, too—even a food that he wouldn't normally try at home! As parents, we can provide a healthy eating environment and send cues that support the habits we are trying to cultivate.

HUNGER AND FULLNESS CUES

One primary cause for the high incidence of **childhood overweight and obesity** is

> **TIP**
>
> Toddlers don't need specialized exercise programs or classes—they just need to be able to explore their inside and outside environments with some adult supervision. Make family time a physical affair: Go for short walks together after meals, take your toddler to the park, or just silly-dance around together to their favorite tunes at home. The American Academy of Pediatrics recommends that children under the age of 2 not watch TV at all.

> **TIP**
>
> Most of the products advertised in the media are for low-quality junk foods with little or no nutritional value. Protect your child from being trained to want these foods by limiting the number of commercials he sees. Limit him to short commercial-free programs, and don't let him watch TV at all while he is eating—that encourages him to tune out his body's fullness signals because he's distracted by watching a show.

that many of today's children tend to overeat. While there are many external factors currently influencing the amount our kids eat, such as the over-large portions typically served in restaurants (more on that in chapter 2), a child will overeat only if he learns to ignore his built-in cues for hunger and **satiety** (satisfaction).

Every child is born with the innate ability to sense both when he is hungry and when he has had enough to eat. The human body is a very sensitive system, with many complex processes governing its growth and functioning. All bodies grow and operate at different rates and in different ways. So each child's energy needs from meal to meal, and even moment to moment, are going to be very individual, and impossible to predict exactly from day to day.

The signals from a very young child's body are the best guide in determining his meal and snack portions. When the fuel levels in his blood drop, the brain releases a signal to the stomach for it to release some digestive juices. This often generates a little tummy rumble or growl and the child will feel a hollowness that is a bit uncomfortable. That's why young children will often cry when they are very hungry. When they've had enough food, the stomach sends a message back to the brain and they feel a pleasant, relaxed sensation of satiety that tells them to stop eating.

These signals are clear to most babies and very young toddlers. Older babies and young toddlers often eat in unpredictable patterns: a lot at one meal, very little at the next. But if they are allowed to eat according to these internal signals,

they do a great job of balancing out their caloric needs with their growth and energy output on their own. Beyond simply portion size, if they eat **calorie**-dense foods at one sitting, they will generally eat fewer calories at the next to balance out their daily intake. But this **natural eating** tends to change by the time they are older toddlers. By then they may not intuitively eat according to their body's needs as effectively as they did when they were younger.

One reason for this is that older toddlers often start ignoring their internal hunger and satisfaction signals in favor of other external cues, such as how much food is on their plate or what others around them are eating. It is at this point, between the ages of 18 months and 2½ years, that you can really support the development of your child's healthy eating habits by helping him to keep honoring his body's internal cueing system for his eating behaviors. If you watch him closely for the subtle signals of true hunger, you can draw his attention inward to his body and help him continue to be conscious of those guiding cues. We will cover what those signals might look like at different ages in the development chapters of this book.

PARENTAL CUES

In addition, you can support his healthy eating habits by sending out supportive signals of other kinds. As parents, we unwittingly send all kinds of messages about food to our children. We might unconsciously make a face if the child eats something we dislike, or we might act surprised if they appear to like a food that we think they won't, such as a bitter green vegetable or unsweetened yogurt. Kids are quick to pick up on these signals, and we have to take care not to accidentally teach them to dislike a variety of healthy foods based on our own preferences and biases!

As your child grows and learns to eat on his own and to follow the guidelines for family mealtimes, the eating cues you send may become more verbal and more directive. You can continue to support healthy eating behaviors by offering a selection of healthy choices for a meal or snack, but then *not* interfering with what and how much your older baby or toddler chooses to eat. *You are responsible for the food choices that you make available to your child, for his eating environment, and even for when the eating will take place.* (See chapter 6 for more tips about creating mealtime environments and rituals that are supportive to healthy eating.) *But it is important that you let your child be responsible for what and how much she chooses to eat at that meal.*

Because young children's appetites are constantly changing, there is truly no cause for alarm when a toddler occasionally skips a meal because he simply is not hungry. Your baby and toddler will likely go through periods of little interest in eating and extra interest in eating. This is normal and natural and based on internal body cues. What you can do is keep supporting him to tune in to those sensations for guidance. Little verbal prompts can be effective reminders: "You're hungry now—do

you feel an empty tummy?" "All done? Your tummy is telling you you've had enough for now?"

Obesity Prevention

Because feeding your child is one of the most important jobs you have as a parent, and because there is valid cause for concern about how poorly many children are eating today, it would be easy to put too much emphasis on getting the "right foods" in the "right amounts" into your child. Paradoxically, that kind of focus and behavior often have the opposite effect of what we are trying to cultivate! We know from research that exerting too much control over what or how much a child eats, for instance, can actually create the eating behaviors you're trying to prevent: overeating sweets, refusing certain foods, etc.

Instead, try to think of this process as cultivating a healthy eating relationship with your child. Relationships are much more generous and flexible than food rules. They can adapt with growth and change, and there is room for learning by you and by your child. Remember that besides establishing healthy eating habits, your eating relationship is to teach your baby and toddler that he is heard and respected, that he is safe in the world, that he is part of a family, and that he can trust that his needs will be met by his caregivers. By learning to honor his body's signals, he is learning that he can trust his body, rather than an external source, for eating guidance.

Quick Chart

OBESITY PREVENTION CHECKLIST

Best practices for building healthy eating behaviors from birth through age 3:

- Breastfeed exclusively for the first 6 months.
- Look for your child's hunger and satisfaction cues to help guide you with breastmilk feeding amounts (more on hunger/satiety cues in chapter 5).
- Introduce solid foods late in the sixth month (more on guidelines for introducing first foods in chapter 5).
- Continue to breastfeed your child until she is at least 1 year old or longer, if both you and your child desire that.
- Offer your young child a varied selection of 3 to 4 healthy, natural food choices in small amounts (a good starter serving size is about 1 tablespoon per year of age) at each meal.
- If he is hungry for more, offer more, but do not offer large portions at first (see chapters 5 and 6 for more information about healthy portion sizes at different ages).
- Never force or bribe your child to eat or to clean his plate if he is not hungry. Forcing may actually cause your child to eat less.
- Be patient with food introductions: Offer a new food up to 15 times, even if it is initially rejected. It will likely take several offerings before your child decides to try it, and several tastes before it becomes familiar and therefore accepted. It may be more effective to spread these offerings out over time rather than at 15 consecutive meals.
- Don't make a fuss when offering your child new foods. There's no need to say anything about it, but try to send the same subtle, encouraging signals (smiling, making "mmm" sounds, etc.) with sour or bitter foods, or other foods that you may not like yourself, as you do when he's eating foods that you like or think he will like.
- Between 9 and 12 months, when he is beginning to learn more words, "name" his hunger and satisfaction at feeding times to give him a language for those feelings: "Oh, you're feeling hungry! Let's have something to eat!" "Now you've had enough? Time to stop eating."
- When he is a little older and eating primarily solid foods, guide him to continue to notice and heed those internal signals for hunger and fullness at mealtimes by **modeling** the language and behaviors with your own actions and with occasional verbal prompts: "You're feeling really hungry for dinner, I see." "Is your stomach feeling calmer now that you've had enough to eat?"
- Do not use food as a reward or a punishment, offering it or withholding it, especially the super-sweet or super-salty junk foods.
- Offer your child only healthy, high-quality food choices. Keep the unhealthy competitive foods (super-sweet, super-salty, or greasy junk foods) out of your pantry.

The Case for Real Food

American Infant and Toddler Diets: The S.A.D. Facts

In 2002, the Gerber Products Company conducted a study of the diets of more than three thousand American infants and toddlers. In 2007, Gerber joined with the Nestlé Nutrition Institute and continued this research, expanding it into what is now known as the Feeding Infant and Toddler Study (FITS). The analyses of the FITS data gave us some surprising information about what and how our young children are eating in this country. The results showed that many babies and toddlers are already eating a poor-quality diet too high in calories and rich in super-sweet or junky food (like soda and french fries), just like older Americans.

On the plus side, many children were found to be meeting the recommended daily **vitamin** and mineral requirements, but often that was happening through supplementation rather than a diet rich in whole, natural foods. In fact, the study clearly showed that infants and toddlers were not eating the recommended amounts of fruits and vegetables. Of the older babies, 25 to 30 percent ate no vegetables or fruits at all on a given day! One-third of the toddlers ate no vegetables either, and over three-quarters were eating too much salt.

Sadly, these statistics don't improve as our children grow up. According to a National Cancer Institute study, only 1 percent of all children between the ages of 2 and 19 years meet all the **U.S. Department of Agriculture (USDA)** food pyramid recommendations for servings of grains, vegetables, fruits, meats, and dairy products! So if our kids aren't eating enough of those foods, what are they eating? Almost half of their daily caloric intake comes from added sugars and extra fat—in other words, super-sweet and super-fatty junk food.

In many ways these statistics define what has become our **Standard American Diet**

(S.A.D.). We eat too few nutrient-rich foods (real food) and too many high-calorie, low-nutrient-density foods (S.A.D. junk food). Eating a lot of poor-quality foods can lead to a lower quality of overall health in our children, and eating primarily high-quality foods helps to foster vibrant health for a lifetime. So what exactly is S.A.D. **junk food**? And how do we know if a food is "real"?

S.A.D. JUNK FOOD DEFINED

Junk food is food that is of very low quality. It typically has a high number of calories in combination with a low concentration of nutrients, with the bulk of the calories in the form of simple sugars or poor-quality fats. Junk foods also frequently contain a lot of additives such as chemical preservatives, artificial colors, sweeteners or flavors, or added sugars and/or salt. The junkiest foods and drinks might fill up the belly, but they do not nourish the body. If your toddler is getting full on junk food, how will she get the nutrients her body needs for energy and growth? The answer is she might not be, or she might feel the urge to keep eating (from a sense that she needs something more to feel good) and end up gaining excess weight.

Poor-quality foods are not found just in grocery or convenience stores, however, and they don't always have a package with a label that you can read to determine if the item is healthy or not. Some of the poorest-quality foods our

Warning

Avoid feeding your baby and toddler poor-quality packaged foods such as the following:
• Foods that contain a lot of ingredients you can't pronounce (chemical preservatives, artificial colors, sweeteners, or flavors)
• Foods that list sugar in any form as the first or second ingredient
• Foods that list a sodium content of more than 20 percent of RDA on the label
• Foods that contain hydrogenated or partially hydrogenated oils
• Foods that contain high-fructose corn syrup
(See page 15 for a list of commonly used names for sugar, and page 38 for information about how to read a food label.)

children are eating come from restaurants: Fast-food restaurants, family-style restaurants, chain restaurants, diners, and even many independently owned restaurants serve primarily foods that are too high in calories and too low in nutrition. To add to the damage caused by the poor quality of restaurant food, the children's portions are generally much larger than what the average child needs to consume at one sitting.

Children usually love the taste of the classic American "kid's meal" because it is typically super-sweet, super-salty, and familiar. Restaurants have developed a S.A.D. "Top Five" meals served to children: hot dog; hamburger;

white pasta with "cheese," butter, or red sauce; chicken nuggets; and pizza. Any one of those entrées could be served with a helping of french fries, but usually not much else—not a piece of fruit or a vegetable in sight!

It's not that hot dogs, hamburgers, chicken, and pasta are terrible meal choices for kids in and of themselves. It's just that most restaurant versions of these meals are of very poor quality. It is quite possible to serve a delicious and healthy mac and cheese meal to your child, but a healthy version won't contain things like artificially colored orange processed cheese "food."

REAL FOOD DEFINED

In contrast to poor-quality junk food, **real food** is of high quality. Remember that human beings are animals, and the foods all animals are designed to eat and thrive on come directly from the natural world. Real food comes from plants and animals in what is essentially their natural state: fresh, nutrients intact, without the unhealthy extras (added sugar; salt; poor-quality fat; chemical preservatives; artificial flavors, sweeteners, or colors).

Up until about fifty years ago, the bulk of what we ate was primarily made up of high-quality real foods. With the advent of large-scale industrial farming and modern food-storage capabilities, however, we started processing and storing our food differently so it could travel farther, to big grocery stores, and have a longer shelf life once it got there.

S.A.D. JUNK FOOD VERSUS REAL FOOD

Today our modern grocery stores are inundated with more than thirty thousand products! The majority of these are processed, packaged foods designed to tickle the taste buds and speed meal preparation. It sounds great, but the problem is that most of those products are poor-quality foods.

Warning

It is vital for the future of our children that we stop sacrificing their health in exchange for the extremely sweet and salty flavors and the preparation ease of poor-quality processed, packaged, and restaurant foods.

Whereas poor-quality junk foods have their nutrients stripped away, high-quality real foods retain them in their original state. Wheat, a healthy grain from a plant, is a staple of many Western diets, and yet the form in which we see it most often is bleached white flour: a low-quality food because it has been stripped of most of its **fiber**, vitamins, and **minerals**. What's left is a simple carbohydrate that turns very quickly into **blood sugar** (**glucose**) in the body (more on **carbohydrates** and blood sugar in chapter 3), so eating white flour products like hamburger buns or pasta is pretty similar nutritionally to eating sugar itself. This also holds true for other poor-quality "white foods" of the Standard American Diet, such as white rice.

If you want to feed your growing child grains like wheat and rice, offer them the higher-quality versions, such as whole wheat or whole-grain products. Serve them brown rice, with its nutritious outer husk intact, rather than refined white rice; whole oats instead of stripped instant oatmeal loaded with sugar and artificial colors. You can also introduce them to some of the less familiar whole grains, like quinoa, that are very high in nutrients.

Whereas poor-quality foods are often packaged so that they have a long shelf life (think of kids' frozen TV dinners or cinnamon apple toaster pastries), high-quality real foods are the fresh, whole version of the same thing (in this example, homemade meat loaf or sliced apples with cinnamon). In addition to having too many calories and too few nutrients, packaged foods are stripped and processed for long shelf life, essentially robbed of their life energy.

Because they've been sanitized and preserved in different ways, packaged foods can be safely consumed after they have been sitting on the shelf for many months, or even years. Preserved "old" foods do not give growing babies and toddlers the same kind of life energy that home-cooked fresh foods will give them.

It is the difference between preserved canned spinach and steamed fresh spinach. The canned version might have been cooked at high heat to kill off any **bacteria** and stored with a preservative and lots of added salt and sat on a shelf for 3 years until you bought it. The fresh version could be steamed lightly with nothing extra about a week after it is picked. In addition to the loss of some of the nutrient content, the canned version *needs* that extra salt to make it palatable because otherwise it would taste lifeless and terrible. The fresh spinach needs no added salt because it still retains a lot of its original flavors and life energy after being harvested.

Although a child would still be getting some good nutrition from eating the canned spinach (the actual nutrient content of canned vegetables is lower than that of frozen or fresh), you can imagine that he would *feel* very different if he was constantly eating canned vegetables, as opposed to having some of them served fresh. He would look and feel perkier getting the energy of the fresher foods. He would be obtaining more nutrients, and also be eating a lot less salt.

THE ADDITIVES

Sugar and Salt

There is no intrinsic need to add extra sugar or salt to an infant or toddler's food. There is no nutritional need for a child to consume simple sugar at all, and the amount of salt a toddler needs is tiny and usually doesn't require any supplementation with table salt if he is eating a wide variety of natural foods. Vegetables like celery have a high salt content, as does tuna fish. Because processed foods are stripped of most of their nutrients and life energy, they don't taste good to people, especially children, unless extra sugars, salt, and other flavors are added back in. Largely as a result of eating these highly processed foods, even our babies are consuming twice as much salt as they need.

Quick Chart

SODIUM RECOMMENDED DAILY ALLOWANCE (RDA)

The Food and Drug Administration (FDA) does not offer sodium recommendations for infants and toddlers, but other U.S. and international health organizations make the following suggestions for daily Adequate Intake.*
 0 to 6 months: 120 mg
 7 to 12 months: 370 mg–1 g
 1 to 3 years: 1 g
This is an extremely small amount (1 teaspoon of salt is about 4 grams). There is no need to salt your infant's or toddler's food in order to meet the nutritional requirements for sodium.
*The term Adequate Intake (AI) is used when there is not enough information to set a Recommended Daily Allowance (RDA).

Warning

WATCH OUT FOR HIDDEN SUGAR!

Sugar is disguised on food labels with many different names. Here is a selection of some of the names you are most likely to see:

corn (or any kind of) syrup
dextrose
fructose
fruit juice concentrate
high-fructose corn syrup
honey
lactose
maltose
sucrose

Hydrogenated Oils

Another additive that is commonly used in processed foods is **partially hydrogenated oils**, which contain **trans fat**. Hydrogenated oils are man-made, designed to help with food preservation. A regular vegetable oil is heated to very high temperatures in order to inject hydrogen molecules into its structure. This process changes the naturally perishable liquid oil into a solid that then has an extended shelf life. The new solid form, however, is very unpalatable and needs to be bleached and deodorized in order to be used in foods. Thus the final result is a chemically altered, highly processed product containing trans fat, which promotes heart disease and type 2 diabetes. It is definitely not a real food.

Warning

Researchers at the Harvard School of Public Health estimate that around 50,000 premature deaths from heart attacks are caused by trans fat. That statistic makes partially hydrogenated oil one of the most dangerous food products on the market.
[Source: Center for Science in the Public Interest Food Additives Chart, www.cspinet.org]

Because hydrogenated oil is inexpensive to manufacture and is such an effective preservative, however, it became a very popular ingredient in thousands of processed foods, especially snack foods like cookies, crackers, and potato chips. It is also used frequently in high-heat restaurant cooking, as with donuts and french fries. Now that its dangers are being made public, more and more fast food restaurants and food-processing companies are working to replace it with a healthier, more natural oil alternative. Some cities have actually banned the use of hydrogenated oils in restaurants.

Artificial Colors, Flavors, Sweeteners, and Preservatives

There are more than 14,000 man-made chemicals in the American food supply. Many of them are quite safe. A few of them, like added vitamins and minerals, even enrich the foods by increasing their nutritional content. Most of them,

however, do not add nutritional value, and some may be harmful to your child's health.

Warning

The Center for Science in the Public Interest recommends avoiding these additives because they are deemed unsafe in the amounts we consume or are not thoroughly tested:
acesulfame potassium, also known as *Acesulfame* K
artificial colorings (Blue 1, Blue 2, Green 3, Red 3, Yellow 6)
aspartame (NutraSweet)
butylated hydroxyanisole (BHA)
cyclamate (not legal in the United States)
hydrogenated vegetable oil/partially hydrogenated vegetable oil
olestra (olean)
potassium bromate
propyl gallate
saccharin
sodium nitrite

Consult www.cspinet.org for the latest research on food safety.

As a general rule, try not to feed your baby or toddler foods that contain artificial coloring, the artificial sweeteners aspartame or saccharin, fats such as olestra, hydrogenated or partially hydrogenated oils, caffeine, or sodium nitrite/nitrate.

Sodium nitrite/nitrate acts as a preservative, adding color and flavor to the food. It's used primarily in cured and processed red meat products like hot dogs, bacon, and lunch meats to extend their shelf life, prevent bacteria growth, turn the meat red, and give them that distinctive S.A.D. salty flavor. There have been several studies that link the consumption of cured meat and nitrite by children with different types of cancer, although none have yet proven that eating cured meat products containing nitrite *directly* causes cancer.

If you decide to feed your child cured or processed meats like hot dogs and cold cuts, try to choose options that are nitrite/nitrate-free, and make it an occasional treat rather than a staple. Choose unprocessed white meat cuts like turkey or chicken breast at the deli and skip the red "pressed" products, such as bologna and salami, which are very high in saturated fats. Many organic brands of hot dogs contain no nitrites/nitrates and also have the added bonus of containing no fillers or animal by-products. You can even find turkey hot dogs (with a lower amount of saturated fat than beef or pork dogs) that your children will love.

S.A.D. FOOD CONSEQUENCES

When babies and toddlers eat the Standard American Diet of too many low-quality junk foods and not enough high-quality real foods, several things are likely to happen. If the child has regularly been fed mostly super-sweet and super-salty foods, he will likely resist those vegetables, and even some fruits, that have strong sour or bitter components in their flavors (which means most of the green stuff) longer than a child who has been raised eating a variety of real foods from the start. He may even refuse vegetables completely.

There may also be some challenges to his endocrine system. Children who are fed a lot of sweet foods, including "liquid sugar" in the form of soda, juice, or even too much milk, can experience an elevation in their blood sugar that is too fast or too high. These elevations in blood sugar may make some babies and toddlers cranky or uncomfortable. They feel out of balance because, in some children, a blood-sugar spike is shortly followed by a blood-sugar crash. When their blood sugar plummets, it may go to a level that's lower than before the child ate the sweets.

Low blood sugar may make a child feel irritable, teary, shaky, or tired. A child with low blood sugar will usually crave, you guessed it, more sugar! She wants something super-sweet (she may ask for a sweet drink, a very sweet fruit, or any version of the white foods—white rice, pasta, bread, cookies, candies, snack foods, etc.) because her body wants to get the blood sugar back up to a normal level quickly. If you give her another super-sweet food, it can start the cycle all over again.

In some children, this is quite dramatic: You can see the blood sugar levels rising and plummeting in a child's shifts of mood from seemingly energetic to cranky and lethargic, sometimes even within an hour. In other children it's more subtle, and the fluctuation in blood sugar may simply manifest itself with them asking for a sugar food at regular intervals throughout the day, with no interest in other types of food. Another consequence of this blood-sugar roller coaster is that it tends to supersede, or even shut down, the stomach's true hunger and fullness signals.

Kids on the blood-sugar roller coaster may never feel actual stomach hunger, but instead may want to graze all day on small amounts of sugary foods or drinks that keep their blood sugar too elevated to send the growl signal to the stomach. Or they may feel what seems to be acute hunger an hour or two after eating, when there still may be food in the tummy. This occurs because the blood sugar has crashed, and low blood sugar is the body's cue to the brain to send the hunger signal.

This type of S.A.D. eating can lead to serious consequences over time. The most obvious is that the child may end up eating too many calories, gain excess weight, and start on a path to a lifetime of poor health. Not every child who is stuck on the blood-sugar roller coaster will gain weight as a baby or toddler, however. Some children may actually be eating a relatively small number of calories, but they are all in the form of different sugars. Or a child's growth rate or natural fat-burning metabolism may be fast. In these cases, it may take several years to see an extra weight gain. Some S.A.D. eaters go well into adulthood before they gain excess weight. A few may never become excessively heavy (they will, however, always be sugar-imbalanced and therefore probably suffer from a lack of vital

nutrients in their diet), but most will eventually gain extra weight from this eating pattern.

With or without an early excess weight gain, a young S.A.D. eater may develop tooth decay in his baby teeth from frequent exposure to sugary foods, or from constantly sucking on a bottle of sweet drinks. He may also develop constipation from a lack of fiber in his diet of overprocessed foods. Although these may seem like relatively small consequences while they are toddlers, these types of problems are cumulative and, as research shows us, can put a child on the road to long-term illness as an adult or even, if the S.A.D. eating is extreme, as an older child.

REAL FOOD BENEFITS: HEALTHY EATING FOR A LIFETIME

When babies and toddlers are breastfed and introduced to a diverse diet of real foods, the results are quite different. Their palates are trained to enjoy a wide variety of flavors and textures. When they are older, they will naturally select the sour and bitter flavors in balance with the more subtly sweet and salty tastes in fruits and vegetables.

They tend to be healthier overall because the bulk of what they eat comes from more intact forms of plant and animal foods packed with natural energy. They are eating a broader variety of foods, which provides them with a better balance of nutrients, including fiber, enabling all their bodily systems to function better. Because they are eating real foods, they are also consuming fewer additives and preservatives.

They will tend to retain their natural energy levels better than S.A.D.-eating kids. Kids who eat a steady diet of nutrient-depleted junky foods for years on end eventually begin to slow down. They don't keep up with their natural-eating peers at sports, on the dance floor, or even at outdoor games like tag. They are more likely to sit out during vigorous physical play and opt for something passive, like television watching, which further increases the likelihood of eventual weight gain. Kids eating real food will maintain the naturally vigorous energy levels of healthy children well into their early adulthood.

Infants and toddlers raised on real food are more likely to continue to eat as humans were designed to eat: in balance and in moderation. As they grow older, they will be able to trust their hunger and fullness cues to guide them to eat the exact amounts of food they need at different ages and stages of their lives. They will intuitively make healthy choices and be able to stay at their healthy natural weight for their whole lives without excessive effort.

Helping your child to honor his internal cues for hunger and fullness and encouraging other good eating habits with a varied diet of real foods can both help to prevent the onset of many of the serious chronic diseases that are plaguing our country, and set your child firmly on a path to a lifetime of healthy eating.

Why, then, aren't we all raising our children in this way? Why do so many of us feed those junky foods to our babies and toddlers? Part of the reason is simply a lack of awareness: *We still don't believe that what and how much we are feeding our children is connected to the obesity crisis.* The problem has crept up on us slowly enough that, now, many of our firmly held beliefs have become outdated.

Busting the Real Food and S.A.D. Food Myths

Let's take a look at some very common, but mistaken, beliefs that are leading many of us into making some feeding decisions for our children that may be detrimental to their health, now and in the future.

MYTH #1: Real food sounds like health food, and kids won't eat health food. Real food as we are describing it is not the same as "health food." "Health food" is an outdated concept that conjures up images of eating lots of bran and other bland, tasteless foods. Many people associate health food with the unfamiliar, foreign, and bad tasting. Real food, by contrast, is readily available almost anywhere, is largely familiar to most people, and it tastes great! Real food is simply naturally grown, minimally processed actual foods from plants and animals, such as vegetables, fruits, grains, legumes, nuts, meats, poultry, fish, eggs, milk, cheese, and oils. Individual humans may eat different diets, but we are all designed to eat from the real food supply.

In today's markets there is such an overabundance of artificial and processed foods with so many chemical, sweet, and salty additives that we have been tricked into thinking our children can thrive on a diet of these types of S.A.D. foods. In truth, overconsumption of S.A.D. foods is damaging our health and our kids' health at an alarming rate. *It is crucial for the future of our children to make the distinction between low-quality junk foods and high-quality real foods so that we can train them to prefer and eat a wholesome diet of actual food, as opposed to the counterfeit products that are weighing down the supermarket shelves.*

TIP

Shop around the perimeter of the grocery store for fresh vegetables, fruit, milk, eggs, cheese, bulk grains and beans, fresh meats, and seafood. Ignore 95 percent of the middle aisles, which typically contain mostly processed and highly refined packaged foods of lower quality.

MYTH #2: Junk food tastes better than real food. Junky super-sweet and super-salty S.A.D. foods don't naturally taste better than real food from plants and animals: Their sweet and salt flavors are just more intense. Those of us who have S.A.D. palates from eating lots of these foods have simply lost our taste for real food. But remember that much of our taste preference is actually a learned thing.

To babies, who haven't yet been exposed to the extreme tastes of junky food, the natural taste of pureed carrots, for instance, is very sweet. And with repeated tastings, they can learn to like the sour and even the bitter flavors of a wide variety of vegetables, beans, and whole grains. Manufacturers spend a lot of money inventing artificial flavors and refined textures for highly processed foods that will hit every pleasurable flavor receptor in your mouth. There is a science to the "layering" of sweet and salty flavors with fats that deliver them directly to the pleasure and reward centers of your brain, turning a food into something that behaves in your body more like an addictive drug than a healthy fuel. But the palate that has been raised on actual real foods can occasionally eat these foods as an adult and still be able to enjoy and even prefer more natural flavors.

MYTH #3: Junk food is cheaper than real food. Okay, on one level this is true. It's hard to beat the cost of a kid's meal at a chain restaurant. And many of the junkiest snack foods are really cheap, especially if they are bought in bulk or at a discount store. But foods such as whole grains, like rice or oats, and dried beans bought in bulk are actually some of the least expensive items you can buy at the grocery store. And to be realistic, you need to consider the cost of the health consequences your child will have to deal with when he is older, such as the discomfort, social stigma, and potential health hazard of

Warning

Conventionally farmed produce is treated with many different kinds of fungicides and pesticides. A significant portion of these chemicals remains on and in the skins of many fruits and vegetables, even if you wash them well with a food-safe cleanser. The following "Dirty Dozen" fruits and vegetables, provided by the Environmental Working Group, a nonprofit consumer protection organization, have been rated the highest in pesticide content. Buy organic varieties of these foods for your baby and toddler, if possible.

Rank	Fruit or Veggie
1 (worst)	Peaches
2	Apples
3	Sweet bell peppers
4	Celery
5	Nectarines
6	Strawberries
7	Cherries
8	Kale
9	Lettuce
10	Grapes (imported)
11	Carrots
12	Pears

You can find this list and also one for the dozen cleanest conventionally farmed fruits and vegetables at www.foodnews.org/walletguide.php.

carrying too much extra weight or a mouthful of fillings.

MYTH #4: Real food takes too long to prepare. Many new parents believe that there is not enough time in the day to cook for a new baby, or that home cooking is an obsolete way for kids to get their meals today. While it's certainly true that there are more time demands on the average family than 25 years ago, it's not true that preparing food for children has to take hours each day. In fact, with some simple planning and preparation, you can make and batch enough food in about an hour to cover the staples of your baby's diet for a week! The key is the three P's: Planning, Purchasing, and Preparing. (See chapter 7 for simple guidelines to easy, time-saving cooking techniques for feeding your baby and toddler with a minimum investment of time.)

MYTH #5: Organic foods are no different than conventionally farmed foods. Organically farmed foods differ from conventionally farmed foods in several significant ways. Foods labeled with the USDA Organic seal are strictly regulated for farmer growing practices. Organic farmers may not use any synthetic forms of pesticides or fertilizers on their crops. Nor can they use any synthetic growth aids on their food animals or feed them any crops grown with synthetic pesticides or fertilizers.

Organic farmers typically use natural techniques such as crop rotation to keep their soil rich, whereas conventional farmers rely on artificial hyper-fertilization to improve the depleted soil. Crops grown in naturally rich soil contain higher concentrations of vital nutrients. They also tend to taste richer than conventionally farmed produce. You'll probably have more success tempting your finicky toddler with fresh organic sweet peas than processed, conventionally grown peas in a can.

MYTH #6: Kids won't eat green vegetables. As we discussed in chapter 1, children are naturally predisposed to dislike sour and bitter tastes at first, which is a natural instinct that helped keep them from accidentally ingesting poisonous plants in our hunter-gatherer era. But children are also predisposed to prefer what is familiar. Therefore if you offer a variety of different green vegetables patiently and consistently over time, most children will learn to enjoy the flavors. Remember, however, that

if you are feeding them too many super-sweet foods, it can put them on the blood-sugar roller coaster and they will be much less likely to ever develop a taste for vegetables with stronger flavors.

MYTH #7: Kids don't like water and will drink only milk or something sweetened, like juice or a soft drink. Water, like vegetables, has gotten a mistaken reputation for being unpalatable to kids. Because babies drink their food at first in the form of breastmilk or formula, older babies are predisposed to liking sweet drinks. As a result, many parents simply keep providing flavored or sweetened juices or milks to their children as they grow and don't introduce them to plain water as a thirst quencher.

If you introduce plain water early on, even in the bottle, children automatically learn to appreciate it as a drink. Because you want to encourage your children to begin taking many of their calories from solid foods after the age of 6 months, it's helpful *not to* give them sweetened caloric drinks when they are thirsty, because the sugar will interfere with their hunger and fullness mechanisms.

Starting Out Right: Natural Nutrition Basics

A Maturing Digestive System

When your baby is born, her digestive system, along with the rest of her body, is still quite immature and not yet ready to handle any food other than breastmilk or infant formula. During the last few months of pregnancy, a fetus swallows **amniotic fluid**, and this helps the delicate intestinal lining to grow. By the time she is born, her digestive system is mature enough to break down and absorb the fats, **proteins**, and simple sugars of breastmilk, but her body does not yet have the complete spectrum of digestive enzymes for a full diet that will develop over the coming months and years.

During a baby's first months, **peristalsis** (the coordinated muscle action required to move food physically through the digestive system) improves steadily, helping the breastmilk move down the throat, into and out of the stomach, and through the intestines, releasing the wastes out into the diaper (hopefully!). This happens at different rates for different babies, and it's usually some hitch in this maturation process that is the culprit behind conditions such as infant colic, reflux, diarrhea, and constipation. Although these conditions are bothersome, they are quite common and generally do not affect nutrient absorption, so they won't interfere with normal growth.

Around the age of 6 months, an infant's digestive system has matured to the point that he will be able to begin to eat and digest solid foods. It's best to introduce solid foods slowly, one at a time, beginning with a simple runny infant cereal made from rice, the most digestible grain. This can be followed by the gradual introduction of single vegetables, then fruits, and eventually combinations of grains, vegetables, and fruits. Around the age of 8 or 9 months, your baby's digestive system will be ready for some foods that are a little higher in protein.

The mouth is an important part of the digestive system, and young babies don't have the teeth or chewing coordination yet to break up large pieces of food, so most of what they eat should be in the form of silky purees. As they mature and their teeth start to come in, they will be able to handle bigger chunks of food and slightly more fibrous textures. By the time they are older toddlers, their digestive systems will be mature enough so that they can eat a diet very similar to our own, just simpler and smaller in portion size.

Baby and Toddler Nutrition

In the first year of life, a baby's nutritional needs are very high. His biggest job after birth is to grow and develop. Over 30 percent of his energy intake will be devoted to the growth of his body. Because a healthy rate of development varies from baby to baby, the best way to ensure optimum nutrition in the first few months of life is to feed him on demand, either breastmilk or formula (see chapter 5 for suggested month-by-month nursing and formula feeding guidelines). Breastmilk and formula (which is designed to mimic the nutritional content of breastmilk) provide an optimum balance of the nutrients your young baby needs.

NUTRIENTS FOR GROWING BODIES

All foods, including breastmilk, are made up of different nutrients that nutritionists have divided into two categories: **macronutrients** and **micronutrients**. They have identified five primary macro- and micronutrients required for basic healthy functioning. Three of these, the macronutrients, make up the largest part of our food: protein, fat, and carbohydrates. The other two, the micronutrients, are found only in trace amounts in the food, but they are essential for the growth and healthy functioning of every human body. These micronutrients are vitamins and minerals.

Protein

Protein is made up of different combinations of **amino acids**. These building blocks support the structural and functional operations that will enable the swift growth of your baby's body during his first year.

Breastmilk or formula provides all the necessary protein for a baby's first 6 months. Between 6 and 12 months, 25 ounces of breastmilk or formula will provide about half the protein a baby needs. It isn't until around 8 or 9 months that a baby will have developed his digestion to the point of being able to break down protein-heavy foods, so it's best to wait until then to begin offering protein-rich foods to complement the breastmilk or formula. Between 6 and 9 months your baby will get enough extra protein from the cereal grains he is eating to meet his needs. Good protein-rich choices for 9- to 12-month-olds include meats, egg yolks, beans, peas, and grains, especially quinoa, which contains eight essential amino acids.

While your child's growth will slow somewhat when he becomes a toddler, he'll still need plenty of protein to help him build new cell tissue (especially muscle and bone) and create vital enzymes and hormones. Protein, like fiber, when it's eaten in combination with carbohydrates, slows the rise of blood sugar. You can think of fiber and protein (and healthy fat, too) as time-release agents for the sugar in carbohydrates. Be sure to create a balance of those three nutrients in your toddler's diet, especially if he is eating simple (and particularly S.A.D.) carbs.

It can be difficult for some toddlers, especially 1- to 2-year-olds or vegetarian toddlers, to get enough protein in their diet. Some toddlers don't like to eat meat or fish, two excellent sources of protein, because they don't like the taste or texture. Or sometimes because their chewing skills haven't matured yet, meat can be difficult for young mouths to break down.

Also, toddlers may sometimes consume very small amounts of food, and without meat or fish it can be challenging for them to get enough protein foods into their diet. Usually this can be handled with a little attentiveness and creativity on your part. See chapters 4 and 6 for lots of ideas for how to ensure adequate protein in your toddler's diet. Good food sources of protein for toddlers include meats, fish,* eggs,* cheese, plain yogurt, beans, peas, and nut butters,* such as almond or cashew.

*Egg yolks, fish, and especially tree nuts and peanuts are very common allergens. It is recommended, therefore, that parents refrain from introducing them into their children's diets until at least their first birthday. Children who are at risk for **food allergies** should wait even longer. Toddlers under 3 years old should not be given whole nuts or seeds because they are a choking hazard. See chapter 6 for a more thorough discussion of food allergies and sensitivities.

Fat

Like protein, fat is also made up of building blocks. These are called **fatty acids**. Two of these fatty acids, **omega-3** and **omega-6**, are called essential fatty acids, meaning that the body cannot produce them on its own like the other building blocks. For your child to get these crucial fats, he will have to consume omega-rich food sources or take them in a supplement form.

Fat has 9 calories per gram, as opposed to carbohydrates and protein, which each have 4 calories per gram. That makes fats a concentrated source of energy. Babies and toddlers need a full range of healthy fats to help fill their large energy needs, build their cell membranes, and help their brains develop.

Restricting fat intake in young children to less than 30 percent of their total calories could reduce growth and visual acuity and might limit mental development. Omega-3 fatty acids are crucial for brain and retina development. It is generally agreed that healthy fats should not be restricted until 5 years of age, at which time the total amount of dietary fat may be gradually reduced, and continue to be reduced throughout the childhood and teenage years. Certain fatty acids are found only in human milk, and, therefore, if formula is used, it is important to choose one that includes the essential fatty acids omega-3 and omega-6.

Essential fatty acids:

- Help maintain a healthy immune system, supporting thyroid and adrenal health.
- Are vital for energy and normal development.
- Help develop healthy hair and skin.
- Support the digestive tract, blood, nerves, and arteries.
- Are very important in the transportation and breakdown of cholesterol and could protect against heart disease.

Good sources of healthy fats for babies include breastmilk or formula (about half the calories of both are from fats), meats, fish, egg yolk, full-fat yogurt, butter, avocado, and oils such as flax, olive, and coconut. Toddlers over 1 year can enjoy the same fat-rich foods along with the addition of nut and seed butters if there is no history of allergies.

Your child's dietary fat requirements will decrease as she grows.

0 to 6 months: About half of her caloric intake should come from fats.

6 months to 2 years: Her total caloric fat percentage may decrease, but you should not restrict her fat or cholesterol intake; use full-fat dairy products such as cheese and yogurt.

2 to 3 years: At this stage, 30 to 35 percent of her caloric intake averaged over a couple of days should come from fats.

FLASH FACT

Even though *coconut* has the word *nut* in it, it really is not a nut in the truest sense of the word, and therefore does not have the typical attributes of nuts. Thus, coconut allergies are very rare. The coconut is a member of the family Arecaceae, or the palm family, and is actually a very healthy food. Some cultures introduce this wonderful food to infants as early as 6 to 8 months in the form of coconut milk.

According to Mark Schauss, noted lab expert and president of Lab Interpretations, LLC, "I haven't seen any evidence that tree nut allergic people are also allergic to coconut. The only way to tell is to test both the mother and the baby. Not that this may not happen, but I haven't seen it yet."

Carbohydrates

Carbohydrates are the components of food that provide your baby's body with its primary source of fuel: glucose. His body breaks carbohydrate foods down into separate nutrients: glucose, fiber, and micronutrients. Glucose is a form of simple sugar. Blood-sugar levels, then, refer to the level of glucose (or fuel) that is in the body at a given time. Carbohydrates (or carbs) are found in many foods, but the best source for your baby from birth through about six months is the lactose (a form of milk sugar) found in breastmilk and formula.

Because your baby's digestive system is just beginning to mature, the first solid food for him needs to be something that is both easy to digest *and* provides simple fuel (glucose) with a good spectrum of micronutrients. A great choice is a milled whole-grain rice cereal. The whole grain provides natural fiber, vitamins, and minerals, and the milling process breaks down the grain to make it easier for his body to digest. Rice is naturally sweet, and mixing the rice cereal with breastmilk will make this first food both appealing and familiar to your baby.

After about 6 months, he can begin to eat additional good sources of carbs, including simple cereals made from whole grains such as oats, rice, millet, and barley; whole-grain pastas from similar grains; purees made from vegetables such as carrots, squash, and sweet potatoes, and from fruits such as apples, bananas, and apricots. As your baby gets a little older and her digestive system is becoming more mature, she can begin eating the more digestible beans, such as lentils and garbanzo beans (at around 9 months of age), which are about half carbohydrate and half protein.

By the time your child is a year old, she will be able to digest nearly all types of grains, vegetables, fruits, and legumes (beans and peas)—although they will still need to be prepared and portioned in ways appropriate to young growing

bodies. The carbohydrate needs of toddlers are highly individual and depend on factors such as how fast they are growing, how big they are, and how much physical activity they are getting.

Intact carbohydrate foods also provide your child with *fiber*, which helps with digestion and elimination. Later in life it also lowers cholesterol and helps prevent the development of certain cancers. Highly refined S.A.D. carbohydrate "white" foods have had most or all of their fiber removed in the processing, so while they are technically carbohydrate foods, they are not the best sources.

It's best to minimize S.A.D. white food products in your toddler's diet. They are low-quality carbohydrates, providing little more than simple sugar and often containing unnecessary additives such as added sugar or salt, preservatives, or artificial flavors or colors. They have usually been stripped of all their fiber, and eating them in place of fiber-filled real foods like whole fruits, vegetables, and grains can lead to constipation and a lack of micronutrients.

Avoid these poor-quality white foods (low nutrient and fiber content) as dietary staples for your toddler:
• White flour foods (cookies, crackers, noodles)
• White rice foods (instant rice, rice cakes)
• White potatoes (french fries, chips)

Another reason you want to choose higher fiber carbohydrate foods for your child is because fiber helps prevent or moderate blood-sugar spikes (and the crashes that can follow). If the glucose (sugar) in a food can be accessed quickly and easily by the body, it will raise the blood-sugar levels much faster. If the body has to work harder at breaking down a food to get to the sugar, the blood-sugar levels will rise more slowly. Gradual rises and falls in blood sugar are optimal, so you want to keep your child off the blood-sugar roller coaster.

Quick Chart

The Institute of Medicine of the National Academies (IOM) recommends 19 grams of fiber per day for 1- to 3-year-olds as the Adequate Intake.

Fiber Comparison in Grains and Breads
1 slice white toast: 0.6 g
1 slice whole-wheat toast: 2.3 g
1 regular (white) cracker: 0 g
1 whole wheat cracker: 0.5 g
1 cup mashed white potato: 3 g
1 cup mashed sweet potato: 4.3 g
1 cup cooked white rice: 0.6 g
1 cup cooked brown rice: 3.5 g
1 cup cooked couscous: 2.2 g
1 cup cooked amaranth: 5.2 g

High-Fiber Fruits
1 cup sliced avocado: 9.8 g
1 cup prunes, stewed: 7.7 g
1 cup raspberries: 8 g
1 cup blueberries: 3.6 g
1 cup sliced strawberries: 3.3 g

High-Fiber Vegetables
1 cup cooked collards: 5.3 g
1 cup cooked spinach: 4.3 g
1 cup cooked green beans: 4 g (really a legume)
1 cup cooked green peas: 8.8 g (really a legume)

Beans
1 cup cooked beans: 12 to 16 g

One way that nutritionists categorize carbohydrates is by how quickly the body can transform them into glucose. The most effective measure we have to date of how quickly a food is transformed into sugar in the body is glycemic load. Foods with a low glycemic load (10 or below) are preferable because they transform slowly into sugar. Those with a high glycemic load (20 or above) transform rapidly into blood sugar. The white foods are perfect examples of low-quality, high-glycemic-load carbohydrates. Green vegetables and beans are great examples of high-quality, high-fiber, low-glycemic-load carbohydrates. A balanced diet rich in high-quality carbohydrates promotes bowel regularity, a key component of healthy digestion. High-quality carbohydrates are also the best source for many micronutrients, including vitamins and minerals.

According to FITS 2008 (see more information about this study on page 11), toddlers are eating too many white potatoes and not enough multicolored vegetables. White potatoes are the most popular vegetable among toddlers, and yet they have the highest glycemic load of all the vegetables, and a low overall level of micronutrients. While white potatoes in and of themselves are not a bad food, because toddlers eat so many of them, mostly in poor-quality form, such as french fries, they fall into the "white food" category of poor-quality carbohydrates.

> **TIP**
>
> Macronutrient Memory Tip: Carbohydrates grow from the ground, and many proteins walk around. Fats have an oily consistency.

Vitamins and Minerals

Vitamins and minerals are two fundamental categories of micronutrients. They are vital to your child's health. They help promote growth, development, and many other essential bodily functions. Each vitamin and mineral has a different but crucial role in the complex interplay of the body's systems.

Breastmilk and iron-fortified formula provide 100 percent of the required vitamins and minerals for your baby's needs through the age of 6 months. In response to an increase in the number of children with rickets in the United States, however, the American Academy of Pediatrics now recommends that exclusively breastfed infants be given 400 IU of vitamin D each day, beginning within the first 2 months of life until they are weaned and are receiving at least 1 liter of formula or whole milk per day (400 IU equivalent).

Dr. Michael Holick, PhD, MD, a highly respected vitamin D researcher, suggests that exposing a child's (over 1 year of age) arms and hands to sunlight for 10 to 15 minutes per week (in 5- to 7-minute sessions, 2 to 3 times a day—best times are between 1 and 3 p.m.) during the summer,

Quick Chart

PRIMARY VITAMINS AND THEIR FUNCTIONS

Biotin: a member of the vitamin B family, it is essential for the metabolism of carbohydrates, fats, and proteins. The most common biotin-deficiency related symptom in infants is known as *cradle cap*, a scaly, crusty skin rash that can occur on the scalp of newborns.

Folic Acid: part of the vitamin B complex, it is best known for its importance during pregnancy in helping prevent neural tube defects in the fetus, which can lead to serious brain and spinal problems in a child. Folic acid works closely with vitamin B_{12} in the synthesis of protein as well as the production of DNA and RNA (genetic materials), and it is a key player in the development of red blood cells.

Niacin (vitamin B_3): important for energy production, metabolism of fats, maintenance of healthy skin, and support of the nervous system and the gastrointestinal tract.

Pantothenic Acid (vitamin B_5): necessary for the metabolism of carbohydrates, fats, and proteins, and support of the immune system.

Riboflavin (vitamin B_2): important for energy production and support of the nervous and immune systems, and necessary for tissue repair and healthy eyes.

Thiamin (vitamin B_1): essential for the metabolism of carbohydrates, for energy production and healthy skin, and support of the nervous system.

Vitamin A: fat-soluble vitamin, important for support of the immune system and for eyesight, and to help increase the body's resistance to infections.

Vitamin B_6: essential for support of the nervous system, healthy blood and blood vessels, and synthesis of many important molecules, including amino acids.

Vitamin B_{12} (cobalamin): is necessary for the production of red blood cells and folate metabolism. Since vitamin B_{12} is found only in animal foods, breastfed infants of vegetarian mothers may be deficient in this vitamin and thus a supplement may be needed. (See page 45 for a discussion of **vegetarianism** and vitamin B_{12}.)

Vitamin C (ascorbic acid): is a powerful antioxidant, supports the immune system, and is vital in helping the body cope with physical and emotional stress.

Vitamin D: plays a major role in calcium absorption and mineralization of bone. It is the only vitamin that can be manufactured in the body. Breastfed infants absorb it very well and usually can make adequate amounts from moderate exposure to sunlight. (See page 29 for a discussion of vitamin D production and supplementation in babies and toddlers.)

Vitamin E: is a fat-soluble vitamin and powerful antioxidant and protects the body from harmful toxins and carcinogens, including mercury, lead, benzene, nitrates, cigarette smoke, and pollution.

Vitamin K: is necessary in the production of prothrombin, an essential substance in blood clotting. Vitamin K is made by intestinal bacteria, and although the gut is sterile at birth, a single dose of vitamin K given to a newborn, along with the amounts of this nutrient supplied by breastmilk and infant formula, should provide adequate levels for infants.

PRIMARY MINERALS AND THEIR FUNCTIONS

Calcium: one of the most abundant minerals in the body, 99 percent of it is stored in bones and teeth, and it is important in maintaining bone density and strength.

Chromium: is very important in glucose metabolism and regulation, and insulin production.

Copper: is important in helping the body use iron to make hemoglobin, necessary for taste sensitivity, and an essential component for bone, cartilage, connective tissue, and skin.

Fluoride: is essential for tooth development. Fluoride supplementation is not recommended for newborns.*

Iodine: is necessary for proper function of the thyroid gland.

Iron: is a mineral needed by every cell in the body, and essential for growth and development. Healthy, full-term babies are born with an adequate amount of iron for 3 to 6 months (provided the mother consumed enough iron during pregnancy), after which these stores begin to decrease. It is recommended that breastfed infants be given an additional source of iron, as an infant must double his iron intake during his first year. Iron-rich foods can be given to infants starting at eight months.

Magnesium: is necessary for healthy bones and teeth, and vital in helping muscles relax.

Manganese: plays a role in carbohydrate, fat, and protein metabolism, and the proper functioning of nerves, and is important for various enzyme systems.

Molybdenum: helps regulate proper pH levels, is involved in carbohydrate metabolism, and is a component of tooth enamel.

Phosphorus: is important for strengthening bones and teeth, and for energy metabolism and muscle contraction.

Potassium: supports the cardiovascular system, and is necessary for proper fluid balance in cells, muscle contraction, and the nervous system.

Selenium: is important for its antioxidant and anticancer properties.

Sodium (chloride): is an electrolyte necessary for making hydrochloric acid in the stomach; it must be in balance with potassium for proper cardiovascular health.

Zinc: supports the immune system and blood-sugar balance, and for taste and smell.

*From an article posted on the Environmental Working Group's Web site, www.ewg.org/node/21416. "Parents may not know that giving fluoridated water to infants younger than 1 has the potential to cause enamel **fluorosis** [emphasis ours] in the child's permanent teeth still in development in the gums. . . . Babies already consume 'more than the optimal amount of fluoride' for their size through formula or food prepared with fluoridated water, according to the American Dental Association." The solution: the American Dental Association recommends using low-fluoride or fluoride-free bottled water labeled "purified," "demineralized," or "deionized" when mixing with powdered infant formulas.

spring, and fall is sufficient for vitamin D production and will not increase the risk of skin cancer or damage the skin. Sunscreens with a protection factor of 8 or more appear to block out vitamin D–producing UV rays. The face is the most exposed area to the sun and doesn't produce much vitamin D, so you can always use sunscreen to protect that delicate area. Babies less than 6 months of age should stay out of direct sunlight, and older babies should wear sunscreen and protective clothing when exposed to the sun. If you can't keep your baby covered and in the shade, sunscreen should be applied. Test sunscreen on a small area of skin first and watch for any reaction before covering your baby. People with darker skin need longer sun exposure for vitamin D production than lighter-skinned people, up to five times or more, according to Dr. Holick, making it potentially more important for darker-skinned children to receive supplemental vitamin D to avoid too much sun exposure without sunscreen.

The American Academy of Pediatrics also recommends supplementing with the mineral iron. It is crucial for a baby to get enough iron during his first year for growth and brain development. Proportionately speaking, a baby under 6 months of age needs more dietary iron than a full-grown man!

TIP

A breastfeeding baby's early stools usually have no odor.

TIP

ZINC-RICH FOODS

Iron supplements may decrease zinc absorption, so when you are supplementing your toddler with iron, be sure to include a variety of zinc-rich foods in her diet, such as:
beef
pork
dark-meat chicken
dark-meat turkey
eggs
yogurt
cheddar cheese
milk
nut butters, especially almond, cashew, tahini (sesame seed), and peanut*
chickpeas (garbanzo beans), kidney beans, and split peas

*Tree nuts and peanuts are very common allergens. It is recommended, therefore, that parents refrain from introducing them into their children's diets until at least their first birthday. Children who are at risk for food allergies should wait even longer. Toddlers under 3 years old should not be given whole nuts or seeds because they are a choking hazard.

The AAP cites low iron as the most common mineral deficiency in American children. **Iron deficiency** can cause *anemia*, hinder your baby's growth, and affect his brain function. If your baby is partially or totally formula fed, the AAP recommends using an iron-fortified brand from birth through 12 months. Although supplemental iron can cause constipation in adults, it is not generally believed to do that in babies.

If your baby is exclusively breastfed, then the combination of your breastmilk and the iron stores he was born with will provide him with ample levels of iron until he reaches about 6 months of age. At that time you can start giving him one or two servings of iron-fortified rice cereal a day or supplement his diet with elemental iron (1 mg/kg per day). According to the American Academy of Pediatrics, for breastfed preterm infants or those with low birth weight, an oral iron supplement (elemental iron) in the form of drops (2 mg/kg once per day) should be given starting at 1 month until the baby reaches 12 months of age.

For all formula-fed infants, only iron-fortified formula should be used during the first year of life, regardless of the age when formula is started (see page 81 for more information about formula recommendations).

The breastmilk from poorly nourished moms still contains enough micronutrients in a high enough volume to provide for a baby's micronutrient needs, but the quality of breastmilk from well-nourished moms is

FLASH FACTS

YOUR CHILD'S SPECIAL SUPPLEMENT NEEDS: IRON
Recommended Daily Allowance (RDA) for iron by age:
0 to 6 months: 0.27 mg (Adequate Intake)
7 to 12 months: 11 mg
1 to 3 years: 7 mg

definitely optimal. (See page 69 for nutritional guidelines for breastfeeding mothers.)

FLASH FACT

Breastmilk is affected by the following vitamins and minerals in Mom's diet:
vitamins A, B_6, B_{12}, and D
riboflavin
thiamin
iodine
selenium

If you are a **vegan** (see chapter 4 for the definitions of vegetarianism and veganism) breastfeeding mom, to ensure enough vitamin B_{12} for your baby, you should take a B_{12} supplement (or consult your pediatrician about supplementing your baby directly) or consult a nutritionist to make sure you are getting adequate amounts in your daily diet. (See chapter 4 for more tips about supplementation.)

As your baby grows into a toddler, her rate of growth will slow and her appetite may decrease. She may need fewer calories for a while, but her body will need *more* vitamins and minerals.

A toddler's micronutrient needs can generally be met by a varied diet of real foods that is rich in fruit and vegetables. You may have to dress up or modify the foods you are offering to ensure that she is getting enough of certain "tricky" vitamins and minerals, namely **vitamin A**, calcium, iron, and zinc. These are found in foods that toddlers are often picky about. In some situations a supplement may be recommended. (See chapter 6 for specific nutritional recommendations for each stage of development.)

Quick Chart

NUTRIENT COMPONENTS OF FOOD

Macronutrients
Carbohydrates: are the body's best source of fuel—glucose or blood sugar. High-glycemic-load carbs are foods that turn rapidly into blood sugar. Low-glycemic-load carbohydrates take more time to break down into sugars and generally have a higher fiber content.
Proteins: help build cells, especially muscles and bones. They also help support the body's communication systems.
Fats: lubricate and protect the organs. They also make up cell membranes and support brain function.

Micronutrients
Vitamins: are organic compounds that support life in the body.
Minerals: are elements that come from the earth and cannot be made by organic life forms.

A Balanced Diet: Baby and Toddler Nutrition Needs

There are no specific USDA Food Pyramid recommendations for babies and toddlers, but other reputable associations offer general guidelines. See chapters 5 and 6 for a monthly breakdown of which foods to introduce when and portion guidelines.

TIP

The American Dietetic Association recommends that for babies aged 6 to 12 months, 5 to 10 percent of their calories should come from protein, 30 to 40 percent from fat, and 50 to 65 percent from carbohydrates.

Quick Chart

CALORIES/SERVINGS BY AGE

The American Heart Association offers general guidelines.

	1 year	2-3 years
Kilocalories[a]	900	1,000
Fat, % of total kcal	30-40	30-35
Milk/dairy, cups[b]	2[c]	2
Lean meat/beans, oz	1½	2
Fruits, cups[d]	1	1
Vegetables, cups[d]	¾	1
Grains, oz[e]	2	3

[a] Calorie estimates are based on a sedentary lifestyle. Increased physical activity will require additional calories: 0 to 200 kcal more a day if moderately physically active; 200 to 400 kcal more a day if very physically active.
[b] Milk listed is fat-free (except for children under the age of 2 years). If 1%, 2%, or whole-fat milk is substituted, this will utilize, for each cup, 19, 39, or 63 kcal of discretionary calories and add 2.6, 5.1, or 9.0 g of total fat, of which 1.3, 2.6, or 4.6 g are saturated fat.
[c] For 1-year-old children, calculations are based on 2% fat milk. If 2 cups of whole milk are substituted, 48 kcal of discretionary calories will be utilized. The American Academy of Pediatrics recommends that low-fat/reduced-fat milk not be started before 2 years of age.
[d] Serving sizes are ¼ cup for 1 year of age, ⅓ cup for 2 to 3 years of age, and ½ cup for 4 years of age and older. A variety of vegetables should be selected from each subgroup over the week.
[e] Half of all grains should be whole grains.

[Source: Gidding, Denison, Birch et al. "Dietary Recommendations for Children and Adolescents: A Guide for Practictioners," American Heart Association, www.americanheart.org]

Decoding Food Labels

One important way to keep track of your child's nutritional intake is to be a savvy label reader. You can make judgments about the quality of a food based partly on its list of ingredients and the amount of nutrients it provides.

All packaged foods are required by both the **Food and Drug Administration (FDA)** and the U.S. Department of Agriculture to list certain nutritional information. This information is labeled "Nutrition Facts" and is usually found on the back or the side of the package. If a food does not come in packaging, like fresh fish or produce, you can usually find the nutritional information on cards on or near the food bins or containers.

INGREDIENTS

You will also find a list of ingredients. That list is in the order of the largest ingredient amount (which comes first) to the smallest ingredient amount (which comes last). So if the first item on the label is sugar, you know that there is more sugar than anything else in that food. This information is also useful in helping you decode misleading label language.

A nutrient that provides less than 5 percent of the RDA is considered "low" in quantity (e.g., low sodium). A nutrient that provides between 10 and 19 percent of the RDA is considered a "good" source (e.g., good source of calcium). A nutrient that provides over 20 percent of the RDA is considered a "high" in quantity (e.g., high in fiber).

For instance, a bread may carry a claim that it's "made with whole grains." That makes it sound like a high-quality real food, right? But if you see whole oats and whole wheat as the last two items in a long list of ingredients, and white flour (which is refined, not whole wheat) as the first, you'll know that this is actually a processed product, probably with a high glycemic load. If you want to make sure that a bread is higher quality, look at the fiber content. If one serving provides 3 or more grams of fiber, that is a better choice.

FLASH FACT

A *calorie* is a unit of energy-producing potential contained in a food.

NUTRITIONAL INFORMATION

At the top of the label you will see the number of total calories in one serving of the food and the calories from the fat in that serving. This information will tell you what percentage of the food is made up of fat.

You will also see the amounts, in total number of grams or milligrams per serving, of the following nutrients:
• Total fat, including a breakdown of saturated, unsaturated, trans fat and cholesterol

- Total carbohydrates, including a breakdown of fiber and sugar
- Protein

At the end, you will also see certain key vitamins and minerals. Their content is given in the form of percent of daily values.

PERCENT DAILY VALUES

The percent daily values for all the nutrients is listed on the right-hand side of the label. The percentages are based on a 2,000-calorie-a-day diet. So for a person with a 2,000-calorie diet, a 45 percent value for vitamin A tells you that one serving of that food contains nearly half of the RDA of vitamin A for the day. You also know that it is a food high in vitamin A (because it contains more than 20 percent RDA).

Because the calorie needs of an average 1- to 3-year-old are much lower than 2,000 calories (about 1,000 calories per day is typical), you can't use the percentages to determine their daily value for him. But those percentages *will* give you a rough idea of whether that food is low, medium, or high in a particular nutrient.

SERVING SIZE

Be sure to pay attention to the serving size. This is given at the top of the label along with the servings per container. You may read all the nutritional information and think that a food is quite low in calories and sugar, but note how many servings there are in one package.

What may look like a single-serving bag of snacks can actually be labeled as two servings, in which case you'd be getting twice the amount of calories and sugar you thought if you consumed the whole bag.

On the other hand, you might find a cereal that looks very high in fiber: 11 grams per serving. But the serving size given is a whopping 1½ cups, too much for a small child to consume in one sitting. In that case, you must divide the nutrient totals according to the amount you might actually serve. So, for example, if you divide by three for ½-cup servings, the fiber content goes down to less than 4 grams.

A High-Quality Diet

While it is important to be familiar with the general nutrition guidelines recommended by well-established pediatric health authorities, remember that providing your child with a high-quality diet of a variety of real foods will provide a strong nutritional foundation for a lifetime of good health.

Here are some general guidelines for building and maintaining a high-quality diet:
- Choose a variety of age-appropriate fresh, whole, minimally processed foods containing an appropriate balance of carbohydrates, protein, and high-quality fats.
- Supplement micronutrients when necessary.
- Be a label detective to avoid chemical or artificial additives or

preservatives, poor-quality fats, or excess salt (sodium) or sugar.

- Prepare the bulk of your child's food at home—it takes only about an hour a week to make the staples (we'll show you how).
- Avoid prepackaged or highly refined white foods—choose whole-grain versions instead.
- Choose predominately whole fruits over fruit juices.
- Avoid all sweetened drinks (including soda, juice "drinks," etc.).

FLASH FACT

Food manufacturers are required to state the presence of any allergens (milk, eggs, peanuts, wheat, soy, fish, shellfish, or tree nuts) in a food on a label following or next to the ingredients list.

16 total pieces in the package

Nutritional breakdown

Allergen alert

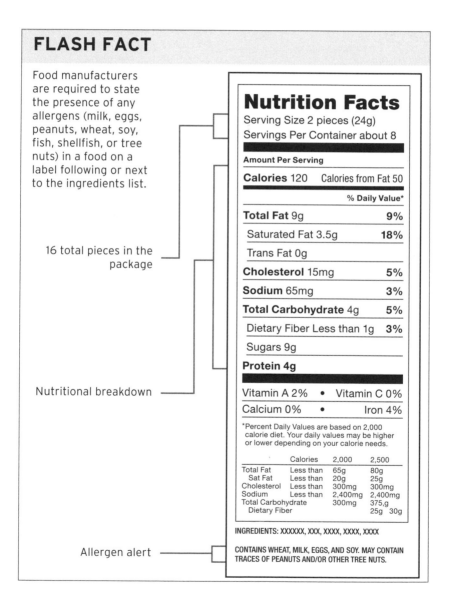

Nutrition Facts

Serving Size 2 pieces (24g)
Servings Per Container about 8

Amount Per Serving

Calories 120   Calories from Fat 50

% Daily Value*

Total Fat 9g	**9%**
Saturated Fat 3.5g	**18%**
Trans Fat 0g	
Cholesterol 15mg	**5%**
Sodium 65mg	**3%**
Total Carbohydrate 4g	**5%**
Dietary Fiber Less than 1g	**3%**
Sugars 9g	
Protein 4g	

Vitamin A 2%   •   Vitamin C 0%
Calcium 0%   •   Iron 4%

*Percent Daily Values are based on 2,000 calorie diet. Your daily values may be higher or lower depending on your calorie needs.

	Calories	2,000	2,500
Total Fat	Less than	65g	80g
Sat Fat	Less than	20g	25g
Cholesterol	Less than	300mg	300mg
Sodium	Less than	2,400mg	2,400mg
Total Carbohydrate		300mg	375,g
Dietary Fiber		25g	30g

INGREDIENTS: XXXXXX, XXX, XXXX, XXXX, XXXX

CONTAINS WHEAT, MILK, EGGS, AND SOY. MAY CONTAIN TRACES OF PEANUTS AND/OR OTHER TREE NUTS.

The Vegetarian Toddler: Pros and Cons

Vegetarianism Defined

The choice of whether or not to eat food from animals is a very individual one. You may already be a vegetarian and wish to raise your child in the same way. Or perhaps you eat meat and other animal foods but may want to start your baby or toddler off as a vegetarian. People choose vegetarianism for a variety of reasons: for health or economic reasons, because of environmental or ecologic concerns, because they do not like the taste or texture of animal foods, for ethical reasons involving the inhumane treatment of animals, or for cultural or religious reasons.

The term *vegetarian* covers several different types of eating styles. A vegetarian diet is primarily a plant-based diet that does not include meat, poultry, or fish, but some vegetarians may choose to eat other animal products, such as dairy (**lacto-vegetarians**), eggs (**ovo-vegetarians**), or both (**lacto-ovo vegetarians**). A vegetarian who chooses not to eat animal products of any kind, including honey, is usually distinguished by the term *vegan*.

> ### Warning
>
> A **fruitarian** is a type of vegetarian who chooses to eat only fruit, seeds, and nuts. This strict diet is not recommended for babies or toddlers because it does not provide adequate amounts of vital nutrients for healthy growth rates.

Vegetarian Diet: Is It Safe?

According to the **American Dietetic Association (ADA)**, a varied, appropriately planned vegetarian diet can meet all of a growing baby's and toddler's nutritional needs, as well as those of children and adolescents. The American Academy of Pediatrics (AAP) is less favorable toward a vegan diet for young children than lacto-ovo vegetarianism because it can be harder to meet all their nutrient needs without including eggs and milk in the diet. Children of different world populations, however, have thrived for centuries on various vegetarian diets, including vegan. Many groups, including the ADA, believe that with careful planning and appropriate food choices, it is perfectly possible to provide a vegan diet for your toddler that offers ample nutrition for her health and growth.

Although research tells us that vegetarian children tend to be leaner than non-vegetarian children, if they eat a **Vegetarian Standard American Diet**, those kids (and adults!) can be more at risk of riding the blood-sugar roller coaster than non-vegetarian kids, which can lead to overeating habits and becoming overweight. S.A.D. vegetarians, like S.A.D. non-vegetarians, eat a lot of super-sweet junk foods, but they have removed some or all of the animal foods from their diets.

Because animal foods provide some of the most concentrated forms of protein, S.A.D. vegetarians are usually not getting enough protein to offset the large amount of simple sugars they consume. In fact, without adequate protein, fiber (stripped away if they are eating S.A.D. refined carbohydrates instead of complex carbs), or good-quality fat, S.A.D. vegetarian children can find

themselves so deeply entrenched in the blood-sugar roller coaster that the more simple sugars they consume, the more they want to eat. This can sabotage or even counteract the health benefits of a vegetarian diet.

If you decide to raise your child as a vegetarian, it is crucial that you feed them high-quality, real plant foods, and not the poor-quality super-sweet refined carbs characteristic of the Standard American Diet.

Getting enough calories and nutrients in a child's diet helps to ensure a healthy rate of growth. Based on the available studies comparing growth rates of vegetarian and non-vegetarian children, there is little difference between the two groups: By age 10 they are growing at about the same rate.

The Health Benefits

The health benefits of a high-quality (balanced and varied) vegetarian diet have been well documented by research. Vegetarian children eat more fruits, vegetables, beans, and nuts than their non-vegetarian peers. Unsurprisingly, their fiber intake is higher, too. They also eat fewer sweets and consume fewer food additives, preservatives, and pesticides, and less saturated fat and cholesterol. As a group they tend to have lower body fat percentages than non-vegetarian kids. A vegetarian diet can lower the risk for heart disease and may even prevent certain types of cancer later in life.

A healthy vegetarian diet for children should include a lot of variety, provide an adequate number of calories for growth and energy, and supply absorbable sources of vital nutrients, particularly protein, vitamin B_{12}, vitamin D, calcium, iron, and zinc.

FLASH FACT

FACTORY FARMING

If a meat or fish does not carry a label saying **"organic,"** **"natural,"** or **"wild caught,"** it is most likely raised in a conventional manner known as **factory farmed**. With this method of farming, fish and livestock (including cows, laying hens, broiler chickens, pigs, veal calves, etc.) are kept indoors throughout most of their lives. Animals are fed "conventional" foods, most often grains such as genetically modified (GMO) corn, with no restrictions on pesticides, herbicides, fungicides, and fertilizers. The animals' living conditions allow for very limited movement, and they may be fed growth hormones, sprayed with fungicides, and given antibiotics in order to avoid potential diseases that may arise from crowded living conditions. There is also a difference, from a nutritional standpoint, between factory farmed and organic meat. Farmed fish, for example, provide lower amounts of beneficial omega-3 fats than wild caught fish.

The Challenges

Many people think that it's too hard to raise a vegetarian toddler. It will take too much time, require a lot of unfamiliar foods, and you'll have to monitor every meal to make sure they don't become malnourished. The truth is, despite the special requirements, it's not much more difficult to feed a toddler a healthy vegetarian diet than it is to feed one a healthy non-vegetarian diet! Typical challenges of providing a vegetarian diet for your toddler can be divided into three main issues: public perceptions (or, more accurately, misperceptions), getting enough calories, and getting enough nutrients.

PUBLIC (MIS)PERCEPTIONS

If you told your neighbors that you've decided to raise your baby or toddler as a vegetarian, you probably wouldn't receive a lot of support. They may even try to warn you that it's dangerous. Many Westerners are entrenched in the idea that a growing child must eat meat, poultry, and/or fish to be healthy. While it's clear that this is a myth, the misperception is still very prevalent.

Although there is statistical information, public polls tell us that only about 2 to 3 percent of the U.S. population does not eat meat, poultry, or fish, and of that group 30 to 50 percent is vegan. Part of the problem with common misperceptions may just be that few of us come in regular contact with vegetarians. If we saw a lot of healthy children being raised without meats, it would probably dispel some of the skepticism about the benefits of vegetarianism.

Despite the fact that research citing the benefits of a non-meat diet is out there, and highly respected nutritional information resources such as the ADA and AAP have deemed vegetarianism healthy for kids, there are even some pediatricians who will hesitate to endorse your decision. That lack of support may make it difficult for you to make this choice, even if you have been living vegetarian yourself for years! It's hard enough if your mom is disapproving, but if your pediatrician warns you about it, too, it's natural to have some concerns.

The best path you can take in that situation is to get as much information about the topic as you can. There are many great educational resources readily available online or in print. (See Resources for a list of excellent Web sites that provide information, research data, helpful food tips, and strategies for raising vegetarian and vegan children.) You might also feel more confident if you explored resources for vegetarian cooking—they often have great ideas for tasty and nutrient-rich meat substitutions or replacements. Over the last 10 years there has been a veritable explosion in vegetarian cookbooks. You can also consult chapters 10 and 11 for many excellent vegetarian recipes.

ENERGY NEEDS VERSUS FIBER BULK

One of the genuine but easily manageable challenges of the vegetarian diet for young children lies in the nature of most plant-based foods: Vegetables, fruits, grains, and beans contain lots of fiber, but are relatively low in calories. Toddler bodies need a high number of calories, and sometimes, on a vegetarian diet, the bulk of the fiber in those foods can fill up little tummies without providing enough actual calories for energy. In a time when most of our children are not eating enough fiber, however, this is a somewhat atypical problem.

You're most likely to encounter this challenge when your child weans off breastmilk entirely, before his diet is filled out with a wide variety of foods. You can remedy the situation in one of several ways. Make sure you regularly provide a selection of calorie-dense food choices at meals and for snacks. Good options include real foods with a high fat content (remember: Fat has more than twice the calories of protein or carbohydrates), such as avocado, olives, vegetable oils, and nut (see nut allergy warning on page 25) and seed butters. Get into the habit of providing a fat-rich food whenever you offer a high-fiber grain or vegetable, such as butter in oatmeal (if your child is lacto-veg), avocado slices with any vegetable, or tahini (sesame seed butter) drizzled on toast.

You can also offer calorie-rich snacks between meals, such as smoothies made with added oils, avocado, full-fat yogurt (if lacto-veg), coconut milk, or nut butters (once past his first birthday if no allergies). Although dried fruits such as apricots, raisins, and apples are high in fiber, they are another high-calorie choice. You can also make fruity puddings by mashing banana with a little full-fat silken tofu. (See chapter 10 for more ideas for other concentrated energy snacks.)

If you need to, you can also reduce her total intake of fiber for a time by peeling some of her fruits and vegetables (there's usually more fiber in the skins than the flesh of produce), or offering her lower fiber grains (rice and millet have fewer grams of fiber than amaranth or quinoa). But this will probably not be necessary. The recommended adequate intake of fiber for 1- to 3-year-olds is 19 grams, and unless your child is eating large quantities of the highest fiber fruits, vegetables, and beans, you are unlikely to encounter any problems. (See page 28 for a chart of foods highest in fiber.)

VEGETARIAN NUTRITION

Because meat, poultry, and fish are rich sources of certain key nutrients, you need to make sure they are replaced with adequate substitutes when they are removed from the diet. The nutrients to monitor most carefully for your vegetarian child are protein, vitamin B_{12}, riboflavin, vitamin D, calcium, iron, and zinc.

Guidelines for Meeting Vegetarian Nutrient Needs

PROTEIN

As a baby, your child will get all of his protein requirements met through breastmilk or formula for the first 6 months. When you begin introducing solid foods to any child, animal protein foods aren't typically offered until his digestive system has matured somewhat, usually around 9 months of age. So all kids really begin their solid diets as vegetarians, usually with simple grain cereals, single-vegetable purees, and then fruit purees.

At 8 or 9 months, you can begin introducing him to some more concentrated protein sources, including cheeses, yogurt, other dairy, and egg yolks, if he is not vegan. But toddlers can meet their protein requirements relatively easily through plant sources. The key is to offer a variety of different foods. You do not have to count grams if you are regularly offering combinations of protein-rich plant foods at regular intervals, including snack time, every day (see chart for some good suggestions for protein-rich vegetarian foods).

Quick Chart

PROTEIN-RICH AND VEGETARIAN FOODS

For babies (introduce at 8 to 9 months): breastmilk, formula, full-fat yogurt (cow, goat, or soy), full-fat cottage cheese, tofu, cooked egg yolks, seed butter (sunflower, tahini), soft-cooked lentil, and garbanzo bean or pea purees.

For toddlers (12 months and older): full-fat dairy (milk, cheese, yogurt–cow, goat, or soy), tofu, whole grains (especially quinoa, which contains 8 essential amino acids), beans, peas, nut and seed butters (with allergy caution), high-quality prepared vegetarian meat substitutes (for hot dogs, lunch meat, ground beef, chicken, etc.), and protein powders (18 months and older; see page 289 for a thorough discussion about choosing and using protein powders).

Quick Chart

RECOMMENDED DAILY ALLOWANCES (RDA) AND ADEQUATE INTAKES (AI)

	AI	RDA
Calcium	Birth to 6 months: 210 mg 7 to 12 months: 270 mg 1 to 3 years: 500 mg	
Iron	0 to 6 months: 0.27 mg 7 to 12 months: 11 mg	1 to 3 years: 7 mg
Vitamin B_{12}	0 to 6 months: 0.4 mcg 7 to 12 months: 0.5 mcg	1 to 3 years: 0.9 mcg
Vitamin D	Birth to 3 years: 200 IU	
Zinc (for non-vegetarians)		7 months to 3 years: 3 mg

TIP

The American Dietetic Association recommends that lacto-ovo vegetarian toddlers 1 to 2 years old get about 13 grams of protein per day, and vegan toddlers get 18 to19 grams. Lacto-ovo vegetarian toddlers 2 to 3 years old need about 16 grams per day, and vegan toddlers need 18 to 21 grams.

FLASH FACT

There are 1,000 micrograms in 1 milligram, and 1,000 milligrams in 1 gram.

VITAMIN B_{12}

Vitamin B_{12} is a crucial nutrient for children's growth and development. It also supports the nervous system and the production of red blood cells. Inadequate amounts can cause anemia. It's the only nutrient to be found (in a form that humans can use) exclusively in animal foods. Good sources are meat, poultry, fish, dairy products, and eggs. Vegetarian babies and toddlers eating milk and eggs will typically get ample vitamin B_{12} from their diet with no supplementation.

Vegan children, however, will need to eat a supplemental form of B_{12} on a regular basis. If you are a lactating vegan mom, you should also be eating B_{12}-fortified foods or taking regular B_{12} supplements to ensure that your breastmilk is providing an adequate supply of B_{12}.

Vitamin B_{12}-Rich Vegetarian and Vegan Foods

For vegetarian babies and toddlers, try egg yolks, full-fat milk (do not boil, boiling can destroy B_{12}), and cheese. (Yogurt and cottage cheese are not the best dairy sources because fermentation reduces the B_{12} content.)

For vegan babies, toddlers, and lactating mothers, try soy milk, veggie burger mixes, non-hydrogenated vegetable oil margarines, nutritional yeast, and some breakfast cereals.

VITAMIN B_2 (RIBOFLAVIN)

Riboflavin is an important nutrient for children because it helps convert macronutrients (protein, fat, and carbohydrates) into energy. It also supports the creation and repair of the tissues of the body. In a few studies, vegans were found to have a low riboflavin intake.

Riboflavin-Rich Vegan Foods

For vegan babies, try whole-grain cereals and yeast extract spreads (such as Vegemite or Marmite)

For vegan toddlers, try almond butter, leafy green vegetables (spinach), yeast extract spread, and fortified breakfast cereals.

VITAMIN D

Vitamin D helps support calcium absorption for the formation of strong, healthy bones. Vitamin D may also support a healthy immune system. Most of the best sources are from animal foods (cod liver oil, salmon, mackerel, sardines, and milk), but with moderate exposure to the sun (about 20 minutes a day on hands and face), the bodies of light-skinned children can manufacture sufficient vitamin D internally. (See the vitamin D supplementation tip on page 29 for guidelines about healthy sun exposure.)

However, if your child lives in a polluted environment that blocks ultraviolet rays, or is dark skinned (requiring prolonged sun exposure to manufacture adequate vitamin D), then he should have supplemental vitamin D. Vegetarian and vegan babies who are exclusively breastfed should also take a vitamin D supplement.

There are a few fortified-food sources of vitamin D that would be appropriate for vegetarian and vegan toddlers.

Vitamin D-Rich Vegetarian Fortified Foods

For vegetarian babies, try cow's, soy, or rice milk.

For vegetarian toddlers, try cow's, soy, or rice milk, and some breakfast cereals.

CALCIUM

Calcium keeps bones strong. Most of it is stored in the bones and teeth, but 1 percent is maintained in the fluids and tissues to help with muscle and blood vessel contraction, hormone and enzyme release, and communication throughout the nervous system. There is more calcium than any other mineral in the body.

Lacto-ovo vegetarian babies and toddlers typically get ample calcium in their daily diet from milk, yogurt, and cottage and other cheese, but vegan children will benefit from the addition of calcium-rich foods to their regular diet.

Calcium-Rich Vegan Foods

For vegan babies, try tahini, mashed tofu (made with calcium sulfate; at 8 or 9 months), beans, and blackstrap molasses.

For vegan toddlers, try tofu (made with calcium sulfate), turnip greens, kale, Chinese cabbage, collard greens, ground nuts (see allergen warning on page 25), blackstrap molasses, and beans.

IRON

Iron-deficiency is the most common nutrient deficiency among both vegetarian and non-vegetarian children. When there isn't enough iron in the body, the amount of oxygen going to the cells is decreased. This can make a child look pale and feel tired and listless. It can also suppress his immune system, making him more susceptible to illness.

There are two types of iron: **heme**, which is present in flesh foods such as beef, poultry, fish, and shellfish, and **nonheme**, which is present in plant foods. While non-heme is more absorbable than heme iron, you need more of it to obtain adequate dietary iron stores. You can increase non-heme iron absorption by offering your toddler a vitamin C–rich food along with an iron-rich food.

Nonheme Iron-Rich Vegetarian Foods

Nonheme iron–rich vegetarian foods appropriate for babies include whole-grain cereals, blackstrap molasses, and mashed tofu.

Nonheme iron–rich vegetarian foods appropriate for toddlers include tofu, beans (lentil, kidney, lima, and navy have high iron concentrations), dark green leafy vegetables, blackstrap molasses, whole-grain cereals, and fortified oatmeal or breakfast cereal.

Vitamin C–rich foods (to enhance nonheme iron absorption when serving iron-rich foods) include citrus fruits (oranges, grapefruit), canta-loupe, strawberries, kiwi fruit, tomatoes, broccoli, and sweet red peppers.

Try these vegetarian iron-rich mini-meals with Vitamin C boosters:
- Hummus with tomato slices and whole wheat crackers
- Lentils and spinach
- Sesame granola with plain yogurt mixed with lemon and blackstrap molasses
- Sweet red peppers and kale

ZINC

Zinc supports normal growth and development in your child. It also supports her immune system and helps speed the healing of wounds. Because there are rich plant-based sources of zinc, vegetarian, vegan, and non-vegetarian children consume about the same amounts of zinc in their diets.

But vegetarian and vegan children tend to eat many more foods that are high in phytates or **phytic acid** (whole grains and legumes), which blocks the absorption of zinc. As a result, veg kids may need up to 50 percent more zinc in their diets than the RDA for non-veg kids. Eating a little miso soup or miso paste with zinc-rich foods will help enhance the zinc absorption.

Phytic acid also binds to other important nutrients, such as iron and calcium, and can block their absorption as well. You can reduce the phytic acid content in grains and beans by soaking them for at least 3 hours or overnight, then throwing away the soak water before cooking. Leavening of grains with yeast also neutralizes phytates somewhat, so yeasted, baked, whole-grain products (in moderate amounts) can provide bioavailable forms of these micronutrients as well.

Zinc-Rich Vegetarian Foods

Foods appropriate for babies (over 8 months) include whole-grain cereals, whole-grain pasta, and mashed tofu.

Foods appropriate for toddlers include whole-grain cereals,

whole-grain pasta, tofu, wheat germ, nut butter (almond, peanut*), beans (soybeans, baked beans, and chickpeas are especially high in zinc), Swiss cheese, and fortified breakfast cereal.

*Peanuts and tree nuts are very common allergens. See chapter 6 for a more thorough discussion of food allergies and sensitivities.

The Soy Controversy

For such a little green bean, soy has been in the middle of a big tug-of-war for the last hundred years. On one side of the debate, soy is viewed as a profitable cash crop with numerous health benefits. On the other side is the view that the huge soy agribusiness industry is clouding the facts about soy: that some of the growth processes (genetic crop modification and heavy pesticide use) may not be safe; that its health benefits are inaccurate or overrated; and that it may, in fact, be harmful to our health, especially in certain forms. The debate surrounding soy is of particular interest to vegetarians because soy and soy products have been touted as a healthy meat substitute based on its high protein content (1 cup of cooked soybeans contains 29 grams of protein).

Special interest groups have worked diligently to find many uses for soy products in the United States, from cheese to burgers to baby formula to livestock feed. Huge amounts of soy are consumed annually by livestock animals, thereby ending up in the American meat-eater's diet indirectly, as well as directly in other food products. With a U.S. production of almost three billion bushels annually, soy is a big business (second to corn, with approximately twelve billion bushels annually). In fact, the Soyfood Association of North America reported that between 1992 and 2006, sales of soy foods skyrocketed from $300 million to *$3.9 billion*. Americans are consuming soy in unprecedented amounts. This is due, in part, to a popularization of the notion that the Japanese have the lowest rate of heart disease because they "eat lots of soy."

Well, yes and no.

The Japanese, in fact, do not eat *lots of* soy. When they do, they typically eat it in small amounts and in a fermented form, such as miso paste and tempeh. The fermentation process makes the soy more digestible and removes its high concentration of phytates. Phytates are compounds that bind to minerals such as calcium, zinc, iron, and copper, causing them to be excreted from the body unabsorbed. But fermenting the soybean destroys the phytates and allows you to get the most nutritional benefits. With this in mind, we recommend using small amounts of soy products sparingly in your toddler's diet to reap the nutritional benefits and avoid the risks. Choose organic to avoid genetically modified (GMO) soy and pesticides, and include some fermented options. We recommend avoiding concentrated forms of soy, such as soy protein powders and lots of soy milk. The best choices are small amounts of organic tofu, miso paste, tempeh, and tamari. Older toddlers can also occasionally snack on the baby form of the fresh beans, edamame. (See page 50 for a discussion of soy-based formulas.)

CONTRADICTORY RESEARCH

The soybean is considered an *isoflavone*, and is one branch of a family of chemical compounds called *phytochemicals* found in all plants, and legumes, including beans, green leafy vegetables, yellow and orange vegetables and whole grains.

Isoflavones are also considered *phytoestrogens* —or weak estrogen compounds—that can exert effects similar to those of the natural estrogen hormone. Many of soy's touted health benefits are related to adults and heart disease, or women and menopausal symptoms. According to Dr. Dixie Mills, who writes for Women to Women, a women's-health Web site by female doctors, phytoestrogens have the ability to interact with estrogen receptors in our bodies, where they can evoke responses similar to the natural hormone estrogen. But the intensity of an estrogen receptor's bond with isoflavones is *much* weaker (a thousand times or so) than the bond with the natural hormone. Isoflavones also function as antioxidants, counteracting free radicals in our tissues, which may be why some research shows they can protect against cancer.

For adults, research suggests that daily intake of soy protein may slightly lower cholesterol LDL levels (the "bad" cholesterol), and some studies have indicated that soy products may reduce hot flashes after menopause. But according to the National Institutes of Health (NIH), the results have been inconclusive. The NIH also cautions that soy may cause stomach and bowel problems because it is difficult to digest for many people, and it is considered an allergenic food. They argue that "the safety of long-term soy has not been established."

Dr. Kaayla Daniel, PhD, CCN, author of *The Whole Soy Story*, disagrees with every argument that is in favor of soy and cites many other studies to support this. She argues that soy does not reliably lower cholesterol, and in fact raises **homocysteine** levels in many people, which has been found to increase the risk of heart disease, stroke, and birth defects. Dr. Daniel also negates previous studies that promoted soy as heart healthy with a study published by the *American Journal of Clinical Nutrition*. The study found that there were no beneficial effects of soy for lowering cholesterol in postmenopausal women. Also, total cholesterol and HDL cholesterol (the "good" cholesterol) levels weren't much different between the soy-consuming group and the untreated group. As a result, she and other experts have sent a sixty-five-page petition to the FDA asking the administration to retract the "soy prevents heart disease" health claim.

SOY FORMULA

There is little documentation to recommend soy formula for babies. It is often promoted as a good alternative when a baby has a milk allergy or sensitivity, but there are other reliable soy-free formulas available for those special circumstances. Dr. Daniel cites numerous studies and references detailing the dangers of soy. She specifically mentions soy baby formula, which uses soy protein isolate (SPI) as the key ingredient. SPI is the result of a manufacturing process that involves high temperatures, high pressures, solvent extraction, and alkaline baths: the soybean is heated, pressurized, chemically altered, and then bleached and flavored. This process has been reported to produce nitrosamine—a known carcinogen.

Soy formula contains levels of aluminum 10 times greater than milk-based formula and 100 times greater than breastmilk. Aluminum can negatively affect bone and nervous system development.

Soy formula contains higher concentrations of the mineral manganese (200–300 μg) than cow's-milk formula (3–10 μg). Newborns exposed to high levels of manganese are vulnerable to brain disorders such as learning disabilities, attention deficit disorders, and other behavioral conditions. Healthy adults and toddlers can eliminate the excess amounts; infants cannot because of their immature livers.

A *Lancet* study showed that daily exposure to "estrogen mimickers" for infants who consume soy formula was six to eleven times higher than for adults consuming soy foods. The blood concentration of these hormones was 13,000 to 22,000 times higher than natural estrogen concentrations.

About 80 percent of soy in the marketplace is from genetically modified beans.

The debate rages on. Some studies support soy; others refute its benefits. Researchers on the pro side claim that in the last 25 years, 20 million infants have been fed soy formula and there have been no ill effects. Others believe that more information about safety is still needed, as phytoestrogen doses given to infants have been shown to cause cancer in some animal studies.

American Family Physician journal reported the results of a recent meta-analysis (a group of studies) related to soy protein formula. The researchers at the Centers for Disease Control, the Food and Drug Administration, and the National Institutes of Health wanted to look more closely at its safety. The panel reviewed 229 studies, which included 38 specifically on soy protein–based formula on human health. Although the panel did not find any detrimental effects of soy, it concluded that the human studies were of limited use because of poor study design. Once again: inconclusive results.

The decision about whether or not to use soy is an individual one. We believe that in this situation, as with so many others in our S.A.D. culture, most of the reported dangers of soy are the result of overconsumption, of high refinement, and of industrial farming and conventional food processing techniques.

[Sources: Kaayla, Daniel, CCN, *The Whole Soy Story.* Washington, DC: New Trends Publishing, Inc. 2005. Kevin Johnson et al., "Effects of Soy Protein-Based Formula in Full-term Infants," *American Family Physician* (January 1, 2008). NIH.gov., Herbs at a Glance: Soy, http://nccam.nih.gov/health/soy/. Dixie Mills, "Nutritional and Health Benefits of Soy: What's in a Bean?" Womentowomen.com.]

Feeding
Your Child

The First Year

Rapid Growth

Your baby's first year is a powerful and delightful time of incredibly rapid growth and development for both of you. The months will go by before you know it, and your baby will be making changes in her eating habits practically every month. It's a wonderful time of learning and it can set the stage for healthy eating habits in the toddler years and beyond.

This chapter is divided into four sections, each one covering a pivotal eating phase in the first year of your baby's life: 0 to 4 months, 4 to 6 months, 6 to 9 months, and 9 to 12 months. Each section begins with a list of best food suggestions for that phase. You'll also find descriptions of what to expect as your baby develops her eating skills. There are tips to help you prepare for any changes or new practices at each age, and lots of suggestions to help you meet common challenges with confidence.

Feeding at Birth to 4 Months

BEST FOOD

Breastmilk or **iron-fortified formula**, exclusively

For the first 4 months of your baby's life, his best food is breastmilk. If you are unable to breastfeed your baby, iron-fortified formula is the next best choice. Breastmilk or formula should be the only foods you give him during this time. If you are able to breastfeed even part of the time, that breastmilk supplementation will benefit your baby's immune system, overall health, and development. Both breastmilk and formula will provide for all of his nutritional needs during these early months as his digestive system is maturing.

FOR YOU: PREPARING TO BREASTFEED

If you are committed to breastfeeding your child, there are several things you can do before the birth to help ensure success in the first days and early weeks. First of all, set up your support network. Getting help when you need it may be the single best thing you can do to ensure nursing success.

Look for a hospital that has been designated baby-friendly and a pediatrician who will support your commitment to breastfeeding. Make sure you will have access to a lactation consultant before, immediately following, and after your baby's birth to support you and answer any questions that may come up.

BREASTFEEDING YOUR BABY

The First 24 Hours

When a healthy baby is born, he takes his first breaths, and then almost immediately begins to look for his first mouthfuls of food: the **colostrum** (early milk) produced by your breasts. Those first minutes after his birth provide a precious window of opportunity for your baby to discover, naturally, how he can find nourishment right from your body. Delivery and birth is a huge amount of work for both of you, but before the resting begins, your baby will experience a short-lived period of alertness, usually lasting anywhere from 30 to 90 minutes. This is an ideal time to breastfeed for the first time.

Colostrum is a thick, low-volume yellowish or clear milk that your breasts will produce for a few days after delivery, before your mature, high-volume milk supply comes in. It is a very nutritious form of first milk that is high in protein and lower in fat and sugars than regular breastmilk. It is loaded with antibodies that will help boost your baby's immune system during her first days. It also helps coat and protect your baby's stomach and intestines in preparation for regular feedings, and stimulates her early bowel movements. Baby's first stool, called meconium, is thick, sticky, and black or greenish in color. Passing the meconium quickly will help prevent jaundice. Lactation consultants often call colostrum "liquid gold" because of its many special benefits for your newborn.

First Nursing Session

When she arrives in this world and you look into her eyes for the very first time, there really are no words to describe all that you might feel. If it's possible, having your baby placed directly onto your bare chest, skin-to-skin, the moment she is born, will provide the best opportunity for her to begin nursing on her own. If it's comfortable for you, have her placed naked directly between your breasts so that she is lying head up along your chest. She will get the warmth she needs from your body heat and will feel or hear your heartbeat and breathing, which are so familiar to her. You can cover the both of you with a blanket if you wish, pouching her in a comfy peaceful space. This natural practice, which has been around for generations, has been coined "**kangaroo care**" because it is similar to the protection a kangaroo mother offers her own newborns. Regular kangaroo care has extra benefits for preemies in that it seems to speed their growth and development.

Your baby may be able to smell the scent of your nipple, and after a little while (usually within the first 20 minutes) she will begin looking for your breast. The darkness of the areola may also help her find the nipple. If left completely undisturbed, healthy newborns are capable of latching on to the breast without outside help. (If you receive heavy medications during the delivery, especially in the last hour before birth, your baby may be somewhat less alert and need a little assistance to get that first latch, but otherwise the process should be the same.)

Nursing causes your body to produce **oxytocin**, which, in these first hours especially, will help stimulate your uterus to contract and return to its original size.

This is such a precious window of opportunity for the mother and baby to establish breastfeeding that in 2005 the American Academy of Pediatrics revised their policy on breastfeeding to include very specific recommendations about post-delivery care for healthy infants. They advise that the baby be in skin-to-skin contact with the mom from the moment he is born until after he has had his first feeding. They recommend that all drying, physical checks, and **Apgar scoring** be performed while the baby is in skin-to-skin contact with his mom. The other common post-delivery practices, such as bathing, weighing, measuring, eye treatment, and other routine pediatric care can wait until after that first feeding. [Source: American Academy of Pediatrics, "Policy Statement: Breastfeeding and the Use of Human Milk," *Pediatrics* 115, no. 2 (February 2005): 496–506.]

TIP

Offering a bottle or pacifier to a newborn learning to breastfeed is generally discouraged because that may confuse him when he is trying to get a latch on the breast.

After a C-section

If you have a caesarean section, you will not be able to have the infant placed along your body directly after birth, because everything below your neck and upper chest needs to be kept sterile. In baby-friendly hospitals, however, the baby is often kept in the same room as you during your postoperative care and is given to you to hold as soon as you are ready to go to your room. Because of the pain of the section cut in your lower abdomen, you still may not be able to place your baby over your chest, but you can have skin-to-skin contact, cradling her under one of your arms and along the side of your upper body. This is sometimes called a football hold, and it's a great nursing position for smaller babies or if you have big breasts, whether or not you've had a c-section delivery.

Breastfeeding using the football hold

Challenge and Success

There are several common challenges to accomplishing that first feeding, and you shouldn't be at all discouraged if your baby doesn't get a great latch or full feeding during the initial period right after delivery. By preparing in advance to be as uninterrupted as possible for about 2 hours after birth, you will definitely maximize your chances of starting the breastfeeding process off more easily. (See page 56 for breastfeeding preparation tips.)

No matter what happens, that first contact alone constitutes success. It will help you create or strengthen the intimacy bond between yourself and your new baby. Skin-to-skin contact especially will comfort, warm, and soothe him after his difficult

trip into the world. Introducing him to your breast at this time is very helpful, even if he isn't able to get a good latch right off the bat. Any nuzzling or licking he does is a great step. If you see a drop or two of colostrum at the tip of your nipple, rub it into his mouth so he can get his first taste of your milk.

Two of the most common challenges to establishing breastfeeding are a mom's discomfort or fatigue and a baby's grogginess following what is often an exhausting birth process. Some new mothers feel elated and energized after delivery. Others feel exhausted or uncomfortable, and the thought of trying to make one more effort can be discouraging. Minimizing visitations or other interruptions during this early period can help with that. Think of it as a precious private time to get to know your new baby and give him a chance to get to know you as well. If you were given pain medication or had a c-section, your baby may not be very alert during those first minutes after birth. But within 30 minutes to 2 hours following birth, most healthy babies will fall into a deep recovery sleep lasting anywhere from 3 to 4 hours or even longer, during which it's much harder to rouse them to nurse.

Stay Close

It's best for your baby to stay as close to you as possible throughout your recovery period and stay in the hospital, so if you can, keep him in your room the whole time. If you are holding him or practicing kangaroo care and feeling drowsy, just ask a nurse or your birthing partner to help prop pillows around your body to stabilize both you and the baby in case you doze off. After that initial alertness phase and recovery sleep, you can begin looking for regular signs of alertness to give your baby more opportunities to latch on to your breast and nurse. You want to offer feeding opportunities about every 2 to 3 hours during the first 24 hours following delivery.

> **TIP**
>
> When timing your baby's feedings, measure from the beginning of a feeding (not the end) to the beginning of the next.

Nursing Opportunities

A brand-new baby may be very sleepy and look like he's dozing for hours at a time. Even when he's asleep, however, you can look for signs that it's a light sleep rather than a deep sleep, and use that window to try nursing. If his eyes are closed, but his eyelids seem to be fluttering a bit, try rubbing him gently to see if he will open his eyes. A very sleepy baby can be lovingly roused by gently opening his blanket wrap, having his back rubbed, or having his cheek gently rubbed to stimulate the rooting response. The **rooting reflex** is your baby's built-in response to open his mouth wide when he is hungry or when his lips or cheeks are brushed. It helps him get a good latch on the nipple for breastfeeding.

Hold him close to one of your breasts and try gently rubbing or touching your nipple on or just above his lips.

Getting a Good Latch

If your baby is sufficiently alert, you want to encourage him to latch on properly to your nipple so his sucking can stimulate the colostrum, and later the mature milk, to let down, so he can nurse effectively and without pain to you. Get into a comfortable, supported position with your back fairly straight. You might use pillows on your lap or under your arm to help support the weight of the baby. Lay him in a comfortable position across your body where you can support his head and upper back with one arm and your breast with the other. Hold your breast with one hand (thumb up, fingers underneath), and squeeze it gently (from behind the areola) to get your areola and nipple to protrude out slightly, making a good "target" about the size of your baby's open mouth. Cradling the baby in your arm, with your wrist supporting his upper back and your hand supporting his head, bring him in close to your breast and stimulate him to root by brushing his lips, cheek, or just under his nose with your nipple. When he opens his mouth wide, bring his head and upper back in close to your breast, aiming your nipple at the roof of his mouth, and help him, chin first, to place his mouth over your protruded areola and nipple. Try to get the entire nipple and as much of the areola as possible into his mouth. You want to get him positioned so his lower gum is clamped over most or all of the areola to work the ducts under the areola. If he gets just the nipple, he may not be able to get enough milk and will put a lot of pressure on the nipple itself, making it very sore. Keep holding your breast until he starts sucking. (During these first feedings, it may be necessary to hold your breast the whole time he nurses, especially if your breasts are large.) His chin might be right up against your breast, and when he starts sucking, you will see his jaw moving back and forth. A proper latch should feel comfortable. If it hurts, release his suction hold by placing your finger into the corner of his mouth and try the process again. Be patient: It can take several tries to get the latch just right.

Getting a Good Latch with Flat Nipples

If you have flat or inverted nipples, it can be even more difficult to get your baby to latch on in those early feedings. Most women with flat nipples are able to breastfeed just fine, but the early feedings can be challenging. Once your baby is able to get a few good latches, her suckling will help draw your nipples out and make them easier to grab as time goes on. After that initial feeding (you want to be as relaxed and casual as possible), you can try a few tricks to make things easier on both of you—ask for use of a manual breast pump from the hospital.

Soak a washcloth with water as hot as you can tolerate, wring it out, and place it over one breast

1. Lightly stroke the midpoint of your baby's upper lip with your nipple to stimulate him to open his mouth.

3. Bring your baby's chin and lower jaw (not his nose) into contact with your breast first, aiming his lower lip as far from the base of your nipple as possible.

2. Repeat the light touch against your baby's lip until he opens his mouth very wide, as if yawning, with his tongue down.

4. When your baby is attached correctly, his jaws should be open wide, his lips flared out, and his chin pressed against the underside of your breast.

for 3 to 4 minutes. You can cover it with a towel to keep the heat from escaping. Try gently massaging your breast from the top down toward the nipple while it is warming. This will help trigger your milk to let down. Remove the washcloth, put a manual breast pump to your breast, and pump it three to five times or until you can see a drop of colostrum. This will help make the colostrum readily available and get your nipple to extend a little bit. Then quickly try the latching techniques with your baby.

If you are anxious about having success with breastfeeding, and things don't go easily from the start, it's important to try to stay relaxed as you work through the process. If you've tried getting your baby to latch on several times and she isn't able to get any milk, both of you can easily become frustrated. Some babies are more tolerant of the process, while others need quick gratification. If she's hungry and she can't get the nipple or any milk, she may express her discomfort by crying. Try not to let that get you upset, too. If she has gotten very upset, just take a break for a while to let both of you calm down and try again a little later. You can try giving her the tip of your little finger to try to suck on (nail-side down)—sometimes that will soothe her. Don't worry if she doesn't get a feeding right away; she is born with enough calorie and liquid stores to hold her over in those early hours.

The Milk Letdown

It usually takes a couple of minutes of vigorous sucking by your baby to get your milk to let down at each feeding. The more relaxed you are, the more quickly this will happen. After going through the process a few times, you will feel more experienced and it will become faster and begin to feel quite natural. Eventually, you may get to the point where your baby's hunger signals alone can trigger a milk **letdown**.

Your milk comes out of your nipple through several small pores, not just a single hole, and may release slowly or spurt strongly once it's let down. As you nurse on one side, your other breast might leak or even spurt some breastmilk. You can wear a **breast pad** to soak it up or try slowing the flow by applying steady pressure over the areola with the palm of your hand.

The Early Weeks

Within 2 to 6 days, the colostrum you produce will be replaced by mature breastmilk. This milk is thin and more watery than colostrum, usually bluish-white in color. If you give your baby plenty of opportunities to nurse on colostrum, your mature milk will come in more quickly. You will typically feel a hot flowing sensation as the milk lets down into your breast.

If your baby isn't yet able to get a good latch or nurse much yet, use a breast pump each time you try to feed him (about once every 2 to 3 hours). A **breast pump** is a manual or electric device that will help you extract the milk from your breasts any time your baby doesn't nurse. They can be very helpful for:
• relieving engorgement

- pumping extra milk to have on hand for a baby sitter or when you return to work
- emptying your breasts (without nursing) after taking medications that are unsafe for your baby
- keeping your milk supply up when your baby is fussy or has a mouth problem and refuses to nurse temporarily

It's very important to find a good breast pump, because many are ineffective. Sometimes a mom may use a poor-quality pump, have no success, and give up breastfeeding because she thinks the problem is with her. Purchasing or renting an electric version that can pump both breasts simultaneously is very convenient and can save you time. Ask a lactation consultant or contact La Leche League for recommendations. (See Resources for more information.)

Pumping Tips

If you are trying to build up a supply of breastmilk for storage while you are breastfeeding, it can be very frustrating trying to find the time to generate extra milk to pump. Here are some helpful tips:

- Your breasts carry the largest volume of milk in the early hours of the day—so pumping for storage may be easiest in the early mornings.
- The late afternoon/early evening milk is the highest in calories—so if you are pumping to give your baby extra calories (for a preemie, slow weight gain, etc.), try pumping your milk or adding the extra feedings in the late afternoon.
- Pumping or nursing in the middle

of the night is the surest way to build up your milk supply.

Engorgement

When your milk first comes in, you may notice a very full sensation in your breasts. This is due in large part to the higher volume of your mature milk (as opposed to the early colostrum), but also because more fluid and blood travel to the breasts in preparation for regular milk production. For some, it's not particularly noticeable; for others, the breasts might feel full to the bursting point. For most cases of breast **engorgement**, frequent, regular nursing will relieve the problem. Also, be sure to allow your baby to empty one breast fully before switching him to the other side.

Usually this will relieve the problem, but if your breasts instead become harder or sore, try one of the following methods to ease the discomfort.

- Use cold compresses between feedings. Soak a washcloth in ice water, wring it out, and apply it to your breast for 3 to 4 minutes to alleviate any aching.
- Stand in a hot shower and let the warm water run down your breasts, massaging them to release a small amount of milk.
- Or you could use the popular folk remedy of cabbage leaf compresses. Peel off the outer leaf layer of a raw, cold-stored cabbage, pull off two large, inner leaves, and rinse them well with cool water. Dry them off and place them over your breasts inside your bra, wearing them until the leaves become wilted. You can repeat until your breast

swelling goes down, but if your skin becomes irritated in any way, discontinue use.

If your symptoms worsen or you develop a low-grade fever, chills, or any redness on your breasts, it may indicate an infection. Contact your doctor.

Nipple Discomfort

Most women will experience some form of discomfort in their nipples at some point during the breastfeeding process. Some lucky women are able to adjust quite easily and breastfeed pain-free; other women can experience quite a bit of soreness, including nipple cracking and even bleeding. In the early stages of breastfeeding, it is quite normal for your nipples to be a little sore as they adjust to being stretched by your baby's nursing. If a little soreness becomes irritation, or outright pain, it's a good idea to contact a lactation consultant for advice. The number one cause of seriously sore and cracked nipples, however, is a poor latch—and that can be avoided. (See page 59 for instructions for helping your baby get a good latch.) Following are some tips for easing the pain and speeding the healing of sore nipples.

For cracked, scabbed, or bleeding nipples, try:
• Increasing your nursing frequency to every 2 hours to reduce your baby's sucking intensity.
• Taking a Tylenol 30 minutes before nursing.
• Beginning with the side that is less sore.
• Inserting your little finger into the corner of your baby's mouth to break the suction before pulling your nipple away from the latch.
• Pumping for a couple of minutes before nursing.
• Using warm water compresses just before and after nursing to ease discomfort.
• Making sure your nipples stay dry: Keep both breasts open to the air while nursing; change any breast pads as soon as they are wet; wear only breathable cotton bras; avoid any breast pads with plastic or synthetic lining; spread a few drops of breastmilk on your nipples and then let them air dry after a nursing session.
• Using a nipple shield when not nursing (make sure it's sized properly).
• Applying a little pure lanolin preparation (100 percent USP modified lanolin lubricant) on your nipples after nursing.
• Not overwashing your nipples or using any harsh soap products; plain warm water is usually best.

If your nipples are sore and also red, burning, or itchy, you may have developed a yeast or other surface infection. Some babies have a yeast overgrowth in their mouths called thrush, and this can easily be passed on to your nipple. These types of infections require medical treatment. For a yeast infection, both you and your baby will need to be treated simultaneously to keep from reinfecting each other. If your nipples are itchy or burning (even when you aren't nursing), and they are red, swollen, shiny, oozing, or cracked, consult your doctor for diagnosis and care.

Mastitis

Mastitis is the medical term for an infection of the breast. Breast infections in nursing mothers can be caused by several factors, but they are most often the result of a blocked milk duct, long-term unalleviated engorgement, a yeast or thrush infection, or ongoing failure to empty the breasts fully during nursing. Bacteria can also enter the breast tissue and cause an infection if the nipple is cracked. The symptoms usually include a red sore or hot spot on one breast (mastitis typically occurs in a specific area on one breast only). Moms may also feel unusually tired and experience one or more flulike symptoms: low-grade fever, chills, nausea, or vomiting.

If you are nursing and develop a painful hot spot on your breast, or you feel unusually fatigued and have a fever over 100° F for more than 24 hours, you should call your doctor to check for mastitis. Once diagnosed, your doctor may prescribe an antibiotic. It's most helpful to continue to nurse regularly if you can tolerate it. The baby won't be affected by your mastitis, but your milk supply on the infected side can taste a little salty and he may be less inclined to nurse on that breast. If that's the case, be sure to pump the milk out of that breast each time he nurses to keep the ducts clear and the milk flowing well.

Lactation experts say that frequently the root cause of mastitis is a mother's exhaustion or high level of stress. Fatigue and stress will lower your immune response and make you more prone to all kinds of infections. Do your best to stay as rested as you can while nursing, to help keep your immune system functioning well. If you do develop an infection, bed rest and frequent nursing will help speed your recovery.

Full Feedings

When your baby has emptied one breast, switch him to the other side to complete his feeding. It's important to allow your baby to get a full feeding on one side before you switch. It's common for your nipples to feel a little sore as they get accustomed to nursing, and you might be tempted to switch off your nursing breasts frequently to try to alleviate that discomfort. You should avoid doing that; it won't help with the soreness, and it will prevent your baby from getting the full benefits of nursing. You want to empty each breast fully because the milk toward the end of the feeding, called **hind milk**, is thicker and richer in fat, helping the baby feel a sense of satiety (satisfaction) and fullness. If you switch him before your breast has emptied, he won't get the benefits of that creamier milk.

Burping Your Baby

Babies can swallow air as they are feeding. Burping helps them stay comfortable by moving the air out of their stomachs. If babies swallow a lot of air and aren't burped regularly, they may spit up or become gassy and cranky or irritable. Try burping your baby about halfway through a nursing or bottle-feeding session, and again when he has finished eating. If you are nursing, burp him before switching to the second side; if bottle-feeding, try halfway through the bottle. Gentle rhythmic patting on your baby's back is usually enough to bring up a burp. You may have to use a firm pat with your baby, but never try to force a burp with hard strikes. Drape a cloth diaper, hand towel, or other clean soft rag over your shoulder to catch any spit-up and, sitting upright, hold him, belly to you, on your upper chest so his chin is resting at your shoulder. Holding him securely with one hand, use the other to pat his back for a couple of minutes or until he burps. If he doesn't, don't worry; just resume feeding. If your baby tends to get gassy, you can try burping him more frequently, but don't get too interruptive with your feeding sessions. You can also try different positions: Lay him facedown across your lap, supporting his head to be higher than his body; or sit him upright in your lap—but be sure to support her by him chest and chin, not his throat.

Feeding Frequency

Once your baby is able to get a few good feeding sessions in, you've made your first big step toward successful breastfeeding. If you are using formula and bottles, you will also be making progress with your feeding rituals. Ideally your baby will be taking 8 to 12 feedings over a course of 24 hours in the early weeks. That usually means she will breastfeed once every 2 to 3 hours, and possibly every 3 to 5 hours at night, with a bit of a longer

sleeping stretch in between. If she isn't getting at least 8 feedings in after the first day, you might have to wake her to nurse after 3 hours of sleep. Formula-fed babies may need to eat slightly less frequently because formula doesn't move through their digestive systems as quickly as breastmilk, but you should begin offering the bottle on the same schedule as the breast; about once every 3 to 4 hours.

Hunger Signs

As time passes, your baby will become more alert for more of the time, and her early signs of hunger will change a little. She might nose around the chest or arm of anyone who is holding her. Her head may move toward the sound of your voice. You might see her open her mouth or stick her tongue out. She might try mouthing her fist or anything else that gets close to her mouth. She may make little sounds, grunts, or snuffles, and wave her arms or move around more than usual. When you see these signs, this is the perfect time to feed her. If you delay, you may see later hunger signs, such as a pinched or furrowed brow, or her head moving rapidly back and forth. Try to feed her before she gets to outright crying. If she is crying with hunger, it usually means that she's been feeling hungry for a while, and it may be harder for her to settle down to feeding if she has become too aroused or upset.

Some babies aren't very demonstrative about their hunger. If you don't regularly see early hunger signs, you should rouse your baby to feed 3 to 4 hours after the start of the last feeding during her first few weeks.

It's good practice during these early weeks to feed your baby on demand, that is, to feed her when she shows signs of hunger as opposed to feeding her on a particular schedule. This will help you provide her with optimal nutrition levels and calorie amounts as she is growing and changing. It will also help maintain her internal connection to her own body's signals for when and how much to eat.

The volume of milk your breasts produce depends on how much demand is placed on them. If your baby is approaching a growth spurt, for instance, she will often intuitively nurse more vigorously, more frequently, or for longer periods to stimulate your breasts to produce more milk. Conversely, if she nurses less frequently, your supply will eventually diminish to accommodate that change as well. It usually takes a day or two for your milk supply to adjust to a change in demand—it's not an instantaneous process. Your supply may increase and diminish many times over the course of your breastfeeding months or years with your baby.

Hold her gently but securely so she can see your face while she is nursing or taking a bottle. You will quickly get to know her feeding behaviors. Usually at the start of a feeding session, you will notice strong sucking and audible swallows. Then she may slow down a bit. Some babies may need to stop sucking and rest for a little while before they've finished, especially in the first weeks.

Sucking is hard work. Think about trying to pull vigorously on a straw for a long time—your mouth gets tired, right? Let her set her own pace and eat only as much as she wants. She may go back to the breast, but less urgently. Her sucking may slow, her expression might soften, and she may look a little blissed out with contentment as she gets closer to full. She might even doze off. Newborns will often eat and doze alternately throughout a feeding in the early weeks.

Fullness Signs

You will know she's had enough to eat when she shows these signs of satisfaction. Most babies will nurse on one side for 10 to 45 minutes. If they finish on one side, try putting her on the other breast. She may simply stop sucking on the breast. She may refuse the nipple on the second side. She might fuss or wiggle a little. You will see similar signs with the bottle: slowing to a stop and looking content, or not taking the nipple. Honor these signs of satisfaction and allow her to stop eating when she's had enough— even if your breast hasn't emptied fully or there's still formula in the bottle. If she falls deeply asleep before she gets full, she will simply show signs of hunger more quickly the next time around.

Your breasts fill with milk based on demand, so if you are nursing on only one side, that breast can become significantly larger and fuller than the other. Offer your baby both breasts during the same feeding. Once she seems to be finished with the first one, offer her the second, but don't be alarmed if she doesn't want to feed as much on that second side. Just start the next feeding session on the side where you finished last. Some moms can tell which breast was last because it feels fuller or heavier at the next feeding, but many wear a little pin or a bracelet to switch from side to side as a reminder of which side was last.

Eating Enough

Many moms feel anxious that their baby isn't eating enough. This may be even more pronounced if you are nursing as opposed to bottle feeding, because you can't see how much milk your baby is actually getting. If your baby is feeding between 10 and 45 minutes 8 to 12 times per day, chances are he's getting plenty of milk. A newborn's stomach is only about the size of a walnut. Until your baby reaches about 10 pounds or so, he will probably need only 1 to 3 ounces of milk per feeding, but every baby is different and some babies may eat more or less at a given feeding.

It's normal for babies to lose weight in their first 3 or 4 days (usually around 5 to 7 percent of their total weight at birth), but they should put that initial loss back on within 10 days to 2 weeks after birth. If your baby loses more than 10 percent of his body weight, he may be underfed and you should see your pediatrician. It's healthy for your baby to gain back about an ounce a day during that initial time period.

Signs That Your Baby Is Getting Enough Breastmilk

If you are feeling nervous about whether or not your baby is getting enough milk, consult your pediatrician. Here are a few signs that his feeding is probably on track:

- He is feeding at least 8 times over 24 hours.
- He nurses for 10 to 45 minutes at a feeding and seems relaxed after eating.
- You can see him sucking vigorously and hear him swallowing.
- Your breasts feel softer or less pressured after a feeding.
- After his first week, he has at least 5 wet diapers in a 24-hour period and the urine is light-colored and mild smelling.
- He is having a few daily bowel movements in his first month. (The meconium will usually be gone after the fifth day, and his stools will turn mustard yellow. They may be small at first, about the size of a quarter, and can be very wet or curdy looking.)

TIP

Keep a ready supply of cloth diapers or other soft, absorbent cloths on hand for feedings. Lay one over your shoulder (or lap, depending on your position), keeping it smooth and flat so it doesn't block the baby's breathing.

Quick Chart

WHAT YOUR BABY IS TELLING YOU

I'm Hungry: Rooting reflex, moving his head from side to side, mouthing his fist or other object, grunting or making other little irritable sounds, wiggling, waving his arms, and, eventually, crying.

I'm Eating Well: Strong, steady sucking at first, sounds of swallowing.

I've Had Enough: Relaxed look, sucking stops or becomes very periodic, dozing, look of contentment, refuses breast or bottle (after a period of feeding). Once he's had enough, a slightly older baby may tell you by turning his face away from the breast or the bottle, or even arching his back in refusal if you continue to try to give him more.

Quick Chart

THE 10 STEPS TO SUCCESSFUL BREASTFEEDING

United Nations Children's Fund (UNICEF) and the World Health Organization (WHO) have developed the following list as part of their worldwide Baby-Friendly Hospital Initiative (BFHI). Hospitals in the United States must meet these 10 criteria to be designated baby-friendly. Consult www.babyfriendlyusa.org for a list of participating hospitals.

1. Maintain a written breastfeeding policy that is routinely communicated to all health-care staff.
2. Train all health-care staff in skills necessary to implement this policy.
3. Inform all pregnant women about the benefits and management of breastfeeding.
4. Help mothers initiate breastfeeding within 1 hour of birth.
5. Show mothers how to breastfeed and how to maintain lactation, even if they are separated from their infants.
6. Give infants no food or drink other than breastmilk, unless medically indicated.
7. Practice "rooming in"—allow mothers and infants to remain together 24 hours a day.
8. Encourage unrestricted breastfeeding.
9. Give no pacifiers or artificial nipples to breastfeeding infants.
10. Foster the establishment of breastfeeding support groups and refer mothers to them on discharge from the hospital or clinic.

Spitting Up

It's actually quite normal for a healthy baby to spit up frequently after eating. The muscle at the bottom of the esophagus that keeps swallowed food in the stomach isn't well developed yet in most young babies, and it will often allow milk to come back up and out after a feeding. Doctors call this **gastroesophageal reflux**, or just reflux, and nearly all babies simply outgrow it. Usually it isn't at all uncomfortable for your baby and is rarely a cause for alarm. If your baby is vomiting forcefully after nearly all feedings, if you think it's getting worse, or if he seems to be losing weight, take him in to see your pediatrician to rule out **pyloric stenosis**, an obstruction of the stomach.

Breast Care

It used to be common advice to twist or tweak your nipples during pregnancy to help toughen them up for nursing. This doesn't have any beneficial effects and may actually irritate sensitive nipples, so it is best to avoid this practice. Also, stimulating your nipples often produces oxytocin, which can stimulate contractions—definitely avoid this if you're at risk for a preterm delivery.

Your breasts will get larger and heavier as your pregnancy progresses, and toward delivery time you may even notice a little colostrum leakage. This is all normal and can be alleviated with a good support bra and possibly the use of breast pads. These are usually round absorbent pads that slide inside your bra cup and over your nipples. They come in washable fabric or disposable versions. It is helpful to have a pack or two of these on hand for your first weeks even if your breasts aren't leaking before.

If you are small-breasted, you may be comfortable just lifting a softer bra up and over one breast to nurse. But this can be awkward, and even smaller-breasted women will need extra support as their breasts become larger during pregnancy and lactation. It can help to find a good **nursing bra**. They are usually well constructed for good support and they have catches over each breast that can be released with one hand to expose your breast(s) without removing the whole bra. Try to find one without constricting underwires. You might also want to sleep in a softer bra at night for support and to help catch any leakage that may occur as you sleep or during night feedings.

Nursing Nutrition

If you're nursing, your body is literally making all the food your baby needs in the form of your breastmilk. It will naturally use any and all available stores of nutrients from itself (your body) to give your breastmilk the correct nutrient balance—so even if you eat a sub-optimal diet, your body will ensure that your baby doesn't. That means you need to take extra care to make sure your own diet is nutrient- and energy-rich for both of you so you don't become drained or listless.

While it does take extra calories to manufacture breastmilk and nurse on a regular basis (especially if you're nursing twins), that doesn't give you carte blanch to continue "eating for two"! If you already eat a healthy diet, you won't have to make many changes while nursing. If you're at a healthy weight, you'll need only about an extra 300 to 500 calories per day (1,000 for twins). It's generally recommended that a nursing mom not go below 1,800 calories while nursing.

Right after your baby is born, you will likely still be carrying some of the weight you gained during pregnancy. The extra fat will help supplement your energy needs while nursing. Don't expect all that weight to just melt away in those first couple of weeks after the baby's birth. Even if your weight gain was moderate and healthy, it will still probably take you several weeks before you can comfortably button your regular pants. Nursing will speed the natural weight loss, and eating a healthy, balanced diet will also help. Going on a diet while nursing, however, is not a good idea, as restrictive eating won't meet your nursing nutrient and energy needs. If you eat when you are hungry, and stop when your hunger ends, your body will gradually return to its natural healthy weight.

Some moms don't have much of an appetite in the first weeks following birth. In that case, make every bite count: Don't snack on poor-quality junk foods. Instead, try eating several small mini-meals with a good balance of complex carbohydrates, protein, and healthy fats. Breakfast and lunch are more important meals than dinner, so if you wish, go lightly at the evening meal, but don't skimp in the morning.

> **TIP**
>
> While you nurse, drink 6 to 8 glasses of water minimum every day to prevent dehydration and constipation. Try drinking a glass when you nurse, and pay attention to your own thirst cues.

A healthy diet for nursing moms includes a good balance of all the primary nutrients: complex carbohydrates, protein, healthy fats, vitamins, minerals, and other key micronutrients such as phytonutrients. Eating 3 moderate meals and 2 to 3 small snacks will provide ample nutrition. See the following chart as a general guide to building healthy meals, and the great snacks list for healthy snacks.

Quick Chart

HEALTHY PLATE FOR THE NURSING MOM

Use a standard dinner plate (the food surface should be about 8 inches in diameter) 3 times per day. Don't pile the food up so high that it's falling off the edges.

Build your plate with a selection of the foods from each column in the chart in the amounts indicated. The food lists are not exhaustive, they are just examples. Choose high-quality, fresh, seasonal, organic, free-range options whenever possible. Choose frozen produce (sauce or additive-free) over canned.

Add a healthy fat to each meal. Include small amounts from among choices like these: organic butter, ghee (clarified butter), oil spreads (trans fat-free), nuts* and seeds, healthy oils (olive oil, avocado oil, coconut oil, macadamia nut oil, and flaxseed oil), avocados, olives, pesto, and hummus.

Avoid fried foods, foods containing hydrogenated or partially hydrogenated oils, and junk foods.

Add 1 to 2 healthy two snacks daily, depending on your caloric needs. See the chart that follows for snack ideas.

Make water your primary drink and get at least 6 to 8 glasses in throughout the day.

(See page 78 for a list of foods to avoid if your baby is exhibiting symptoms of colic.)

Caution: If you have food allergies, or there is a family history of food allergies, you may want to avoid eating tree nuts while breastfeeding.

½ PLATE	¼ PLATE	¼ PLATE
Low-Glycemic Carbs: High-Fiber- and High-Water-Content Vegetables	*Low-to-Medium-Glycemic Carbs: "Sweet Carbs"*	*Protein*
Vegetables: artichokes, asparagus, bok choy, broccoli, broccoli rabe, brussels sprouts, cauliflower, celery, cucumbers, eggplant, escarole, fennel, garlic, green beans, kale, leeks, lettuce, onions, peas, peppers, radishes, spinach, sprouts, summer squash, Swiss chard, tomatoes, zucchini	Fruits: apples, bananas, blueberries, cantaloupe, grapes, melons, oranges, papayas, peaches, pears, raspberries, strawberries, watermelon Sweet Vegetables: beets, carrots, parsnips, sweet potatoes, pumpkin, turnips, winter squash Whole Grains: amaranth, barley, buckwheat, millet, oats, quinoa, whole-grain pasta, whole-grain bread, whole-grain rice	Beans:** adzuki, black, garbanzo, great northern, kidney, lentils, lima, navy Dairy: low-fat cottage cheese, low-fat cow or goat cheese, plain low-fat yogurt, low-fat milk** Meat (Lean Cuts): beef, lamb, pork Poultry or Eggs: chicken, turkey, eggs Seafood (low in mercury and PCBs):*** farmed bay scallops, farmed blue mussels, sardines, tilapia, wild Alaskan salmon Soy: edamame, tempeh, tofu, miso soup

**Note: Both beans and milk are about half carbohydrate and half protein.

***Note: Avoid fresh tuna fillets, swordfish, tilefish, shark, king mackerel, sea bass, marlin, halibut, pike, white croaker, largemouth bass, or oysters from Gulf of Mexico in order to minimize mercury and PCB exposure.

Food Preparation

Making a lot of complicated meals for yourself is the last thing most nursing moms feel like doing. Keep your meals simple, and always cook extra for leftovers and to freeze so you can cut back on meal prep time. Have friends or family that have offered to help?

Take them up on their offer and ask them to bring you nutritious meals and snacks.

Try to avoid the lure of fast food and highly processed foods and snacks. They provide very poor-quality nutrition, and while they may save you time, they can rob you of energy and slow your weight loss: not a good trade-off.

Quick Chart

GREAT SNACKS FOR NURSING MOMS

- Smoothies
- Hummus and veggies
- Guacamole or vegetarian bean dip with veggies, rice crackers, or organic baked corn chips
- Greek yogurt with granola and fresh fruit
- Mochi with fruit spread or nut butter*
- Cottage cheese with diced tomato, cucumber, red pepper, salt, pepper, and onion powder or, for a sweeter flavor, with peaches, pineapple, berries, etc., cinnamon, and a dash of honey or maple syrup.
- Celery or carrot sticks with almond or cashew butter,* hummus, or peanut sauce
- Sliced raw veggies—red peppers, carrots, celery, endive, raw broccoli, cauliflower, etc.—with cilantro or dill yogurt sauce
- Hard-boiled eggs, deviled eggs
- Apple or pear slices with nut butter*
- Applesauce or fresh fruit with Swiss or Cheddar cheese cubes
- Cheese and whole-grain crackers
- Dried fruit and nuts or seeds*
- Nut-free trail mix, by itself or mixed with yogurt
- Bowl of soup, such as miso with tofu, chicken, vegetable barley, or cream of broccoli
- Fresh salad with beans or sliced cooked meats
- High-quality granola, or fruit-and-nut bars: low-sugar and low-fat granola bars, Lara Bars, etc.
- Whole-wheat wrap: hummus and veggies, fruit and nut butter,* chicken or turkey breast and Muenster, Caesar salad with chicken, etc.

*Caution: If you have food allergies, or there is a family history of food allergies, you may want to avoid eating tree nuts while breastfeeding.

Vitamins and Minerals

While it is a good idea to try to get the bulk of your nutrients from the foods you eat, that can be easier said than done. Most obstetricians recommend that you continue to take your prenatal vitamins while you are nursing. If you aren't eating a varied, high-quality diet, if you are eating fewer than 1,800 calories per day, if you are vegan, or if you don't get moderate sun exposure or eat vitamin D–enriched foods (such as cow's milk, orange juice, or commercial cereal), then you will probably need to take a vitamin supplement to ensure that you're meeting the RDA for all the vital nutrients. See your doctor for specific recommendations about supplementation. Taking high doses of micronutrients could create undesirably high levels of certain vitamins and nutrients in your breastmilk, which could be irritating and potentially harmful to your baby, so stick with your doctor's recommendations.

Drugs, Alcohol, and Cigarettes

Before you begin nursing, be sure to check with your doctor about any regular medications you take, both prescription and over the counter, to see whether or not they will pass into the breastmilk or be harmful to your baby. (See the chart on page 76 for a list of common drugs and their known breastfeeding risks.) Definitely avoid any illegal or street drugs, as many of those can be harmful or even toxic to your baby.

A portion of any alcohol you drink will pass into your breastmilk, so moderate to heavy drinking (2 or more alcoholic drinks per day) should be avoided. The alcohol from a moderate to heavy drinker who breastfeeds can slow a baby's weight gain or even affect her motor development. Having 2 or more drinks can also slow your nursing reflexes (such as the milk letdown and ejection reflexes) the same way it affects all your other reflexes. Having an occasional glass of wine or other drink of moderate alcoholic content is fine. It's best to wait at least 2 hours after having your drink before you nurse, however.

According to the U.S. Department of Health and Human Services National Women's Health Information Center, if you want to nurse and you're a smoker, you should try to quit as soon as possible. Your doctor can direct you to resources for help. The nicotine from cigarettes transfers to your breastmilk and may affect your milk production. The effects of nicotine in your breastmilk and the secondhand smoke in your home can include an increased risk of **sudden infant death syndrome (SIDS)**, or higher rates of ear and respiratory infections in your baby. Because the benefits of breastfeeding while smoking outweigh the risks to your baby, you should still nurse even if you can't quit smoking. But don't smoke around the baby (to minimize secondhand smoke risks)—go outside if you can; smoke after, not before a nursing session; and keep trying to stop. It will be better for both of you in the short and the long term.

Medications and Breastfeeding

If you take medications, or if a drug is prescribed to you while you are breastfeeding, it's natural to be concerned about the potential danger of passing medications along to your baby through your breastmilk. In fact, any drug you take while you are breastfeeding will appear in your milk to some degree. The amount depends on the drug dose and how often you take it, how the drug is taken (by mouth versus by injection), the physical and chemical properties of the drug, the amount of breastmilk your baby drinks, how often you nurse your baby, and the duration of treatment. Fortunately most medications are safe for your nursing baby because their presence in your breastmilk is usually minimal. Whenever your doctor prescribes a medicine for you, ask whether it is safe for breastfeeding. Notify your baby's doctor about medications you take, and observe your baby carefully for possible side effects that should be reported promptly to her doctor.

In the vast majority of cases, the benefits of breastfeeding outweigh temporary, minor effects of medication on a nursing baby (such as diarrhea, irritability, or drowsiness). Newborns—especially sick or premature babies—are at greatest risk of being affected, while older infants are able to handle medications more easily. In each instance, you and your health-care provider must weigh the compelling benefits of breastfeeding against the risks of a particular medication.

Resources for your doctor. If your physician prescribes a drug for you that might pose a risk to your nursing infant, ask whether a pharmacist could suggest an alternative medication that is safe for breastfed infants. Unfortunately lack of information about drugs passing into breastmilk frequently results in exaggerated concerns about the risks. For example, your doctor may advise you to wean your baby when the medication being prescribed for you actually is compatible with breastfeeding. Here are two up-to-date comprehensive sources of information about medications and breastfeeding that your physician may appreciate knowing about:

- *Medications and Mothers' Milk*, a popular reference for health professionals written by a clinical pharmacologist, Dr. Thomas Hale, contains the latest information on hundreds of drugs and their relative safety in breastfeeding mothers and infants.
- Lactmed, a free online government database, offers information on hundreds of drugs, including possible effects on breastfed infants and safer alternatives to consider. Information about breastfeeding and medications also is available to health professionals at Dr. Hale's Web site, http://neonatal. ttuhsc.edu/lact/.

Guidelines for breastfeeding women who need to take medications. Take only medications that are necessary and clearly effective. Take the lowest effective dose for the shortest period of time. Avoid "sustained-release" or "long-acting"

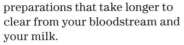

preparations that take longer to clear from your bloodstream and your milk.

Opt for single-ingredient over-the-counter medications that target your major symptom(s), rather than drugs with multiple ingredients. Choose a nasal decongestant spray over an oral formulation to reduce the amount that gets into your milk. Use it only a few days.

Generally, it is preferable to take a medication right after nursing your baby. For most short-acting drugs, the amount that appears in your milk reaches a peak level 1 to 2 hours after taking the medication. The level in milk then starts to decline, so that much of it will be cleared before your baby nurses again.

Take once-daily medications just prior to your baby's longest sleep period at night. However, most long-acting drugs will maintain a fairly constant level in breastmilk throughout the day.

As a general rule, a medication that was considered safe to take while you were pregnant will continue to be safe during breastfeeding. Similarly, drugs, such as many antibiotics, that commonly are prescribed for infants are safe for nursing mothers to take.

Keep in mind that some medications, such as estrogen-containing contraceptives, decongestants, or antihistamines, may decrease your milk supply.

Quick Chart

COMMON DRUGS THAT ARE COMPATIBLE WITH BREASTFEEDING WHEN TAKEN IN USUAL DOSES*

Acetaminophen
Anesthetics (local, for dental work, etc.)
Antacids
Antibiotics (most)
Antihistamines (most)
Anti-seizure medications (many)
Asthma medications (most)
Blood pressure medications (many)
Blood thinners (most)
Corticosteroids
Decongestant nasal spray
Diuretics (most)
Ibuprofen
Insulin
Laxatives (bulk forming and stool softening)
Over-the-counter medications (most)
Prescription pain medications (most)
Thyroid replacement hormone
*This list is not comprehensive.

Warning

Psychiatric medications taken by nursing mothers appear in breastmilk. A low dose of a single psychiatric medication usually is considered relatively safe during breastfeeding. The risks and benefits should be carefully weighed, and babies should be observed closely for possible adverse effects.

Quick Chart

DO NOT TAKE THESE DRUGS WHILE BREASTFEEDING*

Some drugs are not safe for infants and babies at any level of use, and breastfeeding is not recommended if you must regularly take a medication that could pose a risk to your nursing infant. If you know in advance that you temporarily need to take a drug that is incompatible with breastfeeding (such as any of those listed below), pump and save your surplus milk so that you can keep your baby well supplied during your course of drug therapy. Fortunately many breastfeeding mothers keep frozen stores of expressed breastmilk just in case they are needed.

- **Cancer chemotherapy**
  Even very small amounts of these drugs can be harmful to babies and suppress their immune systems. You can pump and dump your milk after each treatment until the drug has cleared.
- **Radioactive drugs used in diagnostic scans**
  You will need to pump and discard your milk until no radioactivity is present. The X-ray department can screen your milk for radioactivity, until it is safe to resume breastfeeding.
- **Certain drugs that suppress the immune system**
  These drugs, including some medications used to treat autoimmune diseases, such as rheumatoid arthritis, decrease the body's defenses against infection. Little is known about their effect on breastfed babies, but they carry a risk of harm and are best avoided while you are breastfeeding.
* This list is not comprehensive.

Warning: Illegal drugs, such as marijuana, cocaine, heroin, methamphetamine, ecstasy, phencyclidine, LSD, and others, pass readily into breastmilk and into your baby's brain. These drugs, as well as the overuse of prescription pain killers, are extremely dangerous to nursing infants and babies and should not be taken under any circumstances during breastfeeding. It cannot be emphasized strongly enough that illicit drugs must *NOT* be taken by nursing women, because of the very real risk such drugs pose to a baby, as well as the danger that exists when a mother attempts to care for her infant while she is high. Several infant fatalities have occurred when babies drank tainted milk from their nursing mothers who used illicit drugs.

Best Positions for Breastfeeding

Because you will spend a lot of time breastfeeding, it's very important to make sure you find positions that are comfortable for you, as well as effective for your baby. There is no right way to position your baby, but you'll want to make sure your arms, and especially your back, are well supported. Use pillows to help prop you or support your baby, if that helps. Also, don't try to bring your breast to the baby, always bring the baby to your breast. It can help to switch positions at different feedings. Many moms enjoy nursing lying down, especially at night. Some common feeding positions

Breastfeeding using the cradle hold

Breastfeeding using the cross-cradle hold

Breastfeeding in a reclining position

that you may find comfortable are illustrated here.

Don't Give Up Too Soon!

Many moms are tempted to give up breastfeeding because they are afraid something is going wrong. The number one thing you can do to help yourself stick with it is to get *support*. If you are feeling nervous or discouraged, know that you are not alone. These are perfectly normal feelings and it can really help to hear other moms talk about their own experiences, or to talk to a professional who has had lots of experiences in all kinds of situations. Here are some tips for supporting your success:

- Join a breastfeeding support group. Bring your partner if you can so they, too, will learn about the benefits of breastfeeding and how to better support you.
- Get in touch with La Leche League (1-800-LALECHE or www.llli.org) or your birthing center to find a lactation consultant.
- Ignore the well-meaning advice from family or friends who tell you that you need to "get him on a schedule," that he "should be sleeping through the night by now," or that breastfeeding is simply not worth the effort.
- Stay rested—not an easy thing to do when you are nursing around the clock, but try to get sleep when the baby sleeps, and put off any chores or other work that isn't a priority, especially during the first month.
- Get help: If friends or family make offers of help, take them up on it! If they ask what they can do, tell them to bring a cooked

meal or help with chores like cleaning, doing a few loads of laundry, or shopping.

- Private time: Remember that your first priority is you and your baby in those early weeks. Many people will likely want to visit and meet your new baby, but don't try to be a star entertainer. When it's time to nurse, ask for some privacy if that makes you feel more comfortable.
- Relax: Anything you do that can help you relax will encourage your milk letdown: quiet, soft music, alone time, etc.

> **TIP**
>
> If you can get through the first month of breastfeeding, chances are that your future months will be much easier. Even if things are smooth sailing from the start, be mentally prepared for a few hurdles to keep you from becoming discouraged.

Baby Gas

It's quite normal for babies, like adults, to have occasional bouts of gas. Some babies seem to have more of a problem with gas than others—getting it more frequently or feeling very uncomfortable with it. Gas in a baby's system is caused by air that's swallowed when he feeds, but it can also be produced as a by-product of his digestion. While most babies do not usually get excessive gas from digesting breastmilk, they will sometimes

have a gassy response to something you ate. And some formulas seem to cause more gassiness than others in particular babies. (See page XX for more information about infant formulas.)

Baby gas: common culprits. If your nursing baby seems to be gassier or fussier after some feedings than others, one thing you might try is eliminating some of the more gas-producing foods in your own diet to see if that makes him more comfortable. It's helpful to keep a chart, jotting down what you ate in the previous 12 hours before the baby's bout with gas—over time a particular food or food group may jump out at you as the culprit. Try eliminating that one from your diet first. Do not eat the food or anything containing the food for two full weeks, and pay attention to whether or not his symptoms improve.

Sometimes the problem is caused by more than one food or a combination, and may not be as easy to identify. Experiment with leaving the following foods out of your diet for at least a week, one at a time or in combination:

- Dairy foods: including milk and all milk products such as cheese, yogurt, sour cream, ice cream, etc.
- Cruciferous and other gas-producing vegetables: bell peppers (especially green), broccoli, Brussels sprouts, cabbage, cauliflower, cucumber, onion, etc. (Raw vegetables are more likely to produce gas than cooked vegetables. Try having your greens steamed for a while instead of raw and in salads.)
- Beans: all kinds. You can minimize the gassy effects of

beans by soaking dried beans overnight and throwing out the soak water before cooking. Make sure they are thoroughly cooked and chew them very well.

- Citrus or other acidic fruits, including lemons, limes, grapefruits, tomatoes, strawberries, etc.
- Pungent spices: hot chilies or hot sauce, hot curry powder, garlic, etc.
- Chocolate: all forms.
- Peanuts or peanut butter.*

* Tree nuts and peanuts are very common allergens. It is recommended, therefore, that parents refrain from introducing them into their children's diets until at least their first birthday. Children who are at risk for food allergies should wait even longer. Toddlers under three years old should not be given whole nuts or seeds because they are a choking hazard.

Colic

If your baby gets fussy and seems to cry for extended periods, his problem may not be gas or even digestive at all. He may have colic. This is a term used to describe regular, extended bouts of crying in a young baby. If your baby cries for 3 or more hours, 3 or more days per week for at least 3 consecutive weeks, your doctor may diagnose him as having colic. The condition used to be attributed to digestive discomfort, but now it's believed to be the result of an immature nervous system or having the trait of high sensitivity (although if your baby is also feeling gassy, this can prolong or intensify his

crying sessions). For some babies, a normal level of daily stimulation is overwhelming to them, and their response is to cry for long periods of time, sometimes intensely and inconsolably.

Colic can appear anytime in young babies, but it occurs most often between 2 weeks and 3 months of age. Colic in most babies seems to go away on its own sometime between 6 and 8 weeks, but it can extend for longer periods. While regular methods of calming babies don't seem to be effective for colicky babies, there are some things you can do to help them settle down. Because they are often overstimulated, try reducing the stimulants in their environment, especially before their typical crying time. If you know your baby tends to melt down in the late afternoon, try carrying him close to your body in a sling before that time. Keep sound and light soft and to a minimum. Highly sensitive babies will also pick up on your stress, so staying relaxed while he is upset can help shorten the episodes. Easier said than done, of course—you might need extra support during this phase. Look for your partner or other family or close friends to take the baby and give you a break occasionally so you don't get burned out.

When Others Want to Feed the Baby

If you are breastfeeding exclusively, you may find that your husband, partner, or even another close member of your family is feeling left out because they "never get to feed the baby." What they are looking for is the intimacy of connecting with that beautiful new being, so try offering them a few alternatives.

- Let others burp the baby during your nursing session.
- Encourage them to be close to the baby during non-feeding times, such as putting her down for a nap, playing with her, or simply holding her.
- Offer them the chance to bathe her. Bathing can be a very sweet time with your baby and can help your family feel more bonded with her.
- You can also just give them the facts: Exclusive breastfeeding is the absolute best thing you can do for the development, health, and future health of the baby you all love. Keep a few informational pamphlets on hand from La Leche League or a baby-friendly hospital about all the benefits of breastfeeding.

Storing Breastmilk

If you have a good breast pump or are able to express by hand, you will be able to pump and store breastmilk for your baby. This is very convenient for the times when you are separated. The care provider can simply thaw and warm your milk to feed the baby with a bottle. Follow these guidelines for safe breastmilk storage:

Always wash your hands before pumping. Make sure all breast pump equipment and your milk storage containers have been well washed in hot, soapy water.

If you know you will use the milk within 4 days, store it in the refrigerator rather than the freezer to best preserve its antimicrobial properties. The best freezer container for breastmilk is a **tempered glass** bottle made for freezer storage, but other freezer-safe containers for liquids may also be used. Never freeze milk or foods in any glass containers that are not made especially for freezer use. Regular glass can crack, depositing tiny shards of glass into the milk.

If your baby bottles are freezer-safe and you have enough of them, you can freeze breastmilk right in the bottles; just be sure to leave an inch of empty space for the frozen milk to expand, and screw the cap on tightly. If you want to freeze the milk in plastic bottles, check to make sure they are freezer-safe first. You can also purchase single-use plastic freezer bags for freezing individual portions of breastmilk—be sure to look for plastic bags that are BPA-free (#2 or #4 plastic).

Freeze the milk in the approximate amounts that your baby will eat at one feeding to minimize waste and thawing time (try 4 ounces per container). Once breastmilk is thawed, it should not be refrozen.

Milk will keep in a cooler with ice for 24 hours or in a fridge for 4 days (best) or up to 1 week, if necessary. Or it can be stored in a freezer for 3 to 4 months or in a freestanding deep-freezer (0° F) for 6 months.

Date your bottles with a marker and a piece of masking tape to keep track. If you have room, store them in order from oldest to newest on a freezer shelf.

To Thaw and Serve

Run lukewarm water over the frozen breastmilk container, gradually warming the water until the milk thaws and reaches room temperature, or place in a bowl or pan of hot water. To prevent hot spots, and to preserve all its health and nutritional qualities, do not heat breastmilk directly over a burner or in a microwave.

Shake the milk to recombine, and test on your inner arm or wrist for temperature—it should be lukewarm or room temperature.

Thawed breastmilk will keep for 24 hours in the refrigerator. Do not refreeze.

Throw away any thawed, unused milk from the bottle after a feeding.

Note: *If milk is frozen in plastic, use cold water only to defrost. Do not use hot water, as any heat can cause chemical leaching into the milk.*

PREPARING TO FORMULA FEED

If you are unable or have chosen not to breastfeed, you will need to feed with formula. You will be able to nourish him well, and you don't have to lose out on the bonding that comes naturally with nursing. There are some bonuses that come with bottle feeding as well: Others can feed the baby, giving them an opportunity to bond with him, and you the chance to take a break once in a while. Babies digest formula more slowly than breastmilk, so they may go longer between feeding times.

Nursing is, by its nature, an act of intimacy because the baby is physically connected to the mother through the latch. Although this obviously isn't possible in the same way with a bottle, you can definitely make feeding a time of special intimacy.

Practice skin-to-skin contact often when feeding, as much as possible in the early weeks. Hold your baby close to you and look into her eyes as she is eating. And since bottle feedings can go faster than breastfeeding sessions, be sure to give her as much cuddle time as she wants before and after eating.

What You'll Need

You'll need to buy some things in advance to formula feed because special equipment is required. You'll need to have formula, bottles, nipples, and bottle-cleaning supplies on hand when your baby is born (or adopted).

Choosing formula. There are several different brands of formula available. Their nutrient content is regulated by the FDA according to preset guidelines from the American Academy of Pediatrics, so you can trust all major brands to be safe for your child. The actual ingredients, however, do differ, and that can make a big difference in how well your baby adjusts to it. There are three basic types of formula: cow's-milk formula, soy formula, and elemental formula. Talk with your pediatrician about which one would be the best for your baby to begin with and why.

In general, most babies will start with a cow's-milk formula, but if there is any allergy present, a soy formula or elemental formula (which contains hydrolysate proteins, which are easier for some infants to digest) may be recommended. You can also find special formulas for preemies, lactose-free, and supplemented with **DHA (docosahexaenoic acid)** and **ARA (arachidonic acid)**, forms of omega-3 fatty acids. This DHA and ARA has been added in an attempt to mimic the naturally-occurring omega-3 fatty acids in breastmilk.

The major provider for DHA and ARA in infant formulas is a company called Martek Biosciences. Martek's branded DHA, life'sDHA, is made from microalgae under tightly controlled manufacturing conditions. Martek differentiates life'sDHA as being free from the contaminants that may be present in fish oils. The company's vegetarian source of omega-3 DHA is used in foods, beverages, infant formula, and supplements, while omega-6 ARA is used only for infant formula.

Formulas come in three types: ready-to-serve (the most expensive), dried (powder that you mix with water—the least expensive), and canned concentrate (thick liquid also mixed with water). While it's nice to have some premixed formula on hand for your first days home and for traveling, that can get costly to use all the time. Powdered or concentrated formula, on the other hand, although not as convenient, is less expensive. Many larger companies will offer coupons for volume purchase, but don't get cases of any one type until you're sure your baby tolerates that type and brand well.

Follow the package directions for mixing your formula exactly. Using too much or too little water can be harmful to your baby. Also follow the package directions for storing your formula once it's been mixed (or opened, if it's the ready-to-feed variety).

Signs of a formula reaction. Every baby is different, and not all formulas work for all babies. If you suspect your baby is reacting to his formula, consult your pediatrician and try switching types or brands. Watch for these signs:

- **Digestion:** Vomiting after every feeding (some spitting up after eating is normal, especially in younger babies; but if you are formula-feeding, it's a good idea to try switching from powder to liquid or changing brands to check whether or not the vomiting is affected); diarrhea or mucus in stool.

- **Crying:** Fierce crying and apparent belly discomfort after eating; unusual night time waking.
- **Skin:** Rashes of any kind, especially around the mouth or on the bottom.
- **Mucus:** Clear discharge from his nose, or recurrent ear or upper respiratory infections.

Safe water for formula. If you are using tap water to mix formula, never use the hot water—there are mineral deposits in most hot water pipes that leach into the hot water. Instead, run the water on the cold side for 2 minutes to clear out excess lead and then use that water.

Some experts recommend boiling tap water for 1 to 5 minutes to kill any existing bacteria, and then cooling before using for formula. Double boiling may concentrate any minerals present, so use fresh water each time.

If you have a cistern or well water, have the mineral content checked. High concentrations of nitrates and other minerals could be unsafe for baby consumption. If the mineral levels are safe, you should still boil any water for formula for 10 minutes and then cool before using. Consult your health-care provider for guidance.

Choosing bottles and nipples. Although there are many different varieties of baby bottles, most are one of three primary types: basic 4- and 8-ounce bottles (the 4-ounce is better for newborns); angled or colic-preventive bottles; or bottles with disposable linings. Some bottles also come with inserts or vents to help minimize the swallowing of air. The basic bottle is easiest to find and clean, and it usually fits with most standardized nipples and bottle warmers. But if they aren't equipped with a vent insert, these bottles allow for air to be swallowed more easily and can contribute to gas bubbles in some babies. They come in plastic or glass. The glass is safest and easiest to clean, but it is heavier than plastic and can break if dropped.

Angled bottles may help prevent your baby from swallowing as much air as basic bottles, but they can be harder to clean. Also, for some reason, some babies just won't take an angled bottle. The liner bottles work well for gas prevention because you can squeeze excess air out of the bag before feeding. They are also a pre-sterilized system, and usually come in a starter set with bottles, nipples, and liners—be sure to look for liners that are free of BPA. The cons are that you have to stay stocked with extra liners so that you never run out, they are more expensive than other bottle types, and they create plastic waste. Bottle liners should be thrown away after a single use, never cleaned and reused.

Nipples come in several different shapes and sizes as well. They are made of either latex or silicone. The **latex nipples** are light brown and softer than the silicone. They also tend to wear out faster, and latex can cause an allergic reaction in some babies. **Silicone nipples** are stiffer, clear, and more resistant to heat. They usually last longer than latex varieties. Both types can tear and will wear out in time, so check the nipples a couple of times a week for any cracks or small tears, and replace if you find any signs of deterioration. All nipples should be replaced regularly, in any case—about every 3 months. Many babies will express a preference for one nipple variety over another, so when you find one that he likes, make sure it fits with the bottle variety you have chosen (to avoid leaks) and stick with that set.

Are plastics safe? The polycarbonate BPA story.

You have very likely heard the warnings about avoiding a certain type of plastic that is commonly found in baby bottles and children's toys. Bisphenol-A (BPA) is a chemical used in hard, clear, plastic baby bottles; sport bottles; sippy cups; metal can linings; and 5-gallon water bottles. It is part of the family of polycarbonate plastics that has been implicated in many potential health conditions that could affect your infant or child (and you, for that matter). Over time, this chemical can seep into the containers and into food and liquids, including your baby's milk. The reason that BPA is harmful is because it mimics the action of the human hormone estrogen. Estrogen mimickers—also called hormone disruptors—have been shown in animal studies to stimulate certain cancer cells, including prostate and breast cancers, as well as ovarian dysfunction. The effect of BPA exposure, even at low levels, has been documented by dozens of government-funded studies. Even though these studies were done on animals, they give us a good clue as to how BPA might be affecting humans.

For instance, reported adverse effects include many conditions that we might associate with a hormone imbalance: early onset of puberty, premature breast development, decreased testosterone levels in males, altered immune function, decreased sperm volume, and increased prostate size. There was also an increase in hyperactivity, aggressiveness, impaired learning, and other changes in behavior. These reactions occurred in adults. For children, the indications are even more dire.

Babies and children have immune systems that are just forming, which makes them more vulnerable when exposed to toxic chemicals. Because BPA can cross the placenta (BPA was found in human fetal umbilical cord blood), exposure while pregnant is as much of a concern as it is once the baby is born. In fact, one study reported spontaneous miscarriages in women whose level of BPA was three times the average level. The National Toxicology Program also noted in a recent report (based on animal studies) that there is some concern that BPA can cause "changes in behavior in the brain, as well as reduce survival and birthweight in fetuses." Because of exposure to chemicals at critical times of development, children are at a much greater risk than adults for toxic overload and subsequent damaging health problems.

It is important to note that

most of the studies that discount the harmful effects of BPA are funded by the plastics industries. In fact, according to the Institute for Agriculture and Trade Policy, out of 115 published animal studies, 81 percent found that BPA significantly caused these side effects, and 90 percent of the government-funded studies reported the same result, while the industry studies reported no side effects.

Currently, Canada has announced that it will be banning BPA in baby bottles, and legislation is underway in the United States to ban the chemical's use in toys. But until these bans take effect, it may be wise to eliminate as much BPA and other harmful plastic as possible from your baby's life, and your own.

Protect your baby and your family. Plastics are classified by different numbers according to the type of resin used. The number is printed or imprinted on the bottom of plastic bottles or plastic wrap containers. If you are ready to start reducing your exposure to polycarbonates, here are some ways to get started:

Avoid PETE number 7. If you see a recycling symbol #7 on the bottom of a bottle, get rid of it. Seven is the number for polycarbonates (PCBs) and BPA. If there is no symbol on the bottom of the bottle, and the bottle is a hard, clear plastic, call the manufacturer and ask. Recycling symbols #1, #2, #4, and #5 are safer plastic alternatives, but do not reuse #1, #3, or #6, as they are harmful plastics. You can typically recycle #1 and #2, but most recycling services will not accept #4 or #5.

Eliminate polycarbonate bottles and opt for safer alternatives. Good alternatives to BPA are plain old glass, or a softer type of plastic that looks cloudy and more pliable, not hard and clear. Some BPA-free alternatives are listed at the *Parents* magazine Web site, www.parents.com—Born Free, Adiri, and Medela are some of the brands. Use alternatives to plastic packaging as well, such as paper bags, wax paper, and cardboard. Baby bottles are not usually labeled for plastics, so check with the manufacturer if you are unsure.

Avoid heating or microwaving. Heating and microwaving these plastics breaks the plastic down and allows the chemical to leach into the food. So avoid putting plastics in the dishwasher, do not microwave food or bottles, and do not leave plastic bottles in a hot car (this also applies to plastic water bottles). Instead, heat foods and liquids in glass containers and then transfer them to a safe plastic once they have cooled a bit.

Do not use plastic wrap over foods in the microwave; use waxed paper or paper towels instead.

Avoid using plastic containers for fatty foods, as there is greater leaching of chemicals into fatty foods.

Note that "microwave safe" does not mean that there is no leaching of chemicals.

Freezing plastics is acceptable, and does not cause the same chemical reaction as heating.

Throw out old bottles. Old bottles and sippy cups that look scratched or worn should be thrown out. One report showed a high BPA exposure after only fifty to one hundred washings.

Limit use of metal cans. The lining in metal cans may also contain BPA, and in some cases, exposure can be up to ten times greater than from plastics that hold liquid formula. If your baby formula comes from one of these cans, you may want to do three things. First, verify that it is indeed metal: Many cans look like they're metal but are actually stiff paperboard. The Environmental Working Group suggests that you hold a magnet up to the can to see if it sticks. If it does, then the can is metal. Second, buy powdered baby formula instead of liquid. Powdered formulas are not distributed in metal containers. And third, reevaluate how much food you have stored in the pantry in metal containers: Soups, beans, and vegetables are not exempt from BPA linings. Note that Eden Organics uses BPA-free cans for their bean products.

BPA is used in cured epoxy resins that line metal cans to maintain the quality of their contents. In most cases it is inert in this form, yet there is some indication that heat and/or time can allow for gradual leaching. Most foods are canned while still hot.

Choose only certain plastics. When plastic wraps or bags are the only choice for food storage, look for options with recycling codes #1 PETE, #2 HDPE, #4 LDPE, and #5 PP. These are frequently recycled plastics, which have not been found to leach toxins into your food. The most common plastic for wraps and bags is #4, and for freezer-safe plastic containers it's #2.

Choose silicone nipples: These are safer than latex, because latex may leach nitrosamines, which have been shown to be carcinogenic.

For more information on plastics, go to www.healthobservatory.org.

[Sources: National Toxicology Program, Department of Health and Human Services. Draft NTP Brief on Bisphenol A. Case no. 80-05-7. April 14, 2008. http://cerhr.niehs.nih.gov/chemicals/bisphenol/BPADraftBriefVF_04_14_08.pdf. Susanne Rust, "FDA Relied on Industry Studies to Judge Safety," Institute for Agriculture and Trade Policy, April 8, 2008. www.healthobservatory.org/headlines.cfm?RefID=102237.]

Warning

Throw your bottle away if you notice any cracking or chipping. These could be dangerous for your baby, especially with glass bottles. Throw away the nipple if it has thinned out, changed color, doesn't return to its original shape when pulled, has any cracks or tears, or allows the milk to pour out in a stream, rather than drip out, when held upside down.

Nipple designs come in several shapes, including varieties for gum comfort (orthodontic), to mimic the human nipple (wider base and natural shape), slow flowing, and **anti-vacuum or vented** (to help reduce gas). In the beginning, choose a standard **slow-flow nipple**. If your baby has trouble taking this nipple, you can try a couple of other varieties until he seems comfortable and relaxed during feeding.

Bottle-cleaning supplies. All new bottles, nipples, and rings should be sterilized by submerging them in a large pan of boiling water for 5 minutes before use. Once they've been boiled, you should wash them thoroughly with a **bottle brush** in hot soapy water after every use, or run them through your dishwasher—the hot cycle on the dishwasher should be adequate for sterilization after first boiling. It can also help to have a **bottle drying rack** and a **nipple and ring cage** for use in your dishwasher to keep from losing those smaller pieces.

Formula Feeding: What to Do

Before your baby comes home, purchase the basics that you'll need to get started: a week's worth of the formula recommended by your pediatrician (we suggest getting ready-to-use for the first few days to simplify things); three or four basic newborn bottles with the same number of silicone, slow-flow, newborn nipples (you will want to buy more when you know your baby likes them); and a bottle brush.

You can serve formula warm, cold, or at room temperature, but never hot or your baby can be burned. Many babies will drink formula at all temperatures, but warming it slightly, especially during the early weeks, may be more soothing to him. To warm a

bottle, place it into a temperature-controlled bottle warmer or a small pan of warm water for about 5 minutes. Your hand is not an accurate gauge of temperature for a newborn. Instead, shake a few drops of warmed formula onto your inner wrist. If it feels gently warm or neutral, it is the right temperature.

Hold him in a position that's comfortable for both of you, skin-to-skin if possible, so that you are both supported and you can look into each other's eyes. Hold the bottle at a 45-degree angle so the milk fills the nipple. Always keep the milk pooled in the bottle neck—you want to avoid having the baby suck at an air pocket in the bottle to help prevent gas.

You can try burping him and switching sides halfway through a bottle feeding, as you would when nursing. But if he seems content, let him finish on one side, and start him on the other side when you next feed him. This will protect your back and neck, and also allow him to work the muscles on both sides of his body equally.

You will usually be encouraged to feed your baby for the first time shortly after birth, and then every 2 to 3 hours on demand. He will likely need only 2 to 3 ounces of formula at a feeding for the first week or so. By the second week, he may increase the amount to 3 to 4 ounces and may feed eight to ten times in a 24-hour period. Feed him when he shows signs of hunger, and let him stop when he shows signs he's had enough. A formula-fed baby typically takes about 20 to 30 minutes for a feeding, but that is highly individual. (See page 65 for typical signs of infant hunger and satisfaction.) Use the signals he is giving you, rather than how full or empty the bottle is, to guide the length of his feeding times. Never force your baby to finish a bottle if he is no longer hungry. Throw away any formula remaining in the bottle.

> **TIP**
>
> To set up your own bottle bar, so you won't have to walk up and down stairs for bottle supplies in the middle of the night, invest in a mini-refrigerator and a bottle warmer. Prepare 2 to 4 bottles (depending on your baby's feeding frequency) before your own bedtime and store them in the fridge, or keep premixed formula at room temperature and sterilized bottles and nipples at the bar.

Formula Feeding: What Not to Do

Never heat formula in a microwave or over direct heat, especially in a closed bottle. Microwaves heat unevenly and you could end up with formula that feels lukewarm but has scalding pockets. If the formula in a bottle gets too hot, it could expand and cause the bottle to explode.

To avoid wasting any of your precious breastmilk, don't mix it with formula in the same bottle. Feed your baby the breastmilk

first, and supplement with a second bottle of formula if he's still hungry.

Don't prop your baby's bottle, either, with a commercial bottle prop or some homemade setup. You should never leave your baby alone while feeding, and having the bottle propped in place might tempt you to get something else done. Propping the bottle increases the risk of him choking. It also encourages milk pooling in his mouth, which can lead to tooth decay or ear infections.

Do not freeze formula, as it will separate when thawed.

FEEDING AT 3 TO 4 MONTHS

Sometime between the third and fourth month, your baby might drop a feeding or two. You may also find that your breasts are feeling softer, even after letdown. These are healthy, natural changes and they do not mean that your baby isn't getting enough milk. On the contrary, it means that the two of you have hit your stride together and you're producing milk very efficiently now. You should still be nursing or bottle feeding seven to eight times in a 24-hour period. If she is gaining weight at the proper pace (between ½ to 1 ounce per day is expected in 3- to 6-month-old babies, but, as always, your pediatrician is the best judge of proper weight gain for your baby), soaking several diapers, and continuing her mustard yellow poops, she is most likely thriving.

All your feeding practices, such as nursing or bottle feeding on demand and holding her close to you during feeding, are helping the two of you develop a healthy feeding relationship. She is learning that her world is safe, and that nourishment feels good. She's able to rely on her own signals for hunger and fullness without having to struggle to be understood. When she feels hungry, she receives food; when she is full, she's allowed to stop. This, in turn, is creating a strong base for a healthy relationship with food and eating.

During the first months with your newborn, it's likely that you will hear a lot of talk about getting your baby to sleep through the night. You may be feeling very tired and hoping that that time will come sooner rather than later. It's important to know that newborn babies aren't made to sleep through the night at first. Their stomachs are very small and they need to eat frequently to keep their nutrient and calorie levels up as they are growing (most newborns can't go for more than 3 to 5 hours without a feeding). While you may feel tired during the day from waking at night, know that this phase is both very important for your baby and also very temporary. Try to think of those nighttime feedings as a special time of intimacy between you and your baby.

TIP

To keep your baby's mouth healthy and free of debris, wipe her gums with a soft, clean, warm, wet cloth before going to sleep at night.

Feeding at 4 to 6 Months

BEST FOODS

Breastmilk
While it has been common practice in the West to introduce solid food between the ages of 4 and 6 months, when the baby shows certain signs of **feeding readiness**, the American Academy of Pediatrics and the World Health Organization recommend waiting to introduce solid foods until sometime in the sixth month. If you do decide to introduce solid foods, breastmilk or formula feeding should not decrease in frequency or volume at this age because the nutrients provided by breastmilk are still required for his development. Solid foods simply can't match breastmilk or formula for baby nutrition before 6 to 9 months of age.

Breast- or Bottle Feeding at 4 to 6 Months

Babies should still be nursing or bottle feeding at least seven times per day at 4 to 6 months, even if they begin having some solid foods. One sign that you may be feeding your baby too much solid food too soon is if he wants to nurse or bottle-feed less frequently.

A common recommendation for formula-fed babies at this age is at least 32 ounces of formula daily, although that has never been backed up by research. Portion needs are very individual and can change from day to day. If your pediatrician is happy with your baby's weight gain, he's doing fine.

Quick Chart

INTRODUCING SOLID FOODS: TOP 5 REASONS TO WAIT UNTIL BABY'S SIXTH MONTH

- Pediatric recommendation: Both AAP and WHO support waiting till the sixth month to start solids.
- It is recognized as obesity preventive.
- Developmental readiness: A 6-month-old is more likely to have resolved the tongue-thrust reflex; his chewing skills will be more advanced and his intestinal tract will be better developed to handle solid foods without triggering an immune reaction.
- Baby may be less likely to develop food allergies.
- Waiting is cheaper and more convenient for you.

FLASH FACT

The American College of Allergy, Asthma and Immunology recommends exclusive breastfeeding during the first 6 months of life, with exclusion of cow's-milk formulas and any supplemental foods. Exclusive breastfeeding protects against the onset of allergic symptoms extending far beyond the period of breastfeeding.

FOODS TO AVOID

The choice of which food to begin with can vary among different world cultures, and there is no one perfect food to choose. There are, however, several foods that you should not offer to your 4- to 6-month-old baby. Because his digestive system is still immature and he has very limited chewing capabilities, avoid any grown-up foods that have not been properly pureed to a silky, runny texture. In addition, you should never offer a young baby any junk foods such as candy or potato chips because of the excess sugar, salt, poor-quality fats, and potentially harmful additives and preservatives.

You should not feed 4- to 6-month-old babies any foods that are known to trigger allergic reactions: cow's milk (or any products made with milk, such as cheese), citrus fruits, chocolate, eggs, fish or shellfish, peanuts or any other tree nuts, nut butters, and anything made with wheat. (See page 110 for a more thorough list of allergenic foods to avoid.)

Babies under 6 months of age should not eat home-prepared beets, carrots, collards, spinach, or turnips. If they are cooked at home, these veggies are quite high in nitrates, which can be converted into nitrites in the bodies of young babies. High concentrations of nitrites in infants can affect their blood's ability to carry oxygen, making it difficult for them to breathe, even causing them to turn blue. Although commercially prepared versions of these vegetables contain only tiny amounts of nitrates and are therefore not considered dangerous for 4- to 6-month-old babies, only carrots make good early foods because they are just slightly harder to digest than the best first foods selections.

Warning

According to the 2005 Dietary Guidelines for Americans developed jointly by the U.S. Department of Health and Human Services and the U.S. Department of Agriculture, infants, toddlers, and pregnant or immune-compromised mothers should avoid raw milk or raw milk products; raw eggs or raw egg products; raw or undercooked meat, poultry, fish, and shellfish; raw (unpasteurized) juice;* and raw sprouts.
*Juice that you squeeze or make in your home juicer from fresh, washed fruits or vegetables and drink immediately is fine for Mom and older babies and toddlers.

It is generally recommended that you avoid giving honey and agave nectar to babies under 12 months of age. Honey may contain the spores of *Clostridium botulinum*, which can cause infant **botulism** in babies. Botulism is a serious illness that attacks the nervous system. After her first birthday, however, your baby is not susceptible to those spores and you can feed her honey safely. Agave nectar is a relatively new product on the U.S. market, and so there is not much available research on it yet. Because it is an **unpasteurized** natural sweetener, however, it may also contain botulism spores. To be safe, treat it like honey and don't feed it to babies until they are at least a year old as well.

The only liquid a 4- to 6-month-old baby needs is breastmilk or formula. Avoid all soda, juices, milk, or large amounts of water.

WHAT TO LOOK FOR IN YOUR 4- TO 6-MONTH-OLD BABY

Although you may have heard stories about mothers feeding babies all sorts of foods at a much younger age, your baby is not developmentally ready to eat solid foods before the age of 4 months. Breastmilk or formula provides all of his nutritional needs, and offering him infant cereal or other first foods too soon to try to get him to sleep through the night (or for any other reason) may actually be harmful to him by depriving him of the nutrition he needs from breastmilk, and contributing to the development of food allergies later in life. There is also a greater danger of him choking.

There are several developmental markers for a baby's readiness to begin eating solid foods. While it is best to wait until your baby is 6 months old to introduce any solids, if you choose to start earlier, look for these milestones sometime between 4 and 6 months.

Head's up. A baby should be able to hold his head up and sit upright on his own in a supportive chair before he's introduced to solid foods. If his head is still drooping when he sits, wait until his neck becomes stronger.

While it is vital to wait to introduce solids until your baby can hold his head up and swallow safely, waiting until the seventh month may make it harder for some babies to learn to chew. Introducing solids in the sixth month is optimum.

I can swallow when I choose. Infants have a built-in **tongue-thrust reflex** (also called the **extrusion reflex**) that helps them suckle at the breast and keeps them from choking. As a result, many young babies will use their tongue to automatically scoot out anything introduced into their mouths. Sometime around 5 or 6 months of age, your baby's ability to swallow will also change from an automatic reflex when he suckles to a voluntary action, and this, plus the resolution of the extrusion reflex, will make it much easier for him to take a bite of solid food from a spoon. While he'll still be more of a "sucker" than a "chewer" at first, he should have the ability to move the food from the front to the back of his mouth to swallow.

FLASH FACT

At age 6 or 7 months, your baby will be capable of making true chewing motions. Before then, she will move her tongue in and out, as if sucking, to swallow solids at first.

I'm watching you. As babies approach the 6-month marker,

they have better muscular control over their heads, and they can look toward, and even reach for, things they want, and turn away from things they don't want. If you see your baby watching you (or others at the table) closely as you eat, if you see his eyes following the food from the plate to your mouth, that can indicate a possible readiness for solids. Some babies are quite intent observers by nature, however, and may be interested in food or eating before they are fully ready for it, so don't use this sign alone as your indicator.

TIP

A young baby who rejects food by pushing it out of his mouth using the extrusion reflex means he is not yet ready for solids, but it doesn't necessarily mean that he doesn't like the taste. Give him another week or two and try again.

I want that! When he's getting very interested in eating, your baby might reach out and grab a handful of food right off your plate! Grabbing your silverware is not the same indicator of readiness, however, because many babies think forks, spoons, or shiny knives look very intriguing as possible playthings, and not because they carry food!

I'm still hungry. One simple way to tell that your baby is ready for solid foods is that he still seems to be hungry after a feeding. If he finishes nursing or bottle feeding and doesn't seem content, if he gets hungry more quickly after eating, or if he suddenly starts waking for a new or extra nighttime feeding, try increasing the frequency of your nursing or bottle sessions. If he wants to keep up this heavier schedule of more nursing sessions or bottles for more than 3 or 4 days in a row, he may be ready for his first bites.

GETTING STARTED

Warning

Check with your pediatrician about when to start offering your baby solid food. In some special cases, such as with preemies, the doctor may recommend delaying first foods for longer than is typically recommended.

Between 4 and 6 months of age, solid foods should be more of a garnish than a main meal. All of her nutrition should still be coming from breastmilk or formula, and you can think of these early feeding weeks as an introduction to eating rather than a replacement of any milk feedings. Introducing solid foods is an exercise in going slow and listening to your baby's messages to you. You may try the first time and discover that she isn't quite ready. No harm done, just wait a week or two, look for readiness signs, and try again.

Baby's First Bites

Wait until the sixth month and/ or look for signs of **feeding** **readiness**. If you think your baby is ready to eat, begin by washing your hands and your baby's hands. Make sure he is sitting up straight in a supported chair, like a high chair. Some parents prefer to hold the baby upright in their lap, but in this position the baby may smell the mom's breasts and become confused about which kind of food you want him to eat! Do not cradle him in your arms as you do when nursing or bottle feeding, as this position could cause him to choke.

You can start by nursing him on one side or giving him half of a bottle first, then trying one or two bites of a single food, letting him be the judge of how many bites he would like at each feeding. After the solid foods, allow him to nurse on the other side or finish his bottle.

While there is no actual research proving that one food is better to start with than another, there are a few foods that most babies traditionally do quite well with. It's good to start with something that's very easy to digest and will taste somewhat familiar to your baby. You'll also want to avoid anything that commonly causes allergic reactions in babies. For this reason, **infant rice cereal** mixed with a little breastmilk or formula is usually recommended as baby's best first food. Rice is a somewhat sweet, gluten-free grain that is very easy to digest. Mixing it with the milk he knows will also make it more palatable to him. Choose an iron-fortified, organic, whole-grain variety to provide the "cleanest" (most organic) version with the most nutrients, and mix no more than 1 tablespoon dry with a couple of tablespoons of room-temperature breastmilk or formula to make a thin gruel. Make sure it is completely smooth, a little runny, and has no lumps.

For the first 3 to 4 days offer all first foods early in the day so you will be able to clearly see whether or not your baby has an allergic reaction. Also, if any problems do occur, he'll have the whole day for it to pass out of his system, rather than disturbing his (and your!) sleep at night.

For his very first bites, you can use an infant spoon or your index finger. While using your finger may be a little messier, it will be warm and familiar to your baby. Talk to him gently and with encouragement. Wait until he is tuned in to you and attentive to what you are doing. To test the waters, let him clearly see you bringing that first bite of food toward his mouth. If he opens his mouth in response, that's a good sign that he's ready to eat. If he clamps his mouth shut or turns his head away from the food, he may not be ready for eating just yet. There's no need to force the issue. If after a couple of tries he remains uninterested, don't make a big deal out of it; just clean things up and try again another day. Remember, all children learn to eat eventually!

If your family has no history of food allergies and your baby is at least 26 weeks, try offering the new food alone for at least 3 days in a row. If there is a history of food allergies, offer the new food for at least 4 days in a row. If your baby is younger than 6 months, offer each new alone food for 4 to 5 days at a time. (See page 96 for the best

feeding practices for babies with a family history of allergies.) If your baby shows no signs of allergy, terrific—add that food into his repertoire. Once you've tested a new food in this way, it's fine to keep offering it in combination with other safe foods—just try each new food one at a time for a few days first. Don't feed your baby just one food for more than a week, as this practice may backfire and actually create a food sensitivity.

Babies under 6 months should not eat home-prepared beets, carrots, collards, spinach, or turnips. These home-cooked vegetables can contain concentrations of nitrates or nitrates that could be harmful to babies younger than 6 months. (See page 90 for more information.)

After the third day, allow him to eat as much as he would like, based on his hunger (most babies will eat 1 to 4 tablespoons at a sitting; younger babies consuming less, and older babies consuming more).

Introduce new foods one at a time thereafter, in the same runny, liquid form as the rice cereal. (See page 95 for a chart of baby's best first foods.) Each new food should be offered for 3 to 5 days (fewer days for babies at least 26 weeks old or with no family history of allergies; more days for younger babies or those at risk for food allergies).

TIP

For baby's first feedings, look for small, oval, infant-size baby spoons with shallow bowls and no hard edges—rubber-coated or molded plastic make good choices. Bowls should also be small, heat resistant, and nonbreakable. Some have a suction cup on the bottom—handy for keeping them attached to the high-chair tray. It's also handy to get a 3 or 4 soft cotton bibs large enough to cover his whole front—baby feeding is a very messy business!

Quick Chart

BEST FIRST FOODS*

Brown rice cereal
Sweet potato puree
Winter squash puree
Applesauce puree
Mashed banana puree
Mashed avocado puree
Pear puree
* See chapter 8 for information about how to prepare baby's first cereals and vegetable and fruit purees.

FOOD ALLERGIES

These last couple of decades have seen an increase in food allergies in children. By some estimates, over 6 percent of all children under the age of 3 years are affected. *Food allergies*, sometimes called **food hypersensitivities**, occur when a body's immune system reacts to normally harmless elements in a food. A big part of the immune system's job is to locate and fight off harmful germs, such as bacteria and viruses. If your child develops a food allergy, his immune system will essentially misfire at a certain food and create an immune reaction that ranges from mild to very severe, sometimes even fatal.

We don't understand all the things that cause food allergies, but allergies can run in families. So if anyone in your family has a history of allergies—not just to food but to environmental or animal allergens such as pollen, mold, dust mites, or pet dander—you should follow a careful allergy-prevention regimen when you introduce all new foods to your baby and toddler. (See "Best Practices for Babies at Risk for Food Allergy" on page 96.) By delaying the introduction of certain foods that seem to cause a lot of allergies, you can help protect your child from developing a hypersensitivity. If he does develop food allergies, introducing the trigger foods later in his life may help make his reactions less severe.

FLASH FACT

THE BIG EIGHT

Any food can potentially trigger an allergic reaction, but these 8 foods are responsible for over 90 percent of all allergy reactions.
Cow's milk
Shellfish
Egg
Fish
Peanuts
Tree nuts (pecans, almonds, walnuts)
Soybean
Wheat

TIP

In 2006, the Food Allergen Labeling and Consumer Protection Act required that all food products, baby formulas, and nutritional supplements clearly label whether a food contains any ingredient from the 8 major food allergens.

Food allergies are not always easy to spot. The allergic reaction can happen just after the food is eaten, a few hours later, or even a few days later. In addition, they can be portion-specific. In other words, your child may not have a reaction to a small amount of egg used in a cookie, but he may have a severe, noticeable reaction to eating a plate of scrambled eggs. Allergic reactions also vary in severity. One child may develop rashes from eating shellfish, while another has trouble breathing and needs to be taken to the hospital immediately.

Best Practices for Babies at Risk for Food Allergy

If your family has any history of allergies—food, environmental, or other—you should delay or avoid the introduction of certain foods in your baby/toddler's diet. While some food allergies are more persistent than others, studies have shown that you can actually prevent a food allergy from developing by delaying the introduction of certain trigger foods (see "The Big Eight" on this page).

The following are the recommendations of the American College of Allergy, Asthma and Immunology for children who have been deemed at risk for food allergies.

Breastfeed your child exclusively for his first 6 months.

Do not introduce any solid foods until he is at least 6 months old.

Begin with low-risk foods (see the "Best First Foods" list on page 95) and offer each one alone, in small amounts.

Do not offer combination foods containing a potential allergy food until each ingredient has been introduced alone and found to be safe.

You can try to carefully introduce dairy products at 12 months and chicken eggs at 24 months.

Wait until your child is at least 36 months old before you introduce fish, seafood, peanuts, or any tree nuts. [Source: Alessandro Fiocchi, Amal Assa'ad, and Sami Bahna, "Food Allergy and the Introduction of Solid Foods to Infants: A Consensus Document," *Annals of Allergy* 97, no. 1 (July 2006): 10–21.]

The American Academy of Pediatrics recommends these additional practices for babies who have two parents or one parent and one sibling with food allergies:

- If breastfeeding is not possible, use a hypoallergenic formula (such as elemental) rather than cow's milk or soy.
- Breastfeeding moms should avoid eating any form of peanuts, peanut butter, or tree nuts while nursing, and possibly egg, cow's milk, or fish as well.

As always, if you are concerned that your child may be at risk for developing a food allergy, consult your pediatrician for guidance.

Signs of Allergic Reaction to a Food

Allergic reactions can be mild or severe, and they can affect several different body systems, such as respiratory, digestive, skin, or cardiovascular. Some reactions happen immediately after the food is eaten, and some have a delayed onset. The reason for introducing each new food alone for a minimum of 3 to 4 days in a row is so you'll have the opportunity to catch any delayed allergic reactions in your baby. Consult your doctor if you notice any symptoms of allergy. Look for:

- Rashes or skin changes, including hives or other itchy bumps, red sandpapery rash on the face, facial puffiness, dark circles under the eyes, or red rash around the anus
- Irritability, crankiness, unusual night waking, unusual crying, unusual fatigue, headache, or sore muscles
- Painful belly, bloated stomach, painful gas, or unusual vomiting
- Diarrhea, mucus in stool, or watery stool
- Respiratory problems, wheezing, coughing, sneezing, itchy or watery eyes, or runny nose

Deadly Allergies

Some food allergies, especially to peanuts, tree nuts, and crustacean shellfish, may actually be life threatening. They can affect your child's ability to breathe or cause an anaphylactic reaction. **Anaphylaxis** is an extreme allergic reaction that can be fatal. Symptoms of an anaphylactic reaction to a food allergen usually show up within a few minutes to a few hours of eating the food. Reactions you can see may include hives; wheezing or difficulty breathing; swelling of the lips, tongue, or mouth area; diarrhea; vomiting; belly pain; or unconsciousness. If anyone in your family has a serious food allergy, or if you or your baby has had a serious reaction to a food, even in rash form, you may want to discuss with your doctor the possibility of getting and carrying an EpiPen. This is a small pen-like syringe that carries injectable adrenaline, and it can save your child's life if you are unable to get to an emergency room immediately. Your doctor or allergist will recommend practicing with the EpiPen so you become adept at administering it. If you have a life-threatening food allergy and know or suspect your child does too, you both should wear a medical ID bracelet for emergency situations.

Milk Allergy versus Lactose Intolerance

Babies who have an allergy to milk are usually allergic to the protein contained in milk. This is different from another type of condition known as lactose intolerance. Allergies are the result of an immune system reaction, while food intolerances are caused by the inability to digest a certain food. Lactose is a natural sugar found in milk, and people who have a lactose intolerance lack a necessary enzyme, called lactase, for digesting that milk sugar.

Milk allergies are more common in infants than adults, while lactose intolerance is rare in infants and more common in children (older than 3 years) and adults. Some researchers estimate that over 3 percent of young babies may have a milk allergy, but most children—although not all—will outgrow it between the ages of 3 and 5. Breastfed babies are less likely to develop a milk allergy than formula-fed babies, even with the use of a non-cow's-milk formula.

The symptoms of a milk allergy, like all other food allergies, may show up immediately after eating or drinking something with milk protein in it, or they may have a gradual onset of up to 10 days. The

symptoms that come on quickly can include bloody diarrhea, vomiting, wheezing, swelling, or hives. Milk allergies can also cause anaphylaxis, but that's much more common with other food allergies, such as peanuts and tree nuts.

Gradual onset symptoms can be similar to the immediate symptoms, such as diarrhea and vomiting, but they also include irritability, persistent colic-like crying, or a rash on the skin. These symptoms may make it seem like other health issues are involved, so an allergy may be a little harder to diagnose. There is no single test to determine whether a child has a milk allergy, but there is a typical protocol for making the diagnosis. If you suspect that your baby might have this problem, see your pediatrician for guidance about how to proceed.

Safer dairy: yogurt and kefir. Yogurt and kefir are healthy, fermented milk products that taste a little sour. Yogurt has a thicker consistency, like pudding, while kefir is more liquidy, like a shake. Yogurt is high in calcium, riboflavin (vitamin B_2), vitamin B_{12}, pantothenic acid (vitamin B_5), zinc, and potassium. Full-fat versions contain relatively equal portions of fat, protein, and carbohydrates (in the form of sugar), making them an excellent source of all the macronutrients. It's best to purchase plain, organic yogurt and kefir, as the flavored varieties are loaded with added sugars. Most babies enjoy the sour taste of plain yogurt and you won't even need to sweeten it with fruit.

Yogurt and kefir may be easier for young children to digest than other dairy products such as milk or cheese. The fermenting process helps break down the *lactose* (milk sugar) and predigest the *casein* (milk protein), making these foods easier to assimilate. Yogurt also contains live cultures, called *probiotics*, which provide beneficial bacteria for the intestinal tract. Look for yogurt that is labeled "live active cultures," or "living yogurt cultures." Probiotics can be very helpful in repopulating the intestinal tract after taking antibiotics. Offering 2 to 3 sugar-free servings of yogurt per day while administering antibiotics (and for at least 2 weeks following), may help prevent the development of diarrhea, thrush, or Candida (yeast infection).

Plain full-fat yogurt is an excellent first dairy product to introduce to your child (at around 8 months). If your baby has a true milk allergy, however, you should not feed them cow's-milk yogurt, but you can find yogurt made with other milks, such as soy yogurt, which, while it doesn't contain the same nutrients, does contain probiotics.

HEALTHY STRATEGIES FOR RAISING A NATURAL EATER (4 TO 6 MONTHS)

Between 4 and 6 months, your loving feeding relationship with your baby is helping her evolve from a totally needy infant into a young baby with new abilities. It's exciting to watch her as she learns to sit upright and reach for things on her own. She is still very tuned in to her own inner signals for hunger and fullness. If you are responsive to those cues by feeding her at the early signs of hunger before she gets upset, this will reinforce her tendency to stop eating when she has had enough.

Comforting Without Food

Feeding and eating can be an act of intimacy, especially breastfeeding. It is, by nature, deeply comforting to your baby. It can be quite tempting to use nursing, bottle feeding, or even spoon feeding as a regular strategy for soothing her whenever she becomes upset, not just when she's hungry. Although there are occasional times of deeper upset, such as intense nighttime teething pain or during an illness, when nursing seems to be the only thing that will calm her down, we don't recommend getting into the habit of offering nursing or bottles as comfort.

While feeding can be the easiest thing to do whenever she cries, that may teach her that eating is the way to calm down when she's upset—a tough habit to break as an older child, or even as an adult. It also may prevent her from learning to self-soothe. If your baby is crying for no clear reason (such as a wet diaper), and she's just had a good feeding, try holding and rocking her first rather than automatically offering your breast or the bottle again. You may find that this contact is all she needs to calm down.

Back to Work: Nursing Strategies

If you need to go back to work but want to continue feeding your baby with breastmilk exclusively, you can take your pump with you to work and use it for one or two regular feeding times each day. Be sure to store the pumped milk for later use. Within a few days, your breasts will adjust accordingly and be ready for pumping at the same time each day. If you have a private office, you can simply lock the door and hang a "Do Not Disturb" sign out for the few minutes it takes. You can also pump in a lavatory, but that's a less sanitary environment. Bring an ice cooler and clean containers to store the milk until you get home. If this is not practical for you, try pumping extra milk over the weekend or in the evening before you go to bed. Be sure to take extra breast pads with you to work to avoid embarrassing leak stains on your blouse.

> **TIP**
>
> Dental decay can occur in your baby's mouth before she even gets any teeth! To protect her future teeth, never put your baby down for a nap or to bed with a bottle of milk (including breastmilk), formula, or fruit juice.

Feeding at 6 to 9 Months

BEST FOODS

Breastmilk or formula
 Vegetables: *asparagus*,* carrot, *green beans, green peas, parsnips, pumpkin, spinach, summer squash,* sweet potato, winter squash, and *zucchini*
 Fruits: *apples, apricots, avocado,* banana, *melon, papaya, peach,* pear, *plums, prunes,* and *raisins*

> **TIP**
>
> Your 6- to 9-month-old may still nurse or have a bottle about every 4 hours during the day, with a possibly longer stretch of 5 to 7 hours at night. Bottle amounts can range from 6 to 9 ounces, but trust your baby's hunger signals to guide you on this.

 Grains: iron-fortified infant brown rice cereal
 Milled grain cereals: *millet, pearled barley,* and *oats*
 Protein: lentils; sunflower seeds, ground or butter; sesame seed butter (tahini); and split peas
 Introduce with allergy caution at 8 to 9 months: hard-cooked egg yolks, yogurt, and tofu
 * Italicized foods are new introductions.
 (See the Mix-and-Match chart on

pages 102–103 for an age-specific guide to preparation, portion, and meal suggestions; and chapter 9 for recipes and more food prep info for your 6- to 9-month-old.)

FOODS TO AVOID

• Any non-mashed or -pureed foods
• Any hard finger foods or soft finger foods larger than ¼ inch in diameter
• Added salt or sugar
• Low-quality processed or packaged foods, especially artificial or other junky foods high in salt, sugar, or poor-quality fats (see chapter 4 for a description of low- and high-quality foods)
• Egg whites, soft-cooked egg yolks
• Cow's milk
• Soft cheeses made from raw milk
• Honey and agave nectar
• Peanuts, tree nuts, or nut butters (see page 95 for a further discussion of food allergy risks)

TIP

Babies 6 to 9 months old will get most of the liquids they need from breastmilk or formula. Avoid giving cow's milk before age 12 months. Also avoid juices or soda as they contain too much sugar. Once your baby starts eating solids, try giving her a few ounces of water each day, with or between meals if she seems thirsty or if it's hot or dry outside.

WHAT TO LOOK FOR IN YOUR 6- TO 9-MONTH-OLD BABY

After the first few weeks of introducing solid foods, you can continue to give her new foods in small amounts, one at a time, for 3 to 4 consecutive days. After the first 2 to 3 weeks of eating single foods, you can start to combine your baby's "safe" foods for more flavor variety and interest.

She will have more and more control over her chewing and swallowing. You might still see your 6-month-old's tongue poking out as she swallows. This is the last vestige of the sucking reflex and will gradually disappear. Her neck will become stronger and her head control will improve. She'll be able to reach for things and try to get food to her own mouth. She'll be sitting up well in her high chair, able to toss her food bowl right off the tray in delight!

As your baby grows a little older and her eating skills progress, encourage her to practice her chewing skills by introducing different textures besides the perfectly smooth purees. Many babies will get their first baby teeth around this age, but most of the chewing they are doing is still really mashing between the gums. You want them to build the tongue skills necessary to move more solid food around in their mouth so they can become adept at eating true solids. After a few weeks of baby purees, try adding in a little food with a slightly coarser texture as well. You can mix a wet puree with a mash, or even finely grate a little fruit or vegetable into her regular puree. Gradually increasing the thickness and coarseness of her purees will make the transition to real solids relatively seamless. (See the Mix-and-Match chart on page 104 for an age-specific guide to best food consistency.)

You may find that at this age your baby would like to help you feed her. She may reach out for the spoon, wanting to hold it, or reach for food in the bowl with her hands. Let her touch the food and eat with her fingers. At 6 or 7 months it's likely that she won't have the dexterity to actually feed herself much food, but it's important to let her do what she can, especially if she's very interested. Over the next 6 months or so, this will let her improve her motor skills and her sense of independence that she can do it herself. Many parents find it helpful to sit down to a meal with two spoons instead of one: one for her to hold and work with, and one for you to feed her regular bites.

BEST FOODS, PORTION GUIDES, AND MEAL PLANNING

While babies and toddlers need a certain number of calories for energy each day, the balance of their nutrition from carbohydrates, protein, and fat can be established over several days. At this age, they do not need to get something from each macronutrient group at every meal, or even every day, but you should encourage them to eat from the three categories over the course of a few days at a time so their nutrition is balanced.

As your baby grows, the amount of solid food she needs will grow as well. While your baby's hunger and fullness cues should be your primary guide, following is a Mix-and-Match chart to give you an idea of a typical range of daily foods, meals, and portions.

Quick Chart

MIX-AND-MATCH SOLID FOOD MEAL GUIDE: 6 TO 9 MONTHS

You can build a balanced meal for your baby by choosing a food from each column (or two from the fruits and vegetables) and serving together. Keep in mind that this is only a general guide; don't force your baby to eat anything he isn't interested in, and always allow him to stop when he's had enough. Serving size is very individual, but it will likely be on the smaller end for younger babies and larger end for older babies.

If he eats applesauce and green beans at one meal, and egg yolk and apricots at another, that's fine. Just do your best to keep offering him a variety of choices from all three categories.

If he doesn't yet seem ready for three servings at one meal, offer him a fruit or vegetable with *either* a grain *or* a protein.

Note that all italicized foods are new foods: Introduce each one early in the day, by itself, in small amounts, for at least 3 consecutive days to check for any reactions.

Best Vegetables and Fruits	Best Cereal Grains	Best Protein Foods
Serving Size: 1-4 tablespoons Choose 1-2 per meal	Serving Size: 1-2 tablespoons dry grain or $^1/_4$-$^1/_3$ cup with added liquid Choose 1 per meal	Serving Size: 1 tablespoon-$^1/_4$ cup 6-7 mos.: Choose 1 per day 8-9 mos.: Choose 2 per day
Cooked and pureed: *asparagus* (because of strong flavor, introduce first with sweet or white potato puree), *carrot, green beans, green peas, pumpkin, spinach, summer squash*, sweet potato, *winter squash, zucchini* Cooked and pureed: applesauce, *apricots, peach*, pear, *prunes, raisins* Raw and mashed: *avocado, banana, melon (including cantaloupe, honeydew, watermelon), papaya*	Ground dried grain or pureed cooked grain cereal: iron-fortified infant brown rice cereal, *millet*	Seeds: *sunflower, ground or butter; sesame butter (tahini)*, (1 tablespoon) 8-9 mos. only: Beans: cooked and pureed: *lentils, split peas*
	Introduce with caution, can be allergenic: *Oats* and *pearled barley* (not generally allergenic, but both contain small amounts of gluten, which some children have trouble digesting—see page 113 for more information about celiac disease). To avoid gluten, buy certified gluten-free oats.	Introduce with caution, can be allergenic: 8-9 mos. only: Egg yolk: hard-cooked and mashed, or cooked into hot cereal (1, not more than 3 times per week) *Plain full-fat yogurt* (up to $^1/_3$ cup) *Medium or soft plain tofu*, mashed (1-2 tablespoons, not more than 3 times per week)

Food Preparation for 6 to 7 Months (after at least 3 weeks of first foods introduction): All solid food should be in wet porridge, puree, or well-mashed form. After his first 3 weeks or so of eating solid foods, your 6- or 7-month-old will be ready for a slightly thicker consistency. Although it should still be completely smooth, with no lumps, the porridge or puree can be a little coarser or thicker in texture, closer to thin yogurt than a liquid.

Number of Meals per Day for 6 to 7 Months: Follow the guidelines on page 93 for the first 2 to 3 weeks of introducing solid foods to your baby. After your 6-month-old has been eating a meal or two of foods per day for those first 3 weeks, you can increase that to two regular meals per day if he seems to want them. At 7 months, your baby may be happy with two meals per day, but may also be ready to go to three. If he seems hungry or eager for more food, offer him an occasional third meal until three meals of solids become his new standard.

Food Preparation for 8 to 9 Months: At 8 to 9 months, the porridge or puree can be thicker still, with a few very soft, small lumps. As he gets closer to the 9-month mark, the texture can be chunky, but should still be quite soft.

Number of Meals per Day for 8 to 9 Months: Sometime between 7 and 9 months, most babies will move to 3 meals per day. Follow his lead for hunger and read the advice on page 117 for developing regular meal routines with your 9-month-old. Eight- or 9-month-olds may also appreciate a small, solid food snack during a longer stretch between meals.

FLASH FACT

Gagging is not the same as choking: Younger babies may gag to prevent choking on solids. It's not uncommon for babies to gag when a new flavor or texture is introduced—they may be sensitive to different foods because everything is new.

THE EATING ZONE: FEEDING GEAR

Those first months of feeding your baby solid foods have one consistent feature: the mess! Between the food going into and out of her mouth, her attempts to touch everything, to feed herself or you, and to throw her spoon or bowl, or even a fistful of oatmeal, at the floor can make for a big cleanup after every meal. It helps to have easy-to-clean, clean gear and a setup that covers enough ground.

High Chair

A good high chair is the centerpiece of your baby's eating zone. Once he can hold himself upright, a high chair will allow him to be part of the food preparation and mealtimes. Your baby will need his high chair at least three times per day for a few years, so choose a model that is well made and will hold up to regular baby treatment. You should look for:

• A stable model that's not too

heavy. The base should be relatively compact so that it doesn't dwarf your kitchen or dining room. Some models can collapse and fold, a nice space-saving feature.

- A sturdy belt that's easy to clip, and possibly a safety harness for younger babies.
- Surfaces that are easy to reach and clean. If it's frilly or it has a cool shape but you can't get to all the surfaces easily, take a pass on that model and go for something simpler. It might not look as fun, but it will save you endless grief during the hundreds of after-meal cleanups. The upholstery should be removable so you can also wash it in the washing machine.
- Some type of crotch post—a bar in the seat that goes between the legs—to keep your baby from sliding under the tray and catching his head or falling out, both dangerous situations that you want to avoid.
- A sturdy tray with a high lip to help keep roving food available and off the floor. The tray should detach and be very easy to remove and reattach.
- Adjustable height—many models can now easily be adjusted to go from stand-alone use with the tray to a lower level without the tray so your baby can sit safely right at the dining room table.

Warning

A good high chair will hold your baby safely while she eats, but it's not a babysitter: Don't leave the room while your baby is in the high chair.

TIP

The Juvenile Products Manufacturers Association (JPMA) tests and certifies children's products for safety standards. Look for the JPMA certification sticker on your high chair and other baby gear.

Clip-on Chair

If you don't have the money or space to invest in a good high chair, another alternative is a clip-on chair that can attach directly to your kitchen or dining room table. As with a high chair, your baby must be old enough to sit up unsupported before you use a clip-on. Look for a lightweight model with sturdy, washable safety straps that include a harness, belt, and crotch strap. The chairs are easy to attach to a table and remove after a meal. Choose only tables that are strong enough to easily support your baby's weight, and make sure the chair is securely attached to the table before placing your baby inside. To prevent slippage, always clip it directly to the table, never over a tablecloth or placemat. The disadvantage of using one of these over a high chair is that it isn't free-standing—which isn't always practical if you don't have a table in the kitchen. Their primary advantage over high chairs is their portability and easy storage.

You can also find plastic high chairs that strap directly onto a regular chair, but these are not as safe as either the high chair or the clip-on chair because they are lightweight enough that one good push on the table can send your baby toppling over backward.

Bibs

Use a bib to keep as much food as possible off your baby's clothes while he eats. In the beginning, a few soft cotton bibs are all you will need. As he gets a little older, however, and begins feeding himself, you'll probably want a little more protection. You can find large bibs that actually have sleeves and tie in the back—great for eating with gusto! Some larger bibs are made of plastic or have a plastic coating on the fabric that you can easily wipe clean.

Floor Mat

It's helpful to lay a large mat of some kind under the baby's eating chair to catch flying or falling food. A large garbage bag can work well, but is a little harder to wipe down than something sturdier. Try using a small plastic tablecloth that doesn't slip.

WEANING FROM THE BREAST

When to wean your baby is a very individual decision. The American Academy of Pediatrics recommends breastfeeding your child for at least 12 months, or longer if it works for you and your toddler. But many factors can affect your ability to continue to breastfeed, and sometimes your

baby will actually wean himself by refusing the breast, especially after he begins taking more of his food in solid form. You may love the intimacy of breastfeeding but decide that your life situation makes it too difficult to continue nursing. When you are ready to wean, it will be easiest for both you and your child if you do it gradually over time, rather than stopping all at once.

Doing it slowly in stages will allow your breasts to adjust. This will reduce the level of breast engorgement when you finally stop completely. Try offering a bottle for one of the daytime nursing sessions for the first couple of days. Then add another. Save the first morning feeding and the last one before bedtime for the last attempts. When your baby is taking a bottle for all the daytime feedings, offer a bottle for that first morning feeding. Finally, when you and the baby are ready, offer a bottle instead of your breast for the final feeding of the night. Although it's not necessary, you may find it helpful for your partner or another family member to offer some of these first bottle feedings.

When you finally stop nursing completely, your breasts will become engorged for a couple of days, then that milk will reabsorb in your body and your breasts will stop producing. Avoid the temptation to pump to relieve the engorgement—that will just keep them producing more milk. Stopping the demand completely will trigger your breasts to stop the supply. Use the tips (except for pumping!) on page 62 to relieve the discomfort of engorgement. You can also try some firm but gentle constriction to speed the process and make yourself more comfortable: Wear a close-fitting sports bra with even pressure all around the breast. You can also try binding your breasts firmly with a wide Ace bandage. Stay cool if you can; cool water and ice packs will help, but heating pads or hot showers can actually trigger a letdown, so avoid those for a couple of days. Avoid any drugs to stop milk production—they don't work any better than natural methods and can have dangerous side effects.

FLASH FACT

There are currently no FDA-approved drugs to stop lactation.

HEALTHY STRATEGIES FOR RAISING A NATURAL EATER (6 TO 9 MONTHS)

Between 6 and 9 months your baby will evolve into a regular eater. This is a period of rapid development—a perfect time to introduce a wide range of new foods. Once he is eating regularly, you can encourage his growing independence by allowing him to feed himself as he is able, and introducing him to a cup as soon as he can hold one on his own.

TIP

TOOTH TIP

Your baby's first teeth can come in as early as 4 months, or wait until well into her first year. Because a baby's new teeth are at risk of decay, it is important to begin brushing them as soon as they appear. Look for a gentle toothpaste made for babies, and use just a tiny bit, smaller than a pea. The fluoride in regular toothpaste should not be ingested. Some pediatric dentists recommend using a non-fluoridated toothpaste until the child has developed an adequate spitting reflex—usually after the child's third birthday. The toothbrush should be made especially for babies: small enough for their little mouths, with a large easy-grip handle, and polished bristles—the softest you can find. Get into the habit of gently brushing the new teeth and surrounding gums each evening before bed, and each morning after breakfast. Make brushing a fun experience for your baby, opening your own mouth wide and pantomiming brushing your teeth, too.

Starting the Cup

Your baby will enjoy holding and banging plastic cups from quite a young age. When he begins to show interest in drinking from a cup, maybe even yours, you can give him a small amount of water to practice with. There are several varieties of baby-training cups; most are made from hard plastic and all have lids. Choosing one with two handles will make it easier for him to grip at first. If your baby is quite young, you may want to start with a cup that has a sucking mechanism similar to a bottle. If not, you can start with one that has a short, stiff spout. As he gets older you may want to shift to one with a built-in straw.

Turn Off the Tube

Mealtime is a special time for interacting with your baby. On a practical level, you need to watch him closely while he eats for signs of hunger and satisfaction, for likes and dislikes, and to make sure he doesn't choke on anything. On a social level, this is early training for family mealtime, when you and your children will have the opportunity to share talk and laughter about the events of your days. Television is a big distraction for both you and the baby. Turn it off during mealtimes to keep the focus on you and him, and not on the screen.

Feeding at 9 to 12 Months

BEST FOODS

Breastmilk or formula

Vegetables: asparagus, *beets*,* broccoli, carrot, cauliflower, *eggplant*, green beans, green peas, *kale*, *onion*, parsnips, pumpkin, *spinach*, summer squash, sweet potato, winter squash, and zucchini

Fruits: apples, apricots, avocado, banana, *kiwi fruit*, *mango*, melon, *papaya*, peach, pear, plums, prunes, and raisins

Cereal grains: iron-fortified brown rice cereal, millet, oats, pearled barley, *quinoa*, and *whole-grain pasta*

Protein foods: beans (lentils, split peas), hard-cooked egg yolks, sunflower seeds (ground or butter), sesame seed butter (tahini), tofu, and yogurt. If you're not raising your baby vegetarian, you can also start introducing some meats: try lean ground or slow-cooked beef, lamb, calf's liver (organic only), chicken, and turkey.

Introduce with allergy caution: *beans (butter, cannellini, navy, and great northern), cottage cheese, and soft cheese*
* Italicized foods are new introductions.

(See the Mix-and-Match chart on page 115 for an age-specific guide to preparation, portion, and meal suggestions; and see chapter 9 for recipes and more food prep info for your 9- to 12-month-old).

While it is important to introduce safe, appropriate foods to babies, there is little scientific data to support the idea that bland food is what's best for a baby's diet. Different cultures around the world have been successfully starting babies on their native cuisines for millennia, including lots of herbs and spices—even pungent, sour, and bitter ones! One of the goals for raising a healthy natural eater is to train the baby's palate to enjoy and appreciate a broad range of flavors. Don't be afraid to offer a wide variety of different flavors to your developing baby. (See chapter 9 for some fun and taste-rich recipes for your little one.)

BREAST- OR BOTTLE-FEEDING AT 9 TO 12 MONTHS

The amount of breastmilk or formula your baby needs will now gradually decrease over the next 3 months in proportion to how much solid food she is eating. Most babies are drinking somewhere from 28 to 39 ounces at 6 months. By 12 months, most babies will have decreased that amount to somewhere between 20 and 30 ounces.

FOODS TO AVOID

• Added salt or sugar
• Low- or reduced-fat foods, such as cheese, yogurt, or tofu
• Low-quality processed or packaged foods, especially

artificial or other junky foods high in salt, sugar, or poor-quality fats (See chapter 4 for a description of low- and high-quality foods)
• Any small hard pieces of food that could get caught in your baby's windpipe and be a choking hazard, such as whole grapes, raisins, whole hot dogs, raw carrot sticks, etc.
• Egg whites, soft-cooked egg yolks
• Cow's milk
• Soft cheeses made from raw milk
• Honey and agave nectar
• Peanuts, tree nuts, or nut butters (see page 95 for a discussion about food allergy risks)

Warning

Soft cheeses such as Brie, feta, Camembert, Roquefort, and bleu are usually made from raw, unpasteurized milk. These can harbor bacteria that are unsafe for your baby. Most U.S. cheeses are made from pasteurized milks, but many imports are not. Check the label to make sure. Also, avoid feeding your baby any cheese that has mold on it.

Quick Chart

HIGHER ALLERGY RISK FOODS

Artificial colors and other
  additives
Baker's yeast
Citrus fruits
Coconut
Corn
Eggs
Fish
Milk and dairy products
Monosodium glutamate (MSG)
Peanuts
Shellfish
Soybeans and soy products
Strawberries
Tomatoes
Tree nuts
Wheat

LOWER ALLERGY RISK FOODS

Apples
Apricots
Asparagus
Avocados
Bananas
Barley
Beets
Broccoli
Carrots
Cauliflower
Chicken
Cranberries
Dates
Grapes, raisins
Lamb
Lettuce
Mangoes
Millet
Ooats
Peaches
Pears
Rice
Squash
Sweet potatoes
Turkey

WHAT TO LOOK FOR IN YOUR 9- TO 12-MONTH-OLD BABY

Between 9 and 12 months, your baby will be gaining lots of new physical ground. He will be able to pull himself up to sitting or even standing. He may begin to creep or crawl. Some babies will even start walking during this time. It's likely that your baby will revel in this new physical independence. You will see that same spirit reflected at feeding times: Your baby will likely want to feed himself most of the time.

Self-Feeding

Although his self-feeding is still going to be a very messy business, he is becoming more adept at fine motor movements. He is able to pick up his food with more dexterity, holding small pieces between his thumb and forefinger. Around this age, most children begin to show a preference for using their dominant hand. He may still enjoy eating mostly with his fingers, or he might be working more with his baby fork and spoon. Most babies can put their hand around a cup at around 9 or 10 months, and can hold it alone by 12 months.

It's important to let your baby experiment with his food and feeding himself. Let him touch and feel his foods, poke and prod them as he's eating. Although it may not look like it, all of these actions are helping him build his independent eating skills. Let his face get messy. You can wipe it down midmeal if he seems uncomfortable, but don't interrupt his meal with constant swipes. If he is getting too vigorous and wants to throw his bowl on the floor all the time, use a bowl with a heavy suction cup on the bottom to keep it in place. You might also invest in a smock-style bib with sleeves and a back tie to keep his clothes relatively un-gooped during this phase.

Getting Enough Food

Although you will see a steady improvement in his use of all the mealtime tools, much of the food will still end up all over him instead of in his belly. He might be quite insistent about feeding himself, and you can encourage that independence while still assisting with some bites off a second spoon. During this time you can gradually replace most of his purees with coarser mashes containing soft pieces. He will enjoy picking delectable morsels right out of the mash with his newfound thumb-and-finger pincer skills. It's the perfect time for stand-alone finger foods as well.

His appetite may grow during this time to keep up with the energy needs of all that new moving around. By around 9 or 10 months, he will most likely be eating a regular three meals every day. Because his stomach is still very small, however, the size of his meals will also still be relatively small, so you'll need to offer her two to three snacks between meals to help him meet all his calorie needs. Snacks will be easier for you to manage because he can now eat soft finger foods, such as cuts of soft fruit or rice crackers.

Quick Chart

HEALTHY SNACKS IDEAS FOR OLDER BABIES

- Slices of soft fruits, such as peach, apricot, or banana, plain or rolled in wheat germ
- Seedless grapes, quartered
- Slices of baked potato, white or sweet
- Steamed vegetable spears, such as zucchini, summer squash spears, or green beans, plain or with a dipping sauce such as hummus or salad dressing
- Peeled cucumber spears
- Thin slices of soft cheese
- Cottage cheese or yogurt, plain or with chunks of soft fruit or peeled cucumber
- Mini brown rice cakes, plain or spread with hummus, apple butter, or tahini

He will be able to show you more clearly what he likes and dislikes, including different preferences at different times—for instance, he may not want fruit at dinnertime, but might welcome the same offering at breakfast the next morning; or he might love green beans for weeks, and then go off them for a while. Honor his choices of what to eat from among the healthy selections you offer him, but continue to offer the new foods and the foods that may have fallen out of favor several times, rather than giving up on them when they're first rejected.

Choking

Older babies are at a higher risk for choking on their food because, while they are beginning to eat coarser mashes and finger foods, they do not yet have all the teeth or chewing skills they need to break down larger or harder pieces of food. For that reason, you want to avoid giving them any hard pieces of food large enough to get stuck in the windpipe, such as hard candies or gum (which you shouldn't give babies anyway because of the sugar content); big chunks of rubbery meat or bread like hot dogs or bagels; whole grapes or raisins; popcorn; or hard vegetables such as raw baby carrots. Also, make sure there is no fibrous material in her vegetable mashes and purees by removing any stringy fibers from sweet potatoes, winter squashes, cooked celery, or leafy greens.

Hard or tough foods should be softened with soaking or cooking and cut into very small pieces. Your

Quick Chart

HOW TO HELP A CHOKING BABY (YOUNGER THAN 1 YEAR)

If a baby younger than 1 year can cough or make sounds, let him cough to try to get the object out. If you are worried about the baby's breathing, call 911. If a baby younger than 1 year can't breathe, cough, or make sounds, then:

Put the baby facedown on your forearm so the baby's head is lower than his chest.

Support the baby's head in your palm, against your thigh. Don't cover the baby's mouth or twist his neck.

Use the heel of one hand to give up to 5 backslaps between the baby's shoulder blades.

If the object does not pop out, support the baby's head and turn him face up on your thigh. Keep the baby's head lower than his body.

Place 2 or 3 fingers just below the nipple line on the baby's breastbone and give 5 quick chest thrusts (same position as chest compressions in CPR for a baby).

Look for an object in the baby's mouth. If you can see something, remove it. Then give 2 rescue breaths.

To give rescue breaths:

Place 1 hand on the baby's forehead, and tilt the baby's chin up to keep the airway open.

Then place your mouth over the baby's mouth and nose and slowly blow air in until the baby's chest rises.

Between breaths, remove your mouth, take a breath, and watch for the baby's chest to rise and fall.

If the object does not come out with these steps and/or the baby faints, call 911 or other emergency services.

Continue with back slaps, chest thrusts, looking for the object, and rescue breaths until the baby coughs up the object and starts breathing on his own, or until help arrives.

For more information, visit www.webmd.com and search for "choking rescue procedure" for a baby younger than 1 year.

baby can handle breaking down softer finger foods, such as pasta noodles or soft raw fruit, or crispy foods that crumble easily into small pieces, such as brown rice cakes. Watch her as she eats to make sure she doesn't put too much food into her mouth at once. Never leave her alone while she's eating, and don't feed her in the car while you are driving. If she started to choke, you wouldn't be able to get to her quickly to help.

If your child does choke, there are very specific techniques for removing the obstruction. If you practice them improperly, you could actually make the situation worse. The most effective way to learn these techniques is to take an infant and toddler CPR class. The class will train you with practical, hands-on experience in the best methods for helping a choking baby or toddler. You will also learn what to do if the choking obstruction cannot be removed. Taking a class like this will not only prepare you to help your child in an emergency, but you will also be able to help if you are nearby when someone else's child is choking. Call your local hospital or Red Cross to find out when their classes are scheduled.

WHAT ABOUT WHEAT?

While wheat is one the eight foods responsible for 90 percent of all allergic reactions, it also contains a protein, called gluten, that can be difficult or even impossible for some children to digest, even if they aren't technically allergic to it. Like milk, wheat can be the cause of both an allergic reaction and a food intolerance.

Because wheat is both highly allergenic and contains gluten, which is impossible for some children to digest, it's best to delay introducing it into your child's diet until around 9 months. You can begin giving wheat in the form of whole-wheat pasta sometime between 9 and 12 months. Watch your child closely for signs of any allergic reactions and to make sure he is digesting the wheat well.

Gluten Intolerance/ Celiac Disease/Sprue

Celiac, also called sprue or gluten intolerance, is an inherited disease involving an inability to digest the protein gluten, which is found in wheat, rye, barley, and in small amounts in oats. (The gluten found in oats is actually a "contamination" from wheat during processing. It is possible to purchase gluten-free oats and oat flour: Look for a "gluten-free" label on the package.) Celiac is currently thought to be much more widespread than previously imagined. Some experts estimate that 3 million Americans are affected, but most are never diagnosed. Eating gluten-containing grains causes intestinal damage in people with celiac, and can lead to serious longer-term health complications.

Signs of gluten intolerance. The signs and symptoms of celiac disease are quite numerous, and sometimes so mild they are easy to miss—this is only a partial list. Consult a good resource for more comprehensive information, such as www.celiac.org.

- Belly pain or swelling
- Gas, diarrhea, or constipation
- Stools that are fatty, bloody, or foul-smelling
- Anemia or other vitamin/mineral deficiencies
- Growth delay
- Weight loss

Celiac can be difficult to diagnose because the symptoms vary from person to person, and they often mimic other problems. If you or a relative have celiac disease, your child is at a higher risk for developing it. If he exhibits some of the symptoms of gluten intolerance, ask your doctor about having him screened for celiac.

If your child has celiac, most, if not all, of the symptoms can be treated by feeding him a totally gluten-free diet. It is easier to go gluten-free now than ever before: Almost every grain-containing food is now available in gluten-free form, even things like pretzels and pizza crust. (See Resources for a list of companies that make gluten-free products.)

TIP

If your baby is irritated, overwhelmed, or just plain not in the mood for eating a meal, you can help him settle into mealtime by (1) eating some of it yourself first, making it look and sound like a real treat, and piquing curiosity about what you've got there that's so yummy; (2) starting with a few bites of a favorite food, quickly followed by a small bite of the new food; (3) placing him on your lap, facing the adult table, and letting him enjoy the novelty of sitting with grown-ups; or (4) playing for a little while away from the kitchen or reading to him. Once he has calmed down a bit, you can try again.

FLASH FACT

GLUTEN-FREE GRAINS
Amaranth
Buckwheat (toasted form: kasha)
Corn
Millet
Quinoa
Rice

BEST FOODS, PORTION GUIDES, AND MEAL PLANNING

As your baby grows, the amount of solid food she needs will grow as well. While your baby's hunger and fullness cues should be your primary guide, following is a chart to give you an idea of a typical range of daily foods, meals, and portions. By 9 months, your baby will likely be eating three meals a day, with a couple of snacks in between. Try feeding her a good balance of all the major macronutrients throughout the day: carbohydrates, protein, and healthy fats.

Quick Chart

MIX-AND-MATCH SOLID FOOD MEAL GUIDE: 9 TO 12 MONTHS

You can build a balanced meal for your baby by choosing a food from each column (or 2 from the fruits and vegetables) and serving them together; the nutrient boosters are optional. Keep in mind that this is only a general guide; don't force your baby to eat anything he isn't interested in, and always allow him to stop when he's had enough. Serving size is very individual, but will likely be on the smaller end for younger babies and larger end for older babies.

If he eats rice and green beans at one meal, and egg yolk and apricots at another, that's fine. Just do your best to keep offering him a variety of choices from the first 3 categories.

Note that all italicized foods are new foods: Introduce each new food early in the day, by itself, in small amounts, for at least 3 consecutive days to check for any reactions.

Best Vegetables and Fruits	Best Cereal Grains	Best Protein Foods	Best Nutrient Boosters
Serving Size: 1-4 tablespoons Choose 1-2 per meal	Serving Size: 1-2 tablespoons dry grain, $\frac{1}{4}$-$\frac{1}{3}$ cup with added liquid Choose 1 per meal	Serving Size: 1 tablespoon to $\frac{1}{4}$ cup Choose 1 per meal	Serving Size: Individual Optional Additions
Cooked and pureed: asparagus, *beets*, *broccoli*, carrot, *cauliflower*, *eggplant*, green beans, green peas, *kale*, *onion*, parsnips, pumpkin, spinach, summer squash, sweet potato, winter squash, zucchini

Cooked and pureed: apples, apricots, peach, pear, plums, prunes, raisins

Raw and mashed: avocado, banana, *kiwi*, mango, *melon* (including cantaloupe, honeydew, watermelon), *papaya* | Ground dried grain or pureed cooked grain cereal: iron-fortified brown rice cereal, millet, oats,* pearled barley,* *quinoa*

10-12 mos. only: Cooked and minced: *whole grain pasta (brown rice, quinoa, spelt)** | Medium or soft plain tofu, mashed (1-2 tablespoons, not more than 3 times per week)

Seeds: butters or ground, sunflower, sesame (tahini), *pumpkin* (1 tablespoon)

Beans: Cooked and pureed: lentils, split peas

Plain, full-fat yogurt (up to $\frac{1}{3}$ cup)

Egg yolk: hard-cooked and mashed, or cooked into hot cereal (1, not more than 3 times per week) *(continued)* | Additional fats: (Your baby will get fats from some of his protein choices, so try to include at least one fat-rich choice per day: tofu, seeds, yogurt, cheese, egg yolk, meats. In addition, you can add small amounts of healthy fats to his vegetables and grains) Cook with olive, grapeseed, or sunflower oil, or add cold flaxseed oil ($\frac{1}{2}$ teaspoon mixed into porridge cereal or puree once per day) *(continued)* |

Best Vegetables and Fruits	Best Cereal Grains	Best Protein Foods	Best Nutrient Boosters
		Cooked and pureed with liquid: *ground or slow-cooked beef, lamb, liver (organic only), chicken, turkey* (if not raising vegetarian)	Nutritional yeast, brewer's yeast ($\frac{1}{2}$ teaspoon mixed into porridge or puree, not fruit, once per day)
	Introduce with caution, can be allergenic: 10-12 mos. only: Cooked and minced: whole wheat pasta,* brown rice pasta *oats (unless labeled gluten-free), barley, spelt, and wheat pasta all contain gluten	Introduce with caution, can be allergenic: *cottage cheese* (up to $\frac{1}{3}$ cup) *mild cheeses* (1 oz., about the size of your thumb) Jack, Colby, cheddar, provolone, Parmesan, ricotta **CAUTION:** Do not feed your baby any cheese that is made with raw milk (check the label). Cooked and pureed with liquid to thin: *butter, cannellini, navy, great northern beans* (1-3 tablespoons) (may be allergenic or may cause digestive disturbance before 12 months—add a small amount of kombu or epazote to the cooking water to increase the digestibility of beans and help prevent gas.)	Introduce with caution, can be allergenic: *wheat germ* (also contains gluten)

Food Preparation for 9 to 12 Months: Throughout this period of 9 to 12 months, try slowly increasing the thickness of the foods you offer. Purees, mashes, and porridges can gradually become chunkier, containing soft, small pieces. Watch your baby's reaction whenever you increase a food's thickness. If she has to struggle at all to swallow it, thin it out for her. Some babies gag on coarser textures at first. If you see this, thin it out and go a little more slowly.

  Sometime in the ninth month you can try small, bite-sized pieces of soft finger food. Avoid offering hard finger foods that could choke your baby, such as uncooked raisins or bites of unpureed meat. Never leave your baby unattended when she is eating.

Number of Meals per Day for 9 to 12 Months: Sometime around the ninth month, your baby will likely be eating 3 meals a day of solid foods. If his regular breastmilk or formula feedings do not seem to allay his hunger until the next meal, it's appropriate to offer a snack between meals. (See the chart on page 111 for ideas for baby snacks.)

HEALTHY STRATEGIES FOR RAISING A NATURAL EATER (9 TO 12 MONTHS)

Regular Mealtimes

At around the age of 9 months, you can begin gradually shifting from on-demand, hunger-based feedings to a more regular three-meal-a-day schedule. If you are able to make the transition slowly, over time, you can train your older baby's body to be hungry at mealtimes. His feedings are probably already pretty regular now and close to normal meal and snack times, so just delay them a little longer or start a few minutes earlier until his feedings are in sync with family mealtimes. Once you have a schedule in place, stick to that routine as much as possible. If he gets hungry between meals, offer him a little snack to tide him over. If he is not hungry at a regular mealtime, don't force him to eat; just offer him a snack a little later when his appetite increases. If you keep his eating routine consistent, you will find that his body adjusts to that schedule so his appetite more or less matches mealtimes.

Food Choices

You want to continue to cultivate her eating independence, so offer her a small variety of foods at each meal and allow her to pick and choose what she'd like to eat for herself. A good general guide is to offer 3 to 4 healthy choices at a meal and 2 to 3 options for a snack. Try to balance her macronutrients throughout the day by offering selections that contain high-quality carbohydrates, protein, and fats. If she just chose fruit at breakfast and lunch, offer her a selection of good proteins and fats with a vegetable at dinnertime to help balance her nutrition.

Transitioning to the Cup

As soon as your baby is able to use a cup with some dexterity, let her use one at each meal. Offer plain water or some of the regular breastmilk or formula in the cup. Some parents find it easier and more convenient to wean directly from the breast to a cup, skipping the bottle stage. If you are already using bottles, regular cup use at meal and snack time can make it easier to transition away from them. While you may still want to retain that soothing nighttime bottle, by the time she gets to her first birthday, it's possible to get most of her daytime liquids in with a cup.

> **TIP**
>
> Supervise your baby with this natural-snack teether: A cleaned and chilled (in the refrigerator) bone from a chicken leg, provided it's too big to swallow. Be sure to remove all cartilage, tendons, and any loose or sharp material while retaining small amounts of meat.

TIP

TOOTH TIP

Several new teeth may emerge between your baby's ninth and twelfth month. Cutting teeth can be uncomfortable and may affect your baby's desire to eat. If he seems resistant to the spoon, try offering him some soft finger foods instead. Chilled or frozen finger foods can be very soothing to sore gums. Try freezing banana wheels, or chilling peach, apricot, or melon slices. If he refuses to eat, try alleviating his gum discomfort with a frozen, child-safe teething ring, or a frozen washcloth: simply wet, wring, and roll a small, soft washcloth, and freeze in a plastic bag.

Remember to also keep brushing the new teeth every morning after breakfast and every night with a pea-sized bit of baby toothpaste. It's a good idea to make his first dentist appointment before his first birthday. A pediatric dentist will be able to check proactively for any problems in dentition, and instruct you in the best methods for brushing and in other elements of dental care. It will also give your baby the chance to have a fun first meeting with this important caregiver.

The Toddler Years (12 Months to 3 Years)

Menu Variety

On his first birthday, your baby officially becomes a toddler and a whole new world of eating opens up to him. The best foods for a toddler's diet are now quite similar to your best foods as an adult, although still prepared to prevent choking and in much smaller quantities. It is now okay to introduce some of the more allergenic foods that can be triggers for babies. Do this with caution, one at a time, and following the 3-to-5-day rule as outlined on page 94.

Because the first months of his toddler years are really a transition period between babyhood and toddlerhood, we separate the period of 12 to 18 months out to give you a few special guidelines for his smaller calorie needs and still-developing digestive system. Around his eighteenth month, however, he will enter into full-fledged toddlerhood, and most tips, suggestions, and guidelines will apply through his third birthday (18 to 36 months).

Feeding at 12 to 18 Months

BEST FOODS (12 MONTHS TO 3 YEARS)

Vegetables: all, in a wide variety, featuring green, yellow, and orange

Fruits: all, in a wide variety, featuring whole fruits over fruit juices

Cereal grains: all, featuring *whole-grain amaranth*, rice, millet, oats, pearled barley, quinoa, whole-grain pasta, *whole-grain breads, and quick breads*

Protein foods: all, featuring beans, hard-cooked egg yolk, cheese, tofu, and yogurt. If you aren't raising your baby vegetarian, you can also offer organic calf's liver, red meats, and poultry.

Fat foods: *chopped olives* and olive oil, grapeseed oil, sunflower oil, and seed butters (tahini, sunflower)

Introduce with allergy caution: *berries, citrus fruits, cow's milk, fish, hard-cooked egg whites, raw honey, raw agave nectar,* and *tomatoes.* If your child is not at risk for food allergies, you can also try introducing some nut foods. Do not feed your child whole nuts, as they are choking hazards. Instead, offer small amounts of nut butters mixed into or spread onto other foods (to avoid the choking hazard of a mouthful of sticky food); ground nuts mixed into cooked cereals, breads, soups, etc.; or nut oils, such as almond, coconut, or macadamia. You can also use coconut milk in your recipes now. *If your child is at risk for food allergies, the American College of Allergy, Asthma and Immunology recommends waiting until after your child's third birthday to introduce any fish, seafood, peanuts, or tree nuts.*

* Italicized foods are new introductions.

(See the Mix-and-Match chart on page 130 for an age-specific guide to preparation, portion, and meal suggestions; and see chapter 10 for recipes and more food prep info for your 12- to 18-month-old.)

Because of the high levels of pollution in our oceans, many varieties of fish and shellfish contain traces of toxins, primarily mercury and PCBs, which are not safe for ingestion, especially by pregnant women and children under 5. On the other hand, seafood is very high in nutrients—it's a great source of protein and B vitamins, and also contains high amounts of omega-3 fatty acids, a crucial, hard-to-find nutrient for healthy growth and development. We recommend feeding your toddler small amounts of the types of seafood lowest in toxins.

Older, larger fish, such as swordfish, shark, tilefish, and king mackerel, have accumulated more toxins in their flesh, so they should be avoided. Smaller fish, such as sardines, are generally considered safer. Much of the tuna that comes in cans is from albacore tuna, which has very high concentrations of mercury. Skipjack or chunk light tuna is significantly lower in mercury, so choose chunk light for your toddler and serve it only once per week, maximum. According to KidSafe Seafood, the safest varieties of fish for toddlers are farmed bay scallops, farmed blue mussels, northern U.S. and Canadian shrimp, sardines, tilapia, and wild Alaskan salmon. Follow the allergy protocols carefully (see page 96) when introducing your child to both fish and shellfish, as they are two of the most allergenic foods.

See www.kidsafeseafood.org and www.cfsan.fda.gov/~dms/admehg3.html for more detailed discussions of this issue.

FOODS TO AVOID

- Added salt or sugar
- Low- or reduced-fat foods, such as cheese, yogurt, or tofu
- Cheese made with raw milk (check the label)
- Low-quality processed or packaged foods, especially

artificial or other junky foods high in salt, sugar, or poor-quality fats (see chapter 4 for a description of low- and high-quality foods)

- Any small, hard pieces of food that could get caught in your baby's windpipe and become a choking hazard, such as whole grapes, raisins, whole hot dogs, and raw carrot sticks

Although there are few restrictions on a toddler who's passed his first birthday, you should wait a little longer before introducing these few foods that are harder to digest:

- Chocolate (which isn't a great food for toddlers, in any case, because it contains caffeine, and most available forms are poor-quality foods: too many calories, not enough nutrition)
- Corn, unless ground, as in cornmeal
- Raw onions or raw green peppers

You may try offering these foods at 18 months, if you wish—just watch him closely to see if they give his system any distress.

BEST DRINKS FOR 12 TO 18 MONTHS

Formula and Cow's Milk

At 12 months you should switch your baby from formula to cow's milk. According to the American Dietetic Association and the National Institutes of Health Office of Dietary Supplements, your 1- to 3-year-old toddler will need about 500 mg of calcium each day, so you can offer 14 to 16 ounces of whole cow's milk, or the equivalent of other dairy or calcium-fortified products. Cow's milk needs to be whole, rather than low-fat or skim, until his second birthday because young toddlers need at least one-third of their total daily calories to come from healthy fats. Milk also provides for a toddler's daily requirement of vitamin D, along with some protein.

If your child won't take milk from a cup, offer him smaller, rather than larger, amounts of milk per bottle: 3 to 4 ounces at a time. Whole milk contains a lot of sugar and some fat, and drinking too much of it throughout the day can easily cause your toddler to lose his appetite for solid foods (and thus rob him of a broader variety of potential nutrients), so remember to keep his overall daily consumption around 12 to 16 ounces. Consuming excessive amounts of milk can also interfere with iron absorption and put your toddler at risk for iron-deficiency anemia. Yogurt and cheese have much less lactose (milk sugar) than milk, so you can offer a couple of servings of those in place of some of the milk, if you think your toddler's appetite is being affected.

> **TIP**
>
> Some children simply don't like the taste of milk. Try mixing it with a little formula or breastmilk initially. Add milk, yogurt, cottage cheese, or other cheese to solid foods such as breads, muffins, pancakes, scrambled eggs, or veggie purees.

Quick Chart

CALCIUM-RICH FOODS

Parmesan cheese, grated (1 oz): 314 mg
Swiss cheese (1 oz): 224 mg
Cheddar cheese (1 oz): 204 mg
Blackstrap molasses (1 tbsp): 172 mg
Mozzarella cheese (1 oz): 143 mg
Whole milk (4 oz [$^{1}/_{2}$ cup]): 138 mg
Plain yogurt (4 oz [$^{1}/_{2}$ cup]): 137 mg
Firm tofu, prepared with calcium sulfate ($^{1}/4$ cup): 127 mg
Rhubarb, cooked ($^{1}/4$ cup): 87 mg
Goat cheese, semi-soft (1 oz): 84 mg
Collard greens, cooked ($^{1}/4$ cup): 66 mg
Soybeans, cooked ($^{1}/4$ cup): 65 mg
Tahini–sesame seed butter (1 tbsp): 64 mg
Cottage cheese, full fat, small curd ($^{1}/4$ cup): 44 mg
Almond butter (1 tbsp): 43 mg
Neufchatel cheese (2 tbsp): 33 mg
Navy beans, cooked ($^{1}/4$ cup): 31 mg
Great northern beans, cooked ($^{1}/4$ cup): 30 mg
Amaranth, presoaked, cooked ($^{1}/4$ cup): 29 mg
Cream cheese (2 tbsp): 28 g
Egg, boiled (1 large): 25 mg
Kale, cooked ($^{1}/4$ cup): 23 mg
Fig, raw (1 large): 22 mg

Breastfeeding

While it's helpful to wean your child from the bottle to the cup sometime between 12 and 18 months if he's using it for formula or breastmilk, there are many health advantages to **extended nursing** beyond 12 months. Nursing continues to supply toddlers with antibodies: Toddlers up to about 30 months have fewer and less-severe illnesses than non-nursing toddlers. Breastmilk continues to provide valuable stores of nutrients, including vitamins A and B$_{12}$, which can be tough micronutrients for toddlers to get enough of if they are picky vegetable or meat eaters. Extended breastfeeding also appears to reduce allergy risk by speeding the development of the baby's protective intestinal barrier and providing anti-inflammatory properties. If your 1-year-old is nursing at least four times per day, there's no need to begin offering cow's milk yet, as he will get ample supplies of calcium and vitamin D from your breastmilk. In addition, breastmilk is higher in important fats than whole cow's milk, and thus aids in brain development. The American Academy of Pediatrics, American Academy of Family Physicians, and the World Health Organization all endorse breastfeeding beyond one year of age, if both the mother and child wish to do so.

Warning

Fruit juice is very high in sugar and can reduce toddlers' appetite for more nutrient-rich foods. To serve a flavored drink as a treat, put a splash of 100 percent fruit juice into their water, keeping it to a maximum of 1 part juice to 5 parts water. Or make a batch of fruity herbal tea (using 100 percent non-caffeinated herbal tea) and keep it chilled in the fridge: tastes great, looks pretty, and has no sugar.

Bottle Feeding: Weaning to the Cup

Most babies are willing to wean from the bottle to a cup sometime between 9 and 18 months. While many babies can hold a cup at around 6 months, they often aren't developmentally ready to drink solely from the cup until they are at least 9 months old. Although there are no hard and fast rules about this, it's generally a good idea to begin gradually weaning your baby to the cup sometime between 10 and 15 months, if you haven't already started. The longer your baby uses a bottle, the harder it may be for him to wean off it. By the age of 2, they often become quite attached to it. Also, extended bottle use can push those new front teeth forward in his mouth,

changing his natural bite.

Give your child plenty of time for the bottle-weaning process. It may take 6 or 7 months before she is getting all her liquids from the cup. The easiest way to begin is to offer her a sippy cup at mealtimes. At first it will just be a novelty, but within a fairly short time, she will be drinking from it in earnest. Start with the midday meal, then the evening meal, and finally the breakfast meal. Give her several days or a few weeks each time you switch a bottle for a cup. The nighttime bottle is often the hardest to switch, so it's a good idea to leave that one until last.

One-year-olds still love to suck on things, so the bottle can easily become a tool for comforting more than for drinking. While there is nothing inherently wrong with this, you don't want the bottle to become your baby's sole means of self-comfort. Gradually decreasing the frequency of bottle use can give her more opportunities to learn other calming strategies, too.

If your child is still firmly attached to her bottle, try offering her special or favorite drinks in the sippy cup to encourage more cup use. You can also try occasionally offering her milk in the cup and plain water in the bottle. Use your judgment about the timing, but don't make yourself crazy trying to force the issue. Just remember, if you do choose to let her keep her nighttime bottle, don't let her take milk or any other sweet drink to bed with her. Instead, hold her or have her sit with that last bottle until it's gone, then help her brush her teeth to help prevent tooth decay before she goes down.

WHAT TO LOOK FOR IN YOUR 12- TO 18-MONTH-OLD

Although the rate at which your baby is growing slows down after the first year, she will continue to grow in size. As a result, her appetite may diminish somewhat, but her need for vitamins and minerals will actually increase, so after her first birthday it becomes even more important to offer her a diet of high-quality, nutrient-rich foods.

Training the Tongue: Toddler Food Preferences

As you've no doubt noticed, older babies and young toddlers love to put things in their mouths. It is one of the primary ways in which they explore their world at this age: through tasting and mouthing whatever is within reach. While this may not be great in the sandbox, it provides a wonderful opportunity at mealtimes! Use this temporary phase to best advantage by encouraging your 12- to 18-month-old to try all sorts of new and different foods, especially vegetables and fruits. By the time toddlers are closing in on 2 years, many of them start to outgrow this tendency, so now is the perfect time to begin training your toddler's tongue to enjoy a broad variety of different tastes and textures.

Many healthy 1-year-olds may also demonstrate a natural preference for variety in their diet. While babies naturally prefer familiar tastes and textures to the unfamiliar, young toddlers begin looking for variety as an instinctive means of getting a broad spectrum of vitamins and minerals in their diet. This can manifest as a seeming delight in one food one day and then an outright refusal to eat it the next day. Although it can drive you crazy, try to see it for what it is: an inborn quest for nutritional variety.

If your child is refusing old favorites, try to resist tempting them to eat with inappropriate foods like low-quality sweets or other junk food. It's distinctly possible that we begin creating a S.A.D. palate in our children at this stage by offering them treats to get them to eat, when what they really want is new and different fruits, vegetables, grains, or protein choices. While you definitely want to be offering a wide variety of new foods, if, for example, he won't eat his beloved grapefruit, and you don't happen to have on hand papaya or kiwi as an alternative, try preparing that familiar food in a new and different way, such as broiling the grapefruit for 5 minutes with a teaspoon of honey and serving it warm that day.

Appetite

Your baby has tripled in weight in his first year, and now, although he will certainly continue to grow in his second year, the rate of growth will be slower, causing a corresponding decrease in appetite. The combination of a decreased appetite and a decreased tolerance for the same foods may make you wonder where your "big eater" has gone. In fact, your older baby may have become a little chubby in those later months, while your toddler will likely grow out of that **baby fat**, stretching and lengthening into a thinner-looking, leggier body over the coming months.

Even though his appetite and eating habits may change at this stage, you can continue to honor your child's signs for hunger and fullness with confidence. If he eats less than he used to, that is generally not a cause for concern. If he's eating a varied diet and his growth is progressing well (your pediatrician is the best one to assess this), he is getting enough food, even though it may not look like much to you.

Make your child's natural craving for variety work for you by offering only one kind of simple cookie or cracker (high-quality whole grain and low-sugar only, of course!), while also offering a broad selection of new and different whole food flavors and textures at meal- and snack times (fruits, vegetables, grains, legumes, dairy, etc.). This may have the effect of encouraging a preference for special fruit and vegetable dishes over the boring old cracker option.

Signs of hunger and fullness in toddlers. Your one-year-old can communicate with you better than your baby could. He may have a few simple words by now, but he will mostly tell you what he wants by pointing or with other gestures. He may pull certain foods he wants toward himself and push others away if he doesn't want them or has eaten enough. There is no single way for a toddler to express his wishes, however, so there is still a certain amount of decoding involved.

Older toddlers have the ability to tell you in words that they are hungry, but they might not always do so. If you notice that your child seems to be slowing down between meals, sitting very still, or becoming cranky when you know he isn't tired, these may be signs that he needs a little snack for extra energy before the next meal. Toddlers' faces can also start to look a little pale if they are extremely hungry.

Very hungry toddlers will typically eat quite rapidly with great focus at the start of a meal, and then slow down as they satisfy their appetites. When they are looking around and talking, they are probably close to feeling satisfied. If your toddler has been **grazing** throughout the day, however, by eating a series of snacks or mini-meals, then you might not see obvious signs of hunger, because he may not be feeling strong hunger at mealtime. Offering meals at the same time each day can help with this issue. (See page 134 for more information about mealtime routines and your toddler's appetite.)

Key Nutrients

Because the amount of food your toddler is eating is probably smaller than what he ate as an older baby, and, like many 1-year-olds, he may have become quite finicky about certain food choices, especially meats, it's very common in this country for young toddlers to develop vitamin or mineral deficiencies, particularly vitamin

A, calcium, iron, and zinc. (See chapters 3 and 4 for a more in-depth discussion of micronutrients and toddler supplements.)

Vitamin A. Many American toddlers are low in vitamin A. This vitamin is crucial for vision, bone growth, tissue cell development, and regulating the immune system, among other functions. Vitamin A compounds are generally divided into two categories: those from animal foods, called **preformed vitamin A** (absorbed by the body as **retinol**); and those from fruits and vegetables, called **provitamin A carotenoids** (such as **alpha-carotene** and **beta-carotene**). The provitamin A carotenoids can be made into retinol by the body (beta-carotene being the most efficient at conversion), but the absorption is not as high as with the preformed vitamin A from the animal food sources. Even though the vitamin A from animal food sources is absorbed better by the body than that from the plant food sources, both types of vitamin A–rich foods are important elements of a balanced toddler diet. Vitamin A–rich plant foods are usually orange or dark green in color: the darker and richer the color, the more carotenoids are present. Try to include some good sources of vitamin A in your toddler's meals and snacks every day.

Recommended Daily Allowances (RDA) for Vitamin A:

Birth to 6 months: 1,320 IU / 400 mcg

7 to 12 months: 1,650 IU / 500 mcg

1 to 3 years: 1,000 IU / 300 mcg

Quick Chart

Good Animal Food Sources of Vitamin A
Calf's liver* (1 oz): 9,061 IU
Chicken liver* (1 oz): 4,108 IU
Egg, boiled (1 large): 293 IU
Whole milk (4 oz): 125 IU
Yogurt (4 oz): 112 IU
*Note: One of the liver's primary functions in the body is to screen out toxins, so it is safest to offer liver from organic meat sources only.

Good Plant Food Sources*
Carrot juice (2 oz): 11,283 IU
Sweet potato, mashed ($^1/_4$ cup): 9,609 IU
Canned pumpkin ($^1/_4$ cup): 9,532 IU (but no retinol)
Carrots, cooked ($^1/_4$ cup): 6,643 IU
Butternut squash, cooked ($^1/_4$ cup): 5,717 IU
Spinach, cooked ($^1/_4$ cup): 4,716 IU
Kale, cooked ($^1/_4$ cup): 4,427 IU
Collard greens, cooked ($^1/_4$ cup): 3,854 IU
Cantaloupe, raw ($^1/_3$ cup): 1,975 IU
*Note: Numbers look high, but plant foods contain no retinol, and they must be converted in the body.

Caution: Excessive amounts of retinol, over 2,000 IU per day for babies and toddlers 0 to 3 years, can cause vitamin A toxicity. Although it's technically possible to overdose on retinol from eating loads of liver, it's more likely that toxicity symptoms would show up only from taking too much of it in supplement form. Signs of acute vitamin A toxicity include nausea, vomiting, headache, dizziness, blurry vision, and loss of coordination.

6

Calcium. Calcium is a particularly important mineral during childhood years because it is necessary for healthy bone and tooth growth and maintenance. In order to fully absorb the calcium available in foods, it is important to get enough vitamin D as well. The primary sources of vitamin D are moderate sunlight exposure (so the body can manufacture its own), and some animal foods, such as cod liver oil, sardines, and milk. (See chapters 3 and 4 for a more detailed description.) It's also helpful to eat calcium-rich foods at intervals throughout the day, since higher amounts eaten at one sitting generally mean that lesser amounts are actually absorbed by the body.

There are two substances in some calcium-rich plant foods that actually inhibit the absorption of the calcium they contain by binding with it so it's excreted out. (It's important to note, however, that these substances don't bind with calcium from other sources—just the calcium contained by that plant.) One of them is called **oxalic acid**, and it's found in high concentrations in plant foods such as spinach, beet greens, Swiss chard, and parsley. Oxalate concentration is usually highest in the leaves of plants, but there is also some oxalic acid in okra, leeks, and quinoa.

The other is called phytic acid, and is contained in the tough outer hull of most grains, beans, seeds, and nuts. You can reduce the phytic acid content of those foods significantly by presoaking or sprouting them before eating or cooking. Beans and long-cooking

grains should be soaked overnight, and the soak water discarded. Nuts, seeds, and shorter-cooking grains can be soaked from 1 to 3 hours, and the soak water discarded. Soaking these foods also shortens their cooking time and makes them more digestible, particularly the nuts and seeds.

Although the calcium content in most grains and legumes is lower than that of many traditional sources of calcium, such as dairy foods, if they are soaked before cooking and consumed frequently, the levels add up over time and can aid greatly in meeting daily calcium levels.

The chart on page 122 contains a list of calcium-rich foods. Other great sources of calcium are flaxseeds, sesame seeds, almonds, Brazil nuts, and filberts (hazelnuts), but these should be crushed or ground to reduce their choking risk. For cooking, ricotta cheese, canned evaporated milk (unsweetened), and buttermilk are also great sources.

Note the differences in protein, fat, and sugar content among the milk alternatives. There is nothing magical about milk; it is simply a convenient food for providing good amounts of calcium and vitamin D along with some fats and proteins. If your child has trouble digesting milk, has a milk sensitivity, or simply doesn't like the taste, it is possible to replace milk with other foods that contain similar amounts of those important nutrients.

Iron. As many toddlers are eating more plant-based sources of iron (nonheme: poorly absorbed) than animal (heme: better absorbed), they often get less than they need on a daily basis, putting them at risk for iron-deficiency anemia. Toddlers up to age 3 need about 7 mg of iron per day. Consuming iron with foods rich in vitamin C will improve their absorption. (See chapters 3 and 4 for more information.)

Zinc. The foods richest in zinc are animal foods that many young toddlers do not like to eat, namely shellfish and dark meats. Also, if you are giving your child an iron supplement, it can decrease her absorption of zinc, so you will need to ensure she's receiving adequate amounts of this mineral. A 1- to 3-year-old toddler needs 3 mg daily. (See chapters 3 and 4 for lists of zinc-rich foods.)

Quick Chart

Iron-Rich Animal (Heme) Foods / 1-ounce portion
Clams: 7.8 mg
Chicken liver:* 3.7 mg
Calf's liver:* 1.8 mg
Anchovies, in oil: 1.3 mg
Anchovies, raw: 0.9 mg
London broil: 0.9 mg
Brisket: 0.8 mg
Lamb, chop: 0.7 mg
Turkey, dark meat: 0.7 mg
Turkey, light meat: 0.4 mg
Chicken, leg: 0.4 mg
Chicken, breast, roasted: 0.3 mg
Pork, loin: 0.3 mg
*Note: One of the liver's primary functions in the body is to screen out toxins, so it is safest to offer liver from organic meat sources only.

Iron-Rich Plant (Nonheme) Foods
Agar (1 tbsp): 3 mg
Blackstrap molasses (2 tbsp): 7 mg
Pumpkin seeds (1 tbsp): 2.1 mg
Spinach, boiled ($1/4$ cup): 1.6 mg
Lentils, cooked ($1/4$ cup): 1.7 mg
Swiss chard, cooked ($1/4$ cup): 1 mg
Tahini (1 tbsp): 1 mg
Kidney beans, cooked ($1/4$ cup): 0.98 mg
Pinto beans, cooked ($1/4$ cup): 0.9 mg
Quinoa, cooked ($1/4$ cup): 0.7 mg

BEST FOODS, PORTION GUIDES, AND MEAL PLANNING

By this age, your toddler can be eating pretty much the same foods you are serving to the rest of the family. As all her grinding teeth have not yet come in, it is still important, however, to cut your toddler's foods into small, bite-sized pieces for her. The most important meals for your toddler are breakfast and lunch. After the long nighttime sleep, little bodies need fueling soon after arising in the morning, so it's important to offer a healthy breakfast within an hour of waking. Most of the calories eaten at the midday meal will be used up by the day's activities, so be sure to provide a good lunch as well. By evening, the body's energy needs are much lower than during the day, so it is perfectly fine for your toddler to eat a very light dinner.

In our culture, unfortunately, the evening meal—when our bodies need the least fuel—is often the biggest of the day. As adults, we may skip breakfast and graze through lunch, only to arrive home starving at dinnertime and eat a huge meal. Metabolically, this pattern can easily lead to weight gain and feelings of low energy throughout the day. It is vital that you reverse this pattern for your toddler; and if that helps you increase your own breakfast size while decreasing your dinner, it will benefit you as well!

Because your toddler's stomach is still very small, it is likely that she will need two to three snacks in addition to her three regular meals each day to meet all her energy and nutrient requirements. Remember to make every bite count, and not waste any precious eating opportunities on poor-quality, low-nutrient density foods. (See page 286 for a list of quick, tasty, and nutrient-rich toddler snack ideas.)

At this age, your young toddler may not be much of a meal eater at all, preferring instead to eat a series of solid snacks or mini-meals throughout the day, or perhaps eating one true meal and snacking lightly at other times. This is fine—his appetite will increase naturally over time as he grows and his calorie needs increase.

Warning

Babies and toddlers often explore their worlds by putting things in their mouths, they are at risk for accidental poisoning. Place the telephone number of your local poison control center near the family house phone in case of emergency. Keep some form of safe emetic, such as ipecac, on hand in case you need to induce vomiting in your child. Ask your pediatrician for a recommendation. If you suspect your child may have ingested a toxin of any kind, call poison control immediately. They will ask you some questions and advise you about what to do. Do not induce vomiting without speaking to poison control first. Contact the American Association of Poison Control Centers at 800-222-1222 or look them up online at www.aapcc.org for local center, first aid, and poison control information.

Quick Chart

MIX-AND-MATCH DAILY NUTRITION GUIDE, 12 TO 18 MONTHS

This chart offers an overview of a very balanced daily diet for toddlers. The guidelines provide for about 1,000 calories per day and a good mix of macro- and micronutrients.

These portions are approximations only. If your toddler is more active, he may need more calories and be hungry for larger portions. If he's more sedentary, he may need slightly fewer calories.

Toddler eating habits and preferences are very erratic. Expecting a balanced plate at every meal is unrealistic. The purpose of this chart is to give you an idea of the types of selections you can offer in balanced proportions—what and how much he actually chooses to eat is a different matter. Offer three meals and one to two snacks throughout the course of the day, spreading out the different food offerings according to his appetite.

If he is on a no-protein jag, you will need to work harder to provide him with adequate stores over the course of the week. (See page 287 for a list of different nutrient boosters and strategies for providing "**invisible nutrition.**")

For drinks, offer water, milk, and cool herbal teas (no caffeine), or very watered-down juices (5 parts water to 1 part 100 percent juice). Avoid sweet drinks, including full-strength juice or extra milk: They can reduce your toddler's appetite and will provide too many calories without enough nutrition.

PROTEIN		CARBOHYDRATES			FATS
Core Protein Total: 1.5 oz 2 servings (.5 to 1 oz)	Calcium Protein Total: 500 mg calcium combination	Vegetables Total: $^3/_4$ cup 3 servings ($^1/_4$ cup)	Fruit Total: 1 cup 4 servings ($^1/_4$ cup)	Whole Grains Total: $^1/_2$ cup 2 servings ($^1/_4$ cup)	Healthy Fats Total: 3 tsp 3 servings (1 tsp)
Beans (30 mg calcium per cup) Meat Fish: wild Alaskan salmon, sardines, tilapia, cod (1 serving per month), and skipjack or chunk light canned tuna (1 serving per week)	Cheese: 200-300 mg per oz Milk: 138 mg per $^1/_2$ cup Yogurt: 137 mg per $^1/_2$ cup Tofu (prepared with calcium sulfate): 127 mg per $^1/_4$ cup Nut or seed butter: 40 to 60 mg per 1 tbsp Egg: 25 mg per 1 large egg	Any Rainbow of color Mix of cooked and raw	Any Rainbow of color Mix of cooked and raw	Cereal grains: amaranth, quinoa, millet, oats, etc. Whole-grain pasta Whole-grain breads and crackers ($^1/_4$ to $^1/_2$ slice bread or 1 to 3 small crackers)	Oil: olive, sunflower, coconut, flaxseed (not heated), etc. Butter, ghee (1 tsp) Avocado, chopped olives (1 tbsp) Coconut milk (1 tbsp)

Quick Chart

RELIEF OF CHOKING IN CHILDREN OVER 1 YEAR OLD

Signs of Choking
Choking occurs when something blocks the airway. When the airway is completely blocked, the child cannot breathe. Choking can be a frightening emergency. But if you act quickly, you can help the child breathe.

If the child can speak or cough loudly, the child's airway is only partly blocked. You should not try to open the airway. If you are worried about the child's breathing, phone 911.

Signs of choking in the child with a completely blocked airway are
• The child suddenly begins to cough, gag, or have high-pitched, noisy breathing
• An older child may make the choking sign (holding the neck with one or both hands)
• The child has bluish lips or skin

Actions to Relieve Choking in a Child
When a child is choking and can't breathe or speak, you must give abdominal thrusts (the **Heimlich maneuver**). The Heimlich maneuver pushes air from the child's lungs like a cough. This can help remove the blocking object. You should give abdominal thrusts until the object is forced out or the victim becomes unresponsive.
1. If you think a child is choking, ask the child "Are you choking?" If he nods, tell him you are going to help.
2. Kneel or stand firmly behind him and wrap your arms around him so that your hands are in front.
3. Make a fist with one hand.
4. Put the thumb side of your fist slightly above the navel (belly button) and well below the breastbone.
5. Grasp the fist with your other hand and give quick upward thrusts into his abdomen.
6. Give thrusts until the object is forced out and he can breathe, cough, or talk or until he stops responding.

If the choking is *not* relieved, the child will become unresponsive. When the child becomes unresponsive, shout for help, lower the child to the ground, and start CPR. If someone else is present, send that person to phone 911 while you start CPR.

The steps of CPR of the child who has become unresponsive after choking are the same, with one addition.
1. Yell for help. If someone comes, send that person to phone your emergency response number (or 911) and get the AED [automated external defibrillator] if available.
2. Lower the victim to the ground, face up. If you are alone with the child victim, start the steps of CPR.
3. Every time you open the airway to give breaths, open the victim's mouth

(continued)

Relief of Choking cont.
wide and look for the object. If you see an object, remove it with your fingers. If you do not see an object, keep giving sets of 30 compressions and two breaths until an AED arrives, the victim starts to move, or trained help takes over.

4. After about five cycles or two minutes, if you are alone, leave the child victim to call your emergency response number (or 911) and get the AED if available.

Chest compressions may force the object out. If you are alone with the child and these steps don't work after about one minute, phone 911.

Note: the Heimlich maneuver is for use on children over the age of 12 months, the AHA does not recommend its use for children under 12 months of age.

[Reprinted with permission www.americanheart.org © 2008, American Heart Association, Inc.]

HEALTHY STRATEGIES FOR RAISING A NATURAL EATER (12 TO 18 MONTHS)

By the age of 1, your toddler can be an active participant at family mealtimes. Making the effort to eat your meals together can be a little challenging with a 12-month-old, but it can also be a lot of fun. Shared mealtimes help model the social element of daily eating. With all the changes occurring during your child's transition from babyhood to toddlerhood, it's possible to turn the dinner table into a battleground. If everyone is eating at the same time, it will be much easier to take the focus off the food your toddler is or isn't eating, and refocus that attention on spending time together. Let your child see and participate in the ways you gather as a family, eat your meals, and connect with laughter and the sharing of stories.

Many families have two parents working full time, and one, or both, may get home too late for a shared family dinner. One practice that some parents enjoy is to switch the family meal to breakfast time. Everyone can be together to share the meal at the start of the day, and there's the added bonus of ensuring that all of your family members begin each day with some solid nutrition.

Skillful Ignoring

We know from experience (and the research bears this out) that the emphasis we place on different foods can have the opposite behavioral effect we're looking for in our toddlers. Some research even indicates that demonstrating approval for healthy foods and disapproval for unhealthy foods can sometimes encourage an avoidance of the healthy and an attraction to the unhealthy! So what can you do to encourage and support acceptance and enjoyment of the healthy foods?

One approach is to simply remove any extra attention from the food and eating.

If you're offering a new food to your toddler, or something she has refused in the past, just offer it alongside the more accepted choices at mealtime and don't draw any special attention to it. Stay neutral when talking about foods; use a casual approach. Never offer one food as a reward for eating another food, as in, "If you eat that broccoli you can have dessert." This will teach your toddler that broccoli is something to be endured, while dessert is something to be coveted. Remember that you may need to offer that food over and over again before your toddler is willing to taste it. Let her hold it and play with it—the more she touches and smells it, the more likely it is that it will eventually make its way into her mouth. Also, give her plenty of opportunities to see the rest of the family eating it as well—that can go a long way toward encouraging her to give it a try herself.

Another simple but important strategy for encouraging your child to accept and enjoy healthy foods is to offer your toddler only foods with a high nutritional impact, in other words, only high-quality foods. Make the treats and desserts as healthy as the meal options. And make some of your meals as tasty and special as dessert. That way you'll know she's getting adequate nutrition no matter what she chooses to eat. (See chapter 10 for some great ideas for healthy desserts and delicious entrées.)

Eating and Drinking When Your Toddler Is Sick

When your child doesn't feel well, his appetite may diminish or even disappear altogether. It's very important to keep your sick toddler from getting dehydrated, so even if he isn't eating, try to get him to drink plenty of fluids. Water is great, but if they have had diarrhea or have been throwing up, they may need fluids with some sugars and salts in them to replace lost **electrolytes**. Drinks specially formulated with these extra nutrients, such as **Pedialyte** or PediaVance, are available in most pharmacies or health-food stores. If your toddler won't take drinks, try freezing some homemade ice pops made with fruity tea (herbal only—no caffeine) or a splash of 100 percent juice (you can also try freezing the Pedialyte). Simple miso broth (see page 292 for how to prepare this) or plain chicken soup are also great alternatives if they'd prefer something warm. If your child's stomach is upset, avoid milk and other dairy products until he is fully well again, as dairy can sometimes irritate upset stomachs.

Diarrhea can dehydrate a young toddler very quickly, so it's crucial to keep the fluids flowing. Throwing up can have the same effect, but it can be harder to get enough fluids back into them because they may not be able to keep drinks down. A simple rule of thumb is to wait for 1 hour after he throws up before offering your child any fluids. If he doesn't throw up for a full hour, begin by offering him 1 tablespoon of Pedialyte. If he keeps that down for 10 or 15 minutes, try offering 2 tablespoons.

If that stays down, you can offer him a bit more. After 2 or 3 successful sipping sessions, you can try offering 3 to 4 ounces or a small ice pop. You don't want to offer too much at once or it might trigger another bout of vomiting.

Dehydration. If you notice any of the following signs in your child, or if the diarrhea or vomiting continues for more than 24 hours, call your pediatrician for guidance.

• Less frequent or smaller amounts of urination: look for a dark yellow color

• Sunken eyes

• Skin doesn't spring back immediately when gently pressed, but retains a light dent for a moment

• Dry lips and tongue

• Decline in energy or lethargy

Once the throwing up has completely stopped and your child has a bit of an appetite again, you can begin offering a diet that is very gentle to the body and easy to digest, emphasizing plain grains, such as brown rice, and bland chicken or low-sodium, low-fat chicken broth. Foods that are high in simple sugars or fats should be avoided.

Offer a few bites of whichever of these foods he is interested in, and if he tolerates it well, you can offer another choice. After a day or so of plain eating, you can begin to offer other simple foods as he is ready—but remember to avoid all dairy products until he is completely recovered.

Constipation. It's very common for toddlers who are eating a poor-quality Standard American Diet to become constipated. The excessive amount of white food carbohydrates can get "sticky" inside, making it difficult for their bowels to move the waste through efficiently. Usually switching them to a diet richer in fruits, vegetables, beans, and whole grains will remedy that problem by gently increasing the amount of fiber in their diet.

When increasing the amount of high-fiber foods in your child's diet (or your own, for that matter!), it's very important to do it gradually, and to also increase the amount of plain water they are drinking. Too much fiber without enough water can actually worsen, rather than alleviate, constipation. Start their morning with a glass of water before they even eat breakfast. Sometimes a small amount (2 to 4 ounces) of prune juice or warm orange juice in the morning can also do the trick. Most toddlers love prunes, and you can cut them up and offer them as a regular snack or as a condiment over cereal, or even baked into cookies to help keep them regular.

Another tip to help get things moving is to offer a small amount of plain flaxseed oil before bedtime: half a teaspoon. If your child will drink it straight from the spoon with or without a 2-ounce juice chaser, that's best. If not, just mix it into the juice and offer it that way.

If your child develops chronic constipation, consult your pediatrician for help.

Setting Reasonable Boundaries

Your 1-year-old is beginning to develop her own distinctive personality. She can now make her preferences more known to you. At the same time, she can also understand simple guidelines for behavior. Now is the perfect time for beginning to implement a few simple rules around mealtime. While it is too soon yet for trying to enforce actual table manners as we know them, you can begin to model asking for things nicely ("More, please"), and declining politely ("No, thank you").

TIP

One of the healthiest snacks for your toddler's teeth is cheese. The calcium and phosphorous in cheese help build strong teeth and remineralize tooth enamel. Some common types of cheese (mozzarella, Swiss, cheddar, Jack) also stimulate the salivary glands in the mouth, rinsing food material away and protecting teeth from acids that can break them down. So give your child a snack of cheese, or serve it to her at the end of the meal as dessert to help protect her precious choppers.

Most 1-year-olds are not able to sit quietly for an extended mealtime. Some toddlers are especially active and find it difficult to even sit still at all. For those children, mealtimes should not become a torturous affair. Try preparing the table and especially his meal completely before asking him to sit. Keep his required mealtime short—10 or 12 minutes is usually plenty. When he has finished eating, you can allow

him to get up from the table. It's a good idea to have some kind of ritual in place, like asking if he'd like to be excused, so even at this young age he understands that there are routines to be followed around mealtimes.

If tossing food from her tray has become a game, you might now want to make a first simple rule: "Food is for eating, not for throwing." Be careful, though, that you make a rule only for something that matters to you, because the most important thing with setting new boundaries is to consistently reinforce them. If you tell her not to throw her food one day, and then laugh at the same behavior the next day—it will confuse her and she won't know what's acceptable.

It's still important developmentally to let your young toddler play with his food—he is engaging all his senses and training his fine motor skills to be a good self-feeder. So trying to get him to keep his hands out of the food can actually be counterproductive. But if the constant mess is driving you nuts, there are a few things you can try to minimize cleanup time. Definitely invest in a couple of smock-style bibs that have sleeves and cover the whole lap—these will protect your toddler's clothes. Also, if she loves to wave her sticky hands around, flinging food everywhere, give her something to do with them to keep them busy: a suction-cup bowl of dry finger foods to grasp, or two baby spoons to hold in her hands. If your older toddler is still throwing her food off the high chair tray as a game, you can simply take the food away as soon as she does that, and feed her every bite yourself—removing her independence—until she makes the connection that throwing the food for fun is not acceptable behavior at mealtime.

Feeding at 18 Months to 3 Years

WHAT TO LOOK FOR IN YOUR 18- TO 36-MONTH-OLD TODDLER

Between 18 months and 2 years, your toddler's growth rate will slow down again. But her movement will seem to speed up! These months often feel like they are mostly about following your toddler around and making sure she doesn't get into trouble on the stairs, or even heading out the door on her own. There are lots of bumps and bruises as she learns to make her way in the world, her sense of independence growing with a ferocity particular to the typical 2- and 3-year-old.

Sometime between 18 months and 2 years, most toddlers will lose their built-in eagerness to put new things into their mouths. In fact, they may become downright stubborn about not putting anything unfamiliar into their mouths, creating a whole new wave of finickiness around food. This may be another inborn adaptive trait: Thousands of years ago, it would have been protective for older toddlers,

growing in independence and able to roam away from their parents, to avoid eating an unfamiliar and potentially dangerous plant.

The Unemotional Approach

You can be ready for this increase in food fussiness with a calm and relaxed attitude. If you try to force your child to eat, you're likely to be met with strong resistance as your toddler works toward establishing his independence. Although it might be tempting to exert your will or to use bribery to get him to eat, try to avoid doing either, as these tactics will backfire in the long run. If possible, you want to minimize any emotional triggering at all around food. In other words, do your best to act casual about his eating, even if you are feeling very frustrated inside.

If he is refusing to eat something, or even to eat at all, just calmly remove the food at the end of meal or snack time and continue on with your day. Don't worry that he will starve—healthy toddlers do not starve themselves! Eventually he will get hungry enough to eat. It can be very tempting at these times to cave in and offer him a treat or something he loves just to make sure he eats. Try to avoid doing this, however, as it will set a bad precedent: You're telling your child, in essence, that if he refuses his regular food, he'll be rewarded with a treat.

Quick Snacks for 2- to 3-Year-Olds

Always have a good supply of simple healthy snacks already prepared and easily available for times when your child suddenly gets hungry between meals. Toddler-sized fruits and cut up vegetables make great light snacks that won't interfere too much with her appetite for an upcoming meal. You can keep some in a bowl on the countertop or in a special container in the fridge so your child can even serve herself. If it will be an hour and a half or more before her next meal, you could bump up the staying power of those fruits and veggies by adding a little protein or fat: Try cubes of cheese, a smear of nut butter, chopped boiled egg, or a small cup of yogurt.

You can extend the **baby food cube** concept (see the Glossary) for toddlers by filling the empty compartments in an ice tray with a selection of different chopped snacks: raisins or other dried fruits, cheese cubes, cucumber slices, halved grape tomatoes, cooked beans, etc., and keep it covered on a low shelf in the fridge. Wash and restock it with alternating selections each morning to keep it fresh.

The Balancing Act

In many ways, this is the most difficult eating phase with your child, because when toddlers get hungry, they truly do need to eat within a short amount of time—you can't ask them to be patient and wait for an hour until dinner. Their blood-sugar level drops very quickly at this age and they can get weepy or frustrated—possibly even launch into a tantrum. But if they have a snack too close to mealtime, then they will likely refuse a regular meal. Developing an eating relationship at this age involves a delicate balancing act of honoring and promptly feeding your child's true hunger, and training that hunger to coincide with regular meal and semi-regular snack times. You can use the tactic of regular routines to help train your toddler's appetite. (See page 143 for ideas.)

Engaging Their Interest

As your toddler gets close to her second birthday, you can begin to engage her in the preparation of the food, and even the dinner table, in new ways. Toddlers' minds are as active as their feet, and if they become involved with food preparation, they will be much more likely to eat and enjoy it. While your toddler's help at this age may be more of a hindrance to the actual work that needs to be done, it will benefit both of you to find ways for her to participate. Ask her to wash the vegetables for the salad, or arrange them in the salad bowl. Give her opportunities to mix ingredients in a big bowl, or to hand you spices or other ingredients to go into soups or stews. Baking is often a big hit with toddlers. They love the messy fun of the flour, mixing ingredients, kneading bread, or rolling out balls of cookie dough. Always make sure you both wash your hands before beginning, and never let her handle knives or any hot food. While she can't work on or near the hot stove, she can stand on a stool in front of your working counter or at the sink.

When it's time to eat, show your older toddler how to set the table. She can fold and place the napkins at each spot, and help to arrange the silverware (except for sharp knives). You can use fun placemats, maybe changing them with the seasons or for special holidays to emphasize the connection between nature and our food.

Encouraging your toddler to take part in the daily cooking and table setting will help them understand the intrinsic connection between plants, animals, cooking, and eating. It will also help them feel like they can contribute something to the family. And best of all for a **finicky eater**, if they helped create it, they will be much more willing to try new foods!

Are They Eating Enough?

At this age, some children pretty much skip one or more of their main meals and seem instead to be just snacking throughout the day. Many parents become worried that their toddlers are not eating enough food. To maximize his appetite for regular food, don't offer your child sweet drinks between meals, such as juice, soda, or even too much milk (more than 2 cups a day). Also, don't give them lots of S.A.D. white food snacks of empty calorie crackers, cookies, or chips. Those drinks or poor-quality snacks will keep their blood-sugar level steadily elevated, causing them to lose their appetites, but not providing them with the varied and balanced nutrition that their growing bodies require.

If they are provided with a good variety of healthy food choices and not given a lot of empty calorie foods, nearly every toddler will eat decently on their own. It may not look like enough food or variety to you, but remember that you should look for nutritional balance for toddlers over a series of days, rather than just one day, never mind one meal. If he seems to be stuck on toast with peanut butter (see nut allergy info on page 95) for several days, let him eat that. Make it high-quality whole-grain bread, and real peanut butter with no additives. You can also try mixing in a little wheat germ or ground flax. Slice bananas and let him make a face with raisins and banana wheels. Add a glass of milk or a cup of yogurt and fruit. Try offering him a small helping of something new in addition to his PB and toast each time you serve it. Don't worry if he ignores it, just let it be there. If you can make it look like fun, he'll be more likely to try it. Colorful dipper sticks of sweet pepper and cool cucumber stuck like soldiers into a cup of bright dipping sauce will be much more appealing to your toddler than a bowl of salad. Don't overwhelm him with too many new offerings at once—keep it simple and straightforward: his requested PB and toast plus one attractive addition. It will help if he sees you or other family members eating the additional choice as well.

Signs that your child is getting adequate nutrition:

Height: The Centers for Disease Control and Prevention, National Center for Health Statistics growth charts (2000) suggest that healthy 12- to 36-month-old children grow an average of 0.3 to 0.4 inches per month.

Activity: Is your child essentially healthy, happy, and active?

Developmental milestones:

Is your toddler meeting the basic developmental milestones within range of the average timing?

Hair: Is your child's hair strong and healthy looking?

Skin: Is your child's skin smooth, with good color?

Nails and teeth: Are your child's nails and teeth smooth and strong?

Underweight Children

If your child tends to be underweight, have his growth closely monitored by your pediatrician. Remember that most healthy toddlers will grow out of the chubbiness they had as babies, and end up looking much leaner at their third birthday than they did at their first. Your pediatrician will also guide you to look for any signs of actual nutritional deficiency. If you truly believe that your toddler is not eating enough food (or a decent balance of nutrition), keep a written record over 2 weeks of exactly what foods he is eating in exactly what amounts. Your pediatrician can refer you to a nutritionist to help you analyze content and amounts to see if your toddler's current diet needs to be modified. Writing down what your child actually eats can be a very enlightening experience for any parent. We have found that many parents were not aware of how much sugar their child was consuming, for example, even when they felt that they were watching the overall intake.

Also, make sure that the foods you are offering are calorically dense choices, such as healthy fats. If he wants a cracker, see if he'll take it with cream cheese or nut butter (as a spread or a dip). If he wants milk, see if he'll accept a smoothie, and add a piece of banana and some full-fat yogurt, coconut milk, nut butter, a slice of avocado, or a teaspoon of a healthy oil, such as flaxseed or coconut. High-fat liquids (yogurt, kefir, coconut milk, healthy oils, etc.) can be added "invisibly" to many other dishes as well (soups, stews, baked goods, ground meat dishes, etc.) to boost their calorie levels. The American Academy of Pediatrics recommends that toddlers eat about 40 calories for every inch of their current height every day (approximately 900 to 1,000 calories for 1- year-olds, and 1,200 to 1,300 calories for 2- to 3-year-olds). You want every bite to count.

Overweight Children

If your pediatrician has indicated that your toddler is overweight, you can work with a pediatric nutrition specialist to give you some advice about specific things you might change. It's helpful to keep at least a 2-week record of exactly when, what, and how much food your child is eating, so that you and the nutritionist are both aware of his current eating habits. Keep that private, however, so as not to bring a lot of attention to the idea that you are concerned about his food. While it's important for all toddlers to have lots of opportunities for active play, it's especially important for overweight toddlers.

Make sure you are providing your child with many chances every day to walk and run around, to dance or play physical games (duck, duck, goose; roll and catch the ball; swing or climb the slide at a park; etc.). It's even better if you do some of these activities as a family, such as taking a short stroll together on most nice evenings. Also, pay attention to how much time your child is sitting in front of the computer or television. Research shows that there is a direct correlation between excess weight and lots of screen time. Don't allow TV watching during mealtimes, as that can encourage your child to eat mindlessly, taking in more food than he needs because his attention is on the show instead of how his body feels. It's also a good idea to put some limits on screen time, because if your child isn't being entertained by the TV, he'll be more likely to engage in active play on his own.

Many toddlers become overweight because they are eating too many poor-quality foods. When the classic toddler pickiness sets in, usually around or shortly after their first birthday, many parents resort to feeding their children lots of milk, sweets, or white food snacks that are high in calories but low in nutrition, just to get them to eat. This can put your child on the blood-sugar roller coaster (see page 17 for more information), making it even more difficult to get them to choose the healthy foods. (See the Healthy Strategies section for 18- to 36-month-olds on page 142 for tips on how to encourage your toddler to snack strategically and eat a healthy variety of foods at regular mealtimes.)

Our Food Beliefs

No matter how good our intentions are, it's pretty much inevitable that our toddlers will learn to eat as we do. If our eating habits as parents are not what we want them to be, what can we do? One strategy is to look closely at your own habits and beliefs about food and eating, both familial and cultural. How did your own family eat as you were growing up? Were you encouraged to clean your plate at every meal, particularly if the reward for doing so was dessert? Were you rewarded with special food treats? If so, you will be likely to pass these same habits onto your own children, often without even knowing it.

Try having an honest discussion with your spouse, partner, or a close friend about your own beliefs about food and eating. Describe your own early childhood mealtimes as well as you can remember them. See if there is any belief or habit you are carrying from that time that you want to change, for yourself and for your child. What is one way you can shift that old pattern for your new family? Sometimes, just bringing an old belief into your awareness is enough to start the pattern of change. While we will never be perfect, as people or as parents, we can make small changes in our own lives that will be of great benefit to our children.

BEST FOODS, PORTION GUIDES, AND MEAL PLANNING

Fruits and Veggies

The U.S. Department of Agriculture and the Department of Health and Human Services work together to provide updated **Dietary**

Quick Chart

DAILY NUTRITION GUIDE, 18 TO 36 MONTHS

This chart offers an overview of a very balanced daily diet for older toddlers. The guidelines provide for about 1,200 calories per day and a good mix of macro- and micronutrients.

These portions are approximations only. If your toddler is more active, he may need more calories and be hungry for larger portions. If he's more sedentary, he may need slightly fewer calories.

Toddler eating habits and preferences are very erratic. Expecting a balanced plate at every meal is unrealistic. The purpose of this chart is to give you an idea of the types of selections you can offer in balanced proportions—what and how much he actually chooses to eat is a different matter. (See page 144 for a list of different nutrient boosters and strategies for providing invisible nutrition over the course of one week to balance out anything your toddler may be avoiding eating.)

Remember that snacks provide the perfect opportunity to offer a serving of fruit, vegetables, and/or a calcium protein—don't waste them on poor-quality, empty-calorie foods.

For drinks, offer water, milk, and cool herbal teas (no caffeine), or very watered-down juices (5 parts water to 1 part 100 percent juice). Avoid sweet drinks, including full-strength juice or extra milk: They can reduce your toddler's appetite and will provide too many calories without enough nutrition.

PROTEIN		CARBOHYDRATES			FATS	
Core Protein Total: 2 oz 1 to 2 servings (1 to 2 oz)	Calcium Protein Total: 500 mg calcium combination	Vegetables Total: 1 1/2 to 2 cups 3 to 6 servings (1/3 cup)	Fruit Total: 1 cup 3 servings (1/3 cup)	Whole Grains Total: 1/3 to 1/2 cup 1 serving plus (1/3 cup)	Healthy Fats Total: 3 tsp 3 servings (1 tsp)	
Beans (30 mg calcium per cup) Meat Fish: wild Alaskan salmon, sardines, tilapia, cod (1 serving per month), and skipjack or chunk light canned tuna (1 serving per week)	Cheese: 200 to 300 mg per oz Milk: 138 mg per 1/2 cup Yogurt: 137 mg per 1/2 cup Tofu (prepared with calcium sulfate): 127 mg per 1/4 cup Nut or seed butter: 40 to 60 mg per 1 tbsp Eggs: 25 mg per 1 large egg	Any Rainbow of color Mix of cooked and raw	Any Rainbow of color Mix of cooked and raw	Cereal grains: amaranth, quinoa, millet, oats, etc. Whole-grain pasta Whole-grain breads and crackers (1/2 slice bread or 2 to 3 small crackers)	Oil: olive, sunflower, coconut, flaxseed (not heated), etc. Butter, ghee (1 tsp) Avocado, pitted chopped olives (1 tbsp) Coconut milk (1 tbsp)	

Guidelines for Americans every 5 years. These give recommendations for dietary intakes for people ages 2 years and older. These guidelines inspired the development of the national **5-A-Day campaign** to encourage all Americans to eat at least five servings of fruit and vegetables every day. In 2007, the campaign became the National Fruit and Vegetable Program. The newest initiative by the program ("Fruit and Veggies—More Matters") reflects the latest recommendations (2005), which call for increased consumption of fruits and vegetables: from 2 to 6½ cups for adults, and 2 cups per day for children 2 to 8 years old. The **MyPyramid** suggestion for the average 2- to 3-year-old is at least 1 cup of fruit and 1 to 1½ cups of veggies each day, varying them to include at least 1 cup of dark green and ½ to 1 cup of orange vegetables each week.

The old 5-A-Day recommendation for fruits and vegetables may be easier to understand in terms of volume. Encourage your 2- to 3-year-old toddler to eat at least 2 cups of varied fruits and vegetables every day. Try to make at least one of those servings a green vegetable almost every day, and include dark orange vegetables at least three times per week.

HEALTHY STRATEGIES FOR RAISING A NATURAL EATER (18 TO 36 MONTHS)

Sometime during this period from 18 to 36 months, your child will make that transition from eating based primarily on the internal cues for hunger and fullness to eating based more on external cues. As we've discussed, you want to keep returning his attention to those internal cues to reinforce his internal guidance system, but you also want to be particularly careful about the type of external cueing he is exposed to. For instance, the portion size in fast food and other restaurants is too large for most toddlers' tummies (which are about the size of their closed fist!). In those settings, toddlers can eat more than they would at home, and can even get into the habit of finishing the whole thing because it's a special treat. They, like adults, are influenced by the amounts of food on the plate and will tend to eat more than they need, if offered more. If you go out to eat, divide your child's meal into portions the size he would normally eat at home and serve it that way, rather than right out of the bag.

Be a Good Role Model

Your own eating behaviors will also influence your toddler's eating habits very strongly now. They will unconsciously be watching how you eat, what you eat, and how much you eat. If you eat several servings of food at one sitting, or reject vegetables, or eat "forbidden" foods that your toddler isn't allowed to enjoy, it will be very difficult to keep him from mimicking those same behaviors. Try to eat in a healthier way yourself, and keep your pantry free of the types of S.A.D. foods that you don't want your child to be eating.

Mealtime Rhythm and Routine

With the particular challenges of toddlerhood, these months are crucial for setting the stage for healthy eating. Use the rhythm of daily routines to help your toddler overcome any unwillingness to eat a variety of healthy foods. Creating consistency in how and when you prepare, serve, and eat your daily foods will help build a firm foundation of security for your toddler. He is looking for the familiar, and trying to avoid the unfamiliar right now. A reliable platform of regular meal and snack routines can help him feel safer about eating different foods.

Regular mealtimes. While you should continue to honor your child's internal sense of hunger to guide his eating, you also need to begin creating some reliable mealtime patterns to help him join the family rhythms. We all need to find the balance between eating according to internal cues and eating when the food is actually served. Setting up regular times to eat each day and sticking to them will help that transition along. Many toddlers prefer grazing on little snacks throughout the day, as opposed to sitting down to regular mealtimes. By the time they are approaching their third birthday, however, there is no reason why he shouldn't be able to join the family's regular mealtimes, even if it's only for a few minutes and he doesn't eat much food. Think about how this will benefit him in the future. Day-care centers, for example, have very specific times for snacks and meals, and there is no grazing allowed. Nearly all toddlers are able to adjust to this strict routine within a matter of days—and no one starves.

Snacking. Consistency in the habit itself seems to be the thing that trains little bodies. It is still very important to feed a hungry toddler when he is truly hungry—they do not have the stamina at this age to wait for very long before refueling. But try to use some care in the types and amounts of between-meal snacks that you offer: If it's right before a mealtime, keep it light (fruit and veggies), or even offer something from the dinner meal as a snack. If they ate little at lunch and got hungry again an hour afterward, give them a small mini-meal that includes some protein or fat to hold them until dinnertime. The key is nutrient balance throughout the day and portion size. If they really want a glass of milk or a white food snack, let them have it, but keep it small. When you give them a white food snack, such as a few white crackers, also offer something with more nutritional bang for the buck, such as cheese slices, or a smear of nut butter (see nut allergy warning on page 95).

Toddler table manners. As you watch your 18-month-old smush his cooked carrots between his fingers, the idea of him having good table manners probably seems like a distant pipe dream. But the truth is, good manners are cultivated over time, and you can begin helping your toddler develop them now.

The best way to begin teaching your toddler appropriate mealtime manners is to use them consistently yourself. Let your toddler see you and your other family members modeling polite eating behaviors:

saying "please" and "thank you"; speaking in a friendly way to one another with an "inside voice" (the low speaking voice that characterizes regular conversation, as opposed to the yelling we do "outside" that characterizes playtime, etc); chewing with your mouth closed; waiting to finish your bite before speaking, etc. This will go a long way toward establishing the mealtime tone that you wish to create.

You can't expect manners miracles from your 18-month-old, but you can definitely begin to ask for acceptable mealtime behaviors. For instance, it's fine to tell her that spitting her food, throwing her food, or grabbing someone else's food are not good table manners. Older toddlers can ask for things politely and say "thank you" when they receive them. They can also ask to be excused from the table, and start learning to use a napkin.

Some toddlers will use bad behaviors at mealtime to get a laugh or some other form of attention. In that case, it's probably best to simply ignore them when they are misbehaving, and acknowledge them with gentle praise when they are using good manners. The lack of attention might be all the discouragement they need to stop doing it. Sometimes simple reminders or a redirection can shift the behavior: "We ask for more food when we want it, we don't grab— would you like some more peas?" Other toddlers need to have those behaviors actively discouraged to learn that they are unacceptable. You can decide which behaviors are not allowed and respond with a consequence that's in balance with

the behavior. If your 3-year-old is banging her plate on the table and yelling, you could remove her to another room until she agrees to sit politely and use only her "inside voice" at the table.

Preparing for meals. It's a good idea to help your child prepare for mealtime by cultivating a few simple habits. Take them to wash their hands before they eat. By removing the germs she's picked up throughout the day, that little routine can go a long way toward keeping your child healthy. If you like, you could also have her set the table, or perhaps just get her own dishes out (be sure to keep them on a low, accessible shelf). It can be very nice to say a little thank-you for the food you will all be eating before the meal begins. Traditional grace is lovely, but it doesn't have to be religious at all. A simple thank-you to the earth and sun for helping to grow the food is perfect for toddlers. You can even make it into a little song. (See Resources for some resources for mealtime thank-yous.) Having them prepare to eat in these simple, consistent ways every day will also help signal their systems that it's time to eat, naturally triggering their body's hunger.

Finesse Your Finicky Eater

Nearly all children will go through a period of picky eating at some point during their toddler years. Try one of the suggestions below to encourage your reluctant toddler to eat a variety of healthy foods without threats, nagging, cajoling, or bribes.

Invisible nutrition. If your child is consistently refusing certain foods that he needs for good nutritional balance, such as green vegetables or dairy foods, try making them invisible. Make a dish you know he enjoys and mix some of the disliked food into it in a way he can't detect. For instance, if your child is refusing protein foods, try mixing a little whey protein powder into his cold cereal milk or hot cereal (oatmeal, etc.). Or if he's been refusing vegetables, grate or puree a bland or sweet combination (zucchini, carrots, sweet potatoes, etc.) and mix it into a dish he enjoys, such as meat loaf or meatballs. (See the Meat Loaf Muffins recipe on page 280.) He'll never know it's there!

You can also get quite creative with baked goods. Because most toddlers enjoy sweet baked goods, they present an excellent opportunity to sneak in all sorts of nutrition. Beans, vegetables, dairy, etc. can all easily be added to cakes, muffins, or quick breads. (See our recipe for Celebration Cupcakes on page 308.) Smoothies also make a great snack or mini-meal that can hide many different nourishing foods: healthy oils, nut butters, protein powders, **pasteurized** eggs, milk, tofu, fruits, vegetables, etc. While it's true that you want to cultivate an active acceptance of these healthy foods, during particularly finicky eating stages, there's nothing wrong with occasional disguises! (See page 287 for invisible nutrition info and tips.)

Divided plates. A picky eater can easily get overwhelmed with a large pile of food on a plate in front of him. Try serving very small, even tiny, portions to tempt him. Many toddlers go through a period when they don't like their food to be mixed up, as in a casserole, or even touching any other foods! For these kids, try preparing simple foods that you know he enjoys and serving them separately, in very small amounts, on a **divided plate** or even in separate, brightly colored bowls. If you have a service online or nearby that allows you to decorate your own dishes, help your toddler design a divided plate of his own, and use his special plate at mealtimes or when you're trying to offer a new food.

Don't give him too many foods at once—that might overwhelm a toddler who's not that interested in eating at the moment. Three or four choices is a good regular average, but if he's very finicky, try offering just two or three. Be sure to include at least one or two healthy foods that you know he usually likes to eat.

Dipping and sprinkling. Condiments hold a special magic for toddlers, and you can use them to great advantage with your picky eater. A plate of baby carrots that he normally wouldn't touch with a 10-foot pole becomes interesting if you serve it with two tiny bowls of different dips. In addition to being fun and tasting good, dipping gives toddlers a sense of control and independence.

You can also sometimes tempt toddlers to eat simple foods by offering a few condiment options for sprinkling on top. Avoid letting your child shake her own salt and pepper because toddlers don't need extra table salt in their food, and pepper can be spicy and irritating to little mouths and noses. A few things you can offer them instead are grated parmesan or other cheeses, cinnamon, wheat germ, gomasio (a Japanese condiment made from crushed sesame seeds and a little salt—look for it in the macrobiotic or Asian section of your grocer or natural foods store), or other ground nuts and seeds (try sunflower seeds, flaxseeds, and almonds but see nut allergy info on page 95). Buy a couple of colored fine shakers at a kitchen supply store and fill them with different choices that your child can sprinkle on his own.

Fun with food. If the food is fun in some way, your toddler will be more likely to eat it. Have your child help in the food preparations—a toddler who has helped decorate a veggie pizza, for example, will very likely try at least a bite or two.

Make his meal or snack presentation attractive or funny: Arrange cut-up fruit into a little design, or make a face with olive eyes and a red-pepper-slice smile on his open- faced sandwich. You might also try calling the food fun and inventive names, such as "ribbons" for zucchini peels, "trees" for broccoli florets, or "buttons" for carrot coins.

Let him touch and play with his food. If he's allowed to experiment with his hands, he'll be more likely to put it into his mouth, even accidentally!

House picnic. If it seems like you and your child are caught in a rut, try having a floor picnic as a novel way to shift the energy. Have your toddler help you pack a picnic basket with foods he would enjoy eating. Spread a beach towel on the kitchen floor (or on the grass or deck in your yard if the weather is nice), and set up a little picnic area where you can both sit and eat. If your regular meals are on a good, steady routine, this is sure to trigger some toddler hilarity and quite possibly invite some good eating, too.

Texture check. Some children are very sensitive, not just to the flavors but also to the textures of foods. It may be that your toddler is refusing a whole category of foods because he doesn't like how they feel in his mouth. The sinewy texture of meat is one of the things that make many toddlers unwilling to eat it. Try changing the texture of a food he won't eat to see if that makes a difference. For instance, if he doesn't like mashed sweet potato or cauliflower, try baked sweet potato fries and raw cauliflower florets (with dip, of course!). You can also try grinding meats if they won't eat cut pieces, or vice versa. If your child won't do crunchy—still likes things with a somewhat pureed consistency—try giving him one or two choices with the texture he likes, while also offering one crispy choice alongside. If he can dip the crunch into the mash, he might eat it.

Minimize distractions. If your toddler isn't very interested in eating his meal, having the TV on will make it nearly impossible for him to focus on the food. Try to keep meals relaxing, social, and fun, without the added distractions of television, loud music, or even answering the phone. Show him with your actions that mealtimes are a time to enjoy eating, and a respite from other regular activities.

Patience. Remember that one meal or snack does not create his whole nutritional palette. Toddlers get the full spectrum of their nutrition over a series of days. And it can also help to remember that nearly all healthy toddlers do actually eat enough food to meet their caloric needs, despite what it looks like!

Remember, too, to be patient when offering new foods—it can take ten to fifteen tries to get him to try something new. If your toddler has tried something several times and consistently rejected it, it's possible that he simply doesn't like it—especially if he has accepted other new foods. But if your toddler takes small tastes and rejects everything new, continue offering new foods and give him more time to build that bridge of familiarity that will make a food acceptable.

Feeding control. Sometimes all it takes is a little control for a toddler to be more willing to eat. Try offering cut-up pieces of food in small bowls and letting your child pick everything up with his fingers. Or give him his own safe set of toddler eating utensils and let him do most of the spooning, scooping, and spearing (if he can). His resistance to eating may be more about a need to feed himself than about pickiness.

Use the familiar to bridge the unfamiliar. Offer only one new food at a sitting, rather than several new things at once. Give it without fanfare, in conjunction with foods that you know he already likes. Also, if possible, prepare that food in a way that is already familiar to him from something else that he has eaten. For instance, if he likes roasted carrots, try offering him beets or parsnips cut and roasted in the same way. If he likes chicken in his soup, but won't eat it baked,

try putting some turkey or even small cubes of beef into the same soup. This play on familiarity will help him feel secure in opening up to new foods.

Positive peer pressure. One of the single most effective ways to get toddlers to try a new food is to surround them with other toddlers who are all eating it. While your toddler may not have a ready circle of veggie-eating friends, it is definitely possible to use the strategy of **positive peer pressure** on a smaller scale. Talk to other moms in your circle about what their children are eating. Discuss this strategy and see if you can share kids for occasional meal- or snack times. If a friend's toddler likes cucumbers but your own won't eat them, have that child over for a playdate and casually serve cukes and dip to both kids at snack time.

Sweets and treats. We call it the "sweets and treats" trap when your toddler consistently says he's not hungry for dinner, but then begs for dessert. We can actually build that trap ourselves by making dessert or sweets seem overly special or exotic. If you decide to offer your child sweets at all (which is optional—many families opt not to eat or serve sweetened foods at all during the toddler years), make them healthy choices and just offer them as part of his regular dinner. If you want to serve stewed fruits or a zucchini muffin as dessert, simply add it to his dinner plate. He might eat it first and skip his veggies, or even skip everything else. That's fine—there's good nutrition in those offerings! If this is a regular occurrence with his lunch or dinner meal, eventually he will get hungry for the other types of foods as well, and may occasionally leave the treat behind because, for example, he wants the whole serving of fish instead. For this to work well, you need to avoid buying any foods you don't want your toddler to eat. If there are forbidden or junky treats in the house, you can be sure your toddler will zero in on those particular foods.

Eating Out and Traveling

If your toddler's eating is already tricky at home, it's likely that it will be even more challenging in unfamiliar territory. Even consistent eaters will often have some difficulties managing all the excitement and stimulation of eating outside the home.

Do your best to make sure your toddler is well rested before venturing out for an event. A tired toddler is a cranky toddler, and the last thing you want is a meltdown at the restaurant table just as your food is arriving. Following are some tips to help you keep your excursions as smooth as possible.

Restaurants. If you are going to a restaurant, you will want your toddler to be hungry so he'll take an interest in his meal, but not so starved that he's unable to wait for the food. Remember that most toddlers have trouble waiting long for food when they are hungry, and many can't sit still for very long. So when choosing a restaurant for a family meal out, look for places that have quick service, booster seats or high chairs, and a good tolerance for toddler energy levels at the table.

Typical restaurant kid's meals are high in calories, low in nutrition, and bigger than what the average toddler needs. Order something that your child likes, and ask for an extra (smaller) plate. You may want to cut down the portion size and put it on the new plate, then try adding something with a little nutrition, such as some cut-up salad from your meal, or a few bites of your cooked veggies as well. Eating out is already challenging enough, so it's not the best place for negotiating about food. You can always bring a healthy snack that you know he likes and will eat in case he refuses his restaurant meal. And it's a good idea to take along a small toy or quiet activity item, like a coloring book, to help while away the time at the table.

Parties. For a non-restaurant event such as a birthday party or a day at the zoo, it's usually best to feed your child before attending. Birthday parties (including their own!) are notoriously **overstimulating** for toddlers. It can be almost impossible for them to settle down enough to eat. If they do eat, it will probably be cake and ice cream, which will often wind them up even more. Even if it's a pizza party, your toddler will probably enjoy himself much more if he has had something solid to eat before heading out the door—just be sure to include some good protein and healthy fat to help balance out all the sugar from the cake and other party goodies.

Traveling. Long trips in the car or by plane are typically very hard on toddlers. They get bored and worn out with the long confinement. When you are planning a trip, be sure to prepare several appealing, healthy snacks that also make good mini-meals (i.e., contain some proteins, fiber, and fat, not just simple carbs) to keep their energy up. Good traveling snacks include cheese sticks, whole-grain crackers, thermoses of cold water (to refill a sippy cup), mini-yogurts, vegetable sticks, sliced fruits (frozen fresh fruits will last longer—good for an extended car trip, as they need time to thaw), etc.

Because you will likely be eating out frequently while traveling, do your best to choose healthy meals for them out of the available selections. Instead of constant kid's meals, you could mix it up with a salad, soup, or an appetizer with a higher nutrient content. To minimize disruption of your toddler's regular routines, whenever possible, try to keep his eating times on the same schedule as at home.

Special rules for flying. The air in a plane's cabin is very dry and can be dehydrating, so be sure to have plenty of liquids on hand for your toddler. There are very specific rules about which foods and liquids are and are not allowed on planes. Usually you are not allowed to bring bottled water (unless you buy it inside the security checkpoint), or any liquid in a bottle exceeding 3 ounces. But there are exceptions to accommodate babies and toddlers. You may bring formula, breastmilk, or juice through the checkpoint in amounts larger than 3 ounces as long as you keep them

separate from any other liquids or gels in zip-closure bags, and tell both the security and the X-ray officers that you are carrying the items. They will not ask you to taste anything, but they may run a special test to check for the presence of explosives. You may also bring baby food in cans or jars. Sandwiches and other finger foods in baggies or Tupperware are also fine. Check www.tsa.gov for more detailed information.

> **TIP**
>
> Keep supervising your child's tooth brushing to make sure he is doing it correctly. When he can dress himself fully, he is old enough to brush without supervision. Remember to use only a pea-sized amount of toothpaste, especially if you're using a fluoride toothpaste. Any more than that, if swallowed, could result in the development of whitish spots on the teeth called flourosis. The American Academy of Pediatric Dentistry recommends that you replace your child's toothbrush every 3 to 4 months for best brushing and to reduce germ transmission.

Real Food for
Real Kids

3

Homemade Baby Food: Cooking with Confidence, Speed, and Ease

Making the conscious decision to prepare the bulk of your baby's food at home is an important first step away from the S.A.D. With so much fast and processed food available so cheaply, you can pat yourself on the back for choosing home cooking (and vibrant health!) as a better alternative for your child. Time and energy are at a premium for most of us, and much of what you have will be absorbed by the everyday tasks of caring for your baby and toddler in these early years. It's important, therefore, to keep the food preparation as simple and streamlined as possible to make it more manageable.

If you have not done a lot of cooking up until this time, you probably feel a lack of confidence in the kitchen. Don't let that worry you—making baby food is a simple and easy way to improve your skills quickly. You will learn about the properties of some basic grains, vegetables, and fruits, which will make it easier for you to graduate to the more sophisticated meals that you'll be cooking for your older toddler. Your food preparation will parallel the growth and development of your child, beginning gradually with small amounts of simple foods, and progressing slowly to more complex meals, until you are preparing and he is eating the same foods as the rest of your family.

Preparing Your Kitchen

You will have some time after your baby is born to prepare your kitchen for making homemade baby food because her diet for the first months will be exclusively breastmilk or formula. Since you will be very tired during those early months of baby boot camp, however, we recommend getting your kitchen ready before the birth,

Quick Chart

COMMERCIAL BABY FOOD VERSUS HOMEMADE
Look at how the nutrient levels compare:

Nutrient	Commercial Baby Food Peas ($^1/_4$ cup)	Home-Cooked Peas ($^1/_4$ cup)
Calories	26 kcal	34 kcal
Protein	1.56 g	2.14 g
Carbohydrate	4.12 g	6.25 g
Fiber	1.6 g	2.2 g
Calcium	8 mg	11 mg
Iron	0.4 mg	0.62 mg
Magnesium	8 mg	16 mg
Potassium	32 mg	108 mg
Phosphorous	27 mg	47 mg
Zinc	0.2 mg	0.48 mg
Vitamin C	2.4 mg	5.7 mg
Niacin	0.34 mg	0.808 mg
Folate	14 mcg	25 mcg
Vitamin A	122 IU	320 IU
Vitamin K	7.2 mcg	10.4 mcg

Every single nutrient value is higher in the home-cooked column than in the commercially prepared column—in a few cases double or even triple the amount.

No contest: Homemade food provides more nutrients for your baby.

if you can—while you're preparing your baby's room and gathering her layette. There are a few kitchen items that make baby food preparation easier, and if you cook you probably already have some or all of them.

BASIC COOKING EQUIPMENT

You may want to do a quick inventory of your kitchen to see what you already have for cooking equipment. Following is a list of basic tools to outfit a family cook's working kitchen. You don't need to have everything on this list to be able to make baby food, but a well-equipped kitchen will save you a lot of time and effort in the long run.

Good knives. It's worth the money to invest in a good set of kitchen knives. If you are going to be cooking real foods from scratch, you will end up doing a lot of cutting, chopping, and dicing. Sharp, well-made knives make this job much easier. Look for a knife with a handle that's comfortable for you, with a full tang: the steel running all the way up through the handle. Sometimes the steel is riveted in the handle, and sometimes it's fully encased by the handle, but make sure it's there. It's a good idea to have these three basic knives: a short (3- or 4-inch) knife for paring, peeling, and small chopping; a longer (6- or 8-inch) chef's knife for slicing, chopping, and opening up larger fruits and vegetables; and a long serrated knife for cutting delicate, thin-skinned produce such as tomatoes, and slicing breads (without squashing them).

Keep your knives sharp. With all that's going on in your life right now, sharpening your knives may seem like a pretty low priority. But dull knives slow cutting time and make it more difficult. Contrary to what you might think, dull knives also cause more injuries than sharp ones. While it's a good idea to have them professionally sharpened once or twice a year, you can do the maintenance yourself with a sharpening stone or electric sharpener once or twice a week. If they are high-quality sharp knives to start with, it will take you less than a minute with a few strokes on the stone.

Cutting boards. We like bamboo cutting boards best. They are harder than hardwood and won't dull your knife blades; have natural antimicrobial properties; and are inexpensive. In addition, bamboo is a renewable resource. Plastic boards, while easy to throw into your dishwasher to sterilize, dull knife blades over time and groove, creating pockets where bacteria can collect.

You'll need one for cutting produce and one for cutting animal foods—it's safer to work with any meats, fish, or shellfish on a separate surface from your produce or breads, to limit any spread of bacteria. You'll also want a smaller board for cutting pungent foods like garlic, onions, and hot peppers, to keep their lingering odors and oils from getting into your apple pie! Don't get boards that are too small—you want them to have plenty of surface area on which to cut and make stacks of foods.

Wash the surface of your cutting boards with soap and hot water after every use— to avoid cracking do not submerge them. Rinse and dry thoroughly to prevent warping. To improve the longevity of your bamboo or hardwood cutting boards, oil your completely dried boards with a small amount of white mineral oil (USP-grade mineral oil) weekly, which will seal the surface and condition the wood.

Regularly sterilize your wood or plastic cutting boards with undiluted white vinegar in a spray bottle: Spray the surface thoroughly and rinse and dry well once weekly for animal food boards and once or twice monthly for the others.

Measuring cups and spoons. It's helpful to get two sets of measuring cups and spoons, if you can afford to—that way you won't have to wash them in between measuring every ingredient. We like stainless steel better than plastic (see page 84 for a discussion of plastic safety), and it's helpful to have them connected on a ring. If you are purchasing two sets of measuring spoons, choose one with rounded spoon bowls for liquids, and one with elongated spoon bowls for pulling food out of jars or narrow box openings, such as a baking soda box.

You'll need both liquid measuring cups (usually one large glass cup with a spout, measurements marked on the side, and calibrated to just under the lip so you can carry it without spilling its contents), and dry ingredient measuring cups (four separate stainless cups clipped to one ring).

Mixing bowls. Look for a set of three or four nesting bowls in different sizes. Glass is safe, does not stain or transfer odors, and is easy to clean, but it's heavier than stainless steel. Stainless bowls are thinner, lighter, and can be used to melt waxy foods: Just put one on top of a saucepan of boiling water to melt chocolate chips, or even reheat a food cube. They also make very satisfactory drums: You can give your older baby or young toddler a short wooden spoon and let him play with the bowls on the floor.

Basic stove-top pans. We prefer stainless steel for most of our pots and pans. It's great to have one cast-iron skillet for perfect pancakes and adding trace amounts of iron into some of your dishes. Enameled cast iron holds and distributes heat very well, but is also quite heavy. Avoid **Teflon**-coated nonstick pans. They may emit toxic fumes when heated dry or at high temperatures. **Anodized aluminum** is a safer nonstick surface. Although aluminum pans should generally be avoided, anodizing seals the metal completely with an electrochemical

process. Look for pots with solid, heavy bottoms for good heat conduction.

Stainless steel is actually a composite of different metals. To avoid any trace metal leaching into your food, upgrade to new pans if your stainless becomes pitted or heavily dented (a rare occurrence with a well-made pan that is properly used and cleaned).

It's helpful to have at least three skillets or sauté pans and three cooking pots. You'll want a 10- or 12-inch skillet or sauté pan for cooking family-size portions (eggs, seafood, meats, vegetables, etc.); a 6- or 7-inch skillet for smaller portions; and a large sauté pan for cooking down greens (4-, 5-, or 6-quart size—choose a lighter model with a lid and a second handle to make lifting easier).

For pots, you'll need:

- A large soup or stockpot (6 to 12 quarts, depending on the size of your family): great for making soups or stews, boiling pasta, or steaming larger vegetables, such as artichokes or corn on the cob (with a steamer basket).
- A medium saucepan or saucier pan (2 or 3½ quart): great for making sauces, reheating soups, or steaming smaller amounts of vegetables (with a steamer basket).
- A small saucepan (1 quart): for making or reheating small amounts of food or melting butter.

All the pots need lids. Glass lids seem nice because you can see what's cooking inside, but we don't generally recommend them because they steam up (making it harder to see the food) and tend to break eventually if you cook a lot.

Basic baking pans. Foods bake most quickly in dark metal or glass bakeware. Shiny pans don't absorb as much heat, and your foods won't get quite as browned. In general, you want to reduce oven temperature by 25 degrees when baking with dark pans, to avoid burning your foods. It's helpful to have a loaf pan, a pie plate, a 9-by-13-inch baking pan, an 8-inch square baking pan, two 8- or 9-inch cake pans (if you want to make cakes), a 12-muffin tin, and two cookie sheets (so you can load up one pan with cookies while the other is baking).

Steamer. Look for a folding stainless steel steaming basket. This will adjust to fit inside different-sized pans and is very effective for steaming most vegetables. We also recommend purchasing a stacking steamer pan—a real help for reheating: The water boils in the saucepan at the bottom, and the upper-tiered pans have holes in their bottoms, so you can steam or reheat several foods at once.

Reheating fridge foods or cooking frozen foods is a snap in a steamer pan. If you use a very small amount of water in the base pan, it will come to a boil very quickly and heat your food in nearly the same amount of time as the microwave—only it will taste better and retain more of its life energy. Steamers are particularly good for reheating and moistening delicate or sticky foods, such as cooked grains or sauced spaghetti. If you wipe them out (carefully!) while they are still hot, clean up takes less than 30 seconds.

Food processor. A food processor is great for chopping or slicing nuts or lots of veggies fast. It's also a key piece of equipment for making purees. Look for a version that has an inset piece allowing you to puree small batches of foods as well as larger ones, or you can buy a smaller version designed expressly for use in making baby food.

Immersion blender. Also called an immersion wand, it allows you to puree soups or other hot foods right in the cooking pot. Transferring hot soup or vegetables to the blender or food processor for pureeing is hot, messy work—the "soup wand" allows you to skip that step and do everything neatly, quickly, and more safely.

Food mill. The food mill is an inexpensive manual tool that allows you to easily remove the tougher hulls and skins from vegetables (that younger babies can't yet digest) for the silkiest first purees. You can purchase a smaller baby food mill to take on the road with you (or to restaurants) to puree and strain foods on the run.

Peeler and box grater. Two important tools for working with produce are the vegetable and fruit peeler and the four-sided box grater. Look for a peeler with a big, slip-proof grip and sharp peeler blade. A box grater should be sturdy and offer you at least four different options for grating: small openings for fine grating hard spices like nutmeg, zest from citrus peels, or hard cheeses like parmesan; larger openings for grating veggies like carrots and zucchini; even larger openings for grating soft cheeses like mozzarella; plus a slicing option.

Colander and sieve. You'll need a colander for tasks like draining pasta and rinsing canned beans. A sieve (or double-mesh strainer) has a mesh bottom with finer openings than the holes of the colander, allowing you to rinse very fine grains, such as amaranth or quinoa, and strain loose herbal teas or fresh juices. Look for one that has a handle on one side and a hook on the other, for laying on the edge of a pan or bowl.

Salad spinner. A salad spinner is an inexpensive but very handy tool that allows you to quickly spin-dry all types of leafy greens and fresh herbs after washing.

High-powered blender. Purchase the best-quality blender you can afford—look for a model with a strong enough motor to crush ice and finely grind grains and nuts. A good blender can be used for many different tasks: grinding grains and beans (for hot cereals); making nut butters; making smoothies; emulsifying (blending and thickening) dressings or sauces; or pureeing cooked or raw foods. (See Resources for a list of brands we like.)

Rice cooker. Look for a rice cooker that is made to accommodate brown rice and other grains (many of the standard models are made for white rice only and will bubble over when cooking whole grains). Rice cookers allow you to simply make up perfect batches of grain. Just add your presoaked and premeasured rice or rice-and-grain combo and the water to the designated line in the cooker. Push a button and return about an hour later to perfect whole grains.

Some models have a timer and/or automatic warming setting as well, allowing you to put the rice on anytime and have it hot whenever you're ready to eat it.

It's simple to combine grains in your rice cooker for creative combinations. Use a whole-grain rice as your base ingredient, and then replace part of the measured amount with other long-cooking grains, such as wheat berries, pearled barley, or even seeds. If your cooker calls for one full measure of rice, for example, fill it three-quarters full with rice and then top it with a combination of wheat berries and pumpkin seeds. You can also add an additional quarter cup or so of chopped dried fruits, such as apricots, tart cherries, or cranberries—just add another quarter cup of water to the designated line. Always combine grains that require similar amounts of water and cooking time.

Slow cooker. The slow cooker is a nearly indispensable tool for family cooking. It allows you to prepare your evening meal sometime in the early day—before leaving for work or when your child is down for a nap, for example—saving you the time and effort in the late afternoon, when toddlers can be cranky and you may be feeling a little frazzled yourself after a full day spent with him or at work. You can also make great oatmeal for breakfast the night before! (See page 232 for the recipe.)

Slow cookers are also the perfect tool for making baby food puree bases. Simply add tender cuts of meat (chicken, lamb, even pot roast will become quite tender if cooked slowly for several hours) and uniform chunks of medium-hard hardy vegetables or fruits (sweet potatoes, winter squashes, green beans, kale, apples, etc.) to the slow cooker with a small amount of broth or water. Within 6 to 8 hours, you will have plenty of food to feed your family, and a good batch of protein and vegetables to puree and freeze for your baby. (See page 173 for tips on batching, and storing baby food.)

Cool containers. Having a good selection of storage containers makes homemade baby food almost as convenient as store-bought (better nutrition—less hassle!). The best containers for refrigerator storage are made of tempered glass, with glass, plastic, or rubber lids. Look for a brand that is oven/freezer/microwave/dishwasher-safe for the most versatility. (You cannot heat things on the stove top in most glass storage containers and need to exercise caution when pouring boiling water in them—read the warning labels about how to make appropriate temperature changes.)

The best containers for freezing are made of freezer-safe, BPA-free plastic, or tempered glass. (See page 84 for a discussion of plastics versus glass and the dangers of BPA.) They must have good, tight-fitting lids. Not all glass is safe for the freezer—it must be tempered or it could shatter or crack, leaving tiny shards of glass in your food, which is a definite no-no!

Plan to stock your kitchen with the following:

- A selection of 1-, 2-, and 3-cup, and 1-quart oven/freezer/microwave/dishwasher-safe glass storage containers (choose shapes that can be packed and stacked easily into your refrigerator)
- Six or more BPA-free ice cube trays with lids (standard size [1 ounce per cube] ice cube trays with lids to keep the food in, odors and germs out)
- Freezer containers that are freezer-safe, nonporous, airtight when sealed, moisture-resistant, stackable, easy to clean, and not odor absorbent
- BPA-free, freezer-safe, gallon- and quart-size zip closure bags
- Wax paper, microwave-safe plastic wrap, and heavy-duty foil (all three are safe for freezer use)

KITCHEN SAFETY

With a hot stove, knives, and toxic cleaning supplies, your kitchen is a true danger zone for babies and young toddlers. Taking a few simple precautions can make it a great deal safer and allow your child to be able to work and play right alongside you during the day. As soon as your baby is able to creep around, invest in a set of **outlet covers** for the electrical sockets, and **safety latches** for the drawers and cabinets within her reach.

Keep all cleaning products locked safely in a cabinet. Keep all plastic wraps, tinfoil, baggies, etc. in a locked drawer or cabinet also. Some of the boxes have razor-sharp edges, and all food wrap items pose a suffocation risk.

Put up high or in locked cabinets any cooking tools or equipment that is stored low. Do not store knives on a magnet or in a block in an accessible area. Get into the habit of laying sharp cooking implements toward the back of your counters and sinks while you are using them—away from the edge.

Once she can pull herself up, put baby-safe covers over the oven knobs. Make sure not to leave anything on the stove, counters, or tables that is dangling over the edge, like a tablecloth that can be pulled off, or a pot handle that can be grabbed. Whenever possible, use the rear burners on your stove top to keep hot burners and pans well out of reach. Don't carry pots of hot food while your toddler is underfoot; strap her into her high chair or bouncy chair if you need to move hot food. Never let your toddler handle knives, meat forks, or any other sharp kitchen tools. Do not let her near electrical equipment, and do not let her touch or work near a hot oven.

Keep a charged fire extinguisher in a permanent, easily accessible spot in your kitchen at all times. Make sure that it is both out of reach of your toddler and in an area that you can get to quickly—do not bury it in the back of your pantry! Check the gauge on the extinguisher each time you check the batteries in your smoke alarms—it should be in the green zone. If it goes into the red, you must have it recharged or replaced. Call your local fire department for information about where to go to recharge it, if you have a rechargeable model.

It's a nice idea to keep one low cabinet safe and unlocked. You can store metal bowls or plastic Tupperware in there for her to be able to take out and play with. You might also consider keeping one set of her dishes and a cup there so she can retrieve her own place settings at mealtime. Some families store placemats and cloth napkins in an area like that so toddlers can help set the places for other family members as well.

You might also get a sturdy stool and place it in front of the kitchen sink. Fill it halfway with bubbly water and give your child some light, safe dishes to wash (metal bowls, plastic cups, measuring spoons, etc.). If you have any funnels, let her use those to pour the water from one container into another. One caution: Make sure she cannot reach or turn on the hot water faucet. Children can be easily scalded by hot tap water.

ANIMAL FOODS SAFETY

To prevent the ingestion of harmful bacteria that can cause serious illnesses in you or your child, it's very important to follow a few safety guidelines when working with animal foods such as meats, fish, poultry, or eggs.

Take the temperature. The USDA states that the only way to ensure that a meat is cooked enough to kill off all the bacteria that may be present is to take its temperature. Color is not an accurate enough gauge of doneness because it is variable and subjective. Invest in a good instant-read **meat thermometer** that has clearly visible temperature settings, and follow individual directions for use. Test a food's temperature near the end of its cooking time. Always insert the thermometer into the thickest part of the meat. Avoid hitting fat, cartilage, or bone, however, as they can run hotter or cooler than muscle and may give an inaccurate reading. Make sure to wash the thermometer in hot, soapy water both before and after using.

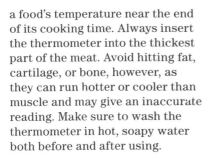

FLASH FACTS

INTERNAL FOOD TEMPERATURES

The following are the USDA recommended minimum internal temperatures that are safe for babies:
Red meat (including ground beef): 160° F
Fish: 160° F
Pork: 160° F
Poultry, white meat: 170° F
Poultry, dark meat: 180° F
Egg dishes: 160° F
Bake all meats at least at 325° F in the oven.

Keep it clean. Make sure to thoroughly wash everything that comes in contact with an animal food product, including your own hands. You should always wash your hands before preparing food. Wash them again in hot, soapy water for at least 20 seconds after working with animal foods and before touching other kitchen tools, surfaces, or foods. Carefully wash all knives, meat forks, cutting boards, serving platters, etc. in hot, soapy water after each use. Wash the counter with hot, soapy water as well, and air-dry it or use a dish towel that has gone through a dryer's hot setting for sterilization. You can actually microwave your wet sponge on high for 2 minutes to kill most foodborne bacteria. Microwave it for 4 minutes to kill everything, but make sure it's soaking wet (and watch it) to avoid any risk of fire! Let it cool before handling it again.

Avoid cross-contamination. Don't set raw animal foods directly on countertops—use platters or plates instead. Do not reuse the same utensils, platters, or counter surfaces you used for raw meat once it's cooked. Use a washed or new knife or fork to test or cut nearly done meat. Use a washed or new platter to serve it. Always use a separate cutting board for animal foods, and follow directions in the cooking equipment section for cleaning and disinfecting.

Defrost frozen animal foods slowly in the refrigerator, never out at room temperature.

Refrigerate or freeze all cooked foods within 2 hours of preparation.

You may refreeze previously frozen raw meat if it has been thawed in the refrigerator and properly handled. You may also cook previously frozen meat, and refreeze the cooked meat. Please note that foods lose moisture when they defrost, so the quality of the food will not be as high after the second freezing.

Signs of Foodborne Illness

Pregnant women, babies, and toddlers are all at an increased risk of developing a **foodborne illness** from bacteria carried on food products. Follow good safety precautions when handling, preparing, and cooking all foods, especially animal foods, and be aware of the typical signs of food-borne illness: upset stomach, nausea, vomiting abdominal cramps, diarrhea, and dehydration. These symptoms range in severity and can even result in death.

Preparing Your Pantry

The key to being able to cook consistently is having a good stock of basic items on hand at all times. In the beginning, you will need to stock only a limited number of pantry and **perishable items** to be able to prepare the simple cereals and purees that will make up your baby's early diet. Over time, as her diet expands, so will the types of foods you need to stock.

REAL BABY FOOD BASICS

For your pantry, you'll want to keep a small collection of fresh whole grains and both dried and canned beans. These foods will form the staples of your baby's early meals. Once you have your basic collection in place, just check it every week or so and replace any items that have gone stale or are getting low. See chapters 9 and 10 for more information about choosing and storing grains and beans.

For the more perishable items, you can shop once or twice a week for the seasonal fruits and vegetables that are safe for him at his age. As your child gets a little older and you begin making baked goods for him, you'll need to keep the baking essentials on hand as well. When he begins eating animal foods, those will need to be purchased once or twice a week, or you can work with frozen meats or fish.

UPGRADING A S.A.D. PANTRY

If you have been eating the Standard American Diet of primarily fast and processed convenience foods, now is a great time to begin improving the quality of the foods you stock at home. By the time your child is eating solid foods, you will not want to have poor-quality junk foods in the house. Remember: The best way to get your baby and toddler to eat healthy foods is to offer him nothing but healthy foods to eat! Also, he will learn many of his eating behaviors by watching what and how you eat, even at a very young age.

Go through your pantry and consider getting rid of the poorest-quality junk foods that offer no nutritional value: candy, soda, and any other processed foods that contain high amounts of sugar, saturated fat, or salt (check the label: a "high amount" is 20 percent or more of your daily calorie requirements for that food value). Also, consider losing or replacing items that list trans fats, hydrogenated, or partially hydrogenated oils, high-fructose corn syrup, or chemical additives or preservatives on their labels or ingredients lists.

You can also begin upgrading the quality of any white foods that you eat regularly. Replace your white pasta with whole-grain pasta, your white bread and rolls with whole-grain varieties, and your white flour with whole-wheat flour.

If it's unrealistic for you to get rid of all the store-bought cookies and chips, then consider replacing them with higher-quality versions. Get cookies made with only real food ingredients, lower in sugar and fat and higher in fiber than their junk-food counterparts. Look for organic snack foods that are baked instead of fried, with no chemical additives or preservatives. Whole-grain chips have more fiber and less fat than corn chips, and sweet potato chips have a few more nutrients than white potato chips—check the labels for comparison. Maybe whole-grain pretzels or organic plain popcorn—both much lower in fat and higher in fiber than all chips—will do the trick. (See Resources for a comprehensive list of natural foods companies that produce all types of higher-quality packaged foods, including snack foods, desserts, ice cream, and frozen meals.) If at all possible, you want to begin retraining your own palate to enjoy the taste of healthier and more natural foods so you can be a great model for your new eater.

In Season

Feeding your child primarily fruits and vegetables at the peak of their growing season is beneficial in many ways. Seasonal foods are at the peak of their freshness: highest in nutrients and vital energy, and richest in taste. They are also the most plentiful, and therefore the least expensive of the available produce. Seasonal foods also help to antidote some common complaints of the season. For instance, fall's root vegetables are warming to little bodies subjected to fall's colder temperatures, while summer's melons help to cool the heat, and spring's early leafy greens help to cleanse the body and flush out some of the mucus accumulated in winter. Eating seasonally will also naturally build variety into your family's diet, increasing the range of nutrients it receives.

See the following list for the peak growing season of some common fruits and vegetables.

Spring produce: Apricots, artichoke, asparagus, avocado, collard greens, fava beans, lettuce, mango, pineapple, spinach, and strawberries

Summer produce: Blackberries, blueberries, beets, baby bok choy, cantaloupe, corn, eggplant, peaches, raspberries, summer squash, peppers, zucchini, tomato, and watermelon

Fall produce: Apples, cauliflower, figs, kale, mushrooms, sweet potato, Swiss chard, winter squash (acorn, butternut, carnival, etc.), pears, and pumpkin

Winter produce: Belgian endive, broccoli, chestnuts, coconuts, leeks, parsnips, radicchio, red currants, rutabagas, and turnips

REAL FOOD SHOPPING GUIDE

Use this basic pantry and perishables outline as a template for creating your weekly shopping list—refer to the age-appropriate charts for the right foods for specific ages (first foods, page 95; 6 to 9 months, page 102; 9 to 12 months, page 115; 12 to 18 months, page 130: 18 months to 3 years, page 141). Notice that the foods are arranged by macronutrient instead of grocery aisles—this is to help you think in terms of creating a balanced daily diet. Always choose the highest quality you can afford: fresh, organic, and unprocessed.

Vegetables and Fruits

Try to make most of your selections from the produce that is in its peak growing season. Choose a selection of five to seven different vegetables and fruits that have a range of color (always try to include at least two dark green and two orange). Look for a variety of different textures as well: light and delicate, heavy and creamy, best raw, best cooked, etc. While fresh is best, make sure you have a good stock of frozen vegetables on hand as well (organic, nothing added).

Vegetables: Asparagus, beets, broccoli, carrots, cauliflower, eggplant, green beans, green peas, kale, onion, parsnips, pumpkin, summer squash, sweet potato, winter squash, zucchini, etc.

Fruits: Apples (dried and fresh), apricots (dried and fresh), avocado, bananas, kiwi fruit, mango, melon, papaya, peaches, pears, plums, prunes, raisins, etc.

Grains

Always have at least three different whole grains, one or two types of pasta, and flour in your pantry. Many whole grains can be purchased inexpensively in bulk, or in smaller amounts in bags. Keep your grains, pasta, and flours in a cool, dry space. For added freshness you can store your grains in the refrigerator or freezer. (See page 173 for more details.)

Amaranth, rice, millet, steel-cut oats, pearled barley, quinoa, cornmeal, whole-grain pasta (different shapes), whole-wheat pastry flour, oat flour, etc.

Proteins

Have four to five protein options available in your larder at all times. Be sure to vary the proteins you offer from meal to meal. It's a good idea to always stock three to five different types of beans, some dried and some canned—dried beans will keep for a year or more if stored in a cool, dry place, and canned beans can last up to 18 months or longer.

Dried and canned beans: lentils, split peas, cannellini, navy, great northern, black, kidney, etc. (If canned, make sure there are no additives—we like Eden Organics best because the beans are cooked with kombu to increase digestibility, and their can liners are BPA-free.)

Eggs (organic, cage-free, omega rich)

Milk (full-fat) and cheese: Swiss, mozzarella sticks, Jack, grated Parmesan, cottage, etc.

Tofu (plain, full-fat, calcium-rich, firm and silken)

Yogurt (plain, full-fat): cow's or goat's milk, Greek, kefir

Red meats: organic calf's liver, 94 percent fat-free ground beef, lean cuts of beef

Poultry: chicken (parts or whole), turkey (parts, whole, or ground), nitrate-free cold cuts–style turkey or chicken breast

Child-safe seafood: farmed bay scallops, farmed blue mussels, northern U.S. and Canadian shrimp, sardines, tilapia, wild Alaskan salmon, chunk light canned tuna

Nuts,* seeds, and butters: almond, sunflower, tahini, walnut, etc.

*Tree nuts and peanuts are very common allergens. It is recommended, therefore, that parents refrain from introducing them into their children's diets until at least their first birthday. Children who are at risk for food allergies should wait even longer. Toddlers under three years old should not be given whole nuts or seeds because they are a choking hazard.

Fats

Choose small bottles of oils in dark-colored glass to keep them from going rancid. Flaxseeds and flaxseed oil should always be stored in the fridge.

Olive oil, grapeseed oil, sunflower oil, coconut oil, butter, ghee, flaxseed oil, pitted olives.

Other

Consider these other items for your pantry.

Condiments: low-sugar and low-sodium ketchup, mustard, pickles, salsa, natural Worcestershire sauce (watch out for high-fructose corn syrup, a common ingredient in many non-organic ketchups, pickles, and sauces)

Broth: free-range chicken broth, vegetable broth, beef broth

Sea vegetables: agar agar, kombu

Sweeteners: agave nectar, blackstrap molasses, date sugar, turbinado sugar, 100 percent maple syrup, rice syrup, honey, apple sauce (nothing added), frozen apple juice concentrate

Vinegars: apple cider, balsamic, red wine, umeboshi plum (Japanese, salty and tangy)

Flavorings and nutrient boosters: wheat germ, nutritional yeast, Bragg Liquid Aminos, sea salt, low-sodium tamari (high-quality, wheat-free soy sauce), mirin (Japanese wine sweetener)

Indispensable Cooking Techniques

Most baby and toddler food can easily be prepared at home using a few basic cooking techniques: sautéing, steaming, blanching, broiling, grilling, baking, roasting, stewing, and puréeing. If you already cook at home, you are probably proficient in most or all of these techniques. If you are a new cook, familiarize yourself with the basic directions outlined in the following sections for preparing different types of foods.

If you tried to make every puree and cereal fresh for your baby at each meal, that would take a lot of time. We have found that the most time-saving and economical way to make your baby food is to prepare larger amounts of the foods in fewer cooking sessions (we call this **batching**), and then store it in the fridge or freezer for several future uses.

WASHING YOUR PRODUCE

It's very important to thoroughly wash all fruit and vegetables before feeding them to your baby or toddler. It is not necessary to wash organic frozen produce, or bagged produce that's been prewashed ("Prewashed" or "Triple Washed" should be clearly written on the packaging), although a rinse just before serving never hurts. Even if the fruit or vegetable has a thick skin, as with oranges or bananas, and you will be peeling it, you should still wash it before peeling. Washing helps remove pesticides and fungicides from conventionally grown produce (although washing can't completely remove them). It also removes microbes, dirt, and other residues accumulated through harvesting and handling, so it's important to wash even fresh organic produce.

Delicate produce, such as leafy greens or fresh herbs, needs to be washed gently. Fill your sink or a large bowl with cold water and submerge the separated greens. Agitate them gently in the water so all the silt and grit falls to the bottom. Finish by spinning them dry in a salad spinner.

Hardier produce, such as root vegetables and cucumbers, should be scrubbed vigorously with a vegetable brush to remove all pockets of dirt and grit.

The Food and Drug Administration advises against using commercial vegetable washes because there hasn't been sufficient research to determine the safety of any residues left on the produce from the wash itself. That said, if all the ingredients in the commercial wash are safe for human consumption, it should be safe to use them on your foods. (See Resources for some "edible" cleansers.)

You can make your own safe produce cleanser very inexpensively by combining equal parts of white vinegar and water. (You can also add 1 tablespoon of baking soda to 1 cup of vinegar and 1 cup of water for a little extra cleaning power.) Make up your mixture and store it in a spray bottle for washing thick-skinned produce: squirt, rub or scrub, then rinse well with cold water. Or you can put equal parts white vinegar and water into your sink or bowl for agitating softer-skinned produce—just be sure to rinse it once more with pure water. The **acetic acid** in the vinegar can help to kill off bacteria; it also helps to dissolve the waxy coating put on some types of conventionally farmed produce for shipping. Adding vinegar to your washing water will also plump slightly wilted greens.

THREE P'S OF SCHEDULING: PLANNING, PURCHASING, PREPARING

With a little organization, you can do the bulk of your homemade baby and toddler food preparation in about an hour per week (plus your shopping time). For the first few weeks you will be cooking more to build your freezer "base," but then you should only have to prepare one to three cereal and puree batches each week to have a varied stock of different options on hand at all times. The key is in Planning, Purchasing, and Preparing.

Planning

Spend a few minutes each week thinking about the types of foods you want to make for your baby or toddler: How old is she now? Which of the foods that she can eat are in season right now? Which new foods would you like to introduce into her diet this week (choose one or two if you are following the 3-to-5-day rule)?

Check your pantry, fridge, and freezer: What staples are running low?

Decide which foods you will batch for your baby this week and build three to four family meals around the same foods.

Make your shopping list based on macronutrients (see page 34).

Purchasing

Plan to shop on a Friday or Saturday so you can do the bulk of your meal preparation on the weekend.

If you have the time, plan an additional, shorter shopping trip midweek to restock any perishables that are running low: vegetables, fruit, milk, meats, etc.

Some grocery stores now offer a relatively inexpensive delivery service. You can make your selections online and have the groceries delivered right to your door, often within a day. You can save favorite items or staple lists so that you don't have to re-create a new list each time. Online grocery shopping can actually save you money by cutting down on impulse buys. Factoring in your saved shopping time and gas money, online grocery shopping and delivery is a convenient and reasonable option for many busy families committed to home cooking. (See Resources for a list of large national grocers that offer this service.)

Preparing

Fresh prep. Set aside an hour or so each weekend to prepare your family's base foods for the week. Coordinate this weekly staples-cooking time to coincide with your shopping day (i.e., shop on Fridays and cook Saturday mornings), and make it a regular habit. Put your grains and beans out to soak the evening before the morning you wish to cook (i.e., Friday evening soak for Saturday morning prep), or put them out the morning before the evening you wish to cook (i.e., Saturday morning soak for Saturday evening prep).

Wash your salad lettuces, hardy crudité vegetables (such as cucumbers, peppers, carrots, etc.), and fruits (except berries) all at once. If it's convenient, do it right after your shopping trip so you put it away clean and ready to eat. Some other delicate fruits and vegetables, such as berries and baby bok choy, will spoil more rapidly if washed early, so wait until just before serving to clean those. (See the individual recipes for cleaning and storage tips about specific produce.)

For your baby (4 to 12 months): In the evening, rinse your grains and beans separately, and place them in separate bowls. Cover them with cold water to an inch above the grains or beans. Put a plate over each bowl and let them soak overnight. You may wish to refrigerate your grains to prevent fermentation. The next morning, grind your grains and beans and prepare the week's hot cereal (¼ cup of dried grain or bean yields about 1 cup cooked cereal).

- 4 to 6 months: 1 cup of soaked brown rice to yield about sixteen ¼-cup servings
- 6 to 9 months: 1 cup of soaked grain (brown rice, millet, pearled barley, or steel-cut oats) and about ½ cup of soaked beans (lentils or split peas) to yield twenty-four ¼-cup servings or twelve ½-cup servings.
- 9 to 12 months: 1½ to 2 cups

of grains (brown rice, milled, pearled barley, steel-cut oats or quinoa) and 1 cup of beans (lentils, split peas, cannellini, navy, great northern, etc.)

Cook and store them according to instructions on page 185 for 3 to 4 days' worth of hot cereal. Double the above amounts for about a full week (you will need to freeze as fresh cereal won't last the entire week).

Choose one to three fruits and vegetables to puree (depending on how many you already have batched and ready), and cook and batch them into freezer cubes. (See batching and freezing directions on page 173.) If you keep a good variety of food cubes on hand, you will need to do this step only every other week or so after the first few weeks.

For your 9-month-old baby to 3-year-old toddler: In the evening, rinse and soak one to three measures of grain (single or mixed) overnight in a covered pot (or the rice cooker, if you have one). Rinse and cook large batch of grain according to instructions on page 230. You can puree these cooked grains for younger babies, or use them over the next couple of days to add to soups, stews, salads, or puddings, or cook them into patties for your toddler or family meals. Cooked grains keep for up to 3 days in the refrigerator. Cooked rice freezes beautifully and lasts for about 3 months (see page 173 for instructions). If you don't freeze any grains, you may want to prepare another batch on Wednesday to get you through the rest of the week.

If you want a fresh pot of beans or bean soup for yourself,

rinse and pick through 2 cups of beans in the evening. Place them in a large pot and cover them with cold water to an inch above the beans. Cover pot and soak overnight. The next morning, drain and rinse the soaked beans. Refill the bean pot with fresh water and cook according to package or recipe directions, or bean chart on page 272. Plain cooked beans will keep for up to 3 days in the fridge.

Mash beans for older babies or add them to soups, stews, salads, or wraps; puree them for dips and spreads; or cook them into patties for your toddler or family meals and snacks.

Cut vegetables to be eaten raw into handy, kid-sized crudités. Put them in accessible containers on a low shelf in your refrigerator that your toddler can reach. Assemble a base salad out of the hardiest salad vegetables: lettuces, carrots, cabbage, radishes, etc. Then you can pull out your base each night and dress it up for that evening's meal with the more perishable additions: cucumbers, tomatoes, mushrooms, avocado, roasted vegetables, cooked grains or proteins (to make a salad meal), etc.

You can also prepare a base meat at this time, such as a simple roasted chicken or poached chicken breasts, if you wish. If you wish to freeze meats for the week(s) ahead, prepare a double batch of your favorite marinades (see recipes for some good ideas), pour over meat or fish, and store in gallon-sized zip closure freezer bags (squeezing all the air out) for up to 3 months (depending on the meat). To prepare, simply thaw overnight in the fridge and grill or bake (and puree or dice) as indicated for dinner for the whole family.

Time savers. Although it costs more, you can save preparation time by purchasing a free-range organic chicken, cooked rotisserie-style from your market. You can also buy prewashed and precut fresh vegetables, everything from triple-washed spinach and julienned carrots to peeled and cubed butternut squash. You can even find high-quality, premixed salads in a bag.

Buy fresh or frozen vegetables. Make sure they are high quality, free of all additives, and raw or blanched. These vegetables are generally frozen shortly after harvest, so they retain high levels of nutrients. They are also prewashed and often precut, which can save you a lot of time.

Buy plain, frozen brown rice. It reheats in minutes for immediate use. You can skip cooking your beans and simply use high-quality canned beans in all the same ways.

Spending about an hour each weekend preparing these base foods will allow you to assemble meals for your child (and the rest of your family!) throughout the week in minutes. Make or warm a cereal, thaw a couple of veggie or fruit cubes, and add a protein: the healthiest "fast food" meal ever!

SAUTÉING

Sautéing is a great technique for quickly cooking a wide assortment of faster-cooking vegetables: carrots (shredded or matchstick), leafy greens (blanch kale for a couple of minutes first to break down tougher fibers), summer squashes, mushrooms, peppers, or tomatoes.

Heat a small amount of water, broth, or a healthy oil in a sauté pan over low to medium heat.

Raise the heat to medium-high and add your vegetables to the pan. If you're using onions (appropriate for older babies, 9 to 12 months), add them first and cook for about 4 minutes until they are translucent. Then add any other vegetables you wish to sauté and cook them to desired softness, turning them over occasionally to prevent sticking and to cook evenly.

Appropriate sautéed vegetables may then be pureed with a little liquid, as necessary, to desired consistency for your baby.

STEAMING

Steaming is an easy, healthy way to cook almost any vegetable while retaining nearly all of the nutrients. Harder or tougher veggies, such as artichokes or sweet potatoes, require more cooking time; while very delicate vegetables, such as baby spinach or bok choy, require only a couple of minutes.

You can steam foods using a steamer pot—some of them come with multiple tiers for steaming several foods at once. You can also steam vegetables in any regular pot using a collapsible steamer basket, because it automatically adjusts to the pot's width when you drop it in. Add water to just below the level of the steamer basket, and bring water to a boil over high heat. Cut your vegetables into uniform pieces for even cooking—smaller pieces will steam faster, while larger ones will take longer. (Frozen vegetables are already precut into uniform pieces.) When the water is boiling, carefully (steam is hotter than boiling water) place your veggies into the basket, and cover.

If you are steaming vegetables for baby food, you want them cooked very soft so they will puree easily. For most softer veggies that will mean between 6 to 12 minutes; while harder veggies, such as carrot chunks, could take 15 minutes or more.

For a young toddler, you'll want the vegetables soft enough to come apart easily in his mouth (remember they don't have all their grinding teeth yet), but firm enough that they still retain some texture. An older toddler can handle a bit more firmness. Shorter cooking times generally mean higher nutrient contents, so steam soft veggies just until their color becomes very bright and they are soft enough to pierce easily.

Full-grown artichokes (which are not appropriate for babies, but lots of fun for older toddlers), require the longest cooking time of the vegetables: 45 minutes to an hour, depending on their size. With extended steaming times, you will need to check on the water levels at least once to make sure your pan isn't going dry.

BLANCHING

Blanching is a good technique for making raw vegetables, such as crudités, more digestible for little tummies. Drop precut and washed vegetables carefully into a pot of boiling water and cook for 2 to 3 minutes. Remove the food carefully from the pot and plunge into a bowl of cold water or ice to stop the cooking process. Blanching has the added benefits of killing off any bacteria and also making produce colors more vibrant. It will not usually make the vegetables soft enough to puree, however.

MICROWAVING

Many young parents consider the microwave an indispensable cooking tool; however, microwaving decreases the vital energy of foods and may decrease their nutrient value as well. We prefer stove-top cooking, and even stove-top reheating in a saucepan or steamer, for babies and toddlers. Steaming foods is easy and surprisingly quick. If you are going to use a microwave, be sure to cook vegetables in smaller, rather than larger, amounts of water to retain the most nutrients possible. Never heat any foods, frozen or otherwise, wrapped or contained in plastic. Harmful chemicals can leach from the plastic into your baby's foods. Always remove food from plastic containers before heating and place in a microwave-safe glass dish.

If you think microwaves don't affect the quality of foods, try this little experiment: Heat a frozen meal in your microwave and cook an identical meal according to oven directions. Compare their

flavor and visual appeal. If you can, eat one of each type and notice if you feel any different afterward. Many people find that they feel less energized when they eat a lot of microwaved food on a daily basis.

BROILING AND GRILLING

Broiling is a method of cooking in the oven with heat from above. Grilling is a similar technique of cooking on a grill but the heat comes from below. Broiling and grilling are good techniques for many different types of meat and fish. They also work well for many vegetables and some fruits, such as pineapple rings. Meat cuts should be relatively tender and less than 2 inches thick. Vegetables should be cut into long slices or chunked, and put on skewers to prevent falling through the cracks of the grill.

To broil, preheat your oven (there is usually a setting for broil) and adjust the rack to about 6 inches below the heating element in the top of your oven. To grill, preheat your charcoal or gas grill to desired temperature. Cook the meat or produce, turning it once during cooking for even browning.

BAKING AND ROASTING

Baking or roasting is a technique for cooking foods uncovered in the oven. Baking is great for things like quick breads, cookies, chicken, and fish. Roasting is a good method for cooking raw nuts, root vegetables, green vegetables, red meats, chicken, and fish. You can bake or roast on a baking pan, sheet pan, or in a loaf or cake pan.

Preheat your oven to the desired temperature. Cook the food for the length of time indicated by the recipe. Roasted meats will continue to cook for about 10 minutes after being removed from the oven.

Soft roasted meats (chicken, lamb, etc.) and vegetables (winter squash, sweet potatoes, etc.) can easily be made into tasty purees by adding a little liquid and processing to desired consistency.

STEWING

Stewing is a method of slow cooking small pieces of meats, vegetables, or fruits (often together) in a liquid. It works especially well for harder vegetables and tougher cuts of meat, but tender vegetables, such as tomatoes, and tender meats, such as fish, can also be stewed. You can stew in a large covered sauté pan, soup pot, or Dutch oven.

Although not required, you can sauté the meat in a small amount of oil over medium heat to brown it on all sides before adding other ingredients. Once browned, add any fruits and vegetables and cover with the liquid (no-sodium chicken, beef, or vegetable broth works best), bringing it to a simmer. Reduce the heat to medium-low and cook the stew according to recipe directions until all ingredients are tender.

PUREEING

To puree a food is simply to blend it well, adding a little liquid if necessary, until it achieves a smooth consistency. There are different methods for making purees, and some foods lend themselves better to one than to another. Purees will make up the bulk of your baby's meals throughout his first 9 or 10 months, until he is old enough to handle and chew foods with more texture.

Grinding

Grains and beans have long cooking times. For faster whole-grain preparations for your child, you can soak and grind dried whole grains and beans into a pasty liquid, and cook them into hot cereal puree in about 5 minutes on the stove top.

Pureeing Precooked Foods

To puree precooked foods, you will blend or process them with a small amount of liquid (cooking water, broth, breastmilk, juice, etc.) until they reach the desired consistency.

Use a blender or food processor to puree cooked grains, meats, and most vegetables. Use a mixer for creamier, softer vegetables, such as cauliflower, sweet potatoes, squash, etc. Use an immersion blender to puree very wet combinations, such as applesauce, stewed peaches or pears, or soups. Use a food mill to remove any unwanted peels or seeds (such as pea or peach skins) for the silkiest first purees.

Make sure to clean all grinding and blending equipment thoroughly after use. Most food processing tools come apart, and the non-mechanical pieces can be cleaned and sanitized in the dishwasher.

BATCHING: COOK ONCE, EAT THRICE

Doubling, tripling, and even quadrupling the puree recipes in this book will provide you with enough to serve at your baby's next meal and batch for later, too. You can store batched food in one unit in the fridge to save space—dishing out individual portions to reheat as you need them. Or you can separate cooked foods into individual portions in the fridge or freezer for easy access. You can use sterilized baby food jars or the smallest glass storage containers to make individual portions for the fridge, or you can freeze the food into cubes in a covered sterile ice tray for individual 1-ounce servings. It's great to have four or five different fruit and veggie "cube" options in your freezer from which to easily build your baby's meals.

Whenever you cook a dish that will keep well in the refrigerator or freezer, consider doubling the recipe to have portions available for a later time when you may not have the time to prepare a meal from scratch. If you make extra-large amounts of simple foods, such as plain quinoa, brown rice, or beans, you can use those in several ways. Use the grain as a hot dish with a meal, then warm

and sweeten leftovers with fruit for breakfast cereal, add a cup to any soup (from scratch or canned), toss some in with a salad, and then use the last bit to make a creamy pudding for dessert. Most cooked grains retain their life energy for only a few days, so plan to use them up quickly. Fresh cooked beans, however, will retain their freshness for longer. Use them in soups and salads, too, and also try mashing them with herbs and spices to form bean cakes or patties that you can serve alone or on a bun.

FLASH FACT

Bacteria and mold proliferate at room temperature or warmer. Boiling temperatures will kill microbes, but refrigerator temps will only slow their growth. Freezing at 0° F will halt their growth as long as it stays at that temp or colder. Once warm, growth continues, speeding up at room temperature or slightly warmer.

FLAWLESS FREEZING

Cooked foods are perishable and must be refrigerated or frozen within 2 hours (and preferably immediately) after their cooking time. To freeze food safely and effectively, make sure you use freezer-safe containers that are thoroughly clean—preferably sterilized in the hot cycle in the dishwasher.

Do not freeze washed baby food jars or any other glass container that is not made specifically for freezer use, as they can crack. Avoid freezing in porous containers, such as milk cartons or yogurt containers, since they do not provide an air-tight seal.

Clean out your freezer. If you're like many people, you probably have a stock of "antique" freezer food. Go through every item in there and ruthlessly dump everything that is past its expiration date, irreparably freezer burned (such as that ice cream in the half-gallon tub with an inch of ice fur on top), unidentifiable, or not a high-quality food. You may even wish to defrost your freezer if it is coated in a thick layer of ice. Clean the surfaces well and put back in only the foods you know will get eaten. Having a well-organized freezer with available space is vital for storing home-cooked baby and toddler foods.

One of the secrets to fresh-tasting freezer food is making sure any food you freeze is cooled at least to room temperature before freezing. While it is possible to skip this step, cooling in the refrigerator first (for an hour to overnight) will help prevent the formation of that unappealing layer of ice on some frozen foods. Simply wipe away any condensation present after refrigeration, reseal (removing all air possible), and place in the freezer.

One exception to this is cooked pancakes or French toast, because they can get rubbery. To avoid this, stack cooled pancakes or French toast slices between sheets of freezer paper or freezer cellophane.

Place the stacks into a freezer bag, press all the air out of the bag, seal, and put the bag directly into the freezer, without chilling first in the fridge.

Freezer burn is caused by exposure to air at freezing temperatures. It leaves dark, leathery spots on frozen foods. Although not harmful, they are ugly and have an unpleasant texture and taste. If your food has a small spot of freezer burn, just cut it off and use the rest. If the food is covered in freezer burn, you're better off just throwing it out.

To avoid freezer burn and ice layers, remove as much air as possible from your container before freezing. If freezing in freezer baggies, seal the bag nearly closed and press or roll as much air out as you can before closing completely. If working with a large container, as for lasagna or soup, for example, you may also lay a sheet of heavy-duty microwave-safe plastic wrap directly on the surface of the cooled food. Then seal the lid as usual over the plastic. Remove the plastic wrap before reheating.

If you are freezing liquids or wet foods (such as stew) in larger amounts, remember that they will expand a great deal when frozen. Be sure to leave about 1 inch of space in all containers (especially glass), to allow for expansion.

If you prefer to freeze your food in a wrap versus a rigid container, use freezer-grade aluminum foil, freezer paper, freezer cellophane, or freezer bags. Don't use regular plastic wrap, tinfoil, or wax paper—they won't stand up well to the freezing temperatures.

Butcher paper is porous: Repackage any meats wrapped in regular butcher paper in freezer-safe materials before freezing.

Do not stack containers to be frozen; instead place them on different shelves to speed individual freezing times. Once the food is in the freezer, you want it to freeze as rapidly as possible to avoid ice crystal formation. Use the quick-freeze shelf, if your freezer has one.

Although it's possible to freeze almost any food, some foods are not appealing after thawing. The following cooked foods do not typically freeze well, because they do not thaw well:

- Cooked egg whites become rubbery
- Gelatin or jam liquefies
- Fried or greasy foods become very wilted and oily
- Pasta without sauce becomes too soft, loses its texture
- Sauces made with mayonnaise, sour cream, or other cream bases separate
- Baked goods made with cream fillings or egg-based icings separate or become runny
- Cooked white potatoes in soups or stews darken and become tougher
- Raw salad greens and salad vegetables (lettuce, tomatoes, cucumbers, etc.) darken and wilt

TIP

Supervised, your teething baby might enjoy the coldness of a frozen mango pit.

TIP

Freeze your baby food purees without breastmilk or formula. Never refreeze breastmilk or formula. Batch your purees with only water, broth, or juice to freeze, and then thin them with breastmilk or formula, if desired, when reheating for immediate use.

TIP

Freeze foods immediately after cooking and cooling. Frozen 3-day-old leftovers do not make great baby meals.

Individual Servings (Food Cubes)

To freeze purees, batched meals, and prepared (soaked and ground) or cooked grains or beans in individual baby or toddler serving sizes, portion them out into ice cube trays. Each cube cup is about 1 ounce; two cubes make about ¼ cup. One ice cube tray holds about 1½ to 2 cups, depending on the number of cube cups—typically twelve on a baby food cube tray and fifteen or sixteen on a standard ice tray. Or you could use small, stackable freezer-safe glass containers. Individual measures of thick foods (like cookie dough) could be frozen in a larger freezer-safe glass container, or on freezer paper on a cookie sheet. Seal each container with its lid, or use freezer paper that is rubber-banded or freezer-taped into place. Be sure to leave at least ½ inch of space between the food and the lid (1 inch for liquids) for food expansion when freezing.

Once the individual servings are frozen solid (usually in 2 to 4 hours or overnight), you can remove them and place them in sealed, freezer-safe bags. Press as much air as possible out of the bag when sealing, to help prevent freezer burn. If the frozen food portions don't easily slip out of their containers, simply let them rest on the counter at room temperature for about 3 minutes—the very slight melting should make it easier. Write directly on the freezer bag or use masking tape to make a label to record the type of food, its initial freezing date, and the expiration date.

Although most food cubes will safely last from 1 to 3 months (depending on whether they contain beans, grains, meat, or produce), their quality will deteriorate over time. For the best-tasting, freshest meals for your baby, try to use your cubes within 4 to 6 weeks.

Thawing or defrosting. Never defrost frozen foods on the counter or outside—your food could become contaminated with mold or bacteria. The only safe ways to defrost foods are in the refrigerator (best method), tightly sealed and submerged in cold water (like in your sink), or in the microwave (which can defrost unevenly and compromise the food's appeal). Heat can cause the leaching of

chemicals from plastic into food, so never use the microwave to defrost foods wrapped or contained in plastic. (See page 84 for a further discussion of plastic safety.)

Reheating. To prevent the spread of bacteria, it is best to reheat frozen baby food directly, without waiting for it to defrost first. This is quite easy with small, individual portions, such as food cubes. Remember, reheated (or any) baby food should only be warm, never hot. Babies' mouths are more sensitive than ours and could easily be burned by improperly heated foods. For that reason, we do not advocate heating baby food in the microwave—it heats very inconsistently and can leave the food with both frozen pockets and burning pockets.

Consider the following methods for warming various kinds of foods:

- Use a stainless steel bowl over a small saucepan of hot water to warm food cubes.
- Use the toaster oven to warm or reheat frozen meats, baked or roasted veggies, dry casseroles, pancakes, or other bread products.
- Use the steamer to warm or reheat sticky foods such as pasta, casseroles, or grains.
- Use a pot to warm or reheat wet foods such as soups or stews, or to reheat grains with some added water.

Quick Chart

FOOD CUBE STORAGE GUIDELINES

Label your homemade frozen baby foods with their content and freezing and expiration dates to keep track of how long they have been in the freezer.

Cooked grains: 2 to 3 days in the refrigerator or 1 month in the freezer

Cooked vegetable or fruit purees: 1 to 3 days in the refrigerator or 2 months in the freezer

Cooked poultry: 1 to 3 days in the refrigerator or 3 months in the freezer

Cooked red meats: 1 to 3 days in the refrigerator or 2 to 3 months in the freezer

Casseroles, soups, and stews: 1 to 3 days in the refrigerator or 2 to 3 months in the freezer

Real Baby Food Guide

Homemade Baby Food

The bulk of what your baby will be eating from 6 to 9 months is a variety of foods in puree form. Although grains, produce, and meats require different techniques, all forms of purees are quite easy to make, even for the avowed non-cook. Remember that purees for the newest eaters should have silky, runny textures. Within a month after she starts eating purees, they can get a little thicker. By the time she is 9 months old, her purees should have more body to their textures, some containing very small, soft chunks that she can pick up with two fingers. Sometime between 9 and 12 months, her foods can be chopped into soft little pieces rather than pureed.

To save time, be sure to consult the Three P's of Scheduling (Planning, Purchasing, Preparing) on page 167 for tips on how to organize your puree preparation by the week instead of by the meal. With a little organization and a few weeks' time, you can have a freezer stocked with enough purees that will make daily homemade food preparation for your baby a snap.

> **TIP**
>
> To prevent food contamination, be sure to wash your hands, all working surfaces, and all tools and utensils with hot soapy water before beginning. Air drying is the most sanitary drying method, or you can use clean dish towels that have been through the hot cycle in the dryer.

PUREEING GRAINS AND BEANS

Cooked Grains and Beans

The simplest technique for making baby grain purees or cereals is to precook the grains or beans and then puree them with a little liquid. (See the charts on pages 230 and 272 for cooking instructions for a variety of different grains and beans.) You may also use rinsed and drained canned beans. (See food charts for ages 6 to 9 months and 9 to 12 months on pages 102 and 115 for best bean and grain choices for baby purees.)

> **TIP**
>
> Grains and beans (dried or cooked) grind and blend best in smaller batches.

To puree cooked grain or beans, blend or process one measure of it with an equal measure of liquid. For instance, combine ¼ cup of cooked brown rice with ¼ cup of breastmilk. Or you could use larger quantities to batch and freeze: 1½ cups of cooked lentils with 1½ cups of water (don't use breast milk for freezing). Puree to desired consistency in a blender or food processor. It's a good idea to begin with smaller amounts of liquid because you can always add more, but you can't take it away once it's been added.

Remember that you should not add any additional salt or sweeteners to baby purees. You should also avoid adding any additional fats from cooked meats, such as gravy, fat drippings, or oily sauces. Although they may taste bland to you, your baby will enjoy the flavors of foods prepared very simply, with no additives. You are also training his palate to enjoy healthy foods in their most natural

forms. As your baby grows, you may wish to begin adding some natural herbs and spices to the purees to continue to develop his palate. Start with combinations that are culturally familiar to your family. Never add honey or agave nectar to food for babies less than 1 year old because they may cause infant botulism. You may wish to add an iron supplement to your cereal or bean purees. (See page 32 for more info on iron supplementation.)

Presoaked Dried Grains and Beans

If you don't wish to precook a batch of grains and beans, you can grind the dried versions and make baby cereal in less than 10 minutes on the stove top. For a higher quality cereal, presoak your dried grains and beans before grinding and cooking them.

Soaking grains and beans thoroughly cleans them; makes them more digestible (a must with beans, especially for babies) by breaking down the complex sugars; decreases phytic acid content, assuring that more of the food's nutrients will be absorbed; and decreases cooking time.

Measure out your grains and beans according to how much cereal you want to make at once. As a general guideline, ¼ cup of dried grains or beans (which will measure approximately ⅓ to ½ cup after it has been soaked overnight) requires about 1 cup of cooking water and will yield around 1 cup of cooked cereal (about four ¼-cup infant portions or two ½-cup baby portions). These measurements are only approximations, as different size grains and beans will require differing amounts of liquid at different ages (your 6-month-old needs a runnier cereal, for instance, while your 10-month-old will be looking for a chunkier cereal).

Rinse your grains and beans well and put them in a bowl on your countertop, covering fully with water to an inch above their tops. Cover the bowls with plates or pan lids and let sit overnight. You may wish to refrigerate your soaking grains to prevent fermentation, but for beans no refrigeration is necessary.

In the morning, drain them well and rinse. Place the grains in a blender and add 1 cup of water for every ¼ cup of dried grain used (remember, your grains will have absorbed water overnight and will now measure more than ¼ cup). Blend at high speed for about 30 seconds to 1 minute, or until the grain has almost dissolved into the liquid.

If making a separate bean mixture, fill the blender half full with water and blend on high to rinse the blades. Pour the water out and place the beans in the blender with 1 cup of water for every ¼ cup of dried beans (dried beans will double or triple in size when soaked) and blend for 30 seconds to 1 minute until the beans have almost dissolved.

If you're making a combination cereal, there's no need to rinse the blender between blending the grains and beans, and you can pour the bean mixture into the same food cubes or saucepan as the grains. A good combination for

9-month-olds and older toddlers is ½ cup dried grain and ¼ cup dried beans. Use 1 cup of water to blend the grain, 1 cup of water to blend the beans, and then pour 1 cup of water into the blender, swish it around, and pour it into the cooking pan or mixing bowl (if using food cube method) to catch any material stuck to the sides.

At this point you may choose to freeze individual portions to cook fresh at mealtimes, or cook them first and then use, refrigerate, or freeze fully prepared grains or beans. The advantage to freezing the uncooked prepared beans or grains is that you can freeze them immediately (no cooling time after cooking), and then cook them "fresh" each time for use. If you precook them at this stage, you will be thawing and warming for use, which is quicker at mealtime, but not as fresh in taste or appearance.

To cook prepared, fresh grains or beans, place your mixture into a saucepan at least twice the size of the liquid. Bring the mixture to a quick boil over medium-high heat. Begin stirring with a whisk to keep the mixture smooth as it nears boiling.

Once the mixture reaches a boil, switch the pan to a second burner and set it to low.

Cook the mixture on low for about 5 minutes, stirring frequently to prevent lumps and sticking. Add more water, a few tablespoons at a time, if the mixture looks too thick.

Allow the mixture to cool for at least 15 minutes before batching for the fridge (will keep for up to 3 days) or for the freezer (will keep for up to 2 months—longer, and the flavor and texture will deteriorate). If you are batching in quantities, be sure to leave at least ½ inch of space at the top of your container for expansion. No need to do this if you're using the food cube method.

Wait until the mixture has cooled almost to room temperature before serving it to your child. Add additional breastmilk or an ice cube to thin further and speed the cooling time, if desired. Placing an individual portion in a bowl in the fridge or freezer will speed the cooling as well.

To freeze uncooked, prepared grains or beans, simply portion out using the food cube method. Two cubes makes ¼ cup.

To cook frozen cubes, place your cubes into a saucepan at least twice the size of the liquid. Add an equal amount of water: For every two food cubes (¼ cup) you will add ¼ cup of water. For a thicker cereal, add less water. Melt the cubes over medium heat. Begin stirring with a whisk to keep mixture smooth as it nears boiling.

Once the mixture thickens and nears a boil, switch the pan to a second burner and set it to low.

Cook the mixture on low for 3 to 5 minutes to the desired consistency, stirring frequently to prevent lumps and sticking. Add more water, a tablespoon at a time, if the mixture looks too thick.

Allow the mixture to cool for at least 15 minutes before batching for the fridge (will keep for up to 3 days). Do not re-freeze the cooked cereal.

Wait until the mixture has cooled almost to room temperature before serving to your child. Add additional breastmilk or an ice cube to thin it further and speed

the cooling time, if desired. Placing an individual portion in a bowl in the fridge or freezer will speed the cooling as well.

Unsoaked Dried Grains and Beans

If you run out of premade grain and you didn't soak any grains or beans the previous night, you can still make a quick baby cereal by grinding dry, unsoaked grains or beans, a technique described and popularized by Ruth Yaron in her excellent book *Super Baby Food*. (Use our presoaked version as your primary cereal, though, because it will be easier to digest and make the nutrients more accessible.) This unsoaked dry grind method is particularly useful for traveling—you can take your preground cereal with you and make a fresh meal once you have arrived at your destination.

Using a high-powered blender, add a measure of dry grain or beans, and blend them at high speed until a fine-sand texture (for babies and toddlers older than 9 months) or a fine powder (for babies up to 9 months) is formed. With the strongest blenders (Vita-Mix, etc.), it takes about 45 seconds for the fine-sand consistency, and 1 minute to achieve the powder consistency. For less powerful blenders, it can take about 2 minutes for the fine-sand consistency, and 2 to 3 minutes to get the powder consistency. Experiment with your machine to find out how long it takes.

With the strongest blenders you can easily grind ½ to ¾ cup of grains or beans at once. You may have to work with smaller amounts at a time with less high-powered blenders. Stop halfway through the grinding to scrape down the corners and bottom of the blender for a consistent texture, if necessary.

> **TIP**
>
> Smaller grains (quinoa, millet, short grain rice) or beans (black, adzuki) tend to need more cooking liquid than larger ones, up to $\frac{1}{2}$ cup of extra water per $\frac{1}{4}$ cup of unsoaked small grain or bean.

Once you've ground the grains and beans, you can make a baby cereal puree by combining ¼ cup of grain or bean powder (or a combination) with 1 cup of water. Using a fork or a whisk, blend them together briskly in a medium saucepan and bring the mixture to a boil over high heat, stirring occasionally to prevent lumps. Once the mixture is boiling, switch the pan to another burner, partially cover it, and continue to cook it over low-medium heat for 8 to 10 minutes until a creamy consistency is achieved. You will need to whisk the mixture several times to prevent sticking or lumps. Add more water, ¼ cup at a time, if the mixture looks too thick. Remove the pan from the heat and let it cool almost to room temperature before serving to your baby. Set aside a portion for that meal, and batch the remainder for up to 3 days in the fridge or 1 month in the freezer.

PUREEING PRODUCE

Carefully clean all fresh produce with cold water before preparing (see page 166 for tips). Peel tough skins or indigestible peels, and remove any pits or seeds. Some fruits and vegetables are easier to peel and pit after cooking, others before cooking.

You may also puree frozen or canned produce, but canned produce is lower in nutrients. If you are using frozen or canned fruits or vegetables, look for plain, organic versions with no additives or salt. All hard frozen and fresh fruits and vegetables must be cooked to softness before pureeing; canned vegetables are precooked, so they can be pureed directly.

You can bake, steam, or sauté produce until it is very tender and can be mashed easily. More nutrients and vital energy are lost in boiling or microwaving, but they are acceptable cooking methods. Use as little water as possible with these methods to minimize nutrient loss.

Once the fruits or vegetables are cooked, you can puree them with a small amount of liquid (cooking water, breastmilk, or formula are best for young babies) to desired consistency. For fibrous or seedy fruits or vegetables, use a food mill to puree—it will strain out the tougher parts.

It is acceptable to peel and mash or puree uncooked fruits (such as avocado, banana, and melon) in the same way if they are very soft (and age appropriate).

> **TIP**
>
> Fruits and vegetables puree best in the blender in larger batches.

PUREEING MEATS

All meats and fish need to be cooked to a certain preset temperature before being pureed into baby food. (See page 161 for the safe-temperature chart and directions for using a meat thermometer.) You should remove the skins and cut away all visible fats from raw meats before cooking. Also remove any bones, cartilage, or tough gristle. A pair of heavy tweezers makes a great tool for removing fish bones.

Cook the meat to its safe temperature without adding fats, salts, rubs, or other tenderizers. The most tender-cooked meats are the easiest to puree: poultry, lamb, and fish puree better than red meats or pork.

> **TIP**
>
> Cooked meats puree best in a blender in smaller batches. Warm cooked meat purees more easily than cold cooked meat, so puree right after cooking and before storing in the fridge or freezer.

Slice, shred, or chop the cooked meat into bite-sized pieces and puree in the blender with a small amount of water or no-sodium cooking broth (chicken or vegetable work well) to the desired consistency.

Recipes for 6 to 9 Months

Remember to use the guidelines on page 93 for introducing first foods for at least 2 weeks before introducing your baby to more complex and varied foods. Once he is 6 months old and eating the first foods regularly, you may begin to incorporate some of the recipes from this chapter. Make sure you introduce each new food following the allergy caution guidelines on page 95.

PREPARED ORGANIC BABY FOOD

While making the bulk of your baby's food fresh is the healthiest and least expensive way to go, it isn't always possible. For the times when you need something ready-to-feed, choose a product you can trust for safety and high levels of nutrition. Frozen food contains more nutrients than jarred food, so go for the freezer aisle if possible. Choose certified organic products to ensure that they are free of any herbicides, pesticides, growth hormones, or other undesirable additives from industrial farming.

Try these choices for high-quality baby food options:

Frozen Food Cubes
- Tastybaby Frozen Organic Foods (3 different stages: single purees, more complex flavors, and chunkier with protein)
- Plum Organics Frozen Baby Food (first and second foods)
- Happy Baby (first and second foods)
- Jack's Harvest (first and second foods)
- Bella Baby (sold in 1.5-ounce packets)

Prepared Jars and Cereals
- Earth's Best Baby Foods (first, second, and third foods, whole-grain cereals and teething biscuits)
- Plum Organics (for 6, 9, and 12 months and up)
- Gerber Organics (first, second, and third foods, whole-grain cereals and premade whole-grain pasta/protein meals)

(See Resources for a more complete list and where to buy them.)

SIMPLE CEREALS

Staple Brown Rice Cereal, Quick-Prep Method

Makes 3 infant servings (¼ cup)

While portion sizes will necessarily be very individual, standard serving sizes for infants, babies, toddlers, and adults will appear in parentheses throughout the recipe sections.

Age: Appropriate for age 4 months and up.

Tips: Brown rice is an excellent source of manganese and a good source of vitamin B, selenium, and magnesium. It is helpful for nausea and diarrhea and is also protective against childhood asthma. Unrefined brown rice has a rice bran coating, making it higher in fiber than refined white rice. The long-cooking method recipe can also be used for toddlers or family meals: Use no-sodium chicken broth to replace the water for a slightly higher protein and mineral content. The AAP recommends adding an iron supplement to baby's first cereal.

See page 33 for more information about iron supplementation.

The simplest, most digestible first cereal to offer your new eater is an organic, iron-fortified, whole-grain rice cereal made especially for young babies. If you are supplementing your child's iron, you can easily make your own simple brown rice cereal. Brown basmati is a fragrant and nutritious choice.

There are three primary methods for preparing rice (and all grain) cereals for your baby. The quick-prep method (most recommended) is quick-cooking, but requires presoaking. The long-cook method is to cook rice as usual and prepare cereal with cooked rice. The dry-grind method is the quickest of the three, but we do not recommend it as a primary method, because unsoaked and lightly cooked whole grains are harder to digest and have higher concentrations of phytates, which inhibit nutrient absorption. (See page 47 for more information on phytates.) Rice cereal is such an early dietary staple that we recommend using primarily presoaked rice with quick or long-cooking methods.

Season: Available year-round

Selection: If buying brown rice in a package, check the date because the natural oils in rice can spoil quickly. If buying in bulk, make sure the grains are dry and the bins are covered.

Storage: Refrigerate in a sealed container or package in a cool dry area for up to 6 months.

¼ cup rice*
1 cup water

Soak rice overnight to speed cooking time and increase digestibility.

Discard soaking water, rinse, and drain.

Add soaked rice and water to a blender and grind for 30 seconds to 1 minute, until rice is almost dissolved.

Bring rice to a quick boil in a small heavy-bottomed saucepan over medium-high heat.

Switch pan to burner on low and cook for 5 minutes or until creamy, whisking to prevent lumps.

Cool and combine ¼ cup cooked brown rice with ¼ cup water or breastmilk. Puree to a fine, thin consistency.

Refrigerate in a sealed container overnight, or batch using the food cube method (if batching to freeze, use water only). Add additional liquid if necessary when rewarming, as the texture of frozen pureed rice can be rubbery.

Double, triple, or quadruple amounts to batch.

Staple Brown Rice Cereal, Long-Cooking Method

Makes 12 infant servings (¼ cup); or 6 adult servings (½ cup)

1 cup brown rice*
2 cups water

Soak rice overnight to speed cooking time and increase digestibility.

Discard soaking water, rinse, and drain.

Add rice and water to a medium saucepan with a heavy bottom and bring to a boil.

Reduce heat to low, cover and simmer for 40 to 45 minutes until rice is tender and all the liquid has been absorbed.

Stir occasionally to prevent burning bottom of pot.

Cool and combine ¼ cup cooked brown rice with ¼ cup water or breastmilk. Puree to a fine, thin consistency.

Refrigerate in a sealed container overnight, or batch using the food cube method (if batching to freeze, use water only). Add additional liquid if necessary when rewarming, as the texture of frozen pureed rice can be rubbery.

(See pages 158 and 175 for information about preparing and freezing rice and other grains with a rice cooker. See page 185 for information about different ways to prepare rice in bulk for batching.)

Double, triple, or quadruple amounts to batch.

Nutrition Facts

Amount Per Serving (¼ cup)
Calories 54   Calories from Fat 4

Total Fat   0.5 g
Saturated Fat   0g
Trans Fat   0 g
Poly Fat   0.2 g
Mono Fat   0.2 g
Cholesterol   0 mg
Sodium   2.5 mg
Total Carbohydrate   12 g
Dietary Fiber   1 g
Sugars   0 g
Protein   1 g

Millet Cereal, Quick-Prep Method

Makes 3 servings (¼ cup)

Age: Appropriate for age 6 months and up.

Tips: High in niacin and magnesium. A good source of phosphorus and manganese. Millet is a smaller grain than rice—a little goes a long way. It looks very similar in size and shape to quinoa, but has a more uniform yellowish color and, unground, takes about twice the time of quinoa to cook.

Season: Available year-round—great for winter warming.

Selection: Millet is available in packages or bulk bins. If buying in bulk, make sure the grains are dry and the bins are covered.

Storage: Store in an airtight container in a cool, dark, dry pantry for up to several months.

¼ cup millet*
1 cup water

Soak millet overnight to speed cooking time and increase digestibility.

Discard soaking water, rinse, and drain.

Add soaked millet and water to a blender and grind for 30 seconds to 1 minute, until millet is almost dissolved.

Bring millet to a quick boil in a small saucepan over medium-high heat.

Switch pan to burner on low and cook for 5 minutes or until creamy, whisking to prevent lumps.

Cool and combine ¼ cup cooked brown millet with ¼ cup water or baby milk. Puree to a fine, thin consistency.

Refrigerate in a sealed container overnight, or batch using the food cube method (if batching to freeze, use water only). Add additional liquid if necessary when rewarming.

Double, triple, or quadruple amounts to batch.

Millet Cereal, Dry-Grind Method (No Presoaking)

Makes about 2 infant servings (¼ cup)

3 tablespoons millet
1 cup water

Place water in a medium saucepan and bring to a boil.

Add 3 tablespoons of dry millet to a blender and grind for about 2 minutes to a fine powder consistency.

Add the ground millet to the boiling water.

Reduce heat to low and cook for 10 minutes, covered.

Stir with a wire whisk frequently to prevent burning.

Cool almost to room temperature before serving or storing.

Refrigerate unused portion for up to 2 days, or batch using the food cube method and store in the freezer for up to 1 month. (When reheating frozen grains, add additional liquid to soften texture.)

Nutrition Facts

Amount Per Serving (¼ cup)
Calories 51   Calories from Fat 4

Total Fat   0.1 g
Saturated Fat   0.1 g
Trans Fat   0 g
Poly Fat   0.2 g
Mono Fat   0 g
Cholesterol   0 mg
Sodium   5 mg
Total Carbohydrate   10 g
Dietary Fiber   0 g
Sugars   0 g
Protein   1.5 g

Baby's Oatmeal, Quick-Prep Method

Makes about 4 servings (¼ cup)

Age: Appropriate for age 6 months and up.

Tips: Oats are high in antioxidants such as selenium, which is helpful in lowering symptoms of asthma and reducing the risk of heart disease. They are also high in manganese and a good source of fiber, phosphorus, and tryptophan.

Use old-fashioned rolled oats or steel-cut oats for this quick-grind cereal. Steel-cut oats are unrefined; they are whole oats cut apart for easier cooking. Old-fashioned or rolled oats have a flatter shape because they are steamed and rolled. Whole oats are called oat groats and typically require a lot of soaking and extended cooking time to prepare. See dry-grind recipe following for a short cut.

Note: It's great to keep giving children homemade oats even as they get older because most packaged, pre-sweetened oatmeal contains a lot of sugar or artificial sweeteners.

Season: Available year-round—great for winter warming.

Selection: Buy oats in small quantities—because of the higher fat content, they can go rancid quickly. If you are avoiding gluten for any reason, look for oats that are marked gluten-free on the packaging. If buying in bulk, make sure the bins are covered and there is no moisture present. Oats should smell fresh.

Storage: Store in airtight containers or sealed packages in a cool, dark place—refrigerator is ideal.

¼ cup oat groats (whole oats) or steel cut oats*
1 cup water

Soak groats overnight to speed cooking time and increase digestibility.

Discard soaking water, rinse, and drain.

Add soaked groats and water to a blender and grind for 30 seconds to 1 minute, until groats are almost dissolved.

Bring groats to a quick boil in a small saucepan over medium-high heat.

Switch pan to burner on low and cook for 5 minutes or until creamy, whisking to prevent lumps.

Cool and combine ¼ cup cooked oat groats with ¼ cup water or breastmilk. Puree to a fine, thin consistency.

Refrigerate in a sealed container overnight, or batch using the food cube method (if batching to freeze, use water only). Add additional liquid if necessary when rewarming.

Double, triple, or quadruple amounts to batch.

Baby's Oatmeal, Dry-Grind Method (No Presoaking)

Makes about 2 infant servings (¼ cup)

¼ cup rolled oats
1 cup water

Place water into a medium saucepan and bring to a boil.

Place dry oats in a blender and process for about 2 minutes to powder consistency. Let oats settle before removing blender lid.

Add oats to boiling water, stirring with a wire whisk to prevent lumps.

Reduce temperature to low and cook for 8 to 10 minutes, stirring frequently, until mixture is soft and creamy.

Cool almost to room temperature before serving or storing.

Refrigerate unused portion for 2 days, or batch using the food cube method and store in the freezer for up to 1 month. (When reheating frozen cooked grains, add additional liquid to soften texture, if necessary.)

Nutrition Facts

Amount Per Serving (¼ cup)
Calories 39   Calories from Fat 6

Total Fat   1 g
Saturated Fat   0.1 g
Trans Fat   0 g
Poly Fat   0.2 g
Mono Fat   0.2 g
Cholesterol   0 mg
Sodium   3 mg
Total Carbohydrate   7 g
Dietary Fiber   1 g
Sugars   0 g
Protein   2 g

Barley Cereal, Quick-Prep Method

Makes 3 servings (¼ cup)

Age: Appropriate for age 6 months and up.

Tips: High in fiber, selenium, phosphorus, and manganese, and a great source of copper.

Barley may help in reducing asthma symptoms. Whole barley (also called hulled barley), although harder to find, contains more nutrients than the commonly used pearled barley. Presoak whole barley for 4 hours or overnight before cooking.

Season: Available year-round.

Selection: If buying in bulk, make sure the bins are covered and dry.

Storage: Store in a sealed container in a dry, cool area. Refrigerate during warmer months.

¼ cup hulled or pearl barley*
1 cup water

Soak barley overnight to speed cooking time and increase digestibility.

Discard soaking water, rinse, and drain.

Add soaked barley and water to a blender and grind for 30 seconds to 1 minute, until barley is almost dissolved.

Bring barley to a quick boil in a small saucepan over medium-high heat.

Switch pan to burner on low and cook for 5 minutes or until creamy, whisking to prevent lumps.

Cool and combine ¼ cup cooked barley with ¼ cup water or breastmilk. Puree to a fine, thin consistency.

Refrigerate in a sealed container overnight, or batch using the food cube method (if batching to freeze, use water only). Add additional liquid if necessary when rewarming.

Double, triple, or quadruple amounts to batch.

Barley Cereal, Dry-Grind Method (No Presoaking)

Makes about 2 infant servings (¼ cup)

¼ cup pearled barley
1 cup water

Place water in a medium saucepan and bring to a boil.

Add barley to blender and process for about 2 minutes to fine

powder consistency.

Add ground barley to the boiling water and reduce the heat to low.

Stir the cereal frequently with a wire whisk for 10 minutes.

Cool almost to room temperature before serving or storing.

Refrigerate unused portion for up to 3 days, or batch using the food cube method and store in the freezer for up to 2 months. When reheating frozen grains, add additional liquid to soften texture, if necessary.

Nutrition Facts

Amount Per Serving (¼ cup)
Calories 48   Calories from Fat 1.5

Total Fat   2 g
Saturated Fat   0.1 g
Trans Fat   0 g
Poly Fat   0.1 g
Mono Fat   0.1 g
Cholesterol   0 mg
Sodium   9 mg
Total Carbohydrate   17 g
Dietary Fiber   2 g
Sugars   0 g
Protein   1 g

SIMPLEST VEGETABLE PUREES

Sweet Potato Puree

Makes 16 servings, 6 to 8 months (¼ cup); or 32 servings, 4 to 6 months (1 to 2 tablespoons)

Age: Appropriate for age 4 months and up (ideal as one of the first foods).

Tip: A great source of vitamins A (beta-carotene), B_6, C, and D, and fiber, iron, manganese, copper, and potassium; high in antioxidants,

which help eliminate free radicals from the body.

Season: Peak for sweet potatoes is fall and winter.

Selection: Look for sweet potatoes that are firm, without cracks, soft spots, or bruises. Yams are generally sweeter and softer than true sweet potatoes, with a deeper orange flesh.

Storage: Store loose in a cool, dark, well-ventilated area. Do not refrigerate or store in plastic bags.

3 medium sweet potatoes
½ teaspoon ground cinnamon (optional)
2 tablespoons water or baby milk (or orange juice for 12 months and up)

To Bake

Set oven to 400° F.

Scrub sweet potatoes clean.

Place potatoes uncovered and unwrapped on a cookie sheet.

Bake for about 45 minutes or until soft when pierced with a fork. Some of the sugar may ooze out.

Allow potatoes to cool until they can be handled comfortably.

Slice potatoes in half.

Scoop out the potato and place in a bowl, discarding skins.

To Boil

Scrub potatoes clean (and peel or follow directions below for removing skins after cooking).

Quarter potatoes or cut into large chunks.

Place unpeeled chunks in a large saucepan.

Add enough water to cover the potatoes.

Bring to a boil and cook on medium-high for about 20 to 30 minutes or until fork tender.

Drain the boiling water.

Place potatoes in cold water and slip the skins off with your fingers.

To Steam

Scrub potatoes clean (and peel or follow directions below for removing skins after cooking).

Quarter potatoes or cut into large chunks.

Place unpeeled chunks in steamer basket.

Place steamer basket into large pot.

Add water up to steamer basket.

Steam for 20 to 25 minutes or until fork tender.

Remove from basket.

Place potatoes in cold water and slip the skins off with your fingers.

To Puree *(After Cooking)*

Once sweet potatoes are cooked, place in a bowl and mash with a potato masher, fork, or mixer.

Add breastmilk or water to thin to desired consistency. (Optional for 12 months and up: Use orange juice for thinning and sweetening.)

Remove any fibrous pieces from the puree, which may present a choking hazard.

Add optional cinnamon for a sweet flavor.

Refrigerate for up to 3 days, or batch using food cube method and store in the freezer for up to 2 months.

Nutrition Facts

Amount Per Serving (¼ cup)
Calories 45   Calories from Fat 1

Total Fat   0 g
Saturated Fat   0 g
Trans Fat   0 g
Poly Fat   0.1 g
Mono Fat   0 g
Cholesterol   0 mg
Sodium   2.75 mg
Total Carbohydrate   10 g
Dietary Fiber   2 g
Sugars   3.25 g
Protein   1 g

Even though your 6-month-old may not be eating a large number of vegetables yet, it is still important to offer him a variety from among the safe foods, to provide him with ample stores of vitamins, minerals, antioxidants, and phytonutrients.

Yellow Squash Puree

Makes 4 to 6 infant servings (¼ cup)
Age: Appropriate for age 6 months and up.
Tips: Yellow squash is very high in vitamin C, manganese, fiber, vitamin A, folic acid, potassium, copper, riboflavin, and phosphorus, and has anti-inflammatory properties.

If desired, add a little chopped mint to the recipe. Chopped mint helps relieve gas and nicely complements the flavor of yellow squash. When making a puree with yellow squash, there is no need for additional liquid because of the large amount of water in the vegetable.
Season: Peak for yellow squash is summer.
Selection: Choose medium or small, slender squash that are bright yellow in color without any markings. (Very large squash are fibrous—indigestible for babies.)
Storage: Store in an unsealed plastic bag and refrigerate in the crisper drawer for up to 7 days. The skin of the squash is very perishable.

2 medium yellow squash
1 teaspoon chopped fresh mint or basil (optional)

Wash squash.
Slice squash into ½-inch coin pieces.
Steam for about 10 minutes until fork tender.
Blend squash and chopped herbs, if using, in a blender to desired consistency.
Refrigerate in a sealed container for up to 3 days, or batch using the food cube method and store in the freezer for up to 3 months.

Nutrition Facts

Amount Per Serving (¼ cup)
Calories 9   Calories from Fat 0

Total Fat   0 .15 g
Saturated Fat   0.1 g
Trans Fat   0 g
Poly Fat   .1 g
Mono Fat   0 g
Cholesterol   0 mg
Sodium   0.5 mg
Total Carbohydrate   2 g
Dietary Fiber   0.6 g
Sugars   0 g
Protein   0.4 g

Carrot Puree

Makes about 4 servings (¼ cup)
Age: Cooked carrots are appropriate for age 6 months and up. Finely grated raw carrots are appropriate for age 10 months and up.
Tips: Carrots are loaded with antioxidants, and high in vitamin A (beta-carotene), fiber, potassium, vitamin C, and vitamin K. They are cardiovascular and cancer protective. Carrots are also good

for eyesight, especially night vision. According to the AAP, lower nitrate concentrations have been found in some organically grown crops when compared with conventional ones. Also, conventional carrots are among the top twelve most highly contaminated fruits and vegetables, so it may be best to buy organic carrots. See page 16 for more information about vegetable nitrate risk in infants.

Season: Peak for carrots is spring and winter.

Selection: Carrots should be firm and have a bright orange color with green tops to ensure freshness. Remove greens right after purchase because they can cause carrots to become soft.

Storage: Remove the tops and place carrots in perforated vegetable or plastic bags in the crisper drawer. They can be refrigerated for up to 2 weeks. Carrots should not be stored with apples or pears as these fruits give off a gas that spoils carrots.

- 2 medium fresh carrots (about 2 cups chopped)
- ¼ to ½ teaspoon raw ginger or sprinkle of ground ginger (optional, aids in digestion, warming)
- 1 tablespoon orange juice (optional for 12 months and up), or water for a thinner puree

Wash, peel, and cut carrots into ¼-inch coins.

Steam the carrot slices for 15 minutes until tender.

Place cooked carrots in the blender, food processor, or food mill.

Add 1 to 3 tablespoons of water (including orange juice, if baby is at least 12 months).

Add ginger, if using, and puree carrots to desired consistency.

Add more water for a smoother texture for younger babies; no need to add more water for older babies.

Refrigerate unused portion for up to 3 days, or batch using food cube method and store in the freezer for up to 2 months.

Nutrition Facts

Amount Per Serving (¼ cup)
Calories 20   Calories from Fat 0

Total Fat   0 g
Saturated Fat   0 g
Trans Fat   0 g
Poly Fat   0.1 g
Mono Fat   0 g
Cholesterol   0 mg
Sodium   12.75 mg
Total Carbohydrate   5 g
Dietary Fiber   2 g
Sugars   2 g
Protein   0 g

Butternut Squash Puree

Makes 6 servings, 6 to 8 months (¼ cup); or about 12 servings, 4 to 6 months (1 to 2 tablespoons)

Age: Appropriate for age 4 months and up.

Tips: Great source of vitamins A and C, potassium, and manganese, and has antioxidant properties.

Season: Peak for squash is September through March, but available year-round.

Selection: Best if stem is still attached to the squash; dropped stem may indicate that the squash has been in storage too long. The squash should feel heavy for its size.

Storage: Store in a cool area away from sunshine for up to 4 months, depending on freshness when purchased. If the squash is cut, refrigerate it for up to 2 days.

1 whole medium butternut squash, or 2 cups peeled and cubed (about 1½ inch square)
½ teaspoon ground cinnamon (optional)
Water (for cooking)
3 tablespoons liquid for pureeing (vegetable or chicken broth, apple cider, or baby milk)

To Bake

Preheat oven to 375° F.

Wash whole squash and cut it in half, lengthwise.

Scoop out the seeds and fibers.

Place squash halves facedown in 13-inch-by-9-inch baking pan.

You may follow the next cooking steps with peeled, precut squash chunks, but add only ½ cup water.

Add ½ inch of water and bake until soft, 30 to 35 minutes (25 to 30 minutes for precut squash chunks).

The water steams the squash to shorten its cooking time. This may discolor the bottom of the squash but does not affect taste.

To Steam

Wash and peel the squash.

Cut it in half and scoop out seeds. Cut the squash into 1-inch chunks (or use peeled, precut chunks).

Add 2 to 3 inches of water to a large saucepan and place the steamer basket in the saucepan. Add the squash chunks to the steaming basket and bring water to a boil,

steaming for 25 minutes, or until squash is soft.

You may also cook squash unpeeled. The peels are easy to remove once the squash is cooked and cooled. Do not feed peels to baby.

To Puree *(After Cooking)*

Puree the squash in a food processor, mixer, or immersion blender for the smoothest texture.

Add a little liquid, if necessary. Add cinnamon, if using.

Refrigerate unused portion for up to 3 days, or batch using food cube method and store in the freezer for up to 2 months.

Nutrition Facts

Amount Per Serving (¼ cup)
Calories 23.5   Calories from Fat 1

Total Fat   0 g
Saturated Fat   0 g
Trans Fat   0 g
Poly Fat   0 g
Mono Fat   0 g
Cholesterol   0 mg
Sodium   1 mg
Total Carbohydrate   5 g
Dietary Fiber   1 g
Sugars   0 g
Protein   1 g

Green Bean Puree

Makes 3 infant servings (¼ cup)

Age: Appropriate for age 6 months and up.

Tips: Green beans are a terrific source of vitamin A (beta-carotene), vitamin C, vitamin K, manganese, potassium, magnesium, fiber, iron, and folic acid. After your baby has been introduced to green bean puree, you may add a dash of fresh or dried dill, basil, or parsley to complement its distinctive flavor.

Season: Peak for green beans is spring and summer.

Selection: Choose bright green, smooth beans that feel substantial. When broken in half, they should make a popping sound. They should be free of bruises and brown marks.

Storage: Do not wash the beans before storing. Refrigerate them in plastic bags in the crisper drawer for about 1 week.

1 cup fresh green beans
2 tablespoons to ¼ cup of the steaming water

Trim off the stems, then wash and cut the beans into 1-inch pieces.

Place a steamer basket in a medium saucepan.

Add 2 to 3 inches of water to saucepan and bring to a boil.

Add the green beans and steam for 12 to 15 minutes or until very tender.

Place the green beans into a blender or use immersion blender. Add 2 tablespoons of the cooking water and puree until a smooth consistency is reached, scraping down the sides and adding more liquid, if necessary.

Refrigerate unused portion for up to 2 days, or batch using food cube method and store in the freezer for up to 2 months.

Nutrition Facts

Amount Per Serving (¼ cup)
Calories 11   Calories from Fat 1

Total Fat   0 g
Saturated Fat   0 g

Trans Fat   0 g
Poly Fat   0 g
Mono Fat   0 g
Cholesterol   0 mg
Sodium   1 mg
Total Carbohydrate   2 g
Dietary Fiber   1 g
Sugars   0 g
Protein   1 g

Zucchini Puree

Makes 3 to 4 infant servings (¼ cup)

Age: Appropriate for age 6 months and up (after first foods)

Tips: Zucchini is very high in vitamin C, manganese, magnesium, folate, copper, riboflavin, potassium, phosphorus, and vitamin A (beta-carotene) and promotes heart health. It's not necessary to peel zucchini because the skin is soft and delicate, and also high in beta carotene.

Season: Peak for zucchini is summer.

Selection: Look for small to medium zucchini that feel heavy, are bright green in color, and free from any bruises. (Small to medium zucchini are the most flavorful and least fibrous.)

Storage: Store unwashed zucchini in an unsealed plastic bag as they bruise easily. Refrigerate in the crisper drawer for up to 7 days.

1 medium fresh zucchini
1 teaspoon diced fresh basil or ½ teaspoon dried (optional)

Wash the zucchini and slice into ½-inch thick circles.

Steam the zucchini for 5 to 8 minutes, until fork tender.

Place the cooked zucchini and basil, if using, into a blender and puree until desired consistency is reached.

Store in the refrigerator for up to 3 days, or batch using food cube method and store in the freezer for up to 2 months.

Suggestion: Great combined with pureed hot cereal of brown rice, quinoa, or millet.

Nutrition Facts

Amount Per Serving (¼ cup)
Calories 10   Calories from Fat 0

Total Fat   0 g
Saturated Fat   0.1 g
Trans Fat   0 g
Poly Fat   0.1 g
Mono Fat   0 g
Cholesterol   0 mg
Sodium   1 mg
Total Carbohydrate   2 g
Dietary Fiber   1 g
Sugars   0 g
Protein   1 g

Pea Puree

Makes about 3 infant servings (¼ cup)

Age: Appropriate for age 6 months and up.

Tips: High in vitamin C, folic acid, vitamin K_1, and vitamin B_6, and a good source of fiber. Snow peas and snap peas can be eaten raw by toddlers, although the cooking process will bring out the sweetness.

Season: Peak for peas is spring.

Selection: Garden peas: Look for fresh pea pods that are firm and bright green in color, with lots of peas in the pod (when shaken, you should hear a noise). Sugar snap peas should be deep green and plump. Snow peas should be flat and crisp, not rubbery. (Garden peas are most easily available canned or frozen, rather than fresh. Frozen peas are typically flash frozen, which preserves many of the nutrients.)

Storage: Place unwashed pea pods in a bag or open container for up to 4 days. Refrigerate right away or use immediately to ensure highest natural sugar content. To freeze, remove shells and blanch fresh peas for 2 minutes. Freeze in plastic freezer bag or freezer container.

1 cup fresh green peas (2 pounds of pods) or frozen

Wash the peas and remove and discard the shell.

Steam the peas for 8 minutes.

Puree the peas in a food mill for the smoothest consistency.

Refrigerate for up to 3 days, or batch using food cube method and store in the freezer for up to 2 months.

Nutrition Facts

Amount Per Serving (¼ cup)
Calories 33   Calories from Fat 1

Total Fat   0 g
Saturated Fat   0 g
Trans Fat   0 g
Poly Fat   0 g
Mono Fat   0 g
Cholesterol   0 mg
Sodium   94 mg
Total Carbohydrate   6 g
Dietary Fiber   2 g
Sugars   2 g
Protein   2 g

Parsnip Puree

*Makes 5 infant servings (¼ cup);
or 4 toddler servings (⅓ cup)*

Age: Appropriate for age 6
months and up.

Tips: Parsnip is a sweet vegetable
that is high in fiber, vitamin C, folic
acid, and manganese. They are
delicious braised with apple cider,
and in soups. Once your baby has
been introduced to parsnip puree,
you may add a dash of curry powder
or ground ginger to complement its
flavor.

Season: Peak for parsnips is
winter. They are also available in
the fall but aren't as sweet.

Selection: Look for parsnips
that are pale yellow in color, firm,
and free of any markings.

Storage: Store in the crisper
drawer of the refrigerator for about
10 days.

1½ cups parsnips, peeled, cored
(if necessary), and diced

Steam parsnips over medium high
heat for 15 to 20 minutes, until soft.

Remove from steamer.

Add ¼ cup cooked parsnip with
2 tablespoons steaming water and
puree in blender or food processor
to desired consistency.

Refrigerate for up to 3 days, or
batch and freeze using food cube
method for up to 3 months.

Nutrition Facts

Amount Per Serving (¼ cup)
Calories 33   Calories from Fat 1

Total Fat   0 g
Saturated Fat   0 g
Trans Fat   0 g
Poly Fat   0 g
Mono Fat   0.1 g
Cholesterol   0 mg
Sodium   113 mg
Total Carbohydrate   8 g
Dietary Fiber   2 g
Sugars   2 g
Protein   1 g

SIMPLEST FRUIT PUREES

Banana Puree (Raw)

*Makes 2 to 3 servings, 6 to 8
months (¼ cup); or about 6
servings, 4 to 6 months (1 to 2
tablespoons)*

Age: Appropriate for age 4
months and up. (One of best first
foods, a banana is the first raw fruit
a baby should have.)

Tips: Bananas are high in
potassium and sugar, making them
a good natural sweetener for other
foods. Very ripe bananas are at their
nutritional peak and mash easily.

Season: Bananas are available

year-round.

Selection: It is best to buy
bananas slightly underripe when
they have greenish to greenish
yellow coloring: ripen at home to
prevent bruising.

Storage: In a fruit bowl or on a
banana hanger on a countertop.

1 medium fresh banana

Wash and peel the banana.

Mash with a fork.

If too thick, add water or
breastmilk for a smoother
consistency.

Refrigerate unused portion for 1 day, or batch using food cube method and store in the freezer for up to 3 months.

Suggestions: Mashed ripe banana will turn brown as it ages. For a baby over 12 months, use 1 tablespoon of lemon juice for 1 cup of banana to prevent darkening. (Discoloration does not affect taste or nutrient content.)

Bananas can also be cut into slices and frozen on a cookie tray: Once frozen, transfer the chunks to a freezer bag. These are great for smoothies.

Whole, overripe bananas can be peeled, halved, and wrapped in wax paper. Place them in plastic freezer bags and freeze for up to 3 months.

Nutrition Facts

Amount Per Serving (¼ cup)
Calories 50   Calories from Fat 4

Total Fat   0 g
Saturated Fat   0.1 g
Trans Fat   0 g
Poly Fat   0.1 g
Mono Fat   0.1 g
Cholesterol   0 mg
Sodium   1 mg
Total Carbohydrate   13 g
Dietary Fiber   1 g
Sugars   7 g
Protein   1 g

> **TIP**
>
> If you need something in a hurry, simply wash, peel, and mash well or puree the fruit from a fully ripe avocado, banana, cantaloupe, or papaya, thinning a bit with water or breastmilk if necessary, and serve it up quick.

Avocado Puree (Raw)

Makes 2 servings, 6 to 8 months (¼ cup); or 4 to 8 servings, 4 to 6 months, (1 to 2 tablespoons)

Age: Appropriate for age 4 months and up. (One of best first foods, avocado is an appropriate first raw fruit.)

Tips: Avocados are high in protein, fiber, monounsaturated fat (healthy fat), and vitamins A, C, and E, and promote heart health.

Season: Peak for avocados is February through May, although they're available year-round. The two most widely available varieties are Hass avocados (small- to medium-sized, oval shaped, with a pebbly texture), and Fuerte avocados (larger, with thinner, smoother, bright green skin).

Selection: Best to buy greenish Hass avocados, they turn dark green to black when ripe. Ripe avocados should indent slightly when pressed with a finger. Or check the stem: If it pulls out, it's ripe.

Storage: Do not store in the refrigerator: The cold turns avocados mushy, black, and stringy. Ripen in a fruit bowl on a counter. Placing avocados in a paper bag quickens the ripening process. Air discolors avocados. For babies 12 months or older, a squeeze of lemon or lime can be used to prevent discoloration. (Discoloration does not affect taste or nutrient content.)

1 fresh Hass avocado

Cut avocado in half lengthwise and twist to separate.

Remove the large pit with a spoon.

Using a spoon, or by cutting the avocado into strips, remove flesh, place in a bowl, and mash well with a fork, thinning with baby milk if desired for a more liquid consistency.

Nutrition Facts

Amount Per Serving (¼ cup)
Calories 96   Calories from Fat 74

Total Fat   9 g
Saturated Fat   1.2 g
Trans Fat   0 g
Poly Fat   1 g
Mono Fat   6.8 g
Cholesterol   0 mg
Sodium   5 mg
Total Carbohydrate   5 g
Dietary Fiber   4 g
Sugars   0 g
Protein   1 g

Papaya Puree (Raw)

Makes 4 to 5 infant servings (¼ cup)

Age: Appropriate for age 6 months and up.

Tips: High in antioxidants like beta-carotene; high in vitamin C, folic acid, potassium, magnesium, and fiber; contains digestive

enzymes that aid digestion; helps reduce inflammation and lowers cholesterol.

Season: Peak for papaya is November through December, harvested in Florida and elsewhere.

Selection: Look for ripe papaya that has orange-red skin and is soft to the touch. If papaya is somewhat yellow in color, it needs to continue to ripen. To quicken the ripening process, put the papaya in a brown bag with a banana for 1 to 2 days.

Storage: Let the papaya ripen at room temperature until soft to the touch. Once it's ripe, it can be refrigerated for up to 2 days.

1 medium fresh papaya

Wash papaya.

Cut in half lengthwise and scoop out black seeds. (The seeds can be ground and added to salad dressings and smoothies.)

Mash papaya to desired consistency and serve immediately; exposure to light and warmth can decrease the available vitamin C.

Nutrition Facts

Amount Per Serving (¼ cup)
Calories 23   Calories from Fat 0

Total Fat   0 g
Saturated Fat   0.1 g
Trans Fat   0 g
Poly Fat   0 g
Mono Fat   0 g
Cholesterol   0 mg
Sodium   2 mg
Total Carbohydrate   6 g
Dietary Fiber   1 g
Sugars   4 g
Protein   0 g

Cantaloupe Puree (Raw)

Makes 1 infant serving (¼ cup)

Age: Appropriate for age 8 months and up.

Tips: Cantaloupe is an excellent summer fruit to cool the body. It is a great source of fiber, potassium, vitamin B, vitamin C, and folic acid, and is high in vitamin A (beta-carotene). Melons have a higher acid content than some of the other fruits recommended for 6 months and up, so it's a good idea to wait to introduce them until around 8 months.

Season: Peak for cantaloupe is June through August.

Selection: Choose a cantaloupe without bruises or soft spots. It should feel heavy and have a slightly sweet smell, while not overly fragrant, which indicates overripeness.

Storage: If the cantaloupe is hard (not ripe), leave at room temperature for a few days. Refrigerate promptly once it is cut, to avoid salmonella.

1 medium fresh cantaloupe wedge (⅛ of medium melon)

Wash and halve the cantaloupe, removing all seeds with a spoon.

Cut it into slices and remove the skins with a knife.

Mash the melon using a fork or immersion blender.

Refrigerate for up to 2 days.

To Freeze *(appropriate for babies over 1 year)*:

Slice into bite-sized pieces and place in a sturdy container. Cover with orange juice: The vitamin C will stop the cantaloupe from changing flavor and prevent it from darkening.

Keep the melon submerged to preserve and do not expose to air.

When melon is thawed it will be a little softer (adults prefer frozen slices).

Other melons can be mixed in the same container.

Store in the freezer for up to 3 months.

Suggestion: Puree frozen melon and orange juice. Mixture will be thin—may add banana and/or yogurt to thicken, plus optional mint to make a smoothie for toddlers or adults.

Nutrition Facts

Amount Per Serving (¼ cup)
Calories 13   Calories from Fat 0.5

Total Fat   0 g
Saturated Fat   0 g
Trans Fat   0 g
Poly Fat   0 g
Mono Fat   0 g
Cholesterol   0 mg
Sodium   6 mg
Total Carbohydrate   3 g
Dietary Fiber   0 g
Sugars   3 g
Protein   0 g

Pear Puree

Makes 4 to 6 servings, 6 to 8 months (¼ cup); or about 12 servings, 4 to 6 months (1 to 2 tablespoons)

Age: Appropriate for age 4 months and up (an ideal first food).

Tips: Pears are high in fiber; contain vitamin C, copper, and vitamin K; are helpful in preventing

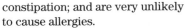

constipation; and are very unlikely to cause allergies.

Season: Peak for pears is August through October.

Selection: Look for pears with smooth skin. If pears are slightly hard to the touch, they can ripen at home. Do not buy pears with bruises or punctures.

Caution: According to the Environmental Working Group's 2006 "Shopper's Guide to Pesticides in Produce," pears are one of the foods highest in pesticide content, so buy organic when you can.

Storage: Ripen pears in a fruit bowl on a countertop. You can speed up the ripening process by placing pears in a paper bag for 1 to 2 days. Once ripened, pears can be refrigerated for up to 5 days.

2 medium fresh pears

Wash and peel the pears. (Leave skins on organic pears for older babies [9 months and up], because they are high in fiber.)

Quarter and core the pears, then cut into chunks.

For babies 4 to 6 months and up: Steam chunks over low heat for about 8 minutes, until fork tender. Puree with an immersion blender or food mill.

For babies 7 months and up: Mash very soft, raw, ripe pears with a fork or an immersion blender or food mill.

Nutrition Facts

Amount Per Serving (¼ cup)
Calories 20   Calories from Fat 0

Total Fat   0 g
Saturated Fat   0 g

Trans Fat   0 g
Poly Fat   0 g
Mono Fat   0 g
Cholesterol   0 mg
Sodium   1 mg
Total Carbohydrate   5.5 g
Dietary Fiber   1 g
Sugars   3.5 g
Protein   0 g

Apricot Puree

Makes 4 infant servings (¼ cup)

Age: Appropriate for age 6 months and up.

Tips: Avoid with diarrhea; helpful for asthma; high in vitamins A (beta-carotene) and C, and they are a good source of fiber and promote good vision.

Season: Peak for apricots is May through August. (Idaho apricots are harvested in the fall.)

Selection: Look for firm apricots with a golden color, and avoid wrinkles, which indicate aging. Best to ripen them at home.

Storage: Store in a warm area on the counter for 5 to 6 days. Once ripe (soft and golden-reddish color), refrigerate for up to 2 days.

6 fresh apricots

Wash, peel, halve, and pit the apricots.

Steam apricots for 6 to 8 minutes, until fork tender.

Puree apricots in a blender or food mill with a little of the steam water, until they are silky smooth with no lumps.

Refrigerate for up to 3 days, or batch using food cube method and store in the freezer for up to 2 months.

Nutrition Facts

Amount Per Serving (¼ cup)
Calories 20   Calories from Fat 1

Total Fat   0 g
Saturated Fat   0 g
Trans Fat   0 g
Poly Fat   0 g
Mono Fat   0 g
Cholesterol   0 mg
Sodium   0.5 mg
Total Carbohydrate   5 g
Dietary Fiber   1 g
Sugars   4 g
Protein   0.5 g

Plum Puree

Makes 2 infant servings (¼ cup)

Age: Appropriate for age 6 months and up (after first foods).

Tips: Not advised for babies with sensitive digestion or gastrointestinal issues; helpful during dehydration. They are high in vitamin C and increase iron absorption. Stewed prunes (dried plums) are helpful in preventing constipation. Purple plums have cooling properties.

Season: Peak for plums is mid-May through August.

Selection: Look for plums that are solid and plump, with nice shades of color; depending on the variety, color can run from red to deep purple. Do not buy bruised fruits.

Storage: Plums can be ripened in a brown bag or on a countertop. Once ripe, they smell fragrant and are soft to the touch. Plums can be refrigerated for up to 5 days.

2 medium fresh plums
2 tablespoons apple juice

Wash plums.

Cut an X on the bottom. (This aids peeling after steaming.)

Steam whole plums over low simmer for 5 minutes, or until very soft.

Rinse with cold water and peel off the skin and discard.

Halve the plums and remove pits.

Puree plums in a blender or food mill to desired consistency.

Sweeten to taste using some of the cooking liquid or apple juice.

Refrigerate for up to 3 days.

Batch using food cube method and store in the freezer for up to 3 months; can also be frozen whole.

Note: Prunes are actually dried plums. They are appropriate for babies 6 months and older—offering your baby small amounts of prunes will help her develop a taste for them. They'll last for a few months in a cool dark place, and up to 6 months if stored in the fridge. Choose pitted prunes and make sure you check them well for any remaining pits. To prepare them for your baby, soak them in hot water for a few minutes, or steam them for 2 to 3 minutes until soft. Puree them with a little water and serve, or try mixing them with chicken, beef, or a grain for an interesting entrée.

Nutrition Facts

Amount Per Serving (¼ cup)
Calories 20   Calories from Fat 0

Total Fat   0 g
Saturated Fat   0 g
Trans Fat   0 g
Poly Fat   0 g
Mono Fat   0.1 g
Cholesterol   0 mg
Sodium   4.3 mg

Total Carbohydrate 5 g
Dietary Fiber 0 g
Sugars 4 g
Protein 0 g

Applesauce

*Makes 4 to 6 infant servings
(¼ cup); 3 to 4 toddler servings (⅓
cup); or 2 to 3 adult servings (½
cup)*
Age: Appropriate for age 6
months and up.
Tips: The best apples for
applesauce are softer apples,
such as McIntosh, Fuji, Gala, and
Cortland.
See page 224 for information on
apples.

>   2 medium fresh apples
>   1 teaspoon fresh-squeezed
>   lemon juice
>   ½ teaspoon ground cinnamon
>   ¼ teaspoon ground nutmeg
>   1 cup water
>   2 tablespoon apple cider
>   (optional, for additional
>   sweetness)

Wash, core, and peel apples.
Cut apples into small chunks.
Combine apples, lemon juice,
cinnamon, nutmeg and water
in small saucepan over medium
heat.
Bring mixture to a simmer and
cook for about 12 minutes or until
apples are soft.
Combine apples and cider, if
using, and puree in a blender or
using an immersion blender.
Refrigerate for up to 3 days in
a sealed container, or freeze using
the food cube method for up to 2
months.

Nutrition Facts

Amount Per Serving (⅓ cup)
Calories 26   Calories from Fat 1

Total Fat 0 g
Saturated Fat 0.1 g
Trans Fat 0 g
Poly Fat 0 g
Mono Fat 0 g
Cholesterol 0 mg
Sodium 0 mg
Total Carbohydrate 9 g
Dietary Fiber 1 g
Sugars 7 g
Protein 0 g

Fresh Pumpkin Puree

*Makes 12 infant servings (¼ cup);
or 3 adult servings (1 cup)*
Age: Appropriate for age 6
months and up.
Tips: Pumpkins are high in
antioxidants, carotenoids, iron,
zinc, and fiber. If eaten regularly,
pumpkins can help to moderate
eczema.
Season: Peak for pumpkins is
fall.
Selection: Look for sugar
pumpkins that are orange in color,
small in size, fairly uniform, and
have few markings.
Storage: Store on countertop
at room temperature for up to 1
month.

>   3 cups fresh pumpkin (about 2
>   small whole pumpkins, or 3
>   pounds cut)
>   1 teaspoon ground cinnamon

Preheat oven to 350° F.
Using a heavy knife, remove
pumpkin stem and cut in half from
stem end to bottom.

Remove seeds and pulp with a heavy spoon. Be sure to save the seeds for roasting.

Place pumpkin halves face down in baking pan. Add water to about ¼ inch in the pan, and bake for 45 to 60 minutes, until soft.

Once pumpkin is cooked, scoop out the soft insides and put in a mixing bowl. Discard the skins.

Add cinnamon and puree to desired consistency, adding a little liquid if necessary.

Freeze pumpkin using food cube method, or store in a larger, container if using for pumpkin bread, cookies, or pie.

Nutrition Facts

Amount Per Serving (¼ cup)
Calories 13   Calories from Fat 0

Total Fat   0 g
Saturated Fat   0.1 g
Trans Fat   0 g
Poly Fat   0 g
Mono Fat   0 g
Cholesterol   0 mg
Sodium   93 mg
Total Carbohydrate   3 g
Dietary Fiber   1 g
Sugars   1 g
Protein   0 g

Roasting Pumpkin Seeds

Makes ½ to ⅔ cup total
   Age: Appropriate for age 5 years and up.

   Seeds from pumpkins used to make puree
   ½ to ¾ teaspoon tamari (optional)

Preheat oven to 170° F.

Boil seeds for 5 minutes to soften hulls.

Drain well, pat dry, and place seeds on a cookie sheet in a single layer.

For a burst of flavor, toss with tamari before roasting (optional).

Roast for 30 minutes, or until lightly browned.

Gently shake the pan a few times when baking to prevent burning.

Nutrition Facts

Amount Per Serving (1 ounce, about ¼ cup)
Calories 125   Calories from Fat 45

Total Fat   5 g
Saturated Fat   1 g
Trans Fat   0 g
Poly Fat   0 g
Mono Fat   0 g
Cholesterol   0 mg
Sodium   5 mg
Total Carbohydrate   15 g
Dietary Fiber   0 g
Sugars   0 g
Protein   5 g

Peach Puree

Makes 4 infant servings (¼ cup)

Age: Peeled and mashed raw peaches appropriate for age 7 months and up (after first foods). For age 4 to 6 months, peaches should be cooked.

Tips: Cooked peach puree is good for gastrointestinal inflammation and cooling the body; high in antioxidants, vitamin C, carotenoids, and pro-vitamin A.

Caution: According to the Environmental Working Group's 2006 "Shopper's Guide to Pesticides in Produce," peaches are one of the foods highest in pesticide content, so buy organic when you can.

Season: Peak for peaches is June through September.

Selection: Look for peaches with an orange blush color; they are usually shipped unripened.

Storage: Ripen on the counter. Peaches are ripe when they have a fragrant sweet smell and yield under slight finger pressure. When fruit is ripe, refrigerate for about 7 days. Keep peaches (and all tree fruits) away from windowsills where they are exposed to sunlight.

3 medium fresh peaches

Ripe peaches can be peeled and mashed well with a fork for babies 7 months and up.

Babies 9 months and up can handle a chunkier peach mash.

To make a cooked puree: Wash and peel peaches using a peeler.

Quarter peaches and remove the pits.

Steam for 5 minutes or until soft.

Puree peaches in a blender or food mill.

Refrigerate for up to 2 days, or batch using the food cube method and store in the freezer for up to 2 months. Whole peaches or chunks of peaches can be covered with orange juice (to prevent discoloration) and frozen in a sturdy container for up to 3 months. Leave 1 inch of space for expansion.

Nutrition Facts

Amount Per Serving (¼ cup)

Calories 20   Calories from Fat 1

Total Fat   0 g

Saturated Fat   0 g

Trans Fat   0 g

Poly Fat   0 g

Mono Fat   0 g

Cholesterol   0 mg

Sodium   0 mg

Total Carbohydrate   5 g

Dietary Fiber   1 g

Sugars   4 g

Protein   0 g

Quick Chart

FRUIT AND VEGGIE PUREE BATCHING COMBOS

Vegetable Combos	Amounts	Cooking Method
Sweet potato and green bean	2 large potatoes, peeled and diced (1-inch chunks) 1 cup green beans (3-inch lengths)	Boil sweet potatoes for 10 minutes, add green beans and boil for additional 10 minutes, or until both are soft.
Carrot and pea	4 large carrots, peeled and cut into thin (¼-inch) coins ¾ cup peas	Steam carrots for 10 minutes. Add peas and steam for 10 minutes, or until all vegetables are soft.
Pumpkin and pear or apple	1 15-ounce can cooked pumpkin puree 2 pears, cored and diced (peeling is optional if skin is tender) lemon (optional)*	Mash 2 ripe pears OR Steam pears/apples for 8 to 10 minutes until soft.
Banana and peach	2 ripe bananas, peeled and cut into chunks 3 ripe peaches, peeled, pitted, and cut into chunks lemon (optional)*	None
Apple and zucchini	2 apples, peeled, cored, and diced 1 large zucchini, or 2 to 3 small, diced fine	Steam apples and zucchini about 10 minutes, or until both are soft.
Carrot and parsnip	3 medium carrots, cut into thin (¼-inch) coins 2 medium parsnips, peeled and diced fine	Steam carrots and parsnips about 15 minutes, or until both are soft.
Spinach and apple	Chopped spinach (2 cups fresh or 1 cup frozen) 2 apples, peeled, cored, and diced	Steam apple for 7 minutes, until soft, then add chopped spinach and steam for 2 more minutes (fresh) or 4 minutes (frozen).
Apricot and butternut squash	2 cups butternut squash, peeled and diced 1 cup fresh or dried (without sulfur or added sugar) apricots, diced	Roast butternut squash at 375° F for 30 to 35 minutes, then add apricots and about ¼ cup water and continue roasting for about 10 minutes, until soft.

Puree Method	Storage
Puree in blender or food processor to desired consistency, adding small amount of liquid if necessary.	Fridge: 3 days Freezer: 2 months
Puree in blender or food processor to desired consistency, adding small amount of liquid if necessary. Do not use water from carrots: could contain nitrates.	Fridge: 3 days Freezer: 2 months
Use hand blender or potato masher and blend together. OR Use potato masher or blender to puree to desired consistency, adding small amount liquid if necessary.	Fridge: 3 days Freezer: 3 months
Combine and puree using blender or food processor to desired consistency, adding small amount of liquid if necessary.	Fridge: up to 2 days Freezer: 2 months
Puree in blender or food processor to desired consistency, adding small amount of liquid if necessary.	Fridge: 2 to 3 days Freezer: up to 2 months
Puree in blender or food processor to desired consistency, adding small amount of liquid if necessary.	Fridge: up to 3 days Freezer: up to 2 months
Puree in blender or food processor to desired consistency, adding small amount of liquid if necessary.	Fridge: up to 2 days Freezer: up to 2 months
Puree in blender or food processor to desired consistency, adding small amount of liquid if necessary.	Fridge: up to 3 days Freezer: up to 2 months

continued on next page

Vegetable Combos	Amounts	Cooking Method
Banana and avocado	2 ripe bananas, peeled and cut into chunks 2 ripe Hass avocados, peeled, pitted, and diced lemon (optional)*	None
Pear and raisin	3 large pears, cored and diced (peeling is optional if skin is tender) ½ cup raisins ¼ cup water	Combine pears, raisins, and water in small saucepan. Simmer lightly over medium heat for 5 to 6 minutes, until pears are soft.

*Optional: Use 1 teaspoon of lemon juice to help prevent browning; appropriate for toddlers 12 months and up.
   Vegetables used can be fresh or frozen.

PROTEIN PUREES

Split Pea Puree

Makes 10 infant servings (2 tablespoons); or 5 toddler servings (¼ cup)

Age: Appropriate for age 9 months and up.

Tips: This puree works well combined with cooked grains, especially rice, quinoa, or oats. Use either yellow or green split peas—yellow peas have a mellower flavor. Split peas are high in protein and fiber—great for keeping blood-sugar levels stable. Split peas require no presoaking.

Turmeric helps make legumes more digestible. It has anti-inflammatory properties and adds a light yellow coloring to foods.

Selection: Split peas are sold in prepackaged containers and in bulk bins. Check to make sure there are no broken split peas, sand, or dirt before purchasing.

Storage: Store in airtight container in a cool, dry place for up to 3 months, or refrigerate to for up to 6 months.

1 cup dry yellow or green split peas
¼ teaspoon ground turmeric
3 cups water

Rinse and sort split peas, discarding any broken ones.

In a large saucepan or soup pot, bring water to a boil.

Add peas and turmeric. Reduce heat to medium-low, cover, and simmer for 45 minutes to 1 hour, until soft.

Watch the pot so water does not foam up and boil over.

Slow Cooker

Combine 3 cups of water, 1 cup of split peas, and turmeric and cook on low for 5 to 6 hours, or on high for about 3 hours.

Puree Method	Storage
Mash well with fork	Fridge: 2 days Freezer: up to 1 month While it is possible to freeze banana and avocado, the result isn't aesthetically pleasing. We prefer to make just enough for one day over batching for this combo..
Puree in blender or food processor to desired consistency, adding small amount of liquid if necessary.	Fridge: 3 days Freeze: up to 4 months

All combos yield approximately 3 cups, enough to fill two baby food cubes or 1½ standard ice cube trays.
Serve with a grain and/or protein to make a complete meal.

For finest consistency, puree with the immersion wand or in a blender to desired consistency.

Refrigerate for up to 3 days, or freeze using the food cube method for up to 2 months.

Nutrition Facts

Amount Per Serving (2 tablespoons)
Calories 23   Calories from Fat 1

Total Fat   0 g
Saturated Fat   0 g
Trans Fat   0 g
Poly Fat   0 g
Mono Fat   0 g
Cholesterol   0 mg
Sodium   47 mg
Total Carbohydrate   4 g
Dietary Fiber   2 g
Sugars   1 g
Protein   2 g

Red Lentil Puree

Makes 20 infant servings (2 tablespoons); or 10 toddler servings (¼ cup)

Age: Appropriate for age 6 months and up.

Tips: Lentils are quick and easy to prepare because they don't need to be presoaked and are among the fastest-cooking legumes. Lentils are high in fiber, folate, and magnesium, and they help with digestion and heart health.

Lentil dip is versatile and can be a puree for babies, mixed with rice, or used as a dip for rice crackers or veggie sticks for older toddlers—a great way to increase the protein content of a snack. Lentils placed directly in boiling water are easier to digest than if they're put in room temperature water and then brought to a boil. Turmeric and bay leaf increase lentil digestibility.

Season: Lentils are available year-round.

Selection: Lentils come in a variety of shapes and colors. When buying in bulk, make sure there is a high turnover rate. Packaging should not have evidence of moisture or be broken. Choose lentils that are bright green, brown, or red in color. Red lentils tend to cook faster, in about 15 to 20 minutes, and form more of a mash. Green and brown lentils hold their shape better once cooked.

Storage: Store fresh lentils in an airtight container in a cool, dry pantry for up to 12 months.

> 2¼ cups water or vegetable broth
> ½ cup diced carrots
> 1 cup dry red lentils
> ¼ teaspoon ground turmeric
> 1 bay leaf
> 1 teaspoon balsamic vinegar

Add water and carrots to a medium saucepan and bring to a boil.

Add lentils, turmeric, and bay leaf and lower heat to a simmer for 20 minutes, until all water is absorbed.

Add vinegar and remove bay leaf.

Puree to desired consistency using the regular or immersion blender.

Refrigerate for up to 3 days, or batch and freeze using the food cube method for up to 3 months.

Nutrition Facts

Amount Per Serving (2 tablespoons)
Calories 26   Calories from Fat 7

Total Fat   1 g
Saturated Fat   0.1 g
Trans Fat   0 g
Poly Fat   0.1 g
Mono Fat   0.5 g
Cholesterol   0 mg
Sodium   82 mg
Total Carbohydrate   4 g
Dietary Fiber   1 g
Sugars   1 g
Protein   1 g

Recipes for 9 to 12 Months

By now your baby is eating purees with more texture to them. While his foods still need to be carefully mashed, he can handle some small, soft pieces mixed into his purees. Sometime around 9 or 10 months, you may find that he prefers to have his food actually minced, rather than fully pureed. By the time he reaches the 1 year mark, he will be able to handle most foods in finely chopped form. Over the course of these next few months, most babies will be looking for more finger foods, soft or crumbly foods they can hold in their hands and safely eat by themselves.

Although most babies will still be eating the bulk of their meals from the spoon, some prefer to have most of their foods in finger form. If you child seems frustrated with spoon feeding/eating, or frequently tries to pick up his purees with his new pincer grasp, experiment with offering him a healthy selection of soft foods that he can pick up with his hands. To prevent choking and minimize mess, limit the number of pieces you put in his bowl or on the high-chair tray at one time. You can keep restocking his supply as he eats, but give him only a few bits at a time.

Finger Foods

All finger foods should be quite soft.

Begin by offering very small pieces of fruits or vegetables mixed into his puree, about ¼-inch square. As he becomes more adept, you can offer him ½-inch pieces of soft foods, gradually increasing the size as he is able to handle it. Remember to avoid feeding him whole tough or rubbery foods that could get lodged in his windpipe: slice fresh grapes in quarters; skin and mince hot dogs (or better yet, skip those until after his first birthday); mash individual cooked beans or peas a little before offering, etc. Dried fruits are very tough and should be served only after cooking to softness first. Be sure to remove all tough skins, peels, and pits before offering.

Chunks of most meats do not make good finger foods—and any pieces of meat containing gristle are a choking hazard. Don't give your older baby large pieces of meat. Babies cannot chew meats, so keep bites small enough to be swallowed whole: about ¼ inch at the most, until he has more of his molars in. The exception to this is soft fish (for 12 months and older), like whitefish, which will fall apart in his mouth (and in his hands!) almost effortlessly. Be sure to remove all bones, however, even the tiny ones, before offering.

He can have larger pieces of finger food if it is something that is crumbly and will break apart easily in his mouth, like a light cracker, or crisp toast.

Once he is old enough to handle larger pieces, think about presenting finger foods in fun, enticing shapes: lay out a face made of veggies on his high chair tray; use cookie cutters to press interesting shapes out of cheeses or toast(stars, triangles, fish, etc.); or build a little structure out of finger foods, like a teepee of toast and cheese slices, or a snowman of melon balls.

Try these suggestions:

Chopped soft fruits: avocado, banana, papaya, mango, kiwi, melon, peach, etc.

Stewed fruits: apples, pears, prunes, raisins, etc.

Frozen fruit or yogurt ices: Some babies really enjoy the novelty of ice-cold sweet treats: try shaving off small pieces of any of your homemade frozen Popsicle-style treats. These can double as gum soothers if he's got a tooth pushing through. (See page 329 for a great recipe for Fruit Pops.)

Chopped soft veggies: roasted winter squash, sweet potato, carrot, eggplant, etc.

Steamed soft veggies: summer squash, zucchini, green beans, asparagus, etc.

Soft cheeses: mozzarella (sticks are rubbery, keep bites tiny), cheddar, feta, etc.

Soft beans and peas: black beans, kidney beans, peas (remember to mash the individual beans slightly before offering)

Grains: round whole-grain crackers (sharp corners can poke baby's mouth), whole-grain toast, cooked whole-grain pasta shapes (elbows, small penne, bowties, small shells, etc.)

Other: sliced egg yolks or breaded fish sticks or fillets (12 months and older for allergy caution)

TIP

When recipes call for broth, such as vegetable, chicken, or beef, use no-sodium varieties to reduce excess salt. For family meals you may add a little salt to the finished recipe, if desired.

Vegetable Recipes

Broccoli Puree

Makes 4 servings (¼ cup)

Age: Appropriate for age 9 months and up.

Tips: Broccoli has a higher amount of vitamin C than citrus sources and is also very high in calcium. If lightly cooked, broccoli will retain its rich chlorophyll content, which offsets gas from its sulfur content. Once your baby has been introduced to broccoli, you might try making his puree with a dash of garlic powder or tarragon to complement its flavors.

Season: Peak for broccoli is fall through winter.

Selecting: Look for broccoli with closed, dark green florets and a firm stalk.

Storage: Wrap in a moist paper towel and refrigerate in the crisper drawer for up to 7 days.

2 cups fresh broccoli florets

Wash and cut broccoli into florets.

Boil water in medium saucepan with steamer basket.

Add florets and steam for 8 to 10 minutes, until bright green and fork tender. (For larger pieces of broccoli and the stems, steam for 15 to 20 minutes.)

Puree the broccoli in blender. Add steaming water as necessary for desired consistency. (The steaming water is highly nutritious and is great to use in purees or to cook pasta or rice.)

Refrigerate for up to 2 days, or batch using the food cube method and store in the freezer for up to 2 months.

Nutrition Facts

Amount Per Serving (¼ cup)
Calories 32   Calories from Fat 3

Total Fat   1 g
Saturated Fat   0 g
Trans Fat   0 g
Poly Fat   0.2 g
Mono Fat   0 g
Cholesterol   0 mg
Sodium   38 mg
Total Carbohydrate   7 g
Dietary Fiber   3 g
Sugars   1 g
Protein   2 g

Broccoli and Sweet Potato Puree

Makes 4 servings (¼ cup)

Age: Appropriate for age 9 months and up.

Tips: If your baby isn't crazy about the strong flavor of broccoli right away, try this combination dish: The sweet potato helps soften broccoli's bitter edge.

See sweet potato information on page 190; broccoli information at left.

1 medium fresh sweet potato, firm with tapered ends
1 cup fresh broccoli

Scrub sweet potato well.

Bake the sweet potato uncovered at 425° F for about 45 minutes until soft and scoop out of peels; or peel and cut into 1-inch chunks and steam for 25 minutes.

Chop broccoli into florets and

steam for 8 to10 minutes, until fork tender.

Puree cooked sweet potato and steamed broccoli together, adding cooking liquid or water until the desired consistency is reached.

Refrigerate for up to 2 days, or batch using the food cube method and store in the freezer for up to 2 months.

OR

Thaw equal parts of previously frozen broccoli puree and sweet potato puree.

Mix in bowl.

Reheat purees using a double boiler over low heat, or microwave.

Do not refreeze thawed puree.

Nutrition Facts

Amount Per Serving (¼ cup)
Calories 32   Calories from Fat 1

Total Fat   0 g
Saturated Fat   0 g
Trans Fat   0 g
Poly Fat   0.1 g
Mono Fat   0 g
Cholesterol   0 mg
Sodium   108 mg
Total Carbohydrate   7 g
Dietary Fiber   2 g
Sugars   3 g
Protein   1 g

Cauliflower Puree

Makes 4 servings (¼ cup)

Age: Appropriate for age 9 months and up.

Tips: Cauliflower is high in antioxidants, vitamin C, folic acid, and fiber, and is a beneficial source of omega-3 fatty acids, manganese, and B vitamins. Cauliflower blends well in mixed purees with apples

and with white potatoes.

Season: Peak for cauliflower is December through March.

Selection: Choose creamy, white-colored florets without discoloration. Clusters should be close together and covered with green leaves for protection.

Storage: Store in a paper bag or perforated plastic bag with the head down to prevent moisture accumulation.

Refrigerate whole cauliflower for up to 1 week. If cut into florets, use within 1 to 2 days for peak nutrient value.

2 cups fresh cauliflower
¼ teaspoon ground turmeric or
curry powder
3 tablespoons low-sodium
vegetable broth or reserved
steaming water

Wash the cauliflower and cut into small florets.

Steam the florets for 15 to 20 minutes, until very soft.

Strain cauliflower (retaining water) and place in a blender or use an immersion blender.

Add the turmeric.

Puree with broth or steaming water until cauliflower is the desired consistency.

Refrigerate for up to 3 days, or batch using the food cube method and store in the freezer for up to 2 months.

Nutrition Facts

Amount Per Serving (¼ cup)
Calories 16   Calories from Fat 3

Total Fat   0 g
Saturated Fat   0 g
Trans Fat   0 g

Poly Fat   0.1 g
Mono Fat   0 g
Cholesterol   0 mg
Sodium   10 mg
Total Carbohydrate   3 g
Dietary Fiber   2 g
Sugars   2 g
Protein   1 g

Cauliflower and Pea Puree

Makes 4 servings (¼ cup)

Age: Appropriate for age 9 months and up.

Tips: Peas are high in folic acid, vitamin B_6, and a good source of fiber. Snow peas and snap peas can be eaten raw by older toddlers, but the cooking process will bring out their sweetness.

The flavors of cauliflower and peas are very complementary.

See page 214 for cauliflower information.

See page 196 for pea information.

1 cup fresh cauliflower
1 cup fresh-shelled or frozen green peas
1 teaspoon chopped mint, dill, or cilantro (optional)
1 to 3 tablespoons of steaming water, breastmilk, vegetable or chicken broth

Wash the cauliflower, cut into florets, and steam for 15 minutes, until very soft.

Wash the green peas and steam them, about 8 minutes for fresh and 5 minutes for frozen.

Puree the cauliflower, green peas, herb (if using), and liquid together until desired consistency.

Serve immediately.

Refrigerate for up to 3 days, or batch using the food cube method and store in the freezer for up to 2 months.

Nutrition Facts

Amount Per Serving (¼ cup)
Calories 41   Calories from Fat 2

Total Fat   0 g
Saturated Fat   0 g
Trans Fat   0 g
Poly Fat   0.1 g
Mono Fat   0 g
Cholesterol   0 mg
Sodium   191 mg
Total Carbohydrate   8 g
Dietary Fiber   3 g
Sugars   3 g
Protein   3 g

Mashed Potatoes with Cauliflower and Leeks

Makes about 20 infant servings (¼ cup); about 10 adult servings (½ cup)

Age: Appropriate for age 9 months and up.

See cauliflower information on page 214.

Tips: Leeks are helpful in balancing blood sugar. They are high in manganese and a good source of vitamins C and B_6, folic acid, and iron. Leeks are members of the allium family, along with onions and garlic, which have cholesterol-lowering effects. Leeks are low on the food allergy list.

Leeks contain a lot of dirt and grit in between the stalk layers and must be thoroughly cleaned before using. Slice into sections and separate, immersing the separated pieces in a sink or large bowl of water to remove all grit. You may substitute ¼ cup chopped sweet onion for the leek in this recipe, if desired.

Season: Peak for leeks is fall through spring, but they are available year-round.

Selection: Choose a leek with a white bulb and dark green stalk. The bulb should be about 1 inch in diameter without any marks.

Storage: Refrigerate unwashed leaks in plastic, which will help hold the moisture in the leek for 1 to 2 days. Leeks are highly perishable and can be refrigerated only for a couple of days. Freeze raw leeks in a plastic freezer bag for up to 3 months.

Tips: White potatoes are high in vitamin B_6, vitamin C, iron, copper, and manganese and contain a good amount of fiber. White potatoes are the most consumed vegetable among toddlers in the United States. Though potatoes do have a good nutrient base, especially in the skin, they also have a high glycemic load, which means they convert quickly into sugar in the bloodstream. Also, the potatoes being consumed are often in poor-quality forms like french fries, with lots of added salts and even sugars. The best way to serve white potatoes to your baby and toddler, then, is to make your own and combine them with a high-fiber vegetable and/or a protein (as in Braised Paprika Chicken and Potatoes, page 240).

Season: Potatoes are available year-round.

Storage: Store in a cool dry place at 45 to 50° F, preferably in a brown bag away from onions, as they both emit gases that will decrease the quality in one or both.

1 fresh leek (bulb and lower leaf portion), about ½ cup
1 small cauliflower head, about 3 cups
3 medium potatoes, peeled and diced, about 3 cups
1 cup broth (chicken or vegetable), add more for thinner consistency
¾ teaspoon paprika
½ teaspoon garlic powder (optional)
½ teaspoon salt

Remove top section of tough leaves and root end of bulb, and slice remaining leek down the middle.

Cut into 2-inch sections.

Separate and immerse the leek pieces in a sink of water, washing thoroughly to remove all dirt and grit.

Fill a large stockpot with 2 quarts water.

Add cauliflower, potato, and leek, and bring to a boil.

Simmer for 10 to 15 minutes, or until vegetables are fork tender.

Drain vegetables in a colander to remove any excess moisture.

Using a mixer or potato masher, blend the vegetables, broth, paprika, garlic powder, and salt until desired mashed potato consistency. Do not puree!

Add salt and pepper to taste for adults. You may also substitute cow's milk for the broth for toddlers, if desired.

Refrigerate for up to 3 days.

Nutrition Facts

Amount Per Serving (¼ cup)
Calories 27   Calories from Fat 1

Total Fat   0 g
Saturated Fat   0 g
Trans Fat   0 g

Poly Fat   0.1 g
Mono Fat   0 g
Cholesterol   0 mg
Sodium   141 mg
Total Carbohydrate   6 g
Dietary Fiber   1 g
Sugars   1 g
Protein   1 g

Greens Puree

Makes 4 servings (¼ cup)

Age: Appropriate for age 8 months and up.

It is a great idea to start introducing your child to green purees so they will get used to the bitter taste at a young age. You may mix green purees with sweet potato, white potato, or a grain to mellow the intense flavors, if desired. This recipe works well with 3 leafy greens: kale, Swiss chard, and collard greens. See page 222 for information on kale.

Swiss Chard

Tips: Swiss chard tastes quite similar to the flavor of beets. Swiss chard is high in vitamins K, E, A, C, and B$_6$, and in magnesium, manganese, potassium, iron, fiber, copper, calcium, and riboflavin. It's extremely high in vitamin K. It is high in oxalates and should be eaten only a few times per week. Quick-boiling chard rather than steaming it will make it taste sweeter and less bitter. To retain maximum minerals and vitamin C, avoid overcooking.

Season: Peak season for Swiss chard is June through August.

Selection: Look for Swiss chard with large, wide leaves that are either vibrant green or red in color with firm, thick stalks. Be sure leaves are not wilted or brown on the edges. If your chard does wilt

before cook time, use 2 tablespoons of vinegar and 5 cups of water to wash—vinegar will replump the leaves somewhat.

Storage: Store Swiss chard in the refrigerator for about 5 days, or blanch and freeze for up to 2 months.

Collard Greens

Season: Peak for collards is spring, fall, and winter.

Tips: Collard greens are a powerhouse vegetable—a great source of calcium, fiber, and iron. High in antioxidants, vitamins C and E, beta-carotene, and more collard greens are also a good source of vitamin B$_6$, riboflavin, and niacin. With their high levels of vitamin A and zinc, collard greens are an immune system booster.

Selection: Look for large, crisp, vibrant green leaves.

Storage: Wrap greens in a damp paper towel, place in a plastic or perforated bag, and place bag in the crisper drawer for up to 5 days. The sooner they are cooked after harvest, the less bitter they are.

> 2 cups chopped kale, Swiss chard, or collard greens, stems removed
> 1 tablespoon water
> 1 tablespoon apple juice
> 1 lemon wedge, squeezed (optional for 12 months and up)

Steam or boil chopped greens for 5 to 10 minutes or until soft.

To reduce bitter taste, steam uncovered.

If necessary (as with curly kale), remove excess water by pressing the greens with the back of a large metal spoon against a shallow bowl or colander. Save the steaming or boiling water for preparing grains, pureeing, or to drink.

Puree all ingredients to desired consistency in a blender or food mill, adding liquid if necessary.

Store in the refrigerator for up to 3 days, or batch using the food cube method and store in the freezer for up to 3 months.

Suggestion: Serve with grain cereal, or mix with potato puree or a sweet fruit such as applesauce or pears.

Nutrition Facts

Amount Per Serving (¼ cup)
Calories 20   Calories from Fat 2

Total Fat   0 g
Saturated Fat   0 g
Trans Fat   0 g
Poly Fat   0.1 g
Mono Fat   0 g
Cholesterol   0 mg
Sodium   200 mg
Total Carbohydrate   4 g
Dietary Fiber   1 g
Sugars   1 g
Protein   1 g

Baked Eggplant and White Beans

Makes 6 infant servings (¼ cup)

Age: Appropriate for age 9 months and up.

Tips: Eggplant is a member of the nightshade family, which includes tomatoes, potatoes, and sweet peppers. Eggplant is high in phytonutrients, fiber, potassium, manganese, copper, and thiamin (vitamin B$_1$); and a beneficial source of folic acid and magnesium. It is helpful with brain functioning.

Once peeled or cut, the white flesh of the eggplant will darken somewhat with exposure to the air, but this will not affect taste or nutrient content.

Caution: Never feed a baby raw eggplant—it is high in oxalates, quite bitter, and difficult to digest.

Season: Peak for eggplant is August through October.

Selection: Look for eggplants that feel heavy, have a glossy appearance, and have a green stem and cap. Eggplant is ripe if it does not indent when pressed gently with the thumb. Avoid eggplants with marks, nicks, or bruises.

Storage: Eggplant is quite perishable and should not be washed before being placed in the crisper drawer of the refrigerator. Do not squeeze it into the drawer, as this may cause damage. Refrigerate for up to 3 days.

1 medium eggplant
2 cloves garlic
1 15-ounce can great northern
    beans, drained and rinsed
1 tablespoon diced fresh basil
¼ teaspoon salt

Preheat oven to 400° F.

Wash the eggplant.

Slightly crush and peel the garlic gloves. Cut into slivers.

Make several slits in the eggplant and place slivers of garlic in slits.

Place whole eggplant into a shallow baking pan and bake for 30 to 45 minutes, depending on size.

The eggplant is done when it looks caved in.

Remove from oven and place in a colander so juices drain off.

When cool enough to handle, cut

in half lengthwise and scoop out the eggplant, discarding the skin.

Add beans, basil, and salt and mash eggplant well with potato masher, large fork, or in the mixer.

Serve mashed, or puree for finer consistency.

Store in the refrigerator for up to 3 days, or batch using the food cube method and store in the freezer for up to 2 months.

Suggestions: Add to plain yogurt with a dash of salt.

For babies 12 months and up: squeeze fresh juice of 1 lemon wedge to prevent discoloration.

To make baba ghanoush, mix cooked eggplant with ¼ cup tahini, ¼ cup lemon juice, 1 clove minced garlic, and ¼ teaspoon salt, and puree it in a food processor or with an immersion wand.

Use as a vegetable dip.

Nutrition Facts

Amount Per Serving (¼ cup)
Calories 33   Calories from Fat 2

Total Fat   0 g
Saturated Fat   0 g
Trans Fat   0 g
Poly Fat   0.1 g
Mono Fat   0 g
Cholesterol   0 mg
Sodium   208 mg
Total Carbohydrate   8 g
Dietary Fiber   2 g
Sugars   3 g
Protein   1 g

Asparagus Puree

Makes 6 infant servings (¼ cup)

Age: Appropriate for age 9 months and up. (If baby has any digestive issues, start asparagus at 10 months.)

Tips: Asparagus is extremely high in folic acid and a great source of potassium, and acts as a natural laxative. Asparagus is cooling to the body.

Asparagus has a strong flavor, which you can mellow initially by mixing with mashed white or sweet potato, if desired. After eating asparagus, you may notice an unusual odor in your child's wet diaper. This is an odd but completely harmless affect of the amino acid asparagine contained in the plant.

Season: Peak for asparagus is spring and summer.

Selection: Asparagus stalks should be deep green, firm, and smooth, and the bottom of the stem can be woody. The thinner male stalks tend to be a little more tender than the larger female stalks, but both will work for a puree. The tips should be green and may have a tinge of purple. They should be dry and compact like a flower bud.

Storage: Wrap in a damp paper towel and place in the back of the refrigerator, since light compromises folic acid content.

12 medium fresh asparagus spears (about a pound)
1 to 2 tablespoons water, depending on asparagus juiciness

Set water to boil in medium saucepan with a steamer basket.

Wash the asparagus.

Hold the asparagus at the base. With the other hand gently bend the stalk until it snaps. It should easily snap apart where the thick part and the tender part meet. Discard the lower end. Do this to all the asparagus spears.

Once water is boiling, place asparagus in steamer basket.

Steam the asparagus for 5 to 8 minutes, or until just mushy. For an older baby, steam about 5 minutes, squeeze a little lemon on, and serve as a finger food.

Puree asparagus and water in a food processor until desired consistency is reached.

Refrigerate for up to 2 days, or batch using the food cube method and store in the freezer for up to 2 months.

Nutrition Facts

Amount Per Serving (¼ cup)
Calories 7   Calories from Fat 1

Total Fat   0 g
Saturated Fat   0 g
Trans Fat   0 g
Poly Fat   0 g
Mono Fat   0 g
Cholesterol   0 mg
Sodium   66 mg
Total Carbohydrate   1 g
Dietary Fiber   1 g
Sugars   0 g
Protein   1 g

Braised Carrot Coins

Makes 8 infant servings (¼ cup)

Age: Appropriate for age 9 months and up.

Tips: The flavor of carrots is enhanced by sweet herbs, such as tarragon or dill.

You can buy pretoasted wheat germ or toast your own. To toast raw wheat germ: Place on a cookie sheet at 325° F for about 15 minutes,

or until lightly browned. Wheat germ is great sprinkled over cooked veggies, on salads, or mixed into yogurt.

See carrot information on page 192.

> 1 pound fresh carrots
> 1 cup water
> 1½ tablespoons ghee (clarified butter) or butter
> 1 tablespoon toasted wheat germ or ground flaxseeds
> 1 teaspoon dried dill, tarragon or parsley (or 1 tablespoon chopped fresh)

Wash, peel, and slice carrots into ¼-inch rounds.

Place carrots, water (or vegetable broth for more flavor), and ghee, in a large sauté pan with a lid.

Place over medium heat, cover, and simmer for about 15 to 20 minutes, or until carrots are fork tender.

(If necessary, add additional 1 to 2 tablespoons of water and continue cooking.)

Add dill, tarragon, or parsley for the last few minutes of cooking.

Sprinkle wheat germ or ground flax over the top for a flavorful crunch.

Allow carrots to cool almost to room temperature.

Chop carrot coins to desired size for finger food. For babies over 6 months: omit wheat germ and flax, and combine ¼ cup cooked carrots with 1 to 4 tablespoons liquid and puree to desired consistency.

Nutrition Facts

Amount Per Serving (¼ cup)
Calories 46   Calories from Fat 23

Total Fat   3 g
Saturated Fat   1.5 g
Trans Fat   0 g
Poly Fat   0.2 g
Mono Fat   0.7 g
Cholesterol   6 mg
Sodium   31 mg
Total Carbohydrate   5 g
Dietary Fiber   2 g
Sugars   2 g
Protein   1 g

Beet Puree

Makes 4 infant servings (¼ cup)

Age: Cooked beets appropriate for age 9 months and up. Grated raw beets appropriate for age 10 months and up.

Tips: High in B vitamins, iron, and folic acid. Benefits circulation. Once your child has been introduced to beets, you may add a dash of parsley, dill, or mint to his puree for complementary flavors.

Beets are unique in that they provide two vegetables in one: the greens and the root.

Don't be alarmed if your child's urine turns red after eating: That's caused by the red pigment from the beet root and is a harmless side effect.

Season: Peak for beets is April through August,

Selection: Beets are best bought when they have brightly colored, crisp greens, and the flesh on the end is red, hard, and firm looking.

Storage: Store with greens on; beets soften faster without the greens.

4 medium fresh beet roots
(about 1 pound)

Preheat oven to 400° F.

Scrub beets well under cold water.

Place whole beets in a baking dish with ¼ inch of water and cover. The steaming effect speeds cooking time.

Bake large beets for 40 minutes; bake small to medium beets for 25 to 30 minutes. Beets are finished when they are fork tender.

Remove the stems and slip off the peels under cold running water before pureeing.

Puree until desired consistency.

Refrigerate for up to 3 days, or batch using the food cube method and store in the freezer for up to 2 months.

Nutrition Facts

Amount Per Serving (¼ cup)
Calories 32   Calories from Fat 1

Total Fat   0 g
Saturated Fat   0 g
Trans Fat   0 g
Poly Fat   0 g
Mono Fat   0 g
Cholesterol   0 mg
Sodium   69 mg
Total Carbohydrate   8 g
Dietary Fiber   2 g
Sugars   7 g
Protein   1 g

See page 193 for information on butternut squash.

> **TIP**
>
> The sweet combination of beets and carrots reduces gas, aids digestion, and can be helpful for relieving colic symptoms. Combine 1 cup of cooked carrots with 1 cup of cooked beets and ¼ teaspoon ground cumin and puree in a blender to desired consistency, adding a little liquid if necessary.

Kale and Butternut Squash Puree

Makes 4 servings (¼ cup)

Age: Appropriate for age 9 months and up.

Tips: Kale is a nutritional powerhouse: very high in calcium; iron; vitamins C, A (beta-carotene), and E; and chlorophyll. It is beneficial to prevention of cancer and heart disease.

Kale is among the tougher and more fibrous of the leafy green vegetables, so generally needs to be boiled instead of steamed. It's a perfect green for soups because it holds up well during extended cooking times. Combining it (or any strong leafy green) with the sweet mellow flavor of a mild root vegetable such as butternut squash is a great way to introduce kale.

Season: Peak season for kale is winter (very sweet flavor after frost), spring, and summer.

Selection: There are a few varieties of kale: Look for a dark green color, crinkled leaves, and a firm stem.

Storage: Store kale, unwashed, in a plastic bag in the crisper drawer for up to 4 days.

See page 193 for information on butternut squash.

> ½ cup fresh kale, washed, stemmed, and sliced into strips
> 1 cup butternut squash, baked or steamed
> ¼ teaspoon ground cinnamon

Boil kale in a medium saucepan with a couple inches of water for 10 minutes until soft and wilted.

Drain well, reserving the boiling water to drink or use as a cooking liquid for rice or pasta.

In a mixer or using an immersion blender, combine kale, squash, and cinnamon, and blend until smooth.

Refrigerate for up to 3 days, or freeze using the food cube and store up to 2 months.

Nutrition Facts

Amount Per Serving (¼ cup)
Calories 24   Calories from Fat 1

Total Fat   0 g
Saturated Fat   0 g
Trans Fat   0 g
Poly Fat   0 g
Mono Fat   0 g
Cholesterol   0 mg
Sodium   4 mg
Total Carbohydrate   6 g
Dietary Fiber   0 g
Sugars   1 g
Protein   1 g

Fruit Recipes

Poached Pears

*Makes 4 toddler servings (¼ cup);
or 2 adult servings (½ cup)*

Age: Appropriate for age 9
months and up (pears are fine for
babies of all ages, but the spices in
this recipe may be a bit much for
younger babies).

Tips: Poached pears are a
comforting dish for the whole family
during the cold months—cooking
them makes the whole house smell
delicious. They work well with
plain yogurt or a yogurt sauce. For
a simple yogurt sauce, combine 3 to
4 tablespoons of cooled poaching
liquid with ½ cup plain yogurt.

You may also serve them as an
accompaniment to cooked poultry.

You may wish to use
nonalcoholic vanilla extract or omit,
unless your child is 12 months and
up.

    4 medium fresh pears
    4 cups water
    2 to 3 slices fresh ginger
    1 cinnamon stick or 1
        teaspoon ground cinnamon
    ½ teaspoon nonalcoholic
        vanilla extract
    1 teaspoon blackstrap
        molasses
    ¼ teaspoon cardamom
        (optional)
    1 tablespoon fresh-squeezed
        lemon juice (optional for 12
        months and up)

Wash, core, seed, and halve pears.
Peel only if pureeing.

In a large saucepan, combine
water, ginger, cinnamon stick,
vanilla, blackstrap molasses, and, if
using, cardamom and lemon juice.

Simmer for 5 minutes.

Add pears, reduce heat to low,
and cook lightly for about 15
minutes.

Flip and cook for an additional
10 to 15 minutes, until fork tender
but not mushy.

Remove pears using a slotted
spoon and place in a baking dish.

Simmer the liquid, uncovered, for
about 5 minutes more, until liquid is
reduced by half.

Remove ginger and cinnamon
stick using a slotted spoon.

Pour liquid over pears.

Serve warm or cold,
refrigerated for about 8 hours to
overnight, with optional yogurt
sauce on top.

Refrigerate in a sealed
container for up to 3 days, or
freeze in airtight container for up
to 3 months.

Nutrition Facts

Amount Per Serving (¼ cup)
Calories 51   Calories from Fat 1

Total Fat   0 g
Saturated Fat   0 g
Trans Fat   0 g
Poly Fat   0 g
Mono Fat   0.1 g
Cholesterol   0 mg
Sodium   4 mg
Total Carbohydrate   14 g
Dietary Fiber   3 g
Sugars   8 g
Protein   0 g

Frozen Applesauce

*Makes 4 infant servings (¼ cup);
or 3 toddler servings (⅓ cup)*

Age: Appropriate for age 9 months and up (because apples are uncooked, and the texture is coarser than that of cooked applesauce).

Tips: This is a great way to make applesauce with no cooking. The freezer breaks down the apples' fiber. Frozen applesauce has a rougher texture than cooked, so it's a good way to get your 9-month-old accustomed to a different feel of a familiar food in his mouth.

Apples are high in antioxidants, fiber, and vitamin C. Insoluble fiber can reduce cholesterol and has anti-inflammatory properties. Apples may help relieve indigestion.

Lemon juice will prevent browning.

Caution: According to the Environmental Working Group 2006 "Shopper's Guide to Pesticides in Produce," apples are one of the twelve foods highest in pesticide concentrations, so buy organic whenever possible.

Season: Peak for apples is late summer to early winter. Available year-round.

Selection: Choose softer apples, like McIntosh, Fuji, Gala, and Cortland, for frozen applesauce recipe. Granny Smith apples are very tart but hold their texture well when cooked. Red, Golden Delicious, and Pink Lady apples are a few of the sweetest "eating apples." McIntosh apples are great for making applesauce (cooked or frozen), pie, and juice.

Storage: Store in a cool area or refrigerate for up to 6 weeks.

4 medium fresh apples (softer apples are best: McIntosh, Fuji, Gala, Cortland, etc.)
1 tablespoon fresh-squeezed lemon juice (optional for 12 months and up)
1½ tablespoons ground cinnamon
¼ teaspoon ground cloves

Peel, core, and slice apples (an apple corer/slicer makes this very quick).

Place apples in a large bowl and add lemon juice, if using, cinnamon, and cloves, mixing to combine well.

Place mixture in wax paper bags or roll into wax paper, and then put in plastic freezer bags.

Freeze for 6 hours to overnight.

Move to refrigerator to thaw for a minimum of 1 hour.

Remove apple mixture from bags and mash with a potato masher or immersion blender.

(Texture will not be as smooth as cooked applesauce.)

Store in the refrigerator for up to 2 days. Do not refreeze.

Nutrition Facts

Amount Per Serving (¼ cup)
Calories 46   Calories from Fat 2

Total Fat   1 g
Saturated Fat   0 g
Trans Fat   0 g
Poly Fat   0 g
Mono Fat   0 g
Cholesterol   0 mg
Sodium   1 mg
Total Carbohydrate   13 g
Dietary Fiber   2 g
Sugars   9 g
Protein   0 g

Fruit Salad Pudding

Makes 8 toddler servings (¼ cup); 4 adult servings (½ cup)

Age: Appropriate for age 9 months and up.

Tips: This "pudding" is actually a combo fruit puree with different fruits with different textures. It works well as a stand-alone treat or as a dip for older toddlers for larger fruit segents, such as apple slices. It would also blend nicely into plain yogurt or into cooked grains for a sweeter cereal. This will initially be a bright green color but it will darken quickly because of the avocado and banana. For an older child you can squeeze a wedge of lime or lemon into the puree to slow the darkening. This mixture won't freeze well, so make just as much as you need for one or two sittings.

Kiwi is high in fiber and vitamin C, and a good source of vitamin E, manganese, magnesium, and potassium.

Season: Peak for kiwi is November through May in California, and June through October in New Zealand.

Selection: Choose kiwis with smooth skins—no wrinkling. If the fruit is pliable when held with your thumb and forefinger, it will be sweet. Kiwis can be bought hard.

Storage: Kiwis can be ripened on a countertop for up to a week. Speed up the ripening process by placing the kiwi in a paper bag with a banana, apple, or pear. Refrigerate ripened kiwi in the crisper drawer for up to 1 week.

2 medium peaches (peeled and
    diced)

½ banana (sliced)
½ cup avocado peeled and diced
    (about 1 small avocado)
2 medium kiwi (peeled and
    diced)
1 teaspoon cinnamon
Dash cardamom

Puree everything together in the food processor or blender to desired consistency or, for a chunkier texture, puree the peach and banana together and stir in diced avocado and kiwi.

Nutrition Facts

Amount Per Serving (¼ cup)
Calories 37   Calories from Fat 13

Total Fat   1 g
Saturated Fat   0.2 g
Trans Fat   0 g
Poly Fat   0.2 g
Mono Fat   0.9 g
Cholesterol   0 mg
Sodium   1 mg
Total Carbohydrate   6 g
Dietary Fiber   2 g
Sugars   4 g
Protein   1 g

Warm Fruit Compote

Makes 16 toddler servings (¼ cup)

Age: Appropriate for age 12 months and up.

Tips: This is a delicious combination of sweet and tart flavors that can be served for breakfast with a grain such as quinoa, oatmeal, or millet, or for lunch with plain yogurt or cottage cheese. It can also be cooked with chicken or turkey, or used as a side dish for cooked meats.

See page 224 for information on apples.

½ cup prunes
½ cup dried apricots
2 cups water
1 cup orange juice or apple cider
2 tablespoons fresh-squeezed
    lemon juice
1 teaspoon ground cinnamon
¼ teaspoon ground nutmeg
    (optional)
2 cups soft apples (such as
    McIntosh), cored, peeled,
    and cut into small pieces

In a large saucepan, combine prunes, apricots, water, juice, lemon juice, cinnamon, and nutmeg (if using).

Bring to a boil.

Reduce heat to a low simmer, cover and cook for about 20 to 25 minutes, until tender.

Add apples and cook for about 10 to 15 minutes, until fork tender.

Add additional water if necessary.

Remove from heat and puree in a blender, or serve as is for an older child. Remove some of the cooking liquid for a thicker consistency.

Refrigerate in a sealed containers for up to 5 days, or batch and freeze in food cubes for up to 3 months.

Nutrition Facts

Amount Per Serving (¼ cup)
Calories 74   Calories from Fat 1

Total Fat   0 g
Saturated Fat   0 g
Trans Fat   0 g
Poly Fat   0 g
Mono Fat   0 g
Cholesterol   0 mg
Sodium   3 mg
Total Carbohydrate   19 g
Dietary Fiber   2 g
Sugars   16 g
Protein   1 g

Pineapple (Puree, Pineapple Boat, and Grilled Pineapple Skewers)

Makes 12 infant servings (¼ cup); or 9 toddler servings (⅓ cup)

Age: Appropriate for age 9 months and up.

Tips: Helps strengthen the immune system; contains proteolytic enzyme, which helps in the digestion of protein; is high in vitamin C, antioxidants, manganese, and thiamin (B_1); helps cool the body.

Season: Peak for pineapples is spring.

Selection: Look for pineapples that are heavy for their size; should have a sweet smell from the stem end. If you can easily pick off a green leaf, the pineapple is ripe. It should not have any dark spots or brown "eyes."

Storage: Pineapples are quite perishable. They stop ripening once they are picked. Pineapples can be left at room temperature for 1 to 2 days. Once cut, refrigerate in a sealed container with some of its juices or water for up to 5 days. Flavor changes when frozen.

1 whole fresh pineapples (1
    medium pineapple yields
    approximately 3 cups of fruit)
1 tablespoon ghee or olive oil
2 tablespoons apple juice or
    apple cider
1 teaspoon ground cinnamon
½ teaspoon ground cloves
    (optional)

Wash the pineapples and cut off and discard the top crown and base.

Standing pineapple on end, cut off the skin by slicing top to bottom.

Remove remaining "eyes" with a paring knife.

Slice the pineapple into large coins, removing the core with a pineapple corer.

OR

Cut the pineapple in half lengthwise and then into quarters; remove the core.

OR

Cut the pineapple into large wedges, and core.

For babies 9 months and up: Puree fresh pineapple in the blender, leaving some small chunks.

Refrigerate for up to 3 days in a plastic container covered with pineapple juice.

Batch using the food cube method and store in the freezer for up to 2 months; or place chunks in a plastic container covered with pineapple juice and freeze for up to 2 months.

For Toddlers: Pineapple Boat
Cut the pineapple in half and scoop out the fruit using a butter knife and spoon.

Remove the core then puree or dice the fruit and add it back into the pineapple skins and serve. (Other fruit can be added as well.)

Grilled Pineapple Skewers
Wash the pineapple and cut off and discard the top crown and base.

Standing pineapple on end, cut off the skin by slicing top to bottom.

Remove remaining "eyes" with a paring knife.

Cut pineapple into 1-inch chunks and place 4 chunks on a skewer.

In a bowl, whisk together olive oil, apple juice or cider, cinnamon, and cloves, if using.

Lightly brush the pineapple with the marinade.

Broil or grill the pineapple skewers for about 5 minutes, or until fork tender, basting once or twice during cooking.

Remove pineapple from the skewers to avoid injury to toddlers.

Skewers go well with grilled chicken, fish, or shrimp.

Nutrition Facts

Amount Per Serving (¼ cup)
Calories 31   Calories from Fat 11

Total Fat   1 g
Saturated Fat   0.2 g
Trans Fat   0 g
Poly Fat   0.1 g
Mono Fat   0.8 g
Cholesterol   0 mg
Sodium   1 mg
Total Carbohydrate   5 g
Dietary Fiber   1 g
Sugars   4 g
Protein   0 g

Pasta and Grains Recipes

Simple Quinoa Cereal, Long-Cooking Method

Makes 8 toddler servings (¼ cup)

Age: Appropriate for age 9 months and up.

Tips: Quinoa is the only grain containing 8 essential amino acids. It has the lowest glycemic load of all the grains. It is very high in calcium, iron, and antioxidants, and a good source of phosphorus and vitamins B and E. It is protective against childhood asthma.

Quinoa is one of the least allergenic grains, and a good balancing food. Quinoa flakes are an easy way to make instant quinoa hot cereal and to enrich baked goods. Quinoa has a mild, nutty flavor and takes on the flavors of foods with which it is cooked.

It combines well with carrots, kale, peas, spinach, broccoli, cauliflower, banana, dried fruit, berries, apples, and pears.

It is actually a tiny seed, which has a bitter protective coating called saponin. Rinse or toast quinoa to remove the saponin's bitter taste.

Season: Quinoa is available year-round.

Selecting: Quinoa comes prepackaged and in bulk. When buying in bulk, make sure there is a high turnover rate to ensure freshness. Containers should be covered and dry.

Storage: Refrigerate in an airtight container for 3 to 5 months.

> 1 cup dry quinoa
> 2 cups water or broth (vegetable or chicken)

Rinse quinoa thoroughly and drain in a fine colander.

Optional (for a nuttier flavor): Heat in a medium saucepan over low heat, stirring occasionally, for about 5 minutes, until a nutty aroma is released (if toasting, no rinsing is required).

Add liquid and bring to a boil.

Lower heat, cover, and simmer for about 15 minutes, until liquid is absorbed and you can see the seeds pop and the spiral tails expand.

Blend ½ cup cooked quinoa with 3 to 4 tablespoons liquid and puree to desired consistency. Serve plain or with an added a dash of salt, nutmeg, cinnamon, or cardamom if desired.

Nutrition Facts

Amount Per Serving (¼ cup)
Calories 56   Calories from Fat 7

Total Fat   1 g
Saturated Fat   0 g
Trans Fat   0 g
Poly Fat   0.5 g
Mono Fat   0.3 g
Cholesterol   0 mg
Sodium   3 mg
Total Carbohydrate   8 g
Dietary Fiber   1 g
Sugars   0 g
Protein   2 g

Kasha and Orzo Pilaf

Servings: 12 infant servings (¼ cup); 10 toddler servings (⅓ cup); or 7 adult servings (½ to ¾ cup)

Age: Appropriate for age 9 months and up.

Tips: This tasty and satisfying dish is a good one for the whole family. To make it a meal, gently stir in cooked diced chicken or soft white beans at the end of cook time.

Buckwheat/Kasha: Kasha is roasted buckwheat. Its name is misleading because it does not contain wheat. Buckwheat, like quinoa, is actually a seed. Buckwheat/kasha does not contain gluten, so is safe for use by people with a wheat intolerance or family history of celiac disease. Buckwheat is high in magnesium and manganese, and also a good source of fiber.

Kasha has a nutty taste and a very soft texture, and cooks up very fast, making it an ideal grain for regular use with your baby and toddler. Cream of buckwheat cereal is a great instant cereal for infants 6 months and older.

Season: year round

Selecting: It can be purchased in a packaged container or in the bulk bins. If purchasing in bulk, make sure there is no moisture in the bins.

Storage: Place buckwheat in an airtight container in a cool, dry place. Buckwheat flour should be refrigerated for maximum freshness, especially in warm climates.

Whole-wheat orzo: Orzo is a tiny pasta, perfectly shaped for the new "pincer" grasp of your older baby. Cook it to full tenderness rather than al dente. Whole-wheat orzo is high in fiber, manganese, and magnesium.

Season: Year-round.

Selecting: Look for the whole-grain stamp on packaged whole-wheat orzo.

Storage: Buy prepackaged and store in a cool dry area.

½ cup whole-wheat orzo
1 cup broth (chicken or
   vegetable)
½ cup water
½ cup finely grated carrot
½ cup kasha
¼ cup minced mushrooms
   (white or button)
1 teaspoon butter
¼ teaspoon dried thyme
¼ teaspoon onion powder
¼ teaspoon salt

In a medium saucepan, bring 3 cups of water to a rapid boil over high heat.

Add the orzo, bring to a second boil and cook, uncovered, for 10 to 12 minutes until orzo is very tender. Drain and set aside.

In a medium sauté pan, add broth, water, and carrots and bring to a low boil over medium heat.

Reduce heat to medium-low and slowly stir in kasha, mushrooms, butter, and salt.

Cover and cook about 12 minutes until kasha is soft and all liquid has been absorbed.

Gently stir in reserved orzo.

Nutrition Facts

Amount Per Serving (¼ cup)
Calories 39   Calories from Fat 4

Total Fat   0 g
Saturated Fat   0.2 g
Trans Fat   0 g
Poly Fat   0.1 g
Mono Fat   0.1 g
Cholesterol   1 mg
Sodium   74 mg
Total Carbohydrate   8 g
Dietary Fiber   2 g
Sugars   1 g
Protein   1 g

Grains Guide

Grain	Ratio of Grain to Liquid	Presoak	Cook Time
Amaranth	1 measure amaranth to 3 measures liquid	No	25 minutes (gelatinous texture)
Pearled barley	1 measure barley to 3 measures liquid	Optional	40 minutes
Brown rice (medium grain)	1 measure rice to 2 measures liquid	Optional	40 to 50 minutes
Buckwheat (kasha is toasted variety)	1 measure kasha to 2 measures liquid	No	15 to 20 minutes (mushy texture)
Millet	1 measure millet to 3 measures liquid	Optional	30 to 40 minutes
Oats (steel cut)	1 measure oats to 4 measures liquid	Optional	30 to 35 minutes
Quinoa	1 measure quinoa to 2 measures liquid	Optional	15 to 20 minutes

Storage: Whole grains still have their germ layer (containing the oil), so they can go rancid more rapidly than refined grains. Keep raw grains in a cool, dry place. If you have space in your fridge, it will extend their shelf life: 2 to 3 months in a cool place, 6 months in the freezer. Once cooked, they will keep up to 3 days in the refrigerator, or 1 to 2 months in the freezer.

Preparation: Rinse your grains in cold water and soak for 3 hours to overnight, if indicated. Drain off soaking water and replace with new cooking liquid. For cooking liquid you can use plain water, no-sodium cooking broth, or 1 part apple cider to 3 parts water or broth for a little sweetness. You can use a 2-quart saucepan with a tight-fitting lid to cook 1 to 2 cups of grain. Combine the rice and liquid and heat to boiling, covered, over medium-high heat. Once boiling, reduce heat to medium-low (keep a low simmer) and cook until the water is almost completely absorbed. After the grains have cooked, remove from heat and let stand, covered, for 5 to 10 minutes to continue absorbing the moisture.

Cooked rice freezes beautifully. Make an oversized batch and spread cooked rice out on a large cookie sheet to cool more quickly. After about 15 minutes, rice can be scooped into quart or gallon-sized zip-closure freezer bags. The rice should fill the bag, but only be about 1 inch thick. Press all the air out of the bag, seal, and label it with contents and the date. One the rice baggies are frozen solid, they can be stored upright to take up less room in the freezer. To reheat, break up frozen rice in the bag, and empty "chunks" into a steamer pan or microwave-safe bowl. Microwave for 1 minute at a time until rice is hot throughout, or steam for 3 to 4 minutes until hot. Do not refreeze thawed rice.

Rice Cooker: No-Brainer Grains

Another way to have fresh, perfect grains with the minimum of effort is to purchase a rice cooker. With a rice cooker, you add the grain and liquid to the machine, set the timer, and leave it alone—no checking required (and no forgotten and burned grains!). The models range from very simple and inexpensive (around $25), to very high tech and pricey (around $175). Look for them in any kitchen supply store, most Asian markets, or online. (See Resources for our favorite models.)

We think rice cookers are a godsend for tired and busy homemade baby food chefs because they really make regular grains prep a no-brainer. Be sure to invest in a model that can handle whole grains, however: If it says suitable for brown rice, you're all set. Many models are equipped to handle only white rice—other grains will boil over.

With a rice cooker, it's also quite simple to combine grains and cook them together, even adding in some chopped dried fruit or veggies. Just combine grains that have comparable cooking times, adjust the liquids as necessary, and push the button. Once they are cooked, you can easily make fresh cereal for your baby by simply pureeing your mixed (or single) grains with a liquid in equal measures. One note: unless you've got the Cadillac model, the rice cooker is not the best method for the shortest-cooking grains (kasha [buckwheat], amaranth, and quinoa), but it works well for everything else on the grains chart.

Basil Pasta with Zucchini and Yellow Squash

Makes 8 infant servings (¼ cup); 6 toddler servings (⅓ cup); or 4 adult servings (½ to ¾ cup)

Age: Appropriate age is 9 months and up.

Tips: The basil in this recipe brings out the natural flavors of the squash and zucchini.

See page 195 for information on zucchini; page 192 for information on yellow squash.

1 tablespoon olive oil
1 medium onion, sliced
1 medium zucchini
1 medium yellow squash
1 teaspoon dried basil
½ cup broth (vegetable or chicken)
¼ to ½ teaspoon sea salt (optional)
Dash garlic powder (optional)
1 16-ounce box whole grain penne, cooked

Cook pasta according to package directions.

In a large sauté pan over medium heat, cook olive oil and onions for 3 to 5 minutes, until translucent.

Cut zucchini and yellow squash lengthwise, quarter, and then chop into ½-inch pieces.

Add zucchini, squash, basil, broth, salt, and garlic powder, if using, to onions and simmer for about 10 to 15 minutes, until vegetables are soft.

Add cooked pasta to the zucchini mixture.

Continue cooking on low heat for about 5 minutes. Stir continually to blend flavors.

Blend or puree for a baby, or chop for an older child.

Nutrition Facts

Amount Per Serving (¼ cup)
Calories 126   Calories from Fat 26

Total Fat   3 g
Saturated Fat   0.2 g
Trans Fat   0 g
Poly Fat   1 g
Mono Fat   0.4 g
Cholesterol   0 mg
Sodium   257 mg
Total Carbohydrate   21 g
Dietary Fiber   3 g
Sugars   3 g
Protein   5 g

Slow Cooker Oatmeal

Makes 12 toddler servings (⅓ cup)

Age: Appropriate for babies 9 months and up.

Tips: This is a terrific way to provide your children with an easy, warm breakfast. Adding nuts or fruit to oatmeal makes this an even more delicious and nutritious food— place them, along with the other ingredients, in the slow cooker at the beginning of cooking time. Some suggestions include crushed pumpkin seeds, minced or crushed sunflower seeds, crushed almonds, crushed walnuts, minced flaxseeds, 1 to 2 diced apples or pears, frozen berries (added right before serving), or any combination of these.

Sunflower oil spray or
    grapeseed oil spray
4 cups water (optional for

added sweetness: Substitute
    1 or 2 cups of the water with
    apple cider)
1 cup oats, steel-cut oats,
    or oat groats (whole,
    unprocessed oats)
1 teaspoon ground cinnamon

Spray slow cooker lightly with vegetable oil.

Add water, oatmeal, and cinnamon to slow cooker and cook on low setting for 8 hours— overnight works well.

Stir well and serve warm.

Refrigerate in a sealed container for up to 3 days.

Nutrition Facts

Amount Per Serving (⅓ cup)
Calories 32   Calories from Fat 2

Total Fat   0 g
Saturated Fat   0.1 g
Trans Fat   0 g
Poly Fat   0 g
Mono Fat   0 g
Cholesterol   0 mg
Sodium   2 mg
Total Carbohydrate   7 g
Dietary Fiber   0 g
Sugars   5 g
Protein   1 g

Quinoa Pudding with Banana and Cinnamon

Makes 9 toddler servings (⅓ cup); or 6 adult servings (½ cup)

Age: Appropriate for babies 9 months and up.

Tips: Makes a great nutrient-packed breakfast, especially enjoyable on a cold winter morning.

Feel free to use other fresh or dried fruits (pears, peaches, cranberries, etc), and/or add age-appropriate nuts or seeds.

See quinoa information on page 227; apple information on page 224; pear information on page 200.

> 1 cup dry quinoa
> 2 cups water
> 2 small ripe bananas, peeled and mashed
> ½ teaspoon blackstrap molasses
> 1 teaspoon ground cinnamon
> 2 tablespoons ground flaxseeds
> 1½ cups water or unsweetened rice milk*

In a saucepan, over medium heat, add the quinoa and dry toast it for a few minutes while stirring. Do not let quinoa burn. You will smell a nutty aroma.

Add water and bring to a slow boil, lower heat, and simmer for about 15 minutes, until all water is absorbed.

Turn heat off and add mashed banana, molasses, cinnamon, flax seeds, and 1½ cups water or rice milk.*

Turn burner back up to medium and cook for 8 to 10 minutes until mixture is thick and creamy.

Refrigerate for up to 3 days, or batch using the food cube method and freeze for up to 2 months.

For babies 9 months and up, combine ¼ cup of cooked quinoa pudding with 1 to 4 tablespoons of water or baby milk and puree to desired texture. Start with less water and add more as needed.

*For toddlers 12 months and up,

rice, soy, or cow's milk can be used for 1½ cup liquid.

Nutrition Facts

Amount Per Serving (⅓ cup)
Calories 97   Calories from Fat 15

Total Fat   2 g
Saturated Fat   0.2 g
Trans Fat   0 g
Poly Fat   0.9 g
Mono Fat   0.4 g
Cholesterol   0 mg
Sodium   3 mg
Total Carbohydrate   18 g
Dietary Fiber   3 g
Sugars   3 g
Protein   3 g

Brown Rice with Peas and Carrots

Makes 4 toddler servings (¼ cup); or 2 adult servings (½ cup)

Age: Appropriate for age 9 months and up.

Tips: Brown rice is a great core dish for older babies as well as younger ones. Use it as a base for adding colorful mixed veggies. Look for frozen mini-cubes of carrot, short-cut green beans, peas, or tender baby onions. These can be steamed and pureed, or lightly chopped for a young toddler.

See page 182 for information on brown rice; page 196 for information on peas; and page 192 for information on carrots.

> 1 cup cooked brown rice
> ½ cup cooked frozen carrot coins or cubes, thawed
> ½ cup cooked frozen green peas, thawed

5 tablespoons water (use less water for a chunkier consistency)

Lightly steam all ingredients over a simmer for 5 minutes.

Blend all ingredients in a blender or food processor to desired consistency.

Refrigerate in a sealed container for up to 3 days, or freeze using the food cube method for up to 3 months.

Nutrition Facts

Amount Per Serving (¼ cup)
Calories 67   Calories from Fat 4

Total Fat   0 g
Saturated Fat   0.1 g
Trans Fat   0 g
Poly Fat   0.2 g
Mono Fat   0.1 g
Cholesterol   0 mg
Sodium   32 mg
Total Carbohydrate   14 g
Dietary Fiber   2 g
Sugars   2 g
Protein   2

TIP

It can be uncomfortable for your toddler to sit with his legs dangling, with no way to alleviate pressure on his rump and thighs. Try seating him at a kid-sized table in a kid-sized chair. Maybe join him there—if you don't fit easily he may find this hilarious.

Apple-Banana Teething Biscuits

Makes 30 toddler servings (1 biscuit)

Age: Appropriate for age 9 to 12 months and up.

Tips: The recipe makes fun and easy-to-hold apple-banana biscuits for babies to teeth on while getting a little added iron from the molasses.

Caution: Hard teething biscuits can be a choking hazard. Always watch your baby with a teething biscuit to ensure that no large pieces break off.

See page 264 for information on blackstrap molasses; page 188 for information on oats; page 224 for information on apples.

> 1 teaspoon butter or cooking spray or butter plus ⅓ cup oil
> 2 cups whole-wheat pastry flour*
> 1 large ripe banana, mashed
> ½ cup unsweetened applesauce
> ⅓ cup unflavored vegetable oil (grapeseed, high-oleic-oil sunflower oil, etc.)
> ¼ cup water
> 1 cup rolled oats
> ½ teaspoon baking powder
> 2 tablespoons ground flaxseeds
> 1 teaspoon ground cinnamon
> 2 teaspoons blackstrap molasses

Preheat oven to 350° F.

Grease cookie sheet with butter or cooking spray.

In a large bowl, combine all ingredients and mix well.

On floured surface, roll dough out to ¼-inch thickness.

Sweet Cereal Grains Mix-and-Match Guide

Choose a grain from the first column and combine in the amounts indicated with selections from the final four columns to create several variations of sweet baby grains.

GRAINS 1 cup	COOK TIME	FRUITS/ VEGGIES ¾ cup Choose any	SPICES 1 teaspoon Choose any	FAT 2 teaspoons Choose any	BOOSTERS 1 tablespoon Choose any
Amaranth (3 cups water)	25 min	Apples, chopped Avocado, peeled (add at end) Banana, peeled and sliced Carrots, grated Parsnips, grated Pears, chopped Sweet potato, peeled and chopped	Allspice Cardamom Cinnamon Ginger Fresh mint leaves	Coconut milk (add at end) Coconut oil Flaxseed oil (add at end) Butter Margarine, non-hydrogenated only	Oat bran Wheat germ Brewer's yeast Flaxseed meal (add at end) For 12 months and up: Finely ground walnuts or almonds (if no history of allergy)
Oats, steel cut (4 cups water)	35 min				
Quinoa (rinse) (2 cups water)	20 min				
Rice, sweet brown (rinse) (2 cups water)	45 min				

Batch Formula
1 cup grain + water + ¾ cup fruit or vegetable + 1 teaspoon spice + 2 teaspoons fat + 1 tablespoon booster

Rinse grain, if indicated.
    In a large saucepan with a tight-fitting lid, bring grain and water to a boil (you can substitute 1 cup of apple cider for 1 cup of the water for a sweeter cereal—makes a great dessert).
    Add your choice of fruit or vegetable, spice, fat, and nutrient booster.
    Reduce heat and simmer for indicated time.
    Mix well, cool for at least 10 minutes, and puree to desired consistency, or serve as is for toddlers, reserving remainder.
    Spoon remaining cereal into glass container and store in fridge for 4 to 5 days. Remove individual portions and reheat in saucepan over low heat. Or freeze using the food cube method for up to 1 month. Thaw and warm in a small saucepan over low heat with a little extra liquid when ready to serve.
Combo Suggestions
    Fruits: amaranth, apples, allspice, coconut milk, and ground almonds
    Vegetables: rice, sweet potato, ginger, butter, and flax meal

Cut with cookie cutters into a shape that is easy for toddlers to hold, with no sharp edges.

Spread biscuits on cookie sheet. Bake for 35 to 40 minutes.

Turn off oven.

Leave cookies in oven to harden for about 2 hours.

Refrigerate baked biscuits in airtight container or plastic bag for up to 5 days, or freeze for 3 months. *You may substitute a gluten-free baking flour mix, such as Bob's Red Mill. Note that they will cook slightly faster with gluten-free flour, so remove at 30 minutes.

Nutrition Facts

Amount Per Serving (1 biscuit)
Calories 70   Calories from Fat 33

Total Fat   4 g
Saturated Fat   0.5 g
Trans Fat   0 g
Poly Fat   0.5 g
Mono Fat   2.6 g
Cholesterol   0 mg
Sodium   2 mg
Total Carbohydrate   8 g
Dietary Fiber   1 g
Sugars   1 g
Protein   2 g

Protein Entrée Recipes

Baby's First Hamburger

Makes 11 infant servings (1 ounce); or 3 to 4 toddler servings (3 ounces)

Age: Appropriate for age 9 months and up.

Tips: This recipe is perfect for introducing your child to ground beef. The raisins will sweeten and complement the flavor of the beef, and the texture and flavor of the rice will make the dish taste more familiar. You can also substitute prunes or cherries (pitted and dried or frozen) for the raisins.

See page 185 for information on brown rice.

1 teaspoon olive oil
¼ cup diced onions
6 ounces ground beef (90 percent lean)
½ cup cooked brown rice
1 tablespoon raisins
1 teaspoon dried thyme
1 tablespoon unsweetened prune juice

Heat the oil in a medium skillet over medium heat.

Add onion and sauté for 2 to 3 minutes, until translucent.

Add ground beef and cook for about 10 minutes, until lightly browned all the way through.

Drain off any excess fat.

Add rice, raisins, thyme, and prune juice. Stir together and cook for 3 to 5 minutes.

Cool and puree to desired consistency.

Refrigerate in a sealed container for up to 3 days, or freeze using the food cube method for up to 1 month.

Nutrition Facts

Amount Per Serving (3 ounces)
Calories 63   Calories from Fat 29

Total Fat   3 g
Saturated Fat   0.9 g
Trans Fat   0 g
Poly Fat   0.2 g
Mono Fat   1.7 g
Cholesterol   14 mg
Sodium   41 mg
Total Carbohydrate   4 g
Dietary Fiber   0 g
Sugars   1 g
Protein   5 g

Poached Chicken

Makes 16 toddler servings (1 ounce); or 4 adult serving (4 ounces)

Age: Appropriate for age 9 months and up.

Tips: It's very easy to poach a good-sized batch of chicken. Skinless white meat works the best, although you can use other cuts. Once the chicken is cooked, you can puree it as is for a quick protein, or use it in a variety of other dishes for your baby, yourself, or the rest of your family. Poached chicken is perfect for making chicken salad, throwing into soup or salad, shredding for wraps, or simply pureeing with grains, vegetables, or even fruit (see recipe for Peachy Chicken following).

4 skinless chicken breast halves
3 cups low-sodium chicken broth
½ small onion, chopped
1 medium carrot, chopped
1 medium celery stalk, chopped
1 bay leaf

In a large saucepan, combine chicken breasts, broth, onion, carrot, celery, and bay leaf and bring to a low boil over medium high heat, turning chicken occasionally.

Reduce heat, cover, and simmer for 10 minutes.

Remove saucepan from the burner and let mixture sit for 30 minutes.

Poaching in the cooking liquid produces very moist chicken.

Nutrition Facts

Amount Per Serving (1 ounce)
Calories 75   Calories from Fat 15

Total Fat   2 g
Saturated Fat   0.5 g
Trans Fat   0 g
Poly Fat   0.4 g
Mono Fat   0.6 g
Cholesterol   37 mg
Sodium   75 mg
Total Carbohydrate   1 g
Dietary Fiber   0 g
Sugars   1 g
Protein   14 g

Peachy Chicken

Makes 4 toddler servings (1 ounce); or 1 adult servings (4 ounces)

Age: Appropriate for age 9 months and up.

Tips: Chicken tastes delicious combined with several different types of fruits. Organic peaches are best because conventional peaches are among the top twelve most highly pesticide-contaminated fruits and vegetables. Try it with apricots (fresh or soaked dried), apples, pears, soaked prunes, etc. Use this recipe to introduce chicken to your baby for the first time.

See page 205 for information on peaches; see above for information on chicken.

4 ounces cooked chicken
(see page 237 for Poached
Chicken recipe)
1 medium fresh or frozen
peach, pitted and chopped
(about ⅓ cup)
¼ cup apple juice
¼ teaspoon ground cinnamon
¼ teaspoon ground ginger

Chop chicken into small pieces.

In a medium skillet combine the peach, apple juice, cinnamon, and ginger and simmer for 3 to 5 minutes over medium heat, until peaches are very soft.

Add chicken, stir, and cook for another 1 to 2 minutes, until mixture is warm.

Puree the mixture in a blender or food processor for a softer consistency, if necessary.

Refrigerate for up to 3 days, or batch and freeze for up to 2 months.

Nutrition Facts

Amount Per Serving (1 ounce)
Calories 95   Calories from Fat 16

Total Fat   2 g
Saturated Fat   0.5 g
Trans Fat   0 g
Poly Fat   0.4 g
Mono Fat   0.6 g
Cholesterol   37 mg
Sodium   75 mg
Total Carbohydrate   6 g
Dietary Fiber   1 g
Sugars   4 g
Protein   14 g

Tofu

Although large amounts of soy are not healthy for babies or toddlers, it is safe to use small amounts of tofu in your baby's foods. Tofu, which is made from soybeans, is an excellent source of protein. If you choose a brand that's been prepared with calcium sulfate, it's also a great source of calcium. Tofu is available in several textures: from silken (the softest, similar in consistency to Greek yogurt) to extra firm, which is almost chewy when cooked and holds its shape well. Bland tasting and white in color, it comes in blocks packed in water, like fresh mozzarella cheese. Once you have opened the package, tofu will stay fresh for a couple of days. Change the water daily to retain maximum freshness.

Because it is virtually flavorless, tofu makes an easy invisible way to add protein to many dishes. Try these suggestions:

Add a little silken tofu to a fruit smoothie.

Dice fine squares of extra-firm tofu and add them to chili, pasta sauce, or soups.

Use silken tofu as a pudding base instead of milk: simply blend it with ripe bananas (in equal portions) and a little juice in your mixer or blender. You can also use it in place of milk with a high-quality pudding mix (keep portions small)—no cooking necessary!

Use silken tofu as a base for creamy salad dressings.

Dice medium tofu into a stir-fry or eggless veggie scramble.

Fruity Cottage Cheese Kugel

Makes 20 toddler servings (1-inch square); or 10 adult servings (2-inch square)

Age: Appropriate for age 9 months and up.

Tips: This is a fruity, sweet noodle pudding high in protein. Feel free to substitute any other fruits for the apples. Peaches, blueberries, and cherries (pitted frozen) are great alternatives.

See page 205 for information on peaches.

1 tablespoon ghee or butter
1 package whole-wheat egg noodles
2 cups cottage cheese
2 cups Greek yogurt
2 eggs
2 medium apples, peeled, cored, and grated
1 tablespoon blackstrap molasses
½ cup raisins (optional)
¼ teaspoon ground cardamom
1½ teaspoons ground cinnamon
2 tablespoons butter cut into small pieces
1 cup wheat germ
½ cup maple syrup

Preheat oven to 350° F.

Cook whole-wheat egg noodles al dente according to package directions.

Grease 9-inch by 13-inch baking pan with butter or ghee.

In the noodle pot or a large bowl, combine cottage cheese, yogurt, eggs, apple, molasses, optional raisins, cardamom, and cinnamon.

Add cooked noodles to cottage cheese mixture and mix well.

Pour into prepared baking dish.

In a small bowl mix together wheat germ and maple syrup and sprinkle mixture over the top of the noodles.

Add cut ghee or butter evenly on top of the wheat germ mixture and bake for 25 minutes.

Refrigerate in a sealed container for up to 3 days, or freeze for up to 2 months.

Nutrition Facts

Amount Per Serving (1-inch square)
Calories 173   Calories from Fat 51

Total Fat   4 g
Saturated Fat   3 g
Trans Fat   0 g
Poly Fat   1 g
Mono Fat   1 g
Cholesterol   50 mg
Sodium   107 mg
Total Carbohydrate   23 g
Dietary Fiber   3 g
Sugars   8 g
Protein   8 g

Veggie Lentil Rice

Makes 10 toddler servings (½ cup); or 5 adult servings (1 cup)

Age: Appropriate for age 9 months and up.

Tips: This is an easy dish to puree for babies. It's great served with the Lemon-Dill Yogurt Sauce (page 282) or Cilantro-Cucumber Yogurt Sauce (page 281) for an older child or adult. Turmeric adds a bright, appealing yellow color and has anti-inflammatory properties—especially helpful during cold season. This dish works well in a rice cooker.

Selection: Lentils come in several varieties. The fastest cooking are red lentils. Red lentils fall apart easily, making a natural puree. The green and brown hold their shape better and are very tasty but take a little longer to cook. They can be found dried in bulk or prepackaged. Organic canned lentils are also a suitable alternative.

See page 272 for bean cooking chart.

Storage: Store in an airtight container in a cool, dry place for up to 1 year.

2 tablespoons olive oil
1 large onion, diced
¾ cup brown, basmati, or jasmine brown rice, rinsed (presoaking for 3 hours to overnight is preferable)
½ ground turmeric (optional)
½ teaspoon ground cumin
½ teaspoon onion powder
½ teaspoon garlic powder
½ teaspoon salt
1¼ cups green or brown lentils, rinsed and sorted
1¼ fresh or frozen carrots, diced or grated
4 cups water, low-sodium broth (vegetable or chicken)

In a large skillet add the oil and onions, and sauté over medium heat until they caramelize, stirring periodically, for 5 to 10 minutes.

Add rice, turmeric, and cumin and sauté for 1 to 2 minutes.

Add lentils, carrots, and liquid and bring to a boil. (If using canned lentils, hold them till the last 5 to 10 minutes of cooking time, below.)

Reduce heat and cook for 40 to 45 minutes.

Puree in food processor or blender to desired consistency, adding water if necessary.

Refrigerate in a sealed container for up to 3 days, or freeze using the food cube method for up to 3 months.

Nutrition Facts

Amount Per Serving (½ cup)
Calories 115   Calories from Fat 30

Total Fat   3 g
Saturated Fat   05 g
Trans Fat   0 g
Poly Fat   0.4 g
Mono Fat   2.2 g
Cholesterol   0 mg
Sodium   77 mg
Total Carbohydrate   18 g
Dietary Fiber   3 g
Sugars   2 g
Protein   4 g

Braised Paprika Chicken and Potatoes

Makes about 16 infant servings (½ thigh and ¼ cup potatoes) 8 toddler servings (1 thigh and ¼ cup potatoes); 4 adult servings (2 thighs and ½ cup potatoes)

Age: Appropriate for age 9 months and up.

Tips: While braising is a technique usually reserved for tougher cuts of meat, it works very nicely with dark meat poultry, bone in or out. Add a garden salad and this dish makes a warming, tasty dinner for the whole family.

½ teaspoon sea salt
¼ teaspoon black pepper
1 tablespoon paprika

2 pounds boneless chicken
    thighs (about 8)
1 tablespoon olive oil
1 large Spanish onion,
    quartered and thinly sliced
1 garlic clove, minced
3 cups russet or yukon gold
    potatoes (about 3 large),
    peeled and diced small
2 cups chicken broth
½ cup balsamic vinegar
Additional salt and pepper to
    taste

In a small dish combine salt, black pepper and paprika.

Rinse and pat chicken dry, then rub mixture over chicken.

Heat olive oil in a 3 or 4 quart Dutch oven or large, heavy-bottom soup pot over medium heat.

Add chicken and brown on each side about 3 minutes.

Transfer chicken to a plate.

Add onions to pan and sauté until translucent, about 5 minutes.

Add garlic and lightly brown 1 to 2 minutes.

Add potatoes and broth, incorporating any browned pieces on the pan into the liquid.

Add chicken and bring to a boil.

Reduce heat to low-medium heat and cover, cooking for about 30 minutes until chicken is cooked through (180° F).

Remove chicken and potatoes to a platter and keep warm.

For a thicker sauce, continue cooking liquids for about 10 minutes, or add 1 tablespoon of kudzu and 2 tablespoons of water.

Add salt and pepper as necessary.

Serve sauce over chicken or in a gravy boat.

Puree the chicken and potatoes with a little sauce or, for older babies, mash the chicken with a fork and a little sauce, and dice the potatoes to desired size.

Nutrition Facts

Amount Per Serving (½ thigh and ¼ cup potatoes)

Calories 140   Calories from Fat 32

Total Fat   4 g
Saturated Fat   1 g
Trans Fat   0 g
Poly Fat   1 g
Mono Fat   2 g
Cholesterol   15 mg
Sodium   162 mg
Total Carbohydrate   21 g
Dietary Fiber   2 g
Sugars   5 g
Protein   7 g

Hummus

Makes 30 toddler servings (1 tablespoon); or 6 adult servings (⅓ cup)

Age: Appropriate for age 12 months and up.

Tips: Canned garbanzo beans can be replaced with 2 cups precooked garbanzo beans. Hummus is great as a dip for veggies or whole-wheat pita strips, in salads, wraps, or as a sandwich spread.

See page 256 for information on garbanzo beans.

1 can garbanzo beans (15
    ounces)
¼ cup sesame tahini
¼ cup cold water
2 tablespoons fresh-squeezed
    lemon juice
½ teaspoon ground cumin
1 to 2 small cloves garlic, minced
2 tablespoons olive oil

Puree garbanzo beans until smooth. If necessary, add water to thin.

Place sesame tahini, cold water, lemon juice, cumin, and garlic in a blender or food processor and blend until smooth.

Add pureed garbanzo beans to mixture and blend until smooth.

Pour mixture into serving bowl, add olive oil, and mix well.

Refrigerate in a sealed container.

Nutrition Facts

Amount Per Serving (1 tablespoon)
Calories 29   Calories from Fat 15

Total Fat   2 g
Saturated Fat   0.2 g
Trans Fat   0 g
Poly Fat   0.6 g
Mono Fat   0.8 g
Cholesterol   0 mg
Sodium   1 mg
Total Carbohydrate   3 g
Dietary Fiber   1 g
Sugars   1 g
Protein   1 g

Pinto Bean Puree

Makes 30 toddler servings (¼ cup)

Age: Appropriate age is 9 months and up.

Tips: This is a versatile puree that can also be served as a dip for quesadillas, nachos, corn chips, rice crackers, or vegetables (steamed and cut into small pieces) such as carrots, broccoli, cauliflower, zucchini, yellow squash, or green beans.

2 15-ounce cans no-salt-added pinto beans, drained and rinsed, or 4 cups cooked
1 tablespoon olive oil
½ cup diced onion

2 cloves garlic, minced
½ cup broth (chicken or vegetable) or water
1 teaspoon fresh minced cilantro
¼ teaspoon salt

In a large sauté pan, add oil and onions and sauté over medium heat for 6 to 7 minutes, until lightly brown.

Add garlic and sauté for another minute.

Add one can of beans or half of the cooked beans (drained), ¼ cup water, and cilantro to the sauté pan and mash using a potato masher or the back of a wooden spoon.

Add the rest of the beans, salt, and water and continue mashing. For an even smoother consistency, blend in a food processor or blender or use an immersion blender.

Nutrition Facts

Amount Per Serving (¼ cup)
Calories 30   Calories from Fat 5

Total Fat   1 g
Saturated Fat   0.1 g
Trans Fat   0 g
Poly Fat   0.1 g
Mono Fat   0.4 g
Cholesterol   0 mg
Sodium   78 mg
Total Carbohydrate   5 g
Dietary Fiber   2 g
Sugars   1 g
Protein   2 g

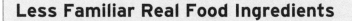

Less Familiar Real Food Ingredients

Agar agar: Originated in Japan, also called kanten. Natural gelling agent made from seaweed (red algae)—used to make fruit gelatin and Japanese jellied sweets. Kanten, unlike American Jell-O gelatin, is a nutrient-rich substance: high in folate, calcium, iron, magnesium, manganese, potassium, and zinc. It is important to buy organic agar agar to ensure no heavy metal exposure from the ocean. Agar can be purchased at natural food stores or grocers, or Asian markets.

Agave nectar: A liquid sweetener similar in consistency to honey (sweeter than sugar, so you need to use less)—made from one of two varieties of Mexican succulents. Agave nectar is unpasteurized and, like honey, should not be given to babies under 12 months of age. It has a lower glycemic load than honey or maple syrup, but because of its high fructose content, should be used sparingly as a sweetener. Many regular grocery stores now carry agave in the sugar or syrup section.

Epazote: A fragrant herb originating in Central America. Very popular in Mexican cooking—adds a distinct flavor to beans and improves their digestibility. When cooking, use 2 teaspoons dried epazote or 6 fresh leaves per pound of beans. You can purchase epazote in Latin markets, or natural food stores or grocers.

Bragg Liquid Aminos: A salty liquid condiment made from soy containing 16 amino acids. Similar in taste to soy sauce, it's a better cooking alternative for children because it contains less sodium. Bragg can be found in natural food stores or grocers.

Flaxseed and flaxseed oil: Very rich sources of an essential fatty acid that can be converted to omega-3s in healthy bodies. Both forms are good for healthy hair and skin, and the seeds are also high in fiber, with a slight laxative quality. Flax can go rancid easily, so all forms should be stored in the refrigerator. Many grocers and natural food stores carry flaxseeds, whole or ground, and flax oil. Look for the oil in the refrigerated section, and for the seeds (vacuum packed for freshness) on the flour or nut shelves.

Ghee: Clarified butter. Has a nuttier flavor than butter and is appropriate for high-heat cooking. Ghee can be found in the oil section of natural food stores or grocers, or Indian markets—it is not refrigerated.

Kombu: A mineral-rich sea vegetable. Very helpful in improving the digestibility of beans. It is important to buy organic kombu to ensure no heavy metal exposure from the ocean. Sea vegetables can be found dried in plastic bags in the macrobiotic section of most natural food stores or grocers.

continued on next page

Kudzu: White powder used as a thickener for hot sauces, stews, and gravies. More nutritious than cornstarch and soothing to the digestive system. Dissolve in cold water before adding to foods: 1 part kudzu to 2 parts water. Add at the end of cooking time—sauce will thicken in about 1 minute while mixture simmers. Kudzu can usually be found hanging in little plastic bags in the macrobiotic section of most natural food stores or grocers.

Miso paste: A salty, strongly flavored paste made from fermented soybeans. The darker the miso, the stronger the flavor. Calming and alkalizing for the body. Great as a salty seasoning for soups, stews, sauces, and vegetables. Miso paste should be added to food just after cooking; it contains live cultures and high heat kills the beneficial bacteria. Store in the refrigerator. Miso paste can be found in the refrigerated section of most natural food stores or grocers, or Asian markets.

Rice syrup: A thick syrupy sweetener made from rice—not as sweet as sugar, mild flavor. Can be used in baking, fruit combos, and other sweet sauces. Rice syrup can be found in the sweetener section of most natural food stores or grocers.

Tamari: A form of fermented soy sauce, some versions are made without wheat. (Most soy sauce contains small amounts of wheat.) Tamari can usually be found in regular grocery stores. Look in the international section (Asian or Japanese), if the store has one.

Tahini: Seed butter made of ground sesame seeds. High in fat (mostly poly- and monounsaturated), protein, and fiber. Delicious alternative to peanut butter in sauces, dressings, and marinades. Tahini can be found in cans or jars in the nut butters section of most grocery stores. The oil and paste will often separate, as with many natural nut butters. Stir well before using.

Turbinado sugar: Raw sugar crystals formed by spinning the sugar in a centrifuge. The juice released is then crystallized to keep the rich molasses color and flavor—less processed than conventional table sugar. Sucanat is a trademark name of the turbinado process. Turbinado sugar can be found in natural food stores and most grocers.

Umeboshi plum vinegar: Not a true vinegar, it is made by pickling umeboshi plums in a brine solution. Salty and tangy, ume vinegar offers a pleasing taste complement to sweet grains and vegetables. Try it on sweet potatoes or corn in place of salt and butter. Use sparingly: A little goes a long way. Available in natural food stores and Asian markets.

Recipes for 12 to 18 Months

By her first birthday, your new toddler will probably be able to eat most regular table foods in chopped form. Feeding her gets easier at around this time, as you can usually dice up what the rest of the family is having for main meals. Although she is now able to eat nearly all of the foods that you eat, it is still important to follow the allergy guidelines when introducing each new food (see page 95).

As she will shortly become quite preoccupied with her new upright status and all the delights that walking provides (if she hasn't already), her eating may take a backseat for a while. Use the tasty recipes in this chapter to tempt her, and load each precious mouthful with a nutrient power punch.

Vegetable Recipes

Roasted Sweet Potatoes

Makes 8 toddler servings (3 ounces); or 6 adult servings (4 ounces)

Age: Appropriate for age 12 months and up.

Tips: Roasting root vegetables brings out their natural sweetness. Toddlers love them warm with dinner, or straight from the fridge as a snack. Smaller chunks make great finger foods plain or dipped. Try roasting carrots and parsnips with olive oil and dill, or sweet potato and white potato with olive oil and rosemary, or several different roots mixed together. Cut vegetable chunks uniformly for even cooking. Larger chunks take longer, smaller take less time.

Sweet potatoes reduce gas, aid digestion, relieve colic, promote energy circulation, and have a cooling effect on the body.

See page 190 for more information on sweet potatoes.

> 2 medium sweet potatoes
> 1 teaspoon ground cinnamon
> ½ teaspoon salt
> 1 teaspoon maple sugar or maple syrup
> ¾ tablespoon vegetable oil
> 1 teaspoon ground cumin (optional)

Preheat oven to 400° F.

Wash, scrub, and peel sweet potatoes.

Dice each potato into ½- or 1-inch chunks.

In a large bowl, combine cinnamon, salt, sweetener, vegetable oil, and cumin, if using, and mix well to combine.

Add potato chunks to mixture and toss to coat evenly.

Arrange potatoes in a single layer on baking sheet and cook for 20 minutes.

Turn them over and bake for an additional 15 to 20 minutes, until potatoes are soft and edges are lightly browned and caramelized.

Refrigerate in a tightly sealed container for up to 5 days.

Nutrition Facts

Amount Per Serving (3 ounces)
Calories 61   Calories from Fat 16

Total Fat   1 g
Saturated Fat   0.1 g
Trans Fat   0 g
Poly Fat   0.9 g
Mono Fat   0.2 g
Cholesterol   0 mg
Sodium   150 mg

Total Carbohydrate   12 g
Dietary Fiber   2 g
Sugars   5 g
Protein   1 g

Sautéed Spinach with Onions

Makes 8 infant servings (¼ cup)

Age: Appropriate for age 12 months and up (after first foods).

Tips: The sweetness of the onions helps mellow the natural bitterness of spinach. This dish is great as a stuffing for baked white or sweet potatoes, or served over a grain.

> 2 tablespoons olive oil
> 1 medium slice sweet onion
> 2 pounds fresh spinach or 10-ounce box frozen, thawed and drained
> ¼ cup water
> 1 wedge fresh lemon

In a large sauté pan with a lid, add 1 tablespoon olive oil and place over medium heat.

Add the onion slice, separating rings and stirring, until they become lightly caramelized, about 6 minutes.

Wash spinach well and drain in a colander.

Remove the dense spinach stems and discard.

Chop spinach leaves.

Add chopped spinach leaves and water to onions.

Cover and cook for about 3 to 5 minutes over medium heat.

Add 1 to 2 additional tablespoons of water if necessary, and continue to cook until spinach is very wilted and onions are completely soft.

Remove from heat and drizzle the remaining tablespoon of olive oil onto the spinach.

Squeeze fresh lemon juice overall.

Refrigerate for up to 3 days, or freeze in a tightly sealed container for up to 2 months.

Nutrition Facts

Amount Per Serving (¼ cup)
Calories 37   Calories from Fat 3

Total Fat   0 g
Saturated Fat   0.5 g
Trans Fat   0 g
Poly Fat   0 g
Mono Fat   0 g
Cholesterol   0 mg
Sodium   20 mg
Total Carbohydrate   1 g
Dietary Fiber   1 g
Sugars   0 g
Protein   1 g

Cooked Carrots with Orange and Dill

*Makes 12 toddler servings (⅓ cup);
or 5 adult servings (¾ cup)*

Age: Appropriate for age 12 months and up.

Tips: This recipe can also be made with tarragon or parsley: Replace dill with 1 teaspoon dried tarragon or parsley or 1 tablespoon chopped fresh tarragon or parsley. Can be pureed for 9 months and up.

1½ cups water
1½ cups orange juice
4 medium carrots, sliced
    (about 2 cups)
¼ teaspoon salt
1 teaspoon minced fresh dill

In a medium saucepan, add water and orange juice and bring to a boil.

Add carrots and salt. Reduce heat and simmer 10 minutes, until tender.

Drain, cool, and place in a serving bowl.

Toss lightly with dill.

Refrigerate in a sealed container for up to 3 days, or freeze for up to 6 months.

Nutrition Facts

Amount Per Serving (¼ cup)
Calories 35   Calories from Fat 1

Total Fat   0 g
Saturated Fat   0 g
Trans Fat   0 g
Poly Fat   0.1 g
Mono Fat   0 g
Cholesterol   0 mg
Sodium   80 mg
Total Carbohydrate   8 g
Dietary Fiber   2 g
Sugars   5 g
Protein   1 g

Stir-Fried Bok Choy

*Makes 8 toddler servings (⅓ cup);
or 6 adult serving (½ cup)*

Age: Appropriate for age 12 months and up.

Tips: Bok choy cabbage is very high in vitamins A and C. It also contains sulforaphane, an enzyme that can reduce the risk of cancer. Baby bok choy is tender and sweet, often a favorite leafy green among toddlers. The leaves of full-grown bok choy are slightly more bitter, but the flavor is still much milder than that of other greens and the white stems are very juicy.

Season: Peak for bok choy is spring and summer.

Selection: Look for baby bok choy with plump, pale green stems and leaves, or full-grown bok choy with firm stalks and dark green leaves.

Storage: Wrap in a damp paper towel, place in plastic or perforated bag, and store in the crisper drawer for up to 7 days.

> 1 large head bok choy (about 2 pounds)
> 1 tablespoon sesame oil or unflavored vegetable oil
> ½ teaspoon fresh ginger, minced
> 2½ teaspoons tamari or soy sauce
> 1 tablespoon sesame seeds, white or black (optional)

Cut off ½ inch of base and separate leaves.

Wash leaves well in a large bowl of water.

Cut stalks into ½-inch pieces.

Stack leaves, roll, and slice into ½-inch strips.

Heat oil in large frying pan over medium-high heat.

Add bok choy stalks and ginger, and toss to coat with oil.

Cover and cook for about 2 minutes, stirring frequently.

Add leaves and cook for an additional 2 minutes until leaves are bright green. If necessary, add water to prevent sticking.

Add soy sauce and toss to coat evenly.

Garnish with sesame seeds.

Refrigerate in a sealed container for up to 3 days.

Nutrition Facts

Amount Per Serving (⅓ cup)
Calories 26   Calories from Fat 17

Total Fat   2 g
Saturated Fat   0.3 g
Trans Fat   0 g
Poly Fat   0.8 g
Mono Fat   0.7 g
Cholesterol   0 mg
Sodium   131 mg
Total Carbohydrate   2 g
Dietary Fiber   1 g
Sugars   1 g
Protein   1 g

Fruit Recipes

Sweet Sautéed Banana

Makes 3 toddler servings (3 ounces)

Age: Appropriate for age 12 months and up.

Tips: This recipe is delicious mashed and mixed with plain yogurt, pureed with chicken, or served with grilled chicken or pork. If desired, butter can be used in place of the ghee; ghee is clarified butter with a nutty flavor and is lower in fat than butter. Ghee is also a lactose-free food.

See page 197 for information on bananas; page 243 for information on ghee.

> 1 medium banana
> 2 teaspoons ghee
> 1 teaspoon ground cinnamon

Wash and peel banana. Cut lengthwise or into coins.

In a sauté pan over medium heat, melt ghee.

Place banana in pan and sauté for about 2½ minutes.

Flip banana and sauté for another 2½ minutes.

Sprinkle with cinnamon.

Puree in a blender or mash with a fork. Dice for an older child.

Serve with plain regular or Greek yogurt.

Nutrition Facts

Amount Per Serving (3 ounces)
Calories 81   Calories from Fat 27

Total Fat   3 g
Saturated Fat   1.8 g
Trans Fat   0 g
Poly Fat   0.1 g
Mono Fat   0.8 g
Cholesterol   7 mg
Sodium   1 mg
Total Carbohydrate   15 g
Dietary Fiber   2 g
Sugars   9 g
Protein   1 g

Blueberry Peach Cobbler

Makes 18 toddler servings (1½-inch piece); or 9 adult servings (2-inch piece)

Age: Appropriate for age 12 months and up.

Tips: Kudzu is a starchy root used as a thickener for sauces, stews, and gravies. It is more nutritious than cornstarch and soothing to the digestive system. Dissolve in cold water before adding to foods: 1 part kudzu to 2 parts water. Add to boiling liquids and stir for 1 to 2 minutes, until thickened.

Selection: Look for the white-powdered chunks in small bags in the macrobiotic or Asian sections of natural food stores or grocers.

Storage: Store in a cool, dry place and check expiration date.

1 teaspoon olive oil or butter
1 tablespoon kudzu root
2 tablespoons water
6 large peaches (fresh or frozen), pitted and sliced (unpeeled)
3 cups blueberries (fresh or frozen)
¼ cup pure maple syrup
1 teaspoon ground cinnamon
¼ cup sunflower oil or organic butter
¾ cup rolled oats
¾ cup whole-wheat flour
¼ cup toasted wheat germ
¼ teaspoon ground ginger
¼ cup pure maple syrup
1 teaspoon ground cinnamon

Preheat oven to 375° F.

Lightly grease an 8-inch by 8-inch pie pan with olive oil or butter.

For the filling: In a small bowl, combine kudzu and water and mix well.

In a large bowl, combine peaches, blueberries, maple syrup, cinnamon, and kudzu and water mixture and mix well.

Pour mixture into pie pan.

For the topping: In a medium bowl, combine sunflower oil, rolled oats, flour, wheat germ, ginger, maple syrup, and cinnamon. Mix with a fork until mixture becomes crumbly.

Sprinkle topping over filling evenly.

Bake for 30 minutes, until fruit is tender and topping is lightly browned.

Nutrition Facts

Amount Per Serving (¹⁄₁₈ of recipe)
Calories 215   Calories from Fat 37

Total Fat   4 g
Saturated Fat   0.6 g
Trans Fat   0 g
Poly Fat   2.3 g
Mono Fat   0.1 g
Cholesterol   1 mg
Sodium   11 mg
Total Carbohydrate   41 g
Dietary Fiber   6 g
Sugars   10 g
Protein   4 g

Pumpkin Banana Custard

Makes 10 toddler servings (¹⁄₂ cup); 5 adult servings (1 cup)

Age: Appropriate age is 12 months and up.

Tips: This is a very simple yet hearty dish that fills and warms—perfect for a crisp fall day as breakfast, a snack, or a dessert. It's also terrific with sweet potatoes. Next time you are baking some, reserve two to use the next morning in this dish. They are much sweeter than pumpkin, so reduce the sweetener down to 2 tablespoons. You can also play with the spicing: add 1 teaspoon grated orange zest or fresh ginger, or use cinnamon, cardamom, and fresh grated nutmeg instead of pumpkin pie spice.

Cooking spray oil
1 cup ripe banana (about 2 large)
1 15-ounce can pumpkin (can also substitute 2 cups baked, peeled sweet potato [about 2 medium])
2 teaspoons pumpkin pie spice
¼ teaspoon salt
1 12-ounce can evaporated skim milk
¼ cup agave nectar or pure maple syrup
1 teaspoon vanilla
3 eggs, beaten
¼ cup ground flaxseed
½ cup rolled oats

Preheat oven to 325° F.

Spray an 8-inch by 8-inch baking dish lightly with oil.

Mash the banana in a large bowl with a fork until creamy.

Mix the pumpkin in with the banana until well blended.

Add the spice and salt and stir to blend well.

Add the milk, agave nectar, vanilla, and eggs and stir or whisk to blend.

Stir in flax and oats until well incorporated.

Pour into prepared casserole dish and bake for 1 hour or until set and center is firm.

Drizzle with additional warmed maple syrup if desired.

Nutrition Facts

Amount Per Serving (¹⁄₂ cup)
Calories 177   Calories from Fat 36

Total Fat   4 g
Saturated Fat   1 g
Trans Fat   0 g
Poly Fat   1 g
Mono Fat   1 g
Cholesterol   80 mg

Sodium   370 mg
Total Carbohydrate   31 g
Dietary Fiber   6 g
Sugars   16 g
Protein   7 g

Baked Apples

Makes 10 toddler servings (¼ cup); or 4 to 5 adult servings (½ cup)

Age: Appropriate for age 9 months and up.

Tips: This is a nutritious and delectable apple dessert. Experiment with toddlers and older children by adding walnuts or granola or replacing raisins with dried cranberries.

See page 224 for information on apples.

> 4 medium fresh baking apples (Granny Smith, Rome, Jonagold, Golden Delicious, etc.)
> ½ cup water
> 1 teaspoon ground cinnamon
> 2 teaspoons blackstrap molasses or maple syrup
> ⅓ cup apple cider or juice
> ¼ cup raisins, dried cranberries, or dried cherries
> ¼ cup wheat germ

Preheat oven to 350° F.

Wash apples and partially core from the stem down, three quarters of the way through. Cut off and discard the top portion of the core.

Prick skins of apples three to five times with a fork to prevent bursting.

Place apples upright in an ovenproof baking dish.

Pour apple juice or water into the baking dish around the apples.

In a small bowl, combine apple juice, cinnamon, molasses, raisins, and wheat germ.

Divide mixture evenly and stuff each apple core.

Bake for 45 minutes, until apples are soft and the mixture is oozing.

Refrigerate for up to 3 days, or double-wrap in freezer-safe plastic and store in the freezer for up to 2 months.

For younger babies: Scoop out 2 tablespoons of the cooked apple and raisin mixture and 1 to 2 teaspoons of the juices. Puree together, cool, and serve.

Nutrition Facts

Amount Per Serving (¼ cup)
Calories 71   Calories from Fat 6

Total Fat   1 g
Saturated Fat   0 g
Trans Fat   0 g
Poly Fat   0 g
Mono Fat   0 g
Cholesterol   0 mg
Sodium   3 mg
Total Carbohydrate   16 g
Dietary Fiber   2 g
Sugars   11 g
Protein   2 g

Jiggly Juice Gelatin

Makes 9 toddler servings (¼ cup); or 4 adult servings (½ cup)

Age: Appropriate for age 12 months and up.

Tips: Vegetarian gelatin made from agar agar originated in Japan and was originally called kanten. Our traditional gelatin is made from boiling bones or hooves.

Agar is a natural gelling material from seaweed (red algae). It is used to make fruit gelatin or jelly. Agar contains a high amount of foliate, calcium, iron, magnesium, manganese, potassium, and zinc. When adding fruit to agar, it needs to be cooked because the enzymes in fresh fruit may dissolve the agar. Agar will gel at room temperature, but it is refreshing when chilled.

Selection: Agar is found in the health food section or Asian section of your supermarket and health food stores. Agar comes in granulated or flaked forms. Use less granulated agar because it expands more than the flakes. To gel one cup of juice or liquid, use 1 tablespoon of agar flakes or ½ tablespoon of granules. You may substitute agar for regular gelatin in any recipe. Try it with different juice and fruit combinations, such as apple juice and peaches, or orange juice and kiwi fruit.

Storage: Store in a cool dry pantry.

2 cups orange juice
1 cup diced or crushed fresh frozen or canned (no sugar added) pineapple or mandarin orange slices, fresh or canned (no sugar added)
1 tablespoon dried agar

In a medium saucepan over medium-low heat, combine orange juice and pineapple.

Stir in agar and simmer for about 5 minutes on low heat.

Remove from heat and use a ladle to pour into individual dishes, an 8-inch by 5-inch Pyrex dish, or gelatin mold.

Cool, then refrigerate for 2 to 3 hours, until chilled.

To speed up the process, place in freezer for 30 minutes before refrigerating.

Refrigerate for up to 4 days.

Nutrition Facts

Amount Per Serving (¼ cup)
Calories 36   Calories from Fat 1

Total Fat   0 g
Saturated Fat   0 g
Trans Fat   0 g
Poly Fat   0 g
Mono Fat   0 g
Cholesterol   0 mg
Sodium   2 mg
Total Carbohydrate   9 g
Dietary Fiber   0 g
Sugars   8 g
Protein   1 g

Fast Frozen Fruit Cream

Homemade frozen fruit cream is a tastier, healthier alternative to traditional ice cream, and you can whip it up in a matter of minutes. Although natural, organic ice cream may have few poor-quality ingredients, it is still very high in sugar. Try this simple treat in its place—great on a hot summer's day!

Simply combine frozen banana with equal amounts of any other peeled and pitted frozen fruit: mango, papaya, peach, berries, cherries, etc., and puree in a blender or food processor until smooth. Serve it up in small amounts and allow your toddler to experiment with the icy cold. The banana is a natural sweetener and will also give the mixture a creamy texture. You can add a tiny pinch of cinnamon, ginger, nutmeg, or cardamom, to deepen the layers of natural flavor, if you wish. Other possible additions include a small amount of fresh mint, a dollop of peanut butter (if not at risk for allergy), or a couple of tablespoons of 100 percent juice: Try black cherry, apple, orange or pomegranate.

Pasta and Grains Recipes

Mac and Cheese

Makes 12 toddler servings (½ cup); or 6 adult servings (1 cup)

Age: Appropriate for age 12 months and up.

Tips: Sweet potato gives this family favorite a sweet twist and increases the fiber and nutritional content. Cheddar cheese is high in calcium, protein, and phosphorus. Hard cheese such as cheddar has less than 1 gram of lactose, which can usually be handled by people who are lactose intolerant.

You will need to bake a sweet potato ahead of time or thaw frozen sweet potato. To bake: Preheat oven to 425° F. Scrub 1 large sweet potato well and bake for 45 minutes until soft.

Selection: Look for organic sharp cheddar cheese or cheese from grass-fed cows without hormones and antibiotics. Avoid cheddar made with raw milk.

Storage: Wrap cheddar tightly in plastic wrap and store in the warmest part of the refrigerator.

See page 190 for information on sweet potatoes.

12 ounces whole-wheat elbow macaroni
1 cup peeled, baked sweet potato (about 1 large) or thawed, frozen sweet potato
½ cup water
½ teaspoon onion powder
½ teaspoon dried mustard
1½ teaspoon umeboshi plum vinegar or apple cider vinegar
1 teaspoon tamari or soy sauce
1 tablespoon miso
1½ cups grated sharp cheddar cheese
½ cup whole-wheat bread crumbs (panko work great)
½ cup Parmesan cheese

Preheat oven to 400° F.

Cook pasta according to package directions.

Whisk or puree together sweet potato, water, onion powder, dried mustard, vinegar, tamari, and miso until very smooth and creamy.

Fold cheese into potato mixture.

Fold macaroni into cheesy mixture.

Spread evenly into a 9-inch by 13-inch pan and sprinkle bread crumbs and Parmesan cheese on top.

Bake for 15 minutes, until lightly browned.

Refrigerate for up to 5 days in a sealed container, or freeze for up to 3 months.

Nutrition Facts

Amount Per Serving (½ cup)
Calories 312   Calories from Fat 68

Total Fat   8 g
Saturated Fat   4.2 g
Trans Fat   0 g
Poly Fat   0.2 g
Mono Fat   1.8 g
Cholesterol   21 mg
Sodium   378 mg
Total Carbohydrate   46 g
Dietary Fiber   7 g
Sugars   3 g
Protein   16 g

Tropical Quinoa Pudding

Makes 12 toddler servings (¼ cup); or 4 to 6 adult servings (½ cup)

Age: Appropriate for age 12 months and up.

Tips: This pudding makes a great breakfast, snack, or dessert. Try adding fresh blueberries, crushed walnuts or almonds (if no allergy), or dried cranberries. These can be put into little cups on the table for toddlers as a "topping bar" for them to add on their own. Coconut milk is a good source of manganese and contains medium-chain fatty acids, which can help improve nutrient absorption.

Season: Available year-round. Nice in summer because it's cooling to the body.

Selection: The coconut shell should not have any cracks or spots, which could mean mold is present. A quick shake should reveal liquid contents.

Storage: Whole coconuts can be stored at cool temperatures for up to 6 months. Shredded fresh coconut should be stored refrigerator for up to 7 days, or in the freezer for up to 6 months.

1 cup dry quinoa
2 cups water
1 14-ounce can crushed pineapple, drained
1 cup rice, cow's, or almond milk
1 teaspoon ground cinnamon
¼ teaspoon ground cloves
½ cup shredded unsweetened coconut (optional)
1 14-ounce can lite coconut milk

In a saucepan over medium heat, dry-toast the quinoa for a few minutes while stirring, being sure the quinoa doesn't burn. You will smell a nutty aroma.

Add water and bring to a slow boil, then lower the heat and simmer for about 15 minutes, until all water is absorbed.

Remove the pan from the heat

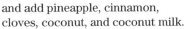

and add pineapple, cinnamon, cloves, coconut, and coconut milk.

Return to medium heat and cook for 5 to 8 minutes, until mixture is thick and creamy.

Nutrition Facts

Amount Per Serving (¼ cup)
Calories 195   Calories from Fat 89

Total Fat   10 g
Saturated Fat   7 g
Trans Fat   0 g
Poly Fat   1.4 g
Mono Fat   0.4 g
Cholesterol   0 mg
Sodium   12 mg
Total Carbohydrate   40 g
Dietary Fiber   5 g
Sugars   4 g
Protein   8 g

Confetti Rice

Makes 10 toddler servings (½ cup); or 6 adult servings (¾ cup)

Age: Appropriate for age 12 months and up.

Tips: Bright and colorful, this tasty dish appeals to a toddler's eyes as well as his tongue. Cooking time may vary according to the type of rice you use. Longer-grain rice may require 5 to 10 minutes more cook time.

See page 185 for information on brown rice.

> 1 cup brown basmati rice (presoaking is preferable, or you can toast according to directions below)
> 1 small onion, grated
> 1 cup grated carrots
> ½ cup grated yellow squash (or an additional ¼ cup of grated carrots and zucchini)
> 1 cup grated zucchini
> 1 teaspoon onion powder
> ¼ teaspoon ground ginger
> ¼ teaspoon cumin (optional)
> ½ teaspoon coriander (optional)
> ½ teaspoon salt
> 1 teaspoon minced fresh cilantro
> 4 cups vegetable or chicken broth (or water)

Rinse rice.

In a medium saucepan, heat rice on low heat until you smell a nutty aroma, about 2 to 3 minutes.

Add onions, carrots, squash, zucchini, onion powder, and ginger and mix well.

Add broth, bring to a boil, reduce heat to medium-low and simmer, covered, for about 45 minutes, until water is absorbed.

Stir in cilantro and cool to serve.

You may also make this dish in a rice cooker.

Refrigerate in a sealed container for up to 3 days.

Nutrition Facts

Amount Per Serving (½ cup)
Calories 99   Calories from Fat 11

Total Fat   1 g
Saturated Fat   0.2 g
Trans Fat   0 g
Poly Fat   0.4 g
Mono Fat   0.4 g
Cholesterol   0 mg
Sodium   187 mg
Total Carbohydrate   20 g
Dietary Fiber   2 g
Sugars   3 g
Protein   2 g

Amaranth with Apples and Cinnamon

Makes 8 toddler servings (⅓ cup); or 5 adult servings (½ cup)

Age: Appropriate for age 12 months and up.

Tips: This makes a rich, filling breakfast cereal or snack. The recipe makes a large portion— freeze using the food cube method or in larger batches in sealed containers for up to 1 month.

See page 301 for information on amaranth.

> 1 cup amaranth
> 3 cups rice or cow's milk
> 2 medium apples, peeled, cored, and diced (may leave apples unpeeled for older toddlers)
> ¼ cup ground or crushed toasted almonds, hazelnuts, or walnuts
> 1 teaspoon ground cinnamon

In a medium saucepan, combine amaranth, milk, apples, almonds, and cinnamon and bring to a simmer.

Reduce heat and cook for 30 minutes, until milk is absorbed.

If necessary, add water to thin.

Nutrition Facts

Amount Per Serving (⅓ cup)
Calories 183   Calories from Fat 36

Total Fat   4 g
Saturated Fat   0.7 g
Trans Fat   0 g
Poly Fat   1.3 g
Mono Fat   1.8 g
Cholesterol   0 mg

Sodium   38 mg
Total Carbohydrate   33 g
Dietary Fiber   6 g
Sugars   4 g
Protein   5 g

Pasta with Pesto and Garbanzo Beans

Makes 8 servings (½ cup); or 4 adult servings (1 cup)

Age: Appropriate for age 12 months and up.

Tips: Garbanzo beans are high in fiber, the trace mineral molybdenum, and manganese. They are also a very good source of folate. Using brown rice pasta with garbanzos lends a unique twist to more traditional rice and beans—with the same good protein content. You may also substitute whole-wheat pasta if desired. Dried garbanzos require longer cooking time than many other dried beans, about 90 minutes and up to 2 hours.

Selection: Dried garbanzo beans can be found packaged or in the bulk bin in health food stores.

Storage: Store dried garbanzo beans in an airtight container in a cool, dry place for up to 12 months.

> 4 quarts water
> 1 tablespoon sea salt
> 1 package whole grain penne pasta
> 2 cups chopped fresh tomatoes (or one 14.5-ounce can diced tomatoes)
> 2 cups canned white (try great northern) or garbanzo beans, no salt added, rinsed and drained

½ cup pesto (packaged or see Pesto Sauce recipe on page 284)

Grated Parmesan, Romano, or asiago cheese (optional)

Cook pasta al dente in salted water according to package directions.

In pasta cooking pot, add drained and rinsed pasta, tomatoes, beans, and pesto sauce, and toss to coat pasta.

If desired, sprinkle with Parmesan, Romano, or asiago cheese.

Nutrition Facts

Amount Per Serving (½ cup)
Calories 374   Calories from Fat 116

Total Fat   3 g
Saturated Fat   1 g
Trans Fat   0 g
Poly Fat   0 g
Mono Fat   2 g
Cholesterol   2 mg
Sodium   186 mg
Total Carbohydrate   22 g
Dietary Fiber   3 g
Sugars   2 g
Protein   4 g

Muffin, Pancake, Cookie, and Cake Recipes

Sunshine Muffins

Makes 24 toddler servings (1 muffin)

Age: Appropriate for age 12 months and up.

Tips: These yummy muffins—a good source of "invisible" veggies—make a well-balanced breakfast meal. Try adding ½ cup sunflower seeds to the batter for older toddlers. Organic hemp protein powder is high in fiber and provides a good balance of omega-3 and omega-6 essential fatty acids with GLA, vitamins E, C, and B_6, calcium, magnesium, potassium, and iron. It is helpful for clearing up eczema.

Storage: Refrigerate hemp protein powder after opening and be sure to check the expiration date on the package.

2½ cups whole-wheat pastry or gluten-free flour mix (such as Bob's Red Mill)

½ cup oat bran

4 tablespoons protein powder (hemp or whey)

¼ cup ground flaxseeds

2 teaspoons ground cinnamon

2 teaspoons nutmeg

1 teaspoon baking soda

¼ teaspoon baking powder

3 extra-large eggs

¼ cup maple syrup

¼ cup blackstrap molasses

¼ cup frozen orange juice concentrate, unsweetened and undiluted, thawed

¼ cup grapeseed or sunflower oil

1 cup grated zucchini

1 cup grated sweet potato

Preheat oven to 325° F.

In a large bowl, combine flour, oat bran, hemp powder, flaxseeds, cinnamon, nutmeg, baking soda, and baking powder.

Stir gently until well mixed.

Beat the eggs in a mixer or food processor for about 2 minutes, until they are light and foamy.

Add maple syrup, molasses, thawed orange juice concentrate, and oil and blend on low until combined.

Stir in zucchini and sweet potatoes.

Fold wet mixture into dry mixture until combined.

Fill paper-lined muffin tins about ¾ full to prevent flat muffin tops.

Bake for about 20 minutes. Test for doneness by inserting a toothpick in the middle of a muffin. When it comes out clean, it's done.

Allow muffins to cool completely on wire rack.

Store in a freezer container or freezer bag for up to 3 months. To thaw, remove condensation, defrost overnight in the refrigerator, and heat in a 325° F oven for 8 to 10 minutes or microwave for 15 seconds.

Nutrition Facts

Amount Per Serving (1 muffin)
Calories 144   Calories from Fat 76

Total Fat   8 g
Saturated Fat   1 g
Trans Fat   0 g
Poly Fat   5.4 g
Mono Fat   1.6 g
Cholesterol   31 mg
Sodium   69 mg
Total Carbohydrate   16 g
Dietary Fiber   3 g
Sugars   1 g
Protein   3 g

Eating for Energy

Toddlers are very busy people. While their tummies are still very small, their activity levels are on the rise. As a result, you may notice your little one's energy flagging from time to time. If you are in the midst of a longer activity, class, or excursion and you notice him slowing down, getting a bit cranky, or even looking a little pale, chances are good that he needs a little nourishment pick-me-up. If it's close to mealtime, you might consider altering your plans to get him to the food a little sooner. Order him (or offer at home) some veggies and a little creamy dip to munch on while he is waiting for his meal. If mealtime is still a ways off, however, you will want to have a few things on hand that will help restore his energy quickly so you can all continue to enjoy your activity. Here's a list of quick pick-me-ups for 12 months and up:
• Sliced apple, pear, peach, or plum, plain or with a yogurt dip
• Whole-wheat or brown rice crackers with nut or seed butter (see nut allergy warning on page 95)
• Sliced grape tomatoes or sliced berries with small cubes of cheese
• Fruit smoothie
• Lightly sweetened yogurt (use mashed banana, applesauce, or a little maple syrup)

Pineapple Upside Down Carrot Cake (egg and dairy-free)

Makes 16 toddler servings (1½-inch piece); 9 adult servings (2½-inch piece)

Age: Appropriate age is 12 months and up.

Tips: This lightly sweetened cake is made with no eggs or dairy. Traditional pineapple upside down cakes are heavy with sugar and syrup, but this one is light, tasty, and adds an extra nutrient punch with the carrots. See page 226 for information on pineapple.

Vegetable spray oil
½ cup vegetable oil
1 cup turbinado sugar
1 cup applesauce, unsweetened
2 teaspoons vanilla extract
2 teaspoons cinnamon
1 teaspoon ginger, ground
1 cup grated carrots
2 cups whole-wheat pastry flour
2½ teaspoons baking soda
1 teaspoon sunflower oil or cooking spray
1 15-ounce can pineapple chunks in juice (not syrup), drained

Preheat oven to 350° F.

Lightly spray an 8-inch by 8-inch baking pan with cooking spray.

In a small bowl combine vegetable oil, sugar, applesauce, vanilla, cinnamon, and ginger and mix well.

Fold in grated carrots.

Stir in flour and baking soda, mixing until just combined.

Lay the pineapple out in a single layer on your prepared baking pan.

Pour batter over the pineapple.

Bake for 30 minutes.

Test for doneness by sticking a tooth pick in the cake. When removed, it should be clean.

Nutrition Facts

Amount Per Serving (1 sllice)
Calories 157   Calories from Fat 67

Total Fat   7 g
Saturated Fat   1 g
Trans Fat   0 g
Poly Fat   5 g
Mono Fat   1 g
Cholesterol   0 mg
Sodium   226 mg
Total Carbohydrate   21 g
Dietary Fiber   3 g
Sugars   8 g
Protein   2 g

Blueberry Muffins

Makes 12 toddler servings (1 muffin)

Age: Appropriate for age 12 months and up.

Tips: These muffins aren't as sweet as conventional blueberry muffins, but they still satisfy toddlers on the lookout for a snack. Add a crumb topping if desired (see page 260 for recipe). You can also try a strawberry or chopped peach version. See page 295 for information on blueberries.

2 cups whole-wheat pastry flour, oat flour, or gluten-free flour blend, divided
1 tablespoon baking powder
½ teaspoon baking soda
¼ teaspoon salt
1 teaspoon cinnamon
1 teaspoon vanilla
¼ cup ground flaxseeds
1 egg, slightly beaten
1 cup milk

¼ cup maple syrup
¼ cup sunflower oil
1 cup blueberries

Preheat oven to 375° F.

Place paper muffin cups in muffin pan.

In a large bowl, combine 1¾ cup flour, baking powder, baking soda, salt, cinnamon, and flaxseeds and mix well.

Add egg, milk, vanilla, and maple syrup to the flour mixture.

Stir just enough to wet the batter.

Add sunflower oil and stir to blend ingredients.

Roll blueberries in ¼ cup reserved flour, add to the batter, and stir.

Fill each muffin cup about ⅔ full.

Bake for about 25 minutes.

Test for doneness by inserting a toothpick in the middle of a muffin. When it comes out clean, it's done.

Cool completely on wire rack.

Nutrition Facts

Amount Per Serving (1 muffin)
Calories 138   Calories from Fat 69

Total Fat   8 g
Saturated Fat   1.2 g
Trans Fat   0 g
Poly Fat   1.3 g
Mono Fat   4.6 g
Cholesterol   20 mg
Sodium   119 mg
Total Carbohydrate   14 g
Dietary Fiber   2 g
Sugars   3 g
Protein   4 g

Banana Oat Muffins

Makes 12 servings (1 muffin)
Age: Appropriate for age 12 months and up.

See page 197 for information on bananas.

1 cup oat flour or gluten free flour mix (such as Bob's Red Mill)
1½ teaspoons baking powder
½ teaspoon baking soda
1 cup oats
⅓ cup ground flaxseeds
½ teaspoon ground cinnamon
¼ cup Sucanat
¼ teaspoon salt
1 cup applesauce
1 teaspoon vanilla
1 egg, well beaten
1 tablespoon sunflower oil
¼ cup milk
1½ cups mashed bananas (very ripe)
¼ cup mini grain-sweetened or semi-sweet chocolate chips (optional for older children)

Crumb Topping (optional)

½ cup rolled oats
⅓ cup Sucanat
1 tablespoon oat flour or gluten-free flour mix
¼ cup wheat germ
¼ cup sunflower oil or melted butter
1½ teaspoons cinnamon

Preheat oven to 375° F.

Place paper muffin cups in pan.

In a large bowl, combine oat flour, baking powder, baking soda, oats, flaxseeds, cinnamon, Sucanat, and salt.

Stir in applesauce, vanilla, egg, sunflower oil, and milk.

Add banana and chocolate chips, if using, by folding into mixture.

Fill each muffin cup about ⅔ full.

For Topping

In a medium bowl, combine all ingredients with a fork until mixture becomes crumbly.

Sprinkle 1 tablespoon of crumb topping on each muffin.

Bake for 25 to 30 minutes.

Test for doneness by inserting a toothpick in the middle of a muffin. When it comes out clean, it's done.

Allow muffins to cool completely on wire rack.

Nutrition Facts

Amount Per Serving (1 muffin)
Calories 260   Calories from Fat 107

Total Fat   12 g
Saturated Fat   1.5 g
Trans Fat   0 g
Poly Fat   3.6 g
Mono Fat   6.2 g
Cholesterol   18 mg
Sodium   115 mg
Total Carbohydrate   34 g
Dietary Fiber   7 g
Sugars   14 g
Protein   7 g

Soft Oatmeal Cookies

Makes 29 toddler servings (1 cookie); or 14 to 15 adult servings (2 cookies)

Age: Appropriate for age 12 months and up.

Tips: Low in sugar, with 2 grams of fiber each, this is a soft and delicious oatmeal cookie. For a smoother cookie and batter that is easier to work with, refrigerate batter until cool before baking cookies, about 30 minutes.

See page 188 for information on oatmeal; page 264 for information on blackstrap molasses.

Grapeseed oil cooking spray
  or 1 teaspoon butter
1¾ cups rolled oats
1¼ cups whole-wheat flour
½ teaspoon baking powder
½ teaspoon baking soda
¼ teaspoon salt
1 to 2 tablespoons ground
  cinnamon
¼ to ½ teaspoon nutmeg
¼ teaspoon cardamom
  (optional)
¾ cup raisins or dried
  cranberries (optional)
¾ cup applesauce
⅓ cup pure maple syrup
2 tablespoons blackstrap
  molasses
2 eggs
1½ teaspoons vanilla extract

Preheat oven to 350° F.

Grease two cookie sheets with grapeseed oil cooking spray.

In a large bowl, mix all dry ingredients together, except raisins and cranberries, if using.

In a medium bowl, mix all liquid ingredients together.

Add liquid ingredients to dry ingredients and mix well, about 2 minutes. If desired, use an electric mixer. Fold in raisins and cranberries, if using.

Drop small balls, about 1 tablespoon batter, onto cookie sheet about 1 inch apart and gently flatten with the back of a spoon.

Bake for 15 minutes, until slightly golden brown.

Cool on a wire rack before serving or storing.

Store cookie batter or cookies in a sealed container in the refrigerator for up to 10 days, or in the freezer for up to 3 months.

Nutrition Facts

Amount Per Serving (1 cookie)
Calories 68   Calories from Fat 8

Total Fat   1 g
Saturated Fat   0.3 g
Trans Fat   0.2 g
Poly Fat   0.2 g
Mono Fat   0.2 g
Cholesterol   15 mg
Sodium   50 mg
Total Carbohydrate   14 g
Dietary Fiber   2 g
Sugars   5 g
Protein   2 g

Pumpkin Cookies

Makes 75 infant servings (1 cookie); or 37 adult servings (2 cookies)

Age: Appropriate for age 12 months and up.

Tips: These warming cookies are low in sugar. Sucanat is a less refined version of conventional table sugar. It is processed with no bleaching or additives.

See page 203 for information on pumpkins.

Vegetable cooking spray
3½ cups whole-wheat pastry
     flour
¼ cup ground flaxseeds
2 teaspoons baking powder
¾ teaspoon baking soda
2 tablespoons ground
     cinnamon
1 teaspoon ground nutmeg
2 teaspoons ground ginger
½ teaspoon ground cloves
2 cups raisins
½ cup butter
¾ cup Sucanat or organic
     brown sugar
2 eggs
2 cups fresh pumpkin puree or
     1 can cooked pumpkin
1 tablespoon vanilla extract
½ cup vegetable oil

Preheat oven to 375° F.

Grease two cookie sheets with cooking spray.

In a large bowl, whisk together flour, flaxseed, baking powder, baking soda, cinnamon, nutmeg, ginger, cloves, and stir in raisins.

In a mixer, cream butter, and sweetener.

Beat in eggs, pumpkin, vanilla, and oil.

Gently fold in dry ingredients. Be careful not to over mix.

Drop small balls, about 1 tablespoon batter, onto cookie sheet about 1 inch apart and gently flatten with the back of a spoon.

Bake for 10 minutes, until slightly golden brown.

Cool on a wire rack before serving or storing.

Store cookie batter or cookies in a sealed container in the refrigerator for up to 10 days, or freeze for up to 3 months.

Nutrition Facts

Amount Per Serving (1 cookie)
Calories 71   Calories from Fat 29

Total Fat   3 g
Saturated Fat   1 g
Trans Fat   0 g
Poly Fat   1 g
Mono Fat   0.7 g
Cholesterol   10 mg
Sodium   26 mg
Total Carbohydrate   10 g
Dietary Fiber   1 g
Sugars   5 g
Protein   1 g

Pancakes

*Makes 10 toddler servings
(2 pancakes); or 5 adult servings
(4 pancakes)*

Age: Appropriate for age 12
months and up.

Tips: Pancakes make a great
finger food: Cut them into strips
and let your toddler dip them into
pure maple syrup, juice-sweetened
fruit jelly or jam, nut butter (see
nut allergy warning on page 95),
blackstrap molasses, or salsa. If you
serve them whole, lightly glaze with a
sweet topping; no need to soak.

You may also top pancakes
with fruit or fold it into the
batter before cooking. Try ¼ to
½ cup strawberries, blueberries,
raspberries, bananas, fresh or dried
cranberries, raisins, dried coconut,
minced nuts (if not allergic), seeds,
beans, cheese, or grain-sweetened
or semisweet chocolate chips.

Untoasted wheat germ is higher
in fiber, B vitamins, folic acid,
thiamin, vitamin E, magnesium,
phosphorus, zinc, and manganese
than toasted wheat germ. Wheat
germ contains agglutinin (WGA), a
lectin that may be related to wheat
allergies. Someone who experiences
allergy symptoms when eating
wheat often will have more severe
symptoms when eating wheat germ.

Selection: It is best to buy
organic wheat germ—can be
purchased in bulk.

Storage: Refrigerate wheat germ
in a glass jar.

1½ cups whole-wheat flour
2 teaspoons baking powder
¼ teaspoon salt
¼ cup ground flaxseeds
¼ cup wheat germ or oat bran
½ teaspoon ground cinnamon
(optional)
1½ cups cow's, unsweetened
rice, or almond milk
2 eggs
½ teaspoon vanilla extract
(optional)
2 tablespoons butter, ghee, or
vegetable oil

In a medium bowl, combine flour,
baking powder, salt, flaxseeds, wheat
germ, and cinnamon and mix well.

In a small bowl, combine milk,
eggs, and vanilla extract.

Pour liquid ingredients over dry
ingredients and whisk lightly until
few lumps are present.

Heat a bit of butter in a large
skillet over medium heat.

Using a ladle or measuring cup,
pour 3½-inch pancakes on griddle
about 2 inches apart.

Cook pancakes for 2 to 3
minutes, until air bubbles show,
flip and cook an additional 1 to 2
minutes, until lightly browned.

Repeat with the remaining batter.

If using an electric griddle, heat
to 350° F.

Refrigerate in a sealed container
with waxed paper between
pancakes, or freeze up to 3 months.
Reheat several on a baking sheet for
5 to 10 minutes at 325° F or toast
individually in a toaster oven.

Nutrition Facts

Amount Per Serving (2 pancakes)
Calories 140   Calories from Fat 21

Total Fat   2 g
Saturated Fat   0.3 g
Trans Fat   0 g
Poly Fat   0.3 g
Mono Fat   1.7 g

Cholesterol 0 mg
Sodium 1,765 mg
Total Carbohydrate 24 g
Dietary Fiber 2 g
Sugars 0 g
Protein 1 g

Sweet Potato Cake

Makes 20 toddler servings (1 slice); or 10 to 15 adult servings (1½ to 2 slices)

Age: Appropriate for age toddlers 12 months and up.

Tips: This recipe makes a great first birthday cake. It is so good that it doesn't need a glaze or frosting, but for special occasions you can coat with Molasses Glaze. Sucanat is the trademark name for unrefined dried cane juice. Sucanat is high in vitamin B$_2$ (riboflavin).

Selection: Demerara Sucanat has a coarser grain—it's a little sticky with a slight molasses flavor. Muscovado has fine, dry crystals and a strong molasses flavor.

Storage: Store in a sealed container in a cool, dry place.

See below for Molasses Glaze recipe.

4 tablespoons butter
½ cup Sucanat
1½ cups oat flour
1 teaspoon baking soda
½ cup toasted wheat germ
¼ cup ground flaxseeds
¼ teaspoon salt
1 teaspoon ground cardamom
1 teaspoon ground cinnamon
2 large eggs
1 teaspoon vanilla extract
1 cup applesauce
3 cups grated sweet potato
1 teaspoon butter

Preheat oven to 375° F.

In a mixer, cream together butter and sugar.

In a medium bowl, combine oat flower, baking soda, wheat germ, flaxseeds, salt, cardamom, and cinnamon.

In another medium bowl, add vanilla extract and applesauce and mix for 2 to 3 minutes.

Add the dry ingredients and mix for about 2 to 3 minutes, until blended.

Fold in the sweet potato.

Grease a 9½-inch Bundt pan or two 8-inch cake pans.

Pour batter in pan and bake for 40 to 45 minutes, until toothpick comes out clean.

Nutrition Facts

Amount Per Serving (1 slice)
Calories 122   Calories from Fat 39

Total Fat 4 g
Saturated Fat 1.9 g
Trans Fat 0 g
Poly Fat 0.9 g
Mono Fat 1.1 g
Cholesterol 28 mg
Sodium 203 mg
Total Carbohydrate 18 g
Dietary Fiber 3 g
Sugars 6 g
Protein 4 g

Molasses Glaze

Makes 16 servings (1 tablespoon)

Age: Appropriate for age 12 months and up.

Tips: Blackstrap molasses is a dark liquid by-product of sugar with the highest nutrient content of all the natural sweeteners. It is high in manganese, copper, iron, calcium, potassium, and magnesium. It has a strong distinctive flavor and very dark color, so may not work as well as the lighter syrups (such as maple or rice) in recipes calling for a liquid sweetener. Molasses Glaze is delicious on Sweet Potato Cake (see page 264 for recipe).

Selection: It is best to buy unsulfured blackstrap molasses because of its smoother taste and because sulfur is a common allergen.

Storage: Opened molasses can be stored in the refrigerator or a cool, dry place for up to 6 months. Unopened molasses can be kept for 1 year.

1 cup confectioner's sugar
1 tablespoon blackstrap
   molasses
2 tablespoons whole or
   evaporated milk
1 tablespoon butter, softened

In a medium bowl, combine all ingredients and whisk until smooth consistency.

Nutrition Facts

Amount Per Serving (1 tablespoon)
Calories 40   Calories from Fat 7

Total Fat   1 g
Saturated Fat   0.5 g
Trans Fat   0 g
Poly Fat   0 g
Mono Fat   0.2 g
Cholesterol   2 mg
Sodium   7 mg
Total Carbohydrate   8 g
Dietary Fiber   0 g
Sugars   7g
Protein   0 g

Protein Entrée Recipes

Egg and Spinach Frittata

Makes 6 toddler servings (1/6 of frittata); or 4 adult servings (¼ of frittata)

Age: Appropriate for age 12 months and up.

Tips: This is an easy high-calcium breakfast or dinner that works well for the whole family. Spinach is high in oxalic acid, which decreases absorption of calcium from the spinach—but does not affect the calcium absorption from feta and cottage cheese.

Tips: Feta cheese adds a burst of flavor to this frittata. Feta is high in protein, riboflavin, vitamin B_{12}, calcium, phosphorus, and sodium. Placing feta cheese in water for

a few minutes before using will decrease the salty flavor.

Selection: Avoid traditional Greek feta cheese as it is not pasteurized. Avoid any feta made with raw milk. Look for feta that is packed in water or tightly sealed packaging.

Storage: Tightly sealed feta cheese will keep in the refrigerator for several weeks due to its high salt content.

See page 127 for more information about oxalic acid. Other vegetables could be used in place of spinach, such as tomato, broccoli, cauliflower, collards, kale, mushrooms, or a combination.

5 large eggs
¼ cup grated crumbled feta
   cheese

1 cup cottage cheese
1 teaspoon diced fresh basil or
dried dill (optional)
Salt and pepper to taste
(optional)
1 tablespoon butter, ghee, or
sunflower oil
¼ cup diced onion
2 cups packed, prewashed
baby spinach, or frozen,
thawed, and drained chopped
¼ cup water

Whisk the eggs in a large bowl.

Add feta cheese, cottage cheese, basil or dill, and salt and pepper, if using, and mix well.

In a large skillet, add butter, ghee, or oil, and onions and sauté over medium heat for 2 to 3 minutes.

Add spinach and water, cover, and cook for 2 minutes.

Spread spinach mixture evenly on the bottom of the pan.

Add egg mixture, spreading it evenly over the spinach.

Cover, reduce heat to medium-low, and cook for 10 to 15 minutes, until egg is set—eggs continue cooking once removed from the heat.

Cut into 6 pieces.

Serve with ketchup (for anyone) or hot sauce (for adults), if desired.

Refrigerate for up to 3 days.

Nutrition Facts

Amount Per Serving (1 slice)
Calories 153   Calories from Fat 70

Total Fat   8 g
Saturated Fat   3 g
Trans Fat   0 g
Poly Fat   1 g
Mono Fat   3 g
Cholesterol   351 mg

Sodium   376 mg
Total Carbohydrate   4 g
Dietary Fiber   1 g
Sugars   1g
Protein   12 g

Scallops and Collards

Makes 8 toddler servings (½ cup); or 4 adult servings (1 cup)

Age: Appropriate for age 2 years and up.

Tips: Scallops are fast cooking and taste great served with greens such as broccoli, baby spinach, or asparagus. They are high in vitamin B_{12}, omega-3 fatty acids, magnesium, and potassium. If you don't want to add the scallops, leave them out for a delicious vegetarian collard dish.

Selection: Look for bay scallops (deemed kid-safe, smaller than sea scallops, the largest, most commonly available variety) that are odorless and pinkish white. When cooked, scallops should have a slightly sweet flavor.

Storage: Place fresh scallops in a lidded container and refrigerate; or place on a bed of ice, wrap tightly and refrigerate. If frozen, defrost in the refrigerator.

See page 217 for information on collard greens.

2 pounds collard greens
2 tablespoons olive oil
1 small onion, chopped
¼ cup water
¼ cup white wine
1½ tablespoons organic
Worcestershire sauce
(Annie's works well)
1 teaspoon ume plum vinegar
or red wine vinegar
12 ounces bay scallops

1 tablespoon lemon juice,
fresh-squeezed or bottled

Wash collard greens well in a large
bowl of water to make sure all sand
is removed.

Fold collard leaves in half. Either
hold the leaf in one hand and pull
off the stem with the other hand, or
use a knife to remove the stem.

Roll the leaves like a cigar and
chop into small pieces.

In a large pan, add 1 tablespoon
olive oil and onion and sauté over
medium heat for 3 to 5 minutes.

Add collard greens and water.

Cover and cook on low-medium
heat for 10 minutes.

Stir greens and add white wine,
Worcestershire sauce, and vinegar.

Cook wilted greens for another 5
to 7 minutes, or longer for increased
tenderness.

Make a hole in the center of the
pan by pushing collard greens to the
edge of the pan. Pour 1 tablespoon
remaining olive oil in hole.

Cook scallops in center of pan
for 1 to 2 minutes, or until firm with
a tinge of pink in the center.

Sprinkle with lemon juice.

Serve immediately as a
standalone dish or over whole-grain
pasta, quinoa, millet, or brown rice.

Nutrition Facts

Amount Per Serving (½ cup)
Calories 308   Calories from Fat 74

Total Fat   8 g
Saturated Fat   1.4 g
Trans Fat   0 g
Poly Fat   1.8 g
Mono Fat   4.4 g
Cholesterol   23 mg
Sodium   2,857 mg

Total Carbohydrate   41 g
Dietary Fiber   3 g
Sugars   1 g
Protein   9 g

Orange Ginger Salmon

*Makes 16 toddler servings (1
ounce); or 4 adult servings (4
ounces)*

Age: Appropriate for age 12
months and up.

Tips: Salmon is high in omega-3
fatty acids, vitamin D, selenium,
niacin, vitamin B_{12}, phosphorus,
magnesium, and vitamin B_6. It is
best to buy wild salmon for lower
levels of mercury and highest levels
of omega-3 fatty acids.

Season: Peak for salmon is early
summer to late fall.

Selection: Salmon should not
smell fishy. If smoked, there should
not be brown around the edges. If
prepackaged, it should not be shiny
and the package should not have
any moisture or leakage. Look for
fillets about 1 inch thick.

Storage: It's best to purchase fish
on cooking day or the day before.
Fresh salmon should be stored
over ice in the coldest part of the
refrigerator. Salmon can be frozen in
a sealed bag for up to 3 weeks.

1 pound salmon filets
1 cup Orange Ginger Marinade
(recipe follows) or any
packaged marinade
grapeseed cooking oil spray

Marinate salmon in the marinade for
about 30 minutes (or overnight for a
stronger flavor).

Preheat grill or oven (set to broil).

Spray clean grill rack or broiling
pan with cooking spray.

Place salmon filets about 2 to 3 inches from broiler heat and 4 to 5 inches from grill heat.

Cook for about 4 minutes, flip, and cook for another 4 minutes, until translucent in center. If leaving fillet unskinned, you may cook, skin side down, for 8 to 10 minutes and lift the flesh right out of the skin when fully cooked.

Salmon will continue cooking when taken off heat.

Nutrition Facts

Amount Per Serving (1 ounce)
Calories 83   Calories from Fat 39

Total Fat   4 g
Saturated Fat   0.7 g
Trans Fat   0 g
Poly Fat   1.2 g
Mono Fat   2 g
Cholesterol   26 mg
Sodium   210 mg
Total Carbohydrate   2 g
Dietary Fiber   0 g
Sugars   1 g
Protein   9 g

Orange Ginger Marinade

Makes 1 cup

Age: Appropriate for age 12 months and up.

Tips: This is a great marinade to add zing to fish, shrimp, poultry, or meat. If using on fish, marinate for 30 minutes—longer and more delicate white fish may fall apart from the acid in the orange juice. Marinate all other foods for 30 minutes to overnight. The longer the food is marinated, the more flavorful it will be. Also, try freezing uncooked protein in the marinade

for up to 3 months. Marinated protein works best when baked in a 375° F oven, broiled under high heat, or grilled.

¼ cup water
1 tablespoon sesame oil
½ cup orange juice
2 teaspoon fresh ginger, minced
¼ cup light soy sauce
1 teaspoon chopped fresh
    cilantro (optional)

In a small bowl, whisk all ingredients together.

Place meat in container, pour marinade on top, seal, and marinate accordingly, depending on the meat.

Nutrition Facts

Amount Per Serving (1 cup)
Calories 226   Calories from Fat 124

Total Fat   14 g
Saturated Fat   1.9 g
Trans Fat   0 g
Poly Fat   5.7 g
Mono Fat   5.4 g
Cholesterol   0 mg
Sodium   2,288 mg
Total Carbohydrate   19 g
Dietary Fiber   1 g
Sugars   17 g
Protein   8 g

Codfish with Garlic, Lemon, and Basil

Makes 15 toddler servings (1 ounce); or 4 adult servings (4 ounces)

Age: Appropriate for age 12 months and up.

Tips: Because of the mercury and PCB contamination in the ocean, codfish should be eaten only once per month by babies and pregnant women. It is a light fish that tastes great flavored simply with olive oil, garlic, and fresh herbs, such as cilantro or parsley. Prepared cod is very soft and flaky, and can be mashed with a fork and a little water to make a puree or sandwich spread, if desired. Add ½ teaspoon mild miso paste for a richer, saltier flavor.

Selection: Make sure you can see and smell the fish before purchasing. It should smell like fresh ocean water. Be sure fish is free of brown spots, which indicate spoilage. If buying frozen fish, make sure there are no signs of freezer burn and thaw fish for one day in the refrigerator prior to cooking.

Storage: It's best to purchase fish on cooking day or the day before. Place fresh fish on a bed of ice, cover, and store in coldest part of the refrigerator.

2 tablespoons olive oil
1 to 2 cloves garlic, chopped
15 ounces Pacific codfish
1 tablespoon fresh-squeezed lemon juice
2 tablespoons minced fresh basil plus additional tablespoon for garnish (optional)

In a medium skillet, heat olive oil and garlic for 2 to 3 minutes, until lightly browned.

Add codfish and lemon juice and cook for 3 minutes.

Gently flip fish and sprinkle with 2 tablespoons of basil.

Cook for another 7 or 8 minutes, until fish is flaky.

If desired, garnish with remaining tablespoon of basil.

Nutrition Facts

Amount Per Serving (1 ounce)
Calories 46   Calories from Fat 18

Total Fat   2 g
Saturated Fat   0.3 g
Trans Fat   0 g
Poly Fat   0.2 g
Mono Fat   1.4 g
Cholesterol   16 mg
Sodium   22 mg
Total Carbohydrate   0 g
Dietary Fiber   0 g
Sugars   0 g
Protein   6 g

Tilapia with Zucchini

Makes 3 toddler servings (½ cup); or 1 adult serving (1½ cups)

Age: Appropriate for age 12 months and up.

Tips: Tilapia is a very delicate and low-fat fish. This tasty puree can also be served baked for the rest of the family. Tilapia is delicious in sandwiches, in tacos, and in fish sticks.

Selection: If you can find it, it's best to buy fresh tilapia from the United States, due to high safety standards. There is a variation in color from pinkish brown to a yellowish color. Make sure you can see and smell the fish before purchasing. It should smell like fresh ocean water. Be sure fish is free of brown spots, which indicate spoilage. If buying frozen fish, make sure there are no signs of freezer burn and thaw fish for one day in the refrigerator prior to cooking.

Storage: It's best to purchase fish on cooking day or the day before. Place fresh fish on a bed of

ice, cover, and store in coldest part
of the refrigerator.

12 ounces filleted tilapia
½ cup vegetable broth
1 bay leaf
2 teaspoons chopped parsley
3 tablespoons grated
    Parmesan cheese
2 cup sliced zucchini

Preheat oven to 350° F.

Make a layer of zucchini in an
ovenproof baking dish.

Place tilapia on top of zucchini.

Add vegetable broth and bay
leaf; sprinkle parsley and Parmesan
cheese on fish.

Bake for 15 minutes, until fish is
opaque and flaky.

Remove bay leaf.

Blend all ingredients in a food
processor or blender for 1 minute,
until pureed, or can be served
as fillets with zucchini for older
toddlers and adults.

Store in the refrigerator for up
to 2 days or freeze in freezer-safe
container for up to 1 month.

Nutrition Facts

Amount Per Serving (½ cup)
Calories 75   Calories from Fat 20

Total Fat   2 g
Saturated Fat   1 g
Trans Fat   0 g
Poly Fat   0.4 g
Mono Fat   0.6 g
Cholesterol   40 mg
Sodium   98 mg
Total Carbohydrate   2 g
Dietary Fiber   1 g
Sugars   1 g
Protein   13 g

Cranberry Tuna Fish Salad

*Makes 3 infant servings (2 ounces);
or 2 adult servings (3 to 4 ounces)*

Age: Appropriate for age 12
months and up.

Tips: This is a simple tuna fish
recipe—great for first tuna tastings.
Tuna fish is high in omega-3 fatty
acids, protein, niacin, selenium, and
vitamin B_{12}. Albacore tuna is higher
in mercury than canned light tuna
(skipjack) and yellowfin tuna; and
Atlantic tuna is higher in mercury
than Pacific tuna. Children 1 to 6
years old should not eat more than 3
portions of tuna per month.

Selection: Canned tuna is
available in chunk light and solid
white usually packed in oil or water.
Tuna packed in oil is higher in fat,
although slightly more moist than
tuna packed in water. Avoid fresh
tuna with brown spots or tuna that
looks dry. It should be displayed
whole and in ice. A clean odor is a
good indication of freshness.

Storage: Be sure to check
expiration date on canned tuna or
tuna in a sealed pouch. Refrigerate
opened canned tuna in a sealed
plastic container for up to 3 days.
It's best to purchase fresh tuna on
cooking day or the day before. Place
tuna on a bed of ice, cover, and store
in coldest part of the refrigerator.
Replace ice at least once a day and
use within 4 days of purchase. Fresh
tuna can be frozen for up to 3 weeks.

1 6-ounce can skipjack or
    chunk light tuna in water,
    drained and rinsed (you may
    also use canned boneless,
    skinless, Wild Alaskan
    salmon)

2 tablespoons prepared
cranberry sauce (such as
Knudsen)
1 tablespoon dried cranberries,
nuts, seeds, or wheat germ
(optional for older toddlers)

In a small bowl, combine tuna fish
and cranberry sauce.

Mix in dried cranberries, nuts,
seeds, and or wheat germ, if using.

Serve with rice cakes, crackers,
on a sandwich, or over greens.

Nutrition Facts

Amount Per Serving (2 ounces)
Calories 55   Calories from Fat 3

Total Fat   0 g
Saturated Fat   0 g
Trans Fat   0 g
Poly Fat   0 g
Mono Fat   0 g
Cholesterol   16 mg
Sodium   24 mg
Total Carbohydrate   4 g
Dietary Fiber   0 q
Sugars   4 g
Protein   8 g

Poached Salmon

*Makes 5 toddler servings (3 ounces);
or 3 adult servings (4 to 6 ounces)*

Age: Appropriate for age 12
months and up.

Tips: Poached salmon is quite
moist. It will continue to cook when
taken out of the liquid, so check
frequently while cooking to avoid
drying out. This dish can be served
at room temperature or cold and is
delicious with Lemon-Dill Yogurt
Sauce (page 282).

See page 267 for information on
salmon.

4 cups water
1 cup orange juice
¼ cup lemon juice
¼ cup apple cider vinegar
1 clove garlic, minced
1 bay leaf
½ teaspoon sea salt
3 to 4 dill sprigs

Rinse salmon under cold running
water.

In a salmon poacher or a large
skillet, add water, orange juice,
lemon juice, apple cider vinegar,
garlic, bay leaf, sea salt, and dill
sprigs and bring to a boil.

Simmer for 15 minutes.

Add salmon with a slotted spoon
or a stainless steel spatula. Make
sure liquid is covering the salmon.

Lower heat and cook at a very
low simmer for 8 to 10 minutes,
until translucent.

Remove skin, cool, and
refrigerate until serving.

Nutrition Facts

Amount Per Serving (3 ounces)
Calories 159   Calories from Fat 48

Total Fat   5 g
Saturated Fat   0 g
Trans Fat   0 g
Poly Fat   1.8 g
Mono Fat   2 g
Cholesterol   40 mg
Sodium   275 mg
Total Carbohydrate   7 g
Dietary Fiber   1 g
Sugars   6 g
Protein   20 g

Beans Guide

Bean	Ratio of Bean to Liquid	Presoak	Cook Time
Adzuki beans	1 measure adzuki beans to 4 measures liquid	Optional	90 minutes
Black beans	1 measure black beans to 4 measures liquid	Optional	90 to 120 minutes (2 hours)
Black-eyed peas	1 measure black-eyed peas to 4 measures liquid	No	45 to 60 minutes
Chickpeas (also called garbanzo)	1 measure chickpeas to 4 measures liquid	Yes	90 to 120 minutes (2 hours)
Kidney beans	1 measure kidney beans to 4 measures liquid	Yes	60 to 90 minutes
Lentils	1 measure lentils to 4 measures liquid	No	20 to 30 minutes (red) or 30 to 45 minutes (brown or French)
Lima beans	1 measure lima beans to 4 measures liquid	Yes	45 to 60 minutes
Navy beans	1 measure navy beans to 4 measures liquid	Yes	90 minutes
Pinto beans	1 measure pinto beans to 4 measures liquid	Yes	60 minutes

Storage: Mason-style glass jars work well. Having a row of jars is attractive and lets you know instantly when you are running low.

Preparation: Pick through for stones and rinse well. Soak overnight (if recommended), drain, rinse, and prepare. Beans should be simmered, covered, in a heavy-bottomed pot. Add a 2-inch piece of kombu or 1 teaspoon epazote to improve digestibility. Remove kombu before serving. Add any salt at the end of cook time only. Beans can also be cooked in a slow cooker. Bring them to a boil on the stove top first, then pour boiling water and beans into slow cooker. Cook on low for about 7½ hours or high for about 5½ hours. Check for tenderness. If still firm, continue cooking, checking for doneness every 30 minutes.

Easy Mexi-Beans

Makes 10 toddler servings (⅓ cup); or 7 to 8 adult servings (½ cup)

Age: Appropriate for age 12 months and up.

Tips: This recipe adds flavor to simple kidney or pinto beans and is great served in a burrito or over brown rice or a salad. Kombu is rich in calcium, iodine and other minerals. In addition, it's a good source of Vitamins A, B, C and E. Kombu and epazote help the digestive system break down the beans. Much of the nutrient and flavor content is on the surface of kombu, so instead of washing, wipe with a cloth.

Storage: Kombu can be stored in a sealed plastic bag in a cool dry area.

2 tablespoons olive oil
1 large chopped onion
1 to 2 minced garlic cloves
1 teaspoon ground cumin
¼ teaspoon chili powder (optional)
2 15-ounce cans kidney or pinto beans, rinsed and drained or 4 cups cooked
1 cup water
3 tablespoons chopped cilantro
1 bay leaf
½ strip kombu or 1 teaspoon epazote
1 to 2 tablespoons red wine vinegar, to taste

Heat oil in a large skillet.

Add onion and cook for about 5 minutes, until soft and translucent.

Add garlic, cumin, and chili powder and cook for 1 minute, stirring constantly.

Add black beans, water, cilantro, bay leaf, and kombu and simmer for 15 to 20 minutes, until consistency of a thick soup.

Remove bay leaf.

Add red wine vinegar and mix.

Nutrition Facts

Amount Per Serving (⅓ cup)
Calories 133   Calories from Fat 34

Total Fat   4 g
Saturated Fat   0.6 g
Trans Fat   0 g
Poly Fat   0.5 g
Mono Fat   2.2 g
Cholesterol   0 mg
Sodium   44 mg
Total Carbohydrate   22 g
Dietary Fiber   6 g
Sugars   2 g
Protein   5 g

Lentil Soup

Makes 11 toddler servings (½ cup), or 5 to 6 adult servings (1 cup)

Age: Appropriate for age 12 months and up.

Tips: This light, flavorful soup cooks up quickly and freezes very well. Makes a great meal on its own or with the addition of a little cooked ham or poultry for a protein boost. Puree completely for babies or partially for a creamier texture.

See page 209 for information on lentils.

6 to 8 ounces spinach or kale, fresh or frozen
1 tablespoons olive oil
1 cup chopped onions
⅓ cup chopped celery
½ cup grated carrots

½ cup parsnips (or omit and
   double carrots)
1½ cups brown or French green
   lentils, rinsed and sorted
½ teaspoon dried thyme
1 bay leaf
10 cups water
2 tablespoons red wine vinegar
1 tablespoon Dijon mustard
1 teaspoon curry powder
Salt and pepper, to taste
3 parsley sprigs (optional)

Wash fresh spinach, remove stems, and slice into 2-inch long ribbons or drain frozen spinach.

In a medium pot, heat oil and onions, stirring frequently over medium heat for about 5 minutes, until lightly browned.

Add vegetables and continue to cook for 3 minutes.

Add lentils, thyme, bay leaf, and water and bring to a boil.

Partially cover, lower heat, and simmer for 25 minutes.

Remove bay leaves.

Add spinach, red wine, and Dijon mustard and stir well.

Simmer gently until greens are just done, about 5 to 10 minutes.

If desired, add salt and pepper to season and garnish with parsley sprigs.

Nutrition Facts

Amount Per Serving (½ cup)
Calories 71   Calories from Fat 24

Total Fat   3 g
Saturated Fat   0.4 g
Trans Fat   0 g
Poly Fat   0.3 g
Mono Fat   1.9 g
Cholesterol   0 mg
Sodium   158 mg

Total Carbohydrate   9 g
Dietary Fiber   3 g
Sugars   2 g
Protein   3 g

Speedy Fake "Baked" Beans

Makes 7 toddler servings (⅓ cup); or 5 adult servings (½ cup)

Age: Appropriate for age 12 months and up.

Tips: This is a quick way to add a lot of flavor to a simple can of beans. The chili powder adds a little bite, so reduce to keep the flavor milder. You can serve these beans as a side with rotisserie chicken, chopped hot dogs (organic and nitrate-free), veggie franks, or, for older toddlers, rolled up in a soft corn tortilla with chopped tomatoes, shredded lettuce, and a slice of avocado

1 15-ounce can black, kidney,
   or pinto beans, rinsed and
   drained*
3 tablespoons water or broth
   (vegetable or chicken)
2 tablespoons mirin (optional)
1 clove garlic, minced
¾ teaspoon cumin
½ teaspoon oregano
¼ to ½ teaspoon chili powder
   (adds heat)
½ teaspoon salt
½ teaspoon smoked paprika
   (optional)
1 tablespoon blackstrap molasses
2 tablespoons tomato paste
2 tablespoons fresh cilantro,
   minced (optional)

Combine all ingredients in a medium saucepan and simmer for 10 to 12 minutes until flavors are well combined.

Black beans will hold their shape, and kidney and pinto beans will soften more easily into a mash.

Nutrition Facts

Amount Per Serving (⅓ cup)
Calories 68   Calories from Fat 3

Total Fat   0 g
Saturated Fat   0 g
Trans Fat   0 g
Poly Fat   0 g
Mono Fat   0 g
Cholesterol   2 mg
Sodium   2,814 mg
Total Carbohydrate   14 g
Dietary Fiber   4 g
Sugars   2 g
Protein   4 g

White Bean and Vegetable Turkey Chili

Makes 19 toddler servings (½ cup); or 9 adult servings (1 cup)

Age: Appropriate for age 12 months and up.

Tips: This is an easy one-pot meal everyone will enjoy. If you like your chili spicy, remove a portion for your toddler, then add more chili powder to taste, stir well, and cook for a few minutes more to integrate the flavors. You can also simply add a few dashes of hot sauce to your own cooked bowl. Garnish with a sprinkle of Jack or cheddar cheese, if desired, and serve with a green salad or slices of cucumber, tomato, and avocado.

1 cup sliced portobello
   mushrooms
1 tablespoon olive oil
1 medium onion, chopped

1½ pounds fresh ground turkey
1 clove garlic, minced
1 teaspoon ground cumin
¼ to ½ teaspoon chili powder
   (adds heat)
1 teaspoon dried oregano
2 15-ounce organic canned
   beans, rinsed and drained, or
   4 cups cooked great northern
   beans
2 14.5-ounce cans diced
   tomatoes
2 tablespoons lime juice
½ teaspoon sea salt
3 tablespoons chopped fresh
   cilantro plus additional for
   garnish
1 cup frozen corn

Stem and wipe mushrooms.
   Heat oil in a Dutch oven over medium heat.
   Add onion and sauté for about 4 to 6 minutes, until translucent.
   Add ground turkey and cook for about 8 minutes until browned, no pink remaining.
   Add mushrooms, garlic, ground cumin, chili powder, oregano, beans, tomatoes, lime juice, and salt and cook for about 10 to 15 minutes.
   Add cilantro and corn and cook for another 10 to 15 minutes.
   Season with salt and pepper.
   If desired, garnish with additional chopped cilantro.
   Puree if necessary or mash with the back of your spoon.

Nutrition Facts

Amount Per Serving (½ cup)
Calories 129   Calories from Fat 27

Total Fat   4 g
Saturated Fat   2.1 g
Trans Fat   1 g

Poly Fat   1 g
Mono Fat   1.8 g
Cholesterol   27 mg
Sodium   128 mg
Total Carbohydrate   12 g
Dietary Fiber   4 g
Sugars   2 g
Protein   11 g

Hearty Slow Cooker Chicken Soup

Makes 40 toddler servings (½ cup); or 12 adult servings (1½ cups)

Age: Appropriate for age 12 months and up.

Tips: This is a rich chicken soup that is great served over cooked barley, whole-grain noodles, brown rice, or quinoa. *It is a hearty dish perfect for when your toddler is under the weather with a cold.* Flavor is best when meal is made ahead and soup can rest for 24 hours. Leftover chicken can be used for a variety of different meals: in chicken salad, over green salad, scrambled into eggs, etc.

Kale is very high in fiber, pro-vitamin A, calcium, vitamin K, vitamin C, and manganese. It is also high in iron, beta-carotene, chlorophyll, vitamin E, and sulforaphane, which fosters the production of cancer-fighting enzymes. It is beneficial to the immune system. Kale is among the tougher of the dark green leafy vegetables, and generally needs to be boiled, not just steamed, to break down its fibers adequately. That hardiness makes it an ideal green for use in soups and stews.

Season: Peak season for kale is spring and summer (very sweet flavor after frost).

Selection: Curly kale has a green color (look for dark green),

crinkled leaves, and coarse stems. It has a slightly astringent, peppery flavor. Dinosaur kale is a dark bluish green color, with smoother edges. It has a more subtle sweet flavor.

Storage: Store kale unwashed in a plastic bag in the crisper drawer for 3 to 4 days.

1 tablespoon olive oil (for stovetop preparation only)
1 whole chicken, 3 to 4 pounds
1 large turnip, scrubbed, top removed and cut in half
4 large carrots, peeled and sliced into ½-inch rounds
1 medium celery stalk, sliced thin
1 leek, halved and rinsed, with ends trimmed (be sure to remove all sand)
2 cups kale, stems removed and chopped
5 sprigs dill, form bunch by tying sprigs with cooking string
1 bay leaf
2 medium parsnips, peeled and sliced into ¼-inch rounds
8 cups water or enough to cover chicken and vegetables

Slow Cooker
Remove neck and giblets from chicken (discard or save for another use), then wash chicken and pat dry.

Add all ingredients to slow cooker, making sure chicken and vegetables are covered with water.

Cook on low for 7 to 8 hours or on high for 4 to 5 hours.

Remove turnip, leek, dill, and bay leaf.

Remove chicken, and refrigerate soup and chicken overnight.

Remove congealed fat from soup and season with salt and pepper, if desired. Separate meat from skin and bones, and add meat to the prepared soup.

Rewarm and serve with a whole grain.

Stove Top

In a large stockpot over low heat, add 1 tablespoon of olive oil and chicken and sear for 2 to 3 minutes on both side.

Add remaining ingredients, making sure chicken and vegetables are covered with water.

Bring to a gentle simmer and cook for 1½ to 2 hours. Remove turnip, leek, dill, and bay leaf.

Remove chicken, and refrigerate soup and chicken overnight.

Remove congealed fat from soup and season with salt and pepper, if desired. Separate meat from skin and bones, and add meat to the prepared soup.

Rewarm soup and serve with a whole grain.

Nutrition Facts

Amount Per Serving (½ cup)
Calories 46   Calories from Fat 13

Total Fat   1 g
Saturated Fat   0.4 g
Trans Fat   0 g
Poly Fat   0.3 g
Mono Fat   0.5 g
Cholesterol   14 mg
Sodium   57 mg
Total Carbohydrate   3 g
Dietary Fiber   1 g
Sugars   1 g
Protein   5 g

Crispy Chicken Tenders

Makes 10 toddler servings (about 1½ tenders); or 8 adult servings (about 2 tenders)

Age: Appropriate for age 12 months and up.

Tips: Chicken tenders are a kid favorite, but they are often fried or coated in a poor-quality breading. This recipe is baked, gluten free, and uses nutrient-rich molasses and ground flaxseeds to boost the iron, fiber, and healthy omegas.

1½ cups cornflakes
¼ cup parmesan cheese (flake version is moister than dried)
1 tablespoon ground flax
¼ teaspoon garlic powder
¼ teaspoon onion powder
¼ teaspoon fresh ground black pepper
¼ teaspoon salt
2 pounds chicken tenders or chicken breast cut into 1-inch strips
1 egg
¼ teaspoon salt
cooking spray
Blackstrap molasses, honey, or applesauce for dipping

Preheat oven to 400° F.

Spray cookie sheet with light coating of high-heat oil.

Combine cornflakes, cheese, flax, garlic, onion, pepper and salt in food processor, and pulse until it makes crumbs.

Pour into a shallow bowl.

In another shallow bowl, lightly beat the egg and salt.

Dip each tender into the egg to thoroughly coat, and then roll it in the cornflake mixture until it's thoroughly covered.

Lay the tenders out uniformly on the prepared cookie sheet and bake for about 12 minutes until coating is crisp, chicken is cooked through (meat thermometer registers 165° F).

Chicken tenders may also be frozen, uncooked, for later use: Place raw tenders on a cookie sheet overnight or until frozen. Once frozen, store in quart- or gallon-sized zip-closure freezer bags (with air removed) for up to 2 months. When ready to use, thaw in the refrigerator overnight and then cook as directed.

Serve tenders warm and cut into bite-sized pieces with small amounts of molasses, honey, or applesauce for dipping.

Nutrition Facts

Amount Per Serving (1 ½ pieces)
Calories 230   Calories from Fat 30

Total Fat   3 g
Saturated Fat   1 g
Trans Fat   0 g
Poly Fat   1 g
Mono Fat   1 g
Cholesterol   62 mg
Sodium   152 mg
Total Carbohydrate   32 g
Dietary Fiber   1 g
Sugars   3 g
Protein   18 g

Turkey Sausage

Makes 6 toddler servings (3-ounce patty); 4 adult servings (4-ounce patty)

Age: Appropriate age is 12 months and up.

Tips: Most store-bought sausage is very high in saturated fat, salt, sugar, and other undesirable additives. This healthy version is easy to make at home and works well as a high-protein accompaniment to a breakfast grain, a snack, or part of a "breakfast for dinner" with scrambled eggs or pancakes.

See page xx for turkey information.

½ pound ground turkey breast
¼ teaspoon basil
¼ teaspoon black pepper
¾ teaspoon coriander
¼ teaspoon fennel
½ teaspoon ginger
½ teaspoon nutmeg
½ teaspoon sage
½ teaspoon sea salt
¼ teaspoon thyme
½ cup applesauce

Combine turkey and spices in a large bowl and mix well.

Add applesauce and place in fridge for 15 minutes.

Form into 6 patties (approximately ½ inch thick).*

Cook in lightly oiled skillet over medium heat (4 to 8 minutes per side until cooked through).

You may also grill patties over medium heat (4 to 8 minutes per side until cooked through.)

*You may also make smaller patties, or even roll the turkey out onto a cutting board and cut out simple shapes with a cookie cutter.

Nutrition Facts

Amount Per Serving (3 ounces)
Calories 187   Calories from Fat 100

Total Fat   11 g
Saturated Fat   2.5 g
Trans Fat   0 g
Poly Fat   2.2 g
Mono Fat   5.2 g
Cholesterol   67 mg
Sodium   71 mg
Total Carbohydrate   3 g
Dietary Fiber   0 g
Sugars   2 g
Protein   18 g

Roasted Chicken

Makes 16 toddler servings (2 ounces); or 8 adult servings (4 ounces)

Age: Appropriate for age 12 months and up.

Tips: This is an easy recipe, and leftovers are great for sandwiches and salads for the week. Try adding vegetables to the pan before roasting, including sweet potato, butternut squash, onions, parsnips, carrots, or any other favorites. Be sure roasting chicken fits nicely in pan. If the pan is too big, the juices will burn on the bottom. You can prepare Roasted Chicken one day ahead and refrigerate before cooking.

> 4- to 6-pound roasting chicken
> ½ organic lemon, rinsed
> 1 tablespoon ghee or butter
> ½ teaspoon salt
> 2 sprigs fresh rosemary, cut in halves

Gravy (optional)
> ¾ cup chicken broth
> 1 tablespoon kudzu

Preheat oven to 400° F.

Remove neck and giblets and save for another use or discard.

Rinse whole chicken inside and out, throwing away fat.

Wipe chicken dry.

Place chicken, breast side up, on a rack in a roasting pan.

Squeeze juice of lemon over chicken and inside cavity.

Leave squeezed lemon half inside cavity.

Working carefully so as not to tear skin, gently push the rosemary sprigs under the skin of the breast, two to a side. Using your finger to break the skin away from the meat first makes this a little easier.

Smooth ghee or butter and sprinkle salt all over the skin of the chicken.

Roasting time for a 4-pound bird is 55 to 65 minutes. For each additional pound, add 8 minutes. Chicken is done when the thickest parts of the thigh, breast, and wing registers 170° F on an instant thermometer.

To carve, let chicken sit on a platter for about 10 minutes.

Cut off the wings using a carving knife or poultry scissors.

Carve between the leg and breast and remove legs by twisting at thigh socket.

Cut the drumstick from the thigh by cutting between the bone.

Remove the breasts by cutting down the breast bone.

For Gravy

After removing chicken from pan, put roasting pan on 2 burners of the stove over medium heat.

Bring juices to simmer, scraping the pan and stirring the bits stuck at the bottom.

Use a gravy separator or pour the liquid into a small glass and remove the fat at the top of the glass.

Pour mixture back into roasting pan.

Mix chicken broth and kudzu together. Add to pan to thicken sauce.

Simmer until thickened, about 2 minutes.

Nutrition Facts

Amount Per Serving (2 ounces)
Calories 20   Calories from Fat 8

Total Fat   1 g
Saturated Fat   0.2 g
Trans Fat   0 g
Poly Fat   0.3 g
Mono Fat   0.3 g
Cholesterol   8 mg
Sodium   8 mg
Total Carbohydrate   0 g
Dietary Fiber   0 g
Sugars   0 g
Protein   3 g

Meat Loaf Muffins

Makes 24 toddler servings (1 muffin)
Age: Appropriate for age 12 months and up.

Tips: This is a clever way to serve veggie-filled meatloaf to your toddler—the individual muffins are always a hit. They freeze beautifully for a quick, healthy protein in a pinch. Use fancy muffin papers to make them even more appealing.

Cooking oil spray
1¼ pounds ground turkey
1 pound ground beef, cooked
1 egg
½ cup rolled oats
1 cup grated carrots

1 cup grated zucchini
1 cup grated yellow squash
2 tablespoons organic Worcestershire sauce
1 tablespoon garlic powder
1 teaspoon mustard powder
1 teaspoon dried basil
½ cup low-sodium tomato juice

Glaze (optional)
1 cup organic ketchup, preferably juice sweetened
2 tablespoons organic Worcestershire sauce
¼ cup apple cider vinegar
1 tablespoon honey
1 teaspoon garlic powder

Preheat oven to 375° F.

Lightly grease muffin tin with grapeseed cooking oil spray.

In a large bowl, mix all ingredients with hands.

Using ⅓ cup measure or ice cream scoop, shape mixture into meatballs and mold into muffin tins.

For Glaze
In a small bowl, mix glaze ingredients.

Separate half the glaze to use as a dipping sauce or sandwich spread, and store in the refrigerator.

Baste top of meatballs with other half of glaze or catsup.

Bake for 25 minutes, until meat thermometer reads 160° F.

Remove from oven and allow to cool for 5 to 10 minutes before removing muffins from tin.

Nutrition Facts

Amount Per Serving 1 muffin)
Calories 163   Calories from Fat 34

Total Fat   4 g
Saturated Fat   1.0 g

Trans Fat   0 g
Poly Fat   0.8 g
Mono Fat   1.5 g
Cholesterol   38 mg
Sodium   1,747 mg
Total Carbohydrate   20 g
Dietary Fiber   1 g
Sugars   5 g
Protein   10 g

Cilantro-Cucumber Yogurt Sauce

*Makes 16 toddler servings
(1 tablespoon); or 8 adult servings
(2 tablespoons)*

Age: Appropriate for age 12 months and up.

Tips: Kids love dipping. This sauce goes well with chicken, beef, veggie burgers, vegetables, and grains.

Selection: Choose a high-quality yogurt with live active cultures.

Storage: Check expiration date and store in original container in refrigerator.

> 8 ounces plain whole milk yogurt
> Juice of 1 lemon
> 1 tablespoon fresh cilantro
> ½ cucumber, peeled and chopped
> ¼ teaspoon salt

In a small bowl, combine all ingredients and mix well.

Refrigerate until ready to serve.

Refrigerate in a sealed container for up to 5 days.

Nutrition Facts

Amount Per Serving (1 tablespoon)
Calories 10   Calories from Fat 4

Total Fat   0 g
Saturated Fat   0.3 g

Trans Fat   0 g
Poly Fat   0 g
Mono Fat   0.1 g
Cholesterol   2 mg
Sodium   43 mg
Total Carbohydrate   1 g
Dietary Fiber   0 g
Sugars   1 g
Protein   1 g

Greek Yogurt

Greek yogurt is strained, making it thicker and creamier than traditional yogurt–also higher in calcium. It is slightly less tart, and may be more palatable plain than standard yogurt to some children.

Creamy Peanut Sauce

*Makes 18 toddler servings
(2 teaspoons); or 12 adult servings
(2 tablespoons)*

Age: Appropriate for age 12 months and up.

Tips: This is a great sauce served over pasta or rice. It also makes a good dipping sauce for grilled chicken, beef, pork loin, or fresh vegetables for an older child. Not appropriate if allergic.

> ½ cup natural, creamy peanut butter
> ¼ cup water
> 3 tablespoons chopped fresh cilantro
> 3 tablespoons rice wine vinegar
> 1 tablespoon sesame oil
> 1 tablespoon light soy sauce
> ¼ teaspoon ground ginger
> ½ teaspoon garlic powder

¼ teaspoon red or cayenne
pepper (optional)

Combine all ingredients in a
food processor and blend until
creamy.
     Refrigerate in sealed container
for up to 3 days.

Nutrition Facts

Amount Per Serving (2 teaspoons)
Calories 50   Calories from Fat 39

Total Fat   4 g
Saturated Fat   0.6 g
Trans Fat   0 g
Poly Fat   1.2 g
Mono Fat   2.1 g
Cholesterol   0 mg
Sodium   59 mg
Total Carbohydrate   2 g
Dietary Fiber   0 g
Sugars   1 g
Protein   2 g

Lemon-Dill Yogurt Sauce

*Makes 16 toddler servings
(1 tablespoon); or 8 adult servings
(2 tablespoons)*
     Age: Appropriate for age
12 months and up.
     Tips: This is a yummy sauce
to use as a dip with vegetables
or on cooked fish. It could also
be thinned and used as a salad
dressing. Yogurt is a fermented
dairy food—bacteria culture is
added to the milk, changing the
milk sugar, lactose, into lactic acid
and making it easier to digest. Be
aware of the high-sugar content in
flavored yogurts.
     Selection: Be sure to buy yogurt
with live active cultures.

Storage: Check expiration date
and store in original container in
refrigerator.

     8 ounces plain whole milk
         yogurt
     1 tablespoon fresh dill weed
     1 ounce fresh-squeezed lemon
         juice
     ¼ teaspoon garlic powder

In a medium bowl, combine all
ingredients and mix well.
     Refrigerate until ready to serve.

Nutrition Facts

Amount Per Serving (1 tablespoon)
Calories 9   Calories from Fat 4

Total Fat   0 g
Saturated Fat   0.3 g
Trans Fat   0 g
Poly Fat   0 g
Mono Fat   0.1 g
Cholesterol   2 mg
Sodium   7 mg
Total Carbohydrate   1 g
Dietary Fiber   0 g
Sugars   1 g
Protein   1 g

Easy Tomato Sauce

*Makes 24 toddler servings
(1 ounce); or 6 adult servings (4
ounces)*
     Age: Appropriate for age 12
months and up.
     Tips: This is a quick, easy, and
versatile tomato sauce. To increase
the protein content of the sauce,
add 1 pound cooked and drained
ground beef or turkey (leanest),
ground chicken, or vegetarian "beef
crumbles" when you add the tomato
ingredients. This recipe makes

approximately 3 cups of sauce and is great over pasta or used in other recipes, such as lasagna. Double and freeze the extra in zip-closure freezer bags for quick red sauce anytime. Tomatoes are very high in vitamins C, A, and B_6, iron, potassium, copper, manganese, and the carotenoid licopene.

Season: Peak for northeast tomatoes is July through September, and Florida tomatoes are best October through July.

Selection: Look for fresh tomatoes that are round in shape, without marks, bruises, or orange coloration. Commercially grown tomatoes ripen in the truck and are usually not as flavorful as vine-ripened tomatoes. It is easy to grow your own tomatoes—if you don't have land for a garden, they will grow well in pots in a sunny area on a small deck, or even in a hanging planter.

Storage: Fresh tomatoes should be stored in a bowl on the counter, stem up. Refrigeration reduces the flavor and nutrients and affects the texture of tomatoes. Flavorful summer tomatoes can be frozen in an airtight freezer bag or sealed container and are easy to peel when mushy and soft. They are great to use for sauces, stews, and soups. Freeze tomato sauce in an airtight freezer container.

> 2 tablespoons olive oil
> 1 small onion, chopped
> 2 cloves garlic, minced
> 1 14.5-ounce can whole or diced tomatoes or 2 cups chopped fresh plum tomatoes
> 1 14.5-ounce can tomato sauce
> 2 tablespoons tomato paste

> 1 tablespoon red wine vinegar
> 1 teaspoon dried basil or 2 tablespoons chopped fresh basil
> ½ teaspoon dried parsley
> ½ teaspoon oregano
> ¼ teaspoon thyme
> ½ teaspoon Sucanat
> Salt and pepper to taste

In a wide skillet, combine olive oil and onions and sauté for 2 to 3 minutes, until translucent.

Add garlic, tomatoes, tomato sauce, tomato paste, vinegar, basil, parsley, oregano, thyme, and Sucanat, and simmer for 20 to 25 minutes, stirring periodically.

If using whole tomatoes, use the back of a spoon to break into smaller pieces.

Add salt and pepper to taste.

If desired, puree sauce with an immersion wand to serve smooth, depending on age of child.

Freeze in a sealed container for up to 3 months.

Nutrition Facts

Amount Per Serving (1 ounce)
Calories 12   Calories from Fat 11

Total Fat   1 g
Saturated Fat   0.2 g
Trans Fat   0 g
Poly Fat   0.1 g
Mono Fat   0.8 g
Cholesterol   0 mg
Sodium   18 mg
Total Carbohydrate   1 g
Dietary Fiber   1 g
Sugars   1 g
Protein   0 g

Pesto Sauce

Makes 16 toddler servings
(1 tablespoon)

Age: Appropriate for age 12 months and up.

Tips: Pesto is a favorite among many young children. You can use it as a marinade for meats, poultry, or fish; as a sauce for pasta or pizza; or as a dipping sauce for raw or cooked veggies. This variation uses walnuts instead of pine nuts, but they are interchangeable. For a nut-free version, simply omit walnuts and just use flaxseeds.

Walnuts are a good source of omega-3 fatty acids, and a very good source of manganese. Walnuts contain melatonin—helpful in regulating sleep. They, like pecans, have a more bitter flavor than other varieties of nuts.

Nuts can be difficult to digest. Soaking them for a few hours up to 24 hours begins the germination process, making them easier to digest. When soaking nuts, rinse 2 to 3 times during the soaking process. After the last rinse of the nuts, they can be refrigerated and used for up to 3 days.

Raw walnuts can also be roasted at low temperature (160° F to 170° F to preserve their perishable oils).

Season: Harvested in December, but available year-round.

Selection: Whole walnuts should feel heavy. They should be odorless—strong odor is an indication of rancidity.

Storage: Because of their high oil content, walnuts should be refrigerated in an airtight container in the refrigerator for up to 6 months or in the freezer for up to 1 year.

2 cloves garlic, crushed
¼ cup shelled English walnuts (or substitute pine nuts for a sweeter, less bitter flavor)
½ teaspoon sea salt
3 cups fresh basil leaves
½ cup olive oil
2 tablespoons ground flaxseeds (if omitting nuts, use ¼ cup ground flaxseeds)
½ cup grated Parmesan cheese

Add the garlic, walnuts, and salt to a food processor or blender and chop until you get a coarse mixture, about 1 minute.

Add the basil and olive oil and process until smooth, about 1 to 2 more minutes.

Add the flaxseeds and cheese and continue to process until blended, about another minute.

Refrigerate pesto for up to 3 days, or freeze using the food cube method or in BPA-free, freezer-safe zip-closure bags: Remove excess air by rolling up into a tube. Store in freezer for up to 3 months.

Nutrition Facts

Amount Per Serving (1 tablespoon)
Calories 107   Calories from Fat 92

Total Fat   10 g
Saturated Fat   2 g
Trans Fat   0 g
Poly Fat   2 g
Mono Fat   6 g
Cholesterol   5 mg
Sodium   119 mg
Total Carbohydrate   1 g
Dietary Fiber   1 g
Sugars   0 g
Protein   3 g

Hoisin Marinade

Makes about 1 cup

Age: Appropriate for age 12 months and up.

Tips: This is a sweet, delicious marinade for pork, chicken, shrimp, tofu, tempeh, and beef. Marinate 1 to 2 pounds of meat for 4 hours to overnight, turning several times to coat. Discard after use.

¼ cup hoisin sauce
2 tablespoons rice wine vinegar
¼ cup orange juice
1 tablespoon organic ketchup
1 teaspoon maple syrup
1 clove garlic, minced
2 tablespoons light soy sauce
¼ cup water

In a medium bowl, combine all ingredients and mix well.

Marinate for at least 30 minutes. If time allows, marinate overnight.

Refrigerate marinade in a sealed container for up to 5 days, or pour over meat and freeze in gallon-size zip-closure freezer bag, air removed, for up to 2 months. To prepare, thaw overnight in the refrigerator, and cook as directed.

Nutrition Facts

Amount Per Total Marinade (1 cup)
Calories 183   Calories from Fat 1

Total Fat   20 g
Saturated Fat   0 g
Trans Fat   0 g
Poly Fat   0 g
Mono Fat   0 g
Cholesterol   0 mg
Sodium   2,384 mg
Total Carbohydrate   40 g
Dietary Fiber   3 g

Sugars   33 g
Protein   6 g

Quick BBQ Sauce

Makes 24 toddler servings (1 tablespoon); or 12 adult servings (2 tablespoons)

Age: Appropriate for age 12 months and up.

1 cup organic ketchup
¼ cup cider vinegar
2 tablespoons molasses
2 teaspoons horseradish mustard (or Dijon for less heat)
2 teaspoons organic Worcestershire sauce
2 teaspoons horseradish, or less for less heat
½ teaspoon salt
Pinch ground cloves

Combine all ingredients in a small saucepan.

Simmer over low heat for 10 minutes.

Sauce will keep in the refrigerator for about 2 weeks.

Nutrition Facts

Amount Per Serving (1 tablespoon)
Calories 60   Calories from Fat 0

Total Fat   0 g
Saturated Fat   0 g
Trans Fat   0 g
Poly Fat   0 g
Mono Fat   0 g
Cholesterol   0 mg
Sodium   260 mg
Total Carbohydrate   12 g
Dietary Fiber   0 g
Sugars   4 g
Protein   0 g

Quick Snacks and Mini-Meals for 12- to 18-Month-Olds

Toddlers often need something to eat in a hurry. Try these:

Yogurt and veggies: 8 ounces plain yogurt or cottage cheese with 1 or 2 thawed vegetable food cubes (leafy greens or root veggies work very well).

Yogurt and fruit: 8 ounces plain yogurt or cottage cheese with chopped bananas, other chopped fruit, or applesauce. Optional for additional fiber and crunch: Add 1 tablespoon of wheat germ, ground flaxseeds, or ground nuts (if no allergies). Optional iron-boosting sweetener: Add 1 teaspoon of blackstrap molasses.

Cottage cheese balls: 1/2 cup of small curd whole milk cottage cheese with 3 tablespoons to 1/4 cup of grated, diced, or pureed apple or pear or a combination, with a dash of cinnamon.

Deviled eggs: 4 hard boiled eggs cut in half. Scoop out the yolks and mash in a small bowl with 1 tablespoon plain yogurt (Greek style works well), a pinch of onion powder, and 1/3 to 1/4 teaspoon of Dijon mustard. Blend well with a fork and scoop mixture back into the egg white halves. Optional: Sprinkle the tops lightly with paprika.

Veggie egg scramble: Sauté or steam 1 to 2 cups of finely diced veggies in a medium pan over medium heat with a little olive oil, butter, coconut oil, or ghee. In a small bowl, scramble 3 to 4 eggs with a whisk or fork and pour over softened veggies. Once the eggs begin to settle, stir the mixture until the eggs are cooked through and the veggies are coated. Eggs continue to cook once off the heat, so there is no need to brown them.

Grains with sauce: Cooked whole-wheat pasta, brown rice pasta, soba noodles, quinoa, or millet mixed with warm tomato sauce and a dollop of ricotta cheese. To add veggies, chop and steam 1/4 to 1/2 cup broccoli, zucchini, yellow squash, tomatoes, or spinach.

Grains, cheese, and fruit: 1 cup whole-grain egg noodles, brown rice pasta, quinoa, or millet mixed with 1/3 cup cottage cheese and 1/3 cup diced fruit, such as apples, peaches, or pears, with 1 to 2 teaspoons of maple syrup or blackstrap molasses and a sprinkle of cinnamon and/or nutmeg.

Fruit dippers: Sliced fruit (bananas, peaches, apples, pears, etc.) served with 1/4 cup of plain yogurt mixed with 1 to 2 teaspoons of maple syrup or blackstrap molasses and a sprinkle of cinnamon and/or nutmeg. Fill a little bowl with 2 to 3 tablespoons of wheat germ or ground sunflower seeds for your child to dip the fruit into after the yogurt.

Cheesy rice and beans: Rinsed canned black beans and cooked brown rice with a sprinkle of cheddar or Mexican blend cheese and/or mild salsa.

Crackers and toppings: Rice crackers with nut butter and/or jelly (100 percent fruit), or with sliced cheese and thinly sliced tomato and avocado.

Dip, veggies, and crackers: Hummus or mild bean dip with lightly steamed vegetable sticks and whole-grain crackers.

Recipes for 18 Months to 3 Years (and the Whole Family!)

Although your growing toddler may still prefer to graze on a series of snacks or mini-meals throughout the day, he will slowly integrate into regular family dining. Over the coming months he will become capable of assisting in the small kitchen tasks of food preparation and table setting and more likely to sit and eat with you as a family at mealtime.

The overall volume of what your toddler is eating is still low, so boost the nutrient content of what she is eating on a regular basis. There are many strategies you can utilize for adding "invisible" nutrition to meals and snacks.

Invisible Nutrition Boosters

In order to help your toddler meet his nutritional needs throughout a week of eating (keep track by the week instead of by the day), you may want to get in the habit of adding some invisible nutrition to dishes that you know he enjoys, especially if he is a finicky or light eater. Remember to use high-quality versions of each food. Organic is best as many are in concentrated form. Try some of the suggestions below.

INVISIBLE VEGGIES

Vegetable purees disappear almost magically into a number of dishes. Continue to make pureed vegetable cubes and add one or two to soups, stews, tomato sauce, etc. No need to thaw: Just throw them in near the end of cooking time.

Hint: If you are truly trying to hide their presence, choose colors that are similar to what you are already making.

Thaw vegetable cubes or simply grate fresh vegetables (onions, sweet peppers, zucchini, summer squash, leafy greens—puree form—etc.), and add to ground meat dishes such as meat loaf, chili, meatballs, etc. You can also add thawed sweet veggie cubes or grated vegetables to many baked dishes, such as muffins or quick breads: Try zucchini, carrots, sweet potato, pumpkin, or beets. Purees are wet, so you may need to add a little extra flour to prevent your batter from becoming too moist.

Add several soft vegetables (zucchini, yellow squash, tomatoes, sweet peppers, etc.) to any slow cooker dish at the start of cooking time and they will cook down into an unrecognizable, flavorful sauce. These are especially tasty when cooked with meats because the meats imbue the vegetables with a rich flavor.

Caution: The best choices for invisible vegetables are those with sweet or relatively mild flavors. Unless he likes them already, your toddler might reject dishes made with strongly flavored invisible veggies, such as green peppers or very bitter greens.

INVISIBLE DAIRY

Add dried milk powder to cookies, cakes, quick breads, and muffins.

Use unsweetened evaporated milk as a healthier cream base for cooked sauces. Use regular or Greek yogurt as a base for uncooked dips, sauces, or salad dressings.

Make pudding or custard (egg, pumpkin, banana, etc.) with whole milk.

Grate small amounts of hard cheese (so that it can melt) into almost any savory dish: soup, stew, casserole, etc.

Make milk-based smoothies with banana, nut butters, canned/cooked pumpkin, or even a small amount of high-quality ice cream.

FIBER BOOSTERS

Add small amounts of wheat germ or ground flaxseed to salads or grain dishes. Sprinkle on peanut butter in sandwiches. Roll or dip melon, banana, apple, pear, or peach slices in small bowls of wheat germ.

Add wheat bran or oat bran to baked breads, cookies, quick breads, and muffins. They are drying, so you may slightly decrease the flour content or add a little liquid to your recipes.

Dust a light crust of wheat germ over baked fruit, cobblers, noodle dishes, fish, or casseroles right before baking. Equal parts of wheat germ and grated Parmesan make a particularly tasty topping for tuna or noodle casseroles.

HEALTHY FAT AND CALORIE BOOSTERS

Sauté sweet or savory spices in a little ghee or butter and use to top individual servings of grain dishes: salty curried ghee on brown rice, or cinnamon-nutmeg butter over cranberry oatmeal.

Add a small amount of flaxseed oil (1 teaspoon), avocado, or seed or nut butter, to your toddler's smoothies (4 ounces).

Sauté vegetables or fruits in a little olive, almond (if no nut allergy), or coconut oil.

PROTEIN BOOSTERS

You can easily boost the protein content of many dishes by adding a small amount of high-quality protein powder. This should be made from organic ingredients, and contain no artificial additives. Choose plain varieties, with no added sweeteners or flavorings. Avoid any protein powders containing other ingredients, such as vitamin and mineral complexes, as for weightlifters or other special populations—they are not appropriate or safe for toddlers.

Check both the ingredients list and the nutrition content label to make sure you are buying nearly pure protein from a good source. The best protein powder for toddlers 18 months to 2 years (and toddlers at risk for food allergies) is made from rice protein: It's virtually nonallergenic and the easiest of all to digest. Best choices for older toddlers (2 years and up) are rice protein powder, undenatured whey protein powder (made from milk), and hemp protein powder. Whey protein powder provides a very clean source of protein and is easy to digest. Hemp protein powder, although slightly higher in carbohydrate content, provides an excellent source of vegan (no animal product) protein. Avoid soy protein powder. (See page 48 for a discussion of soy.) Add 1 teaspoon rice, whey, or hemp protein powder to:
- 4 ounces (½ cup) of any smoothie
- individual servings of warm cereal grains, such as oatmeal
- cold cereal milk or yogurt
- ¼ cup nut or seed butter (see nut allergy warning on page 95)

You can also use protein powder in baked goods, such as cookies, muffins, and quick breads—also great in pancakes.

Note: Although undenatured whey protein should technically not be heated, it holds its structure at low heat temperatures, so you can add it to baked goods provided they are cooked at temperatures of 350° F or lower.

Crack eggs into sautéed vegetables, boiling soups, or stir-fried grains, such as rice. Be sure to cook eggs all the way through.

Replace ¼ of the regular flour you use in a baking recipe with soy flour.

Add 1 tablespoon of silken tofu to 4 ounces of smoothie. Use silken tofu as a base for salad dressings, puddings, or custard pie fillings. (See page 238 for more tips on using tofu.)

GENERAL NUTRIENT BOOSTERS

For additional essential amino acids (protein), B complex vitamins, and folic acid: Add 1 teaspoon nutritional (brewer's) yeast) to individual servings of soups, stews, etc.

For additional iron: Use blackstrap molasses as a sweetener for warm cereal grains, baked goods, meat marinades or sauces, etc.

Vegetable Recipes

Rutabaga Fries

Makes 16 toddler servings (1 ounce; about ⅛ cup); or 4 adult servings (3 ounces)

Age: Appropriate for age 18 months and up.

Tips: Rutabagas have half the carbohydrate content of a potato and are high in fiber. Rutabaga fries are a tasty and much healthier alternative to notoriously high-fat, high-glycemic-load french fries.

Season: Peak for rutabagas is spring, fall, and winter.

Selection: Avoid rutabagas that are giant, shriveled, or cracked.

Storage: Store rutabagas in a plastic bag in the refrigerator or in a cool, dry place.

> 1 large rutabaga
> 1 tablespoon grapeseed oil
> ½ teaspoon salt
> 1 teaspoon paprika
> 1 tablespoon olive oil

Preheat oven to 400° F.

Wash, peel, and slice rutabaga into long, thin french fries.

In a plastic bag, combine sliced rutabaga, grapeseed oil, salt, and paprika. Shake to mix thoroughly.

Spread rutabaga fries on a cookie sheet and bake, turning occasionally, for 35 to 40 minutes, until lightly browned and soft.

Once cooked, brush fries with olive oil.

Sprinkle with an extra pinch of salt for taste, optional.

Refrigerate in a sealed container for up to 3 days.

Nutrition Facts

Amount Per Serving (1 ounce)
Calories 33   Calories from Fat 16

Total Fat   2 g
Saturated Fat   0.2 g
Trans Fat   0 g
Poly Fat   0.7 g
Mono Fat   0.8 g
Cholesterol   0 mg
Sodium   185 mg
Total Carbohydrate   4 g
Dietary Fiber   1 g
Sugars   3 g
Protein   1 g

Fiesta Corn and Broccoli

Makes 8 toddler servings (½ cup); 4 adult servings (1 cup)

Age: Appropriate age is 12 months and up.

Tips: This attractive dish will appeal to your toddler's eyes as well as his taste buds. Broccoli "trees" are often a toddler favorite. See page 213 for information on broccoli.

> ¼ cup butter
> ¼ cup chicken or vegetable broth (or water)
> 1 teaspoon dried basil
> ¼ teaspoon garlic powder
> ½ teaspoon salt
> 1 6-ounce can diced green chilies (mild), drained
> ¼ cup finely diced red bell pepper, optional
> 2 cups frozen corn
> 1 bunch broccoli, stemmed and cut into 1-inch florets

(or 1 10-ounce package frozen broccoli florets)

In a large saucepan, melt butter over medium heat.

Stir in broth, basil, garlic powder, and salt.

Add chilies, red pepper, if using, corn, and broccoli and cover.

Reduce heat to medium low and cook, stirring occasionally, for about 10 minutes until broccoli reaches desired tenderness.

Nutrition Facts

Amount Per Serving (¼ cup)
Calories 71   Calories from Fat 39

Total Fat   4 g
Saturated Fat   3 g
Trans Fat   0 g
Poly Fat   0.2 g
Mono Fat   1 g
Cholesterol   11 mg
Sodium   266 mg
Total Carbohydrate   8 g
Dietary Fiber   2 g
Sugars   1g
Protein   2 g

Baked Winter Squash

Toddler servings (½ cup); adult servings (1 cup)

Age: Appropriate for age 18 months and up.

Tips: Beautiful winter squash look a little intimidating, but actually they are relatively easy to prepare and provide a sweet, warming, and satisfying meal base or side dish for toddlers. The simplest cooking method is to wash the squash and cut it in half; many stores will halve the squash for you if you ask. Using a heavy chef's knife or cleaver, work it gently at first until it breaks through the tough outer skin. Cut it all the way through and then scoop out the seeds and pulp with a spoon. Place the squash cut-side down on a baking pan with a little water. Roast at 375° F until the flesh is tender (it will indent when nudged with a spoon or fork), usually 30 to 50 minutes. Once cooked, you may scoop the flesh out of the skin and serve any way you like (mashing with a little butter, apple, or orange juice, and cinnamon is a toddler favorite), or serve smaller squashes (such as carnival or smaller acorn squash) intact as a "boat" you can stuff with grain and ground meat, applesauce, and raisins, or just a little olive oil and salt.

Varieties: Some of the best for kids are delicata (small, oblong yellow with thin green stripes), butternut, buttercup (larger and deep green with a creamier, sweeter flesh than butternut), acorn, and spaghetti squash (large, pale yellow, and oblong).

Selection: Look for firm squash with smooth skin and no soft spots. They should feel heavy and should be odorless or have a light, earthy smell.

Storage: Most varieties have a long shelf life, up to 6 months in a dry cool area (about 50° F to 60° F, away from direct sunlight). Once squash is cut it should be covered with plastic wrap and refrigerated. Freeze winter squash in portion sizes that are convenient to use for roasting or other recipes. For tougher-skinned varieties, baking or roasting first and removing skins after cooking is the easiest way to peel them.

Nutrition Facts

Amount Per Serving ($\frac{1}{2}$ cup)
Calories 41   Calories from Fat 1

Total Fat   0 g
Saturated Fat   0 g
Trans Fat   0 g
Poly Fat   0 g
Mono Fat   0.2 g
Cholesterol   0 mg
Sodium   4 mg
Total Carbohydrate   11 g
Dietary Fiber   0 g
Sugars   2 g
Protein   1 g

Miso Soup with Bok Choy

Makes 8 toddler servings ($\frac{1}{2}$ cup); or 4 adult servings (1 cup)

Age: Appropriate for age 18 months and up.

Tips: Originating in Japan, miso is made from fermented soybean paste. It is very high in B_{12}, zinc, copper, and iron. A small amount of miso makes a great salt substitute in soups or stews, but it is high in sodium. Due to its high mineral content, miso is soothing to the stomach. This soup will work well with many different types of vegetables. Try shredded carrots, chopped onions, ribbons of leafy greens, mushrooms, or broccoli. In cold weather, miso soup makes an excellent savory breakfast for toddlers. Do not heat miso directly as it will destroy the delicate cultures. You may omit the kombu step and make the soup with plain water as well. Add an egg for additional protein: Add it raw to simmering water at the end of cooking time and whisk it for a couple of minutes until the pieces are cooked through.

Selection: Miso is sold in sealed plastic or glass containers. Check the label to make sure there is no MSG in the miso you are purchasing. When choosing, consider the following: the darker the miso, the saltier and stronger the flavor. The mildest is sweet white miso.

Storage: Check expiration date and refrigerate accordingly.

See page 247 for information on bok choy.

> 3 cups water
> 1 4-inch piece organic kombu
> $\frac{1}{4}$ cup sweet white miso
> 2 cups shredded or chopped bok choy
> $\frac{1}{2}$ cup diced soft tofu
> 1 tablespoon chopped scallions (optional)

Add water and kombu to a large saucepan over medium heat to make a mineral broth.

Simmer covered, on low for 10 minutes.

Add bok choy, tofu, and scallions, if using, to large saucepan and simmer for 5 minutes, until bok choy is tender.

Remove from heat and add miso to saucepan, whisking gently to combine.

Refrigerate in a sealed container for up to 3 days.

Nutrition Facts

Amount Per Serving ($\frac{1}{2}$ cup)
Calories 24   Calories from Fat 8

Total Fat   1 g
Saturated Fat   0.1 g

Trans Fat   0 g
Poly Fat   0.5 g
Mono Fat   0.2 g
Cholesterol   0 mg
Sodium   262 mg
Total Carbohydrate   3 g
Dietary Fiber   1 g
Sugars   1 g
Protein   2 g

Roasted Greens

Roasting green vegetables caramelizes their sugars and gives them a chewy or crispy texture that may appeal to toddlers who won't eat them in more traditional ways. The simplest method is to wash the veggies and pat them dry. Cut them into appropriate sizes, if desired, and toss them with a tablespoon or two of olive oil in a bowl. You can also add a pinch or two of salt and pepper. Once they are lightly coated, spread them out in a single layer on a baking sheet and cook in a 375° F oven.

Brussels sprouts: Halve them and roast for about 25 minutes, until you can pierce them with a fork.

Asparagus: Snap off tough stem bases and leave whole. Roast for about 15 minutes, until soft.

Broccoli: Remove tough lower stems and cut lengthwise into long, thin strips. Roast for about 20 minutes, until tender.

Kale: Remove ribs and chop into bite-sized pieces. Roast for 15 to 20 minutes, turning at least twice. Kale should be soft and slightly browned and crispy around the edges.

Veggie Pancakes

Makes 18 toddler servings (2½ inch, about 3 ounces); or 9 adult servings (6 ounces)

Age: Appropriate for age 12 months and up.

Tips: Coconut oil contains 45 percent lauric acid, which has antiviral and antibacterial properties. The fatty acids caprylic and lauric acid help boost the immune system. When coconut oil is used in small amounts, it does not have a distinctive coconut flavor.

Storage: Store in a cool area for up to 2 years.

> 1 cup grated sweet potato
> ¼ cup grated onion
> 1 cup grated carrot
> 1 cup grated zucchini
> ¼ cup flaxseeds
> 1 teaspoon minced ginger
> 1 egg
> 4 tablespoons water
> ¾ cup whole-wheat flour
> 1 teaspoon baking powder
> 3 tablespoons coconut oil

In a large bowl, combine sweet potato, onion, carrot, zucchini, flaxseeds, and ginger and mix well.

In a small bowl, whisk egg, water, whole-wheat flour, and baking powder.

Pour egg mixture into vegetable mixture and mix to a pasty consistency.

In a large skillet over medium heat, heat coconut oil.

Use an ice cream scoop to drop batter into the skillet, and press down gently to form into small pancakes about 2½ inches wide.

Cook pancakes for about 5 minutes on each side, until lightly browned.

Serve immediately, or freeze on a cookie sheet and store in a tightly sealed container with wax paper separating pancakes.

To reheat, cook at 450° F for 5 to 10 minutes if defrosted, and 15 to 20 minutes if frozen.

Nutrition Facts

Amount Per Serving (3 ounces)
Calories 66   Calories from Fat 29

Total Fat   3 g
Saturated Fat   2.1 g
Trans Fat   0 g
Poly Fat   0.5 g
Mono Fat   0.4 g
Cholesterol   12 mg
Sodium   66 mg
Total Carbohydrate   9 g
Dietary Fiber   2 g
Sugars   1 g
Protein   2 g

Fruit Recipes

Frozen Banana Dreams

Makes 8 toddler servings (½ banana); or 4 adult servings (1 banana)

Age: Appropriate for age 12 months and up.

Tips: Frozen Banana Dreams are high-fiber snacks that are fun to make with your child. You can also try dipping bananas in nut* or seed butter instead of yogurt, or cutting bananas into thick rounds before serving, for less mess. In addition, you may use low-fat yogurt instead of whole milk yogurt, and low-fat granola if child is over 2 years old. See page 197 for information on bananas.

*If your child is at risk for food allergies, the American College of Allergy, Asthma and Immunology recommends waiting until after your child's third birthday to introduce any fish, seafood, peanuts, or tree nuts.

4 medium bananas
1 cup plain whole-milk yogurt
2 teaspoons maple syrup
1 teaspoon ground cinnamon
2 cups granola
½ cup wheat germ or blend of wheat germ and ground flaxseeds, almonds, or walnuts

Peel bananas and cut in half.

In a medium bowl, combine yogurt, maple syrup, and cinnamon.

In another medium bowl, combine granola and wheat germ.

Dip bananas in yogurt mixture, turning to coat completely.

Dip in granola, turning to coat completely.

Place on cookie sheet lined with wax paper and freeze for at least 3 hours before serving.

Store pops for up to 1 month.

Nutrition Facts

Amount Per Serving (½ banana)
Calories 244   Calories from Fat 82

Total Fat   9 g
Saturated Fat   3 g
Trans Fat   0 g
Poly Fat   3.6 g

Mono Fat   2.0 g
Cholesterol   4 mg
Sodium   96 mg
Total Carbohydrate   38 g
Dietary Fiber   6 g
Sugars   19 g
Protein   5 g

Berry Yogurt Parfait

Makes 4 toddler servings (½ cup);
or 2 adult servings (1 cup)

Age: Appropriate for age 18 months and up.

Tips: Both blueberries and strawberries contain anthocyanins, an antioxidant found in fresh and frozen berries but not in processed foods containing strawberries.

Blueberries are a super food high in antioxidants and phytonutrients. Studies have shown blueberries to be highest among fruits and vegetables in their ability to remove free radicals. Blueberries are also helpful in relieving diarrhea, constipation, and urinary tract infections.

Strawberries are a good source of dietary fiber and contain high amounts of phenol, which helps protect against cancer and heart disease. Strawberries are high on the food allergen list. If allergies run in your family, wait until your child is older to introduce.

Caution: Strawberries are one of the twelve foods on the Environmental Working Group's 2006 "Shopper's Guide to Pesticides in Produce," so buy organic whenever possible.

Season: Peak for blueberries is late summer. Peak for strawberries is spring and early summer.

Selection: Look for blueberries that are bright blue with a white seed. Shake container to make sure berries are fresh; looking to see that there is no mold or excess moisture in container. If using frozen blueberries, shake bag. If berries do not move, this may indicate that they have previously been thawed and refrozen. Do not thaw frozen berries if using them in cooked food. If they are not being cooked, thaw and drain before adding to recipe.

Fresh blueberries freeze beautifully. They are often very inexpensive during the summer, when they are in season. Buy extra pints and put them directly into your freezer in their original plastic containers. Wash them while frozen, just before use.

Look for strawberries that are bright red and heart shaped. Medium-sized berries are the most flavorful.

Storage: Do not prewash berries before storage, as that will speed spoilage.

Wash blueberries immediately before using to prolong freshness. Store in a sealed container for up to 1 week. Blueberries have the most nutrients if eaten within the first few days.

Wash strawberries immediately before using to prolong freshness. Remove any molded or bruised strawberries before refrigerating for up to 2 days in the original container or spread out in a dish covered with plastic wrap.

> ½ cup fresh blueberries plus a
>   few for garnish
> ½ cup fresh strawberries plus
>   a few for garnish
> 1 cup plain whole milk yogurt
> 2 tablespoons ground flaxseeds
> ½ teaspoon ground cinnamon
> 2 teaspoons maple syrup or
>   honey*

Wash blueberries and strawberries.

Hull and slice strawberries in half. If large, slice in quarters.

In a medium bowl, combine yogurt, flaxseeds, cinnamon, and maple syrup and mix well.

Using a parfait glass or monkey dish, fill with three-quarters of the blueberries.

Add ½ cup yogurt mixture.

Add three-quarters of the strawberries.

Top with remaining yogurt and extra berries.

*If the berries are very tart, add a little extra sweetener or more banana slices.

Nutrition Facts

Amount Per Serving (½ cup)
Calories 322   Calories from Fat 133

Total Fat   15 g
Saturated Fat   5.8 g
Trans Fat   0 g
Poly Fat   4.5 g
Mono Fat   3.5 g
Cholesterol   32 mg
Sodium   125 mg
Total Carbohydrate   39 g
Dietary Fiber   9 g
Sugars   24 g
Protein   13 g

Apple Pear Fruit Bake

Makes 10 toddler servings (½ cup); or 7 to 10 adult servings (¾ cup)

Age: Appropriate for age 18 months and up.

Tips: This is an easy cold-weather dessert that makes the house smell wonderful. Try serving with plain or Greek yogurt.

1 tablespoon butter
2 cups apple chunks, unpeeled
2 cups pear chunks, unpeeled
1 tablespoon 100 percent maple syrup
1 teaspoon ground cinnamon
1 cup low-sugar granola (see page 303 for Granola with Sunflower Seeds and Cranberries recipe)

Preheat oven to 350° F.

Place butter in an 8-by-10-inch baking dish and put in oven to melt butter.

In a medium bowl, combine apples, pears, maple syrup, and cinnamon and stir well to coat fruit evenly. Put mixture into pan.

Bake for 20 minutes, until fruit is soft.

Sprinkle granola evenly over fruit and bake for another 5 minutes.

Nutrition Facts

Amount Per Serving (½ cup)
Calories 93   Calories from Fat 27

Total Fat   3 g
Saturated Fat   1.1 g
Trans Fat   0 g
Poly Fat   0.9 g
Mono Fat   0.7 g
Cholesterol   4 mg
Sodium   11 mg
Total Carbohydrate   16 g
Dietary Fiber   3 g
Sugars   10 g
Protein   2 g

Pasta and Grains Recipes

Spinach Lasagna

Makes 16 toddler servings (2½-square-inch piece); or 9 adult servings (2½-by-3½-inch piece)

Age: Appropriate for age 18 months and up.

Tips: Ricotta cheese is high in phosphorus, selenium, and calcium and an excellent source of protein.

Lasagna is a very simple dish to make, and an easy medium for loading up on the veggies. You can make this version with many other vegetables. Sliced zucchini and sweet peppers work well. Or try shredded broccoli and carrots. If you have ready vegetable cubes, you may thaw and add 3 to 5 to the sauce as additional "invisible veggies." Try carrot, squash, or zucchini. For a higher protein content, you may also add 1 pound of cooked and drained ground turkey or beef (leanest) to the sauce before assembling the lasagna.

Selection: Look for organic ricotta cheese.

Storage: Refrigerate according to package date.

1 package whole-grain lasagna noodles
2 pounds fresh baby spinach or 2 10-ounce packages frozen spinach, thawed and drained
2 cups ricotta cheese
1 egg
2 teaspoons garlic powder
½ teaspoon salt
2 cups Easy Tomato Sauce (see recipe on page 282) or prepared sauce

2 cups shredded part-skim mozzarella
Grated Parmesan cheese for topping (optional)

Preheat oven to 350° F.

Cook lasagna noodles according to package directions, rinse with cold water, and drain well.

Steam spinach for 2 to 3 minutes in a large pot, then drain well. If using thawed frozen spinach, squeeze out excess water.

In a medium bowl, add ricotta cheese, egg, garlic powder, and salt and mix well.

Spread a thin layer of sauce on the bottom of a large casserole dish.

Place a layer of noodles.

Spread half of ricotta cheese mixture, half of the spinach, a third of the sauce, and half of the mozzarella.

Place another layer of noodles, remaining ricotta cheese and spinach, a third of the sauce, and a third of the mozzarella.

Place the last layer of noodles and remaining sauce and mozzarella.

Sprinkle with grated Parmesan, if desired.

Bake uncovered for 40 minutes.

Refrigerate in a sealed container for up to 3 days, or freeze for up to 2 months.

Nutrition Facts

Amount Per Serving (2½-square-inch piece)
Calories 311   Calories from Fat 108

Total Fat   12 g
Saturated Fat   5.7 g
Trans Fat   0 g
Poly Fat   0.6 g
Mono Fat   4.1 g
Cholesterol   54 mg
Sodium   290 mg
Total Carbohydrate   35 g
Dietary Fiber   3 g
Sugars   3 g
Protein   18 g

Lentil Oat Loaf

Makes 16 toddler servings (1-inch slice) or about 4 adult servings (2-inch slice)

Age: Appropriate age is 12 months and up.

Tips: Making loaves from your cooked beans is another great serving option. Patties or loaves are easily made with mashed, cooked beans, a small amount of binder (egg and rolled oats or whole grain bread crumbs), and any combination of herbs, spices, or condiments you enjoy. They are also a great place to hide "invisible nutrition" such as pureed vegetables or extra fiber. Lentil loaf is also great with a mushroom topping in place of the tomato below. Bean loaves and patties are easy to serve and freeze well.

See page 287 for information on "invisible nutrition." See page 209 for information on lentils.

Tomato Mixture
1 6-ounce can tomato paste
1 tablespoon balsamic vinegar
1 teaspoon garlic powder
1 teaspoon onion powder

Loaf Mixture
1 cup finely diced onions
1 tablespoon olive oil
3 cups cooked lentils, (if using canned, drain and rinse)
1 cup rolled oats
½ cup walnuts, ground
1 tablespoon balsamic vinegar
1 tablespoon soy sauce
½ teaspoon garlic powder
½ teaspoon sea salt
1 large egg, beaten

Preheat oven to 350° F.

In a small bowl mix together the tomato paste, vinegar, garlic powder and onion powder. A portion will be used in the loaf and the rest will be used to coat the top.

Heat 1 tablespoon of olive oil in a medium skillet over medium heat.

Add chopped onion and cook, stirring frequently, until onions are transparent, about 5 minutes.

In a mixing bowl, combine cooked onions, 6 tablespoons of the tomato mixture, oats, lentils, walnuts, vinegar, soy sauce, garlic powder, and salt and mix well.

Add egg to bind the mixture and mix well.

Using a cooking spray, spray a loaf pan (8½ by 4½ by 2½)

Spoon lentil mixture into pan to form a loaf shape.

Coat top with remaining tomato mixture.

Cook for 20 minutes, then cover with foil and cook an additional 10 to 15 minutes.

Nutrition Facts

Amount Per Serving (1-inch slice)
Calories 218   Calories from Fat 75

Total Fat   8 g
Saturated Fat   1 g
Trans Fat   0 g
Poly Fat   4 g
Mono Fat   2 g
Cholesterol   26 mg
Sodium   269 mg
Total Carbohydrate   28 g
Dietary Fiber   8 g
Sugars   5 g
Protein   10 g

Simple Fried Rice

Makes 10 toddler servings (½ cup); or 6 adult servings (⅔ cup)

Age: Appropriate for age 18 months and up.

Tips: Napa cabbage is a cancer-fighting vegetable. It is a great source of calcium, fiber, beta-carotene, vitamins C and B, provitamin A, and alpha linolenic acid.

Season: Peak for napa cabbage is spring and summer.

Selection: Look for crisp, fibrous leaves with a pale green and white coloring and a wide leaf stalk.

Storage: Store in the crisper drawer for up to 2 weeks. The sooner cabbage is cooked after harvest, the more nutritious it is.

> 1 tablespoon sesame oil
> 1 tablespoon chopped
>   scallions
> 2 tablespoons finely chopped
>   ginger
> ½ cup shredded carrots
> ½ cup diced red pepper
> ½ cup shredded napa cabbage

> 4 cups cooked brown rice
> 1 cup fresh or frozen peas
> 2 teaspoons water
> 2 eggs
> 3 tablespoons tamari or soy
>   sauce

Heat sesame oil in a large sauté pan over medium heat.

Add scallions and ginger and sauté for 2 minutes.

Add carrots, red pepper, and cabbage and sauté for another 3 minutes.

Add cooked rice, peas, and water and cook on low heat for 10 minutes.

In a small bowl, whisk eggs.

Add egg mixture to rice, stirring quickly to distribute egg evenly.

Add soy sauce and stir.

Continue cooking and stirring until egg is cooked through.

Refrigerate in a sealed container for up to 3 days.

Nutrition Facts

Amount Per Serving (½ cup)
Calories 132   Calories from Fat 29

Total Fat   3 g
Saturated Fat   0.6 g
Trans Fat   0 g
Poly Fat   0.5 g
Mono Fat   1.8 g
Cholesterol   42 mg
Sodium   290 mg
Total Carbohydrate   21 g
Dietary Fiber   3 g
Sugars   2 g
Protein   5 g

Mochi

Makes 16 toddler servings (1-inch square); or 8 adult servings (2-inch square)

Age: Appropriate for age 24 months and up.

Tips: Mochi is a traditional Japanese food made from mashed and steamed short grain sweet rice. When cooked, mochi puffs up and has a chewy texture with a crispy outside. It can be savory or sweet, depending on the flavor. You can stuff it with nut butter, jam, cheese, chopped olives, hummus, etc. You do not have to use the whole package of mochi at one time.

Mochi is sticky, so be sure to cut it into very small bites for your toddler.

Selection: Mochi is found in the refrigerated section of natural food stores and some natural food sections of grocery stores and Asian markets. Different flavors include raisin and cinnamon, cashew date, chocolate brownie, plain, and sesame garlic.

Storage: Mochi can be stored in the refrigerator or freezer and thawed for use. Once open, mochi should be tightly sealed and refrigerated for up to 10 days.

See page 185 for information on brown rice.

> 1 square package mochi, plain or cinnamon apple flavor
> ½ cup cottage cheese
> 2 teaspoons maple syrup, blackstrap molasses or honey
> ¼ teaspoon ground cinnamon
> Preheat oven to 450° F.

Using a sharp knife, cut mochi into 1-inch squares.

Place squares on a baking sheet about 1 inch apart.

Bake for 8 to 10 minutes, until squares puff up and browns.

In a small bowl, combine cottage cheese, sweetnener, and cinnamon.

Once cooked, allow to cool.

Make small slit in side of mochi pieces and add cottage cheese mixture. Slice cooled pieces before serving.

Nutrition Facts

Amount Per Serving (1-inch square)
Calories 82   Calories from Fat 19

Total Fat   2 g
Saturated Fat   0.9 g
Trans Fat   0 g
Poly Fat   0.1 g
Mono Fat   0.6 g
Cholesterol   7 mg
Sodium   198 mg
Total Carbohydrate   10 g
Dietary Fiber   0 g
Sugars   9 g
Protein   6 g

Pesto Millet Meal

Makes 16 toddler servings (½ cup); or 5 adult servings (1½ cup)

Age: Appropriate for age 18 months and up.

Tips: This is a nutrient-rich, vegetarian, one-pot meal. Tastes great cold or warm. Parmesan cheese is high in protein and calcium.

Selection: The higher quality Parmigiano Reggiano cheeses are imported from Italy. These are more expensive and a little less salty than standard Parmesan cheese.

Consider buying it in a block and grating it yourself for freshness. All Parmesans should be free of spots or mold and smell nutty.

Storage: Wrap fresh Parmesan cheese tightly in plastic wrap and store in the least cold section of the refrigerator for up to 2 weeks for a chunk, and 1 week if grated.

See page 187 for information on millet; page 192 for information on carrots.

2 tablespoons olive oil
½ cup diced onions
1 cup millet, rinsed
2½ cups water, vegetable broth, or chicken broth
1 cup grated carrots
1 15-ounce can cannellini beans, rinsed and drained
1 cup frozen corn
4 tablespoons pesto sauce (packaged or see Pesto Sauce recipe on page 284)
Salt and pepper to taste
1 to 2 basil leaves for garnish (optional)
Parmesan cheese for garnish (optional)

In a wide sauté pan, heat olive oil over medium heat.

Add onions and millet and cook for 3 to 4 minutes while stirring, until onions are transparent.

Add water, bring to a boil, and lower heat immediately. Cover and simmer for 10 minutes.

Add carrots and cannellini beans, cover, and simmer for 20 minutes.

Add corn and beans, cover, and cook for an additional 5 minutes, until all liquid is absorbed.

If the millet is still crunchy, add ¼ cup water and continue cooking until tender.

Add pesto and toss to coat evenly.

Is desired, add basil leaves and a sprinkle of Parmesan cheese to garnish.

Nutrition Facts

Amount Per Serving (½ cup)
Calories 83   Calories from Fat 41

Total Fat   5 g
Saturated Fat   0.8 g
Trans Fat   0 g
Poly Fat   0.7 g
Mono Fat   2.7 g
Cholesterol   1 mg
Sodium   128 mg
Total Carbohydrate   8 g
Dietary Fiber   3 g
Sugars   2 g
Protein   3 g

Amaranth, Carrots, and Parsnips

Makes 8 toddler servings (⅓ cup); or 5 to 6 adult servings (½ cup)

Age: Appropriate for age 18 months and up.

Tips: Amaranth is a tiny, highly nutritious ancient grain that originated with the Aztecs. It is high in protein and contains lysine and methionine, essential amino acids that are not frequently found in grains. It is also high in fiber, calcium, iron, potassium, phosphorus, and vitamins A and C. Amaranth seeds can be cooked with other whole grains, and added to stir-fries, soups, and stews. Do not rinse before cooking. When cooked, amaranth has a sticky texture, more like a thick pudding than separate grains, which makes it a great base for fruit dishes as well.

Selection: Amaranth is found in health food stores.

Storage: Refrigerate in a tightly sealed container for up to 6 months.

> 1 cup amaranth seeds
> 2 teaspoons tamari or soy
> sauce
> ½ teaspoon ground ginger
> 1 cup diced carrots
> 1 medium parsnip, diced
> 3 cups water
> 1 tablespoon sweet miso

Combine all ingredients except miso in a small saucepan and bring to a boil.

Simmer for about 30 minutes, stirring occasionally. Remove from heat, stir in miso, and cover to dissolve.

Freeze in a sealed container, or batch using the food cube method for up to 1 month.

Nutrition Facts

Amount Per Serving (⅓ cup)
Calories 114   Calories from Fat 16

Total Fat   2 g
Saturated Fat   0.4 g
Trans Fat   0 g
Poly Fat   0.8 g
Mono Fat   0.4 g
Cholesterol   0 mg
Sodium   177 mg
Total Carbohydrate   21 g
Dietary Fiber   5 g
Sugars   2 g
Protein   4 g

Cheesy Bean Quesadillas

Makes 2 toddler servings (½ quesadilla); or 1 adult serving (1 quesadilla)

Age: Appropriate for age 18 months and up.

Tips: Kids love quesadillas. Try making them with different beans, meats, and vegetables. You can be creative with your combinations. This recipe calls for soft corn tortillas, but you can also use whole-grain wheat or rice tortillas, and they come in a variety of sizes. Try these variations: cheddar cheese and grated apple with a smear of pumpkin puree; Jack cheese with roasted sweet potato and cinnamon honey; provolone with lean ground beef or shredded chicken and mild barbecue sauce. You can add additional cooked veggies or a sprinkle of chopped nuts as well.

See page XX for information on pinto beans.

> ¼ cup mashed pinto beans or
> canned vegetarian refried
> beans*
> 2 6-inch corn tortillas
> ¼ cup shredded four-cheese
> Mexican blend (or grated
> Jack cheese)
> Cooking oil spray
> 2 to 3 slices avocado
> 1 slice tomato
> 1 tablespoon mild salsa
> (optional)

Spray a skillet with oil and place on medium heat.

Spread pinto beans onto 1 corn tortilla and place in pan.

Add cheese, avocado, tomato, and salsa, if using.

Cover with remaining tortilla and flatten slightly.

Cook for 1 to 2 minutes, flip, and cook for an additional 1 to 2 minutes, until golden brown.

Slice into halves and serve.

* Double, triple, or quadruple to feed the whole family.

Nutrition Facts

Amount Per Serving (½ quesadilla)
Calories 47   Calories from Fat 23

Total Fat   6 g
Saturated Fat   3 g
Trans Fat   0 g
Poly Fat   0.2 g
Mono Fat   1.6 g
Cholesterol   12 mg
Sodium   156 mg
Total Carbohydrate   8 g
Dietary Fiber   2 g
Sugars   0 g
Protein   4 g

Granola with Sunflower Seeds and Cranberries

Makes 20 toddler servings (¼ cup); or 5 to 10 adult servings (½ cup to 1 cup)

Age: Appropriate for age 24 months and up.

Tips: Granola is great over yogurt, baked fruit, hot grains (such as quinoa or rice), or alone as a snack. This version does not include nuts and uses cinnamon and dried fruits as sweeteners. For toddlers who haven't been exposed to the super-sweet commercial granolas, this mild version will taste just right.

1 tablespoon butter
2 cups rolled oats
½ cup sunflower seeds
½ cup raw wheat germ
¼ cup white or black sesame
    seeds
¼ cup ground flaxseeds
1 teaspoon ground cinnamon
1 tablespoon maple syrup
1 tablespoon molasses
1 cup dried cranberries
½ cup dried apricots, chopped

Preheat oven to 300° F.

Add butter to a 13-by-9-inch baking dish and place in the oven for 2 to 3 minutes to melt the butter.

Remove baking dish and swirl to spread the butter evenly.

Add the oats and bake until lightly brown, about 15 minutes.

In a large bowl, mix together sunflower seeds, wheat germ, sesame seeds, flaxseeds, cinnamon, maple syrup, and molasses.

Pour the mixture over the oats and stir to combine.

Bake for an additional 10 minutes.

Add dried apricots and cranberries for the last 5 minutes.

Cool before serving.

Store in a sealed container for up to 1 week or in the refrigerator for about 1 month.

Nutrition Facts

Amount Per Serving (¼ cup)
Calories 112   Calories from Fat 40

Total Fat   4 g
Saturated Fat   0.9 g
Trans Fat   0 g
Poly Fat   2.2 g
Mono Fat   1 g
Cholesterol   2 mg
Sodium   6 mg
Total Carbohydrate   16 g
Dietary Fiber   3 g
Sugars   7 g
Protein   3 g

Muffin, Quick Bread, and French Toast Recipes

Applesauce Oat Muffins

Makes 12 toddler or adult servings (1 muffin)

Age: Appropriate for age 12 months and up.

Tips: These muffins are high in fiber and healthy fats. They are delicious and make a quick easy breakfast or snack, and are great for Mom and Dad, too. Make a double batch and freeze the extras to have on hand for another busy morning.

See page 224 for information on apples; and page 262 for information on Sucanat.

1½ cups whole-wheat pastry flour
¾ cup rolled oats
3 tablespoon oat bran
3 tablespoons ground flaxseeds
1 tablespoon baking powder
⅔ cup Sucanat
2 teaspoons ground cinnamon
¾ cup whole milk or ½ cup cow's milk plus ¼ cup almond milk
⅓ cup no sugar-added applesauce
2 tablespoons vegetable oil
3 egg whites
1 teaspoon vanilla extract

Preheat oven to 400° F.

Place paper muffin cups in muffin pan.

In a large bowl, combine all dry ingredients and mix well.

In a medium bowl, combine all liquid ingredients and whisk together.

Pour wet mixture into dry mixture and mix until just combined.

Fill each muffin cup about ⅔ full.

Bake 18 to 20 minutes, until a toothpick comes out of muffin clean.

Nutrition Facts

Amount Per Serving (1 muffin)
Calories 169   Calories from Fat 39

Total Fat   4 g
Saturated Fat   0.7 g
Trans Fat   0 g
Poly Fat   0.9 g
Mono Fat   2.4 g
Cholesterol   2 mg
Sodium   23 mg
Total Carbohydrate   30 g
Dietary Fiber   4 g
Sugars   12 g
Protein   4 g

Pumpkin Spice Bread

Makes 32 toddler servings (1 slice); or 16 adult servings (2 slices)

Age: Appropriate for age 18 months and up.

Tips: Cook up Halloween pumpkins to make the freshest tasting base for this tasty bread. Or use canned if you're in a hurry. Either way, this loaf won't last long!

See page 203 for information on pumpkin.

1 cup agave nectar or pure maple syrup

½ cup softened butter

1 can pumpkin or 2 cups fresh
pumpkin puree (see page
203 for recipe)

2 eggs

½ teaspoon ground cloves

3½ cups oat or whole-wheat
pastry flour

2 teaspoons baking powder

1 tablespoon vanilla extract

4 teaspoons ground cinnamon

1 teaspoon ground ginger

1 teaspoon baking soda

1 teaspoon salt

1 teaspoon ground nutmeg

½ cup ground flaxseeds

Preheat oven to 350° F.

In a large bowl, cream agave
nectar and butter until mixture is
light and fluffy.

Stir in pumpkin.

One at a time, beat in eggs until
thoroughly mixed.

In large bowl, sift together
remaining ingredients and stir into
pumpkin mixture.

Pour mixture into 2 well-greased
9-by-5-inch loaf pans.

Bake for 1 hour, until lightly
browned.

Remove from oven and let loaves
cool in pans for 10 minutes.

Remove loaves from pans and
allow to finish cooling on racks.

Nutrition Facts

Amount Per Serving (1 slice)
Calories 104   Calories from Fat 41

Total Fat   5 g
Saturated Fat   2.1 g
Trans Fat   0 g
Poly Fat   0.9 g
Mono Fat   1.3 g
Cholesterol   21 mg

Sodium   124 mg
Total Carbohydrate   14 g
Dietary Fiber   2 g
Sugars   6 g
Protein   2 g

Cornbread

*Makes 16 toddler servings (1 slice);
or 8 adult servings (2 slices)*

Age: Appropriate for age 18
months and up.

Tips: Cornbread makes a
delicious snack or side dish. You
can sweeten it by adding 2 extra
tablespoons honey or ½ cup
blueberries or chocolate chips to
the batter. Or go savory by adding
½ cup fresh or frozen corn kernels
and/or ¼ cup chopped broccoli to
the batter. Give it a richer texture
and boost the protein content by
adding ¼ cup cottage cheese to the
batter.

1 tablespoon butter

1 egg

¼ cup vegetable oil

5 tablespoons honey

1 cup plain whole milk yogurt,
Greek style works well

2 teaspoons vanilla extract

¼ cup whole milk

2 cups whole-grain
cornmeal

¼ teaspoon salt

Preheat oven to 425° F.

Add butter to 8-inch-square
baking dish and melt in oven.

In a small bowl, whisk egg, oil,
honey, yogurt, vanilla, and milk.

In a large bowl, combine
cornmeal and salt.

Pour egg mixture into cornmeal
mixture and mix until just
combined.

Pour into prepared pan and bake for 25 minutes, until lightly browned and edges have pulled away slightly from pan.

Nutrition Facts

Amount Per Serving (1 slice)
Calories 129   Calories from Fat 50

Total Fat   6 g
Saturated Fat   1.4 g
Trans Fat   0 g
Poly Fat   2.6 g
Mono Fat   1.3 g
Cholesterol   17 mg
Sodium   60 mg
Total Carbohydrate   17 g
Dietary Fiber   1 g
Sugars   6 g
Protein   2 g

French Toast Faces

Makes 8 toddler servings (½ slice); or 4 adult servings (1 slice)

Age: Appropriate for age 18 months and up.

Tips: There's no need to drench French toast with maple syrup. You can use any fruits, chopped nuts (see nut allergy warning on page 95) or seeds, or spreads. You can also use the toast to make a baked sandwich for lunch: Try ham and melted Swiss, nut butter and fruit-sweetened jelly, or a mixture of half cream cheese and half cottage cheese with a little honey and cinnamon.

2 eggs
1 cup cow's, rice, or almond milk
2 medium bananas, mashed
2 teaspoons cinnamon
1½ teaspoons vanilla extract
¼ cup ground flaxseeds
2 tablespoons butter or ghee
4 slices whole-wheat challah bread or 6 slices whole-wheat or sprouted-grain bread
¼ cup nut butter, fruit butter, or fruit spread
½ cup dried cherries or cranberries
1 apple, peach, plum, or orange, cored and sliced
2 tablespoons dried coconut flakes

In a medium bowl, lightly beat eggs.

Add milk, banana, cinnamon, vanilla extract, and flaxseeds and mix well.

In a skillet, melt butter or ghee over medium heat.

Dip slices of bread in milk mixture so that both sides are coated completely and place on skillet.

Cook for 3 to 4 minutes on each side, until lightly browned.

Cut each slice of bread in half and decorate with nut butter, dried cherries, apple, and coconut flakes to create faces, or put the "decorations" in bowls and let your toddler do it himself.

Nutrition Facts

Amount Per Serving (½ slice)
Calories 217   Calories from Fat 94

Total Fat   10 g
Saturated Fat   4.3 g
Trans Fat   0 g
Poly Fat   2.1 g
Mono Fat   3.1 g
Cholesterol   64 mg
Sodium   128 mg
Total Carbohydrate   26 g
Dietary Fiber   4 g
Sugars   13 g
Protein   7 g

Fun and Healthy Birthday Cakes

The foods we typically serve children at birthday parties and holiday celebrations are notoriously high in sugars and poor-quality fats: Think chocolate birthday cake with shortening icing! Because kids love bright colors, you will often find holiday treats decorated with artificially colored and artificially flavored sprinkles, icings, or even ice cream ("crazy vanilla" in the DayGlo play dough colors is nothing more than plain vanilla ice cream loaded up with a huge amounts of artificial and chemical colorings).

Technicolors are not found in real foods—they belong in the decorations, not in your child's treats. It's easy to dress up a healthy, nutritious cake in several fun ways without using poor-quality ingredients. Use any healthy cake recipe (see the recipe for Celebration Cupcakes on page 308) and cook it in rectangular pans. Try dressing it up in the following easy ways, and come up with your own creative ideas, too.

Gift Cake Make your cake look like a wrapped present by frosting it with chocolate and simply laying two lengths of white ribbon across the cake in a cross shape and placing a bow in the middle. (Be sure to remove the ribbon before cutting and serving!)

Pirate Treasure Chest Cake You can make a pirate treasure chest by cutting away a rectangle in the center of the cake. Make the lid out of a piece of clean, white cardboard and prop it up with two wooden toothpicks. Then frost the outside of the cake and top of the cardboard with white frosting. Place a small amount of chocolate frosting into a gallon-sized zipper-seal bag and snip off one corner, creating an opening about $1/4$ inch thick. Pipe the frosting out in the shape of a skull and crossbones on top of the chest's cardboard lid. If you like, on a clean piece of white paper you can draw a treasure map with simple directions to follow to a special prize, roll it into a tight cube, and place it inside the chest. X marks the spot!

Design Your Own Cupcakes Another fun option for older toddlers is to let them decorate their own cupcakes (see the delicious and nutritious recipe for Celebration Cupcakes on page 308). Frost them white, and give the children a selection of small treats in little bowls with which to decorate: raisins, chocolate chips, cereal balls or squares, halved grapes, dried cranberries, dollops of fruit-sweetened jelly, etc.

Your toddler truly does not need a lot of fanfare for his birthday. Keeping the celebrations relatively low-key will help prevent overexcitement and allow him to actually enjoy it without getting too stimulated. A good basic rule of thumb is to invite one friend for each year of age: two children for his second birthday, three for his third, etc.

Make sure he is well rested and has had some nutritious food, preferably with a little protein, before the party begins.

(See Resources for a list of fun food coloring and decorative products made with all-natural ingredients.)

Puffy Pancakes

Makes 4 toddler servings (¼ pancake); or 3 adult servings (⅓ pancake)

Age: Appropriate for age 18 months and up.

Tips: This special pancake is a snap to whip up. Whole-wheat flour and cow's milk make the pancake extra puffy. Be careful not to overmix the batter. Try substituting blueberries for apples, pears, or peaches.

See page 262 for information on Sucanat.

> 4 tablespoons butter, cut into small pieces
> ½ cup whole-wheat pastry flour, oat flour, or gluten-free flour mix (such as Bob's Red Mill)
> ½ cup cow's, rice, or almond milk
> 2 eggs
> ½ teaspoon ground cinnamon
> 1 cup frozen blueberries, no sugar added
> 2 tablespoon Sucanat
> ¼ fresh lemon

Put butter in cast-iron skillet.

Preheat oven to 425° F. Place pan in oven so butter will melt while preheating.

Place frozen fruit in a metal bowl on top of the oven to partially thaw.

In a small bowl, combine flour, milk, eggs, and cinnamon.

Mix with a fork until combined, leaving some lumps.

Remove pan from oven and pour batter into melted butter.

Replace pan and cook for 15 minutes.

Spread blueberries, sprinkle Sucanat, and squeeze lemon over pancake.

Put pan back in oven and cook for another 5 minutes, until edges are lightly browned.

Remove, cut into quarters, cool, and serve.

Nutrition Facts

Amount Per Serving (¼ pancake)
Calories 257   Calories from Fat 140

Total Fat   16 g
Saturated Fat   8.7 g
Trans Fat   0 g
Poly Fat   1 g
Mono Fat   4.2 g
Cholesterol   139 mg
Sodium   131 mg
Total Carbohydrate   25 g
Dietary Fiber   4 g
Sugars   11 g
Protein   7 g

Celebration Cupcakes

Makes 18 toddler servings (1 cupcake)

Age: Appropriate for age 18 months and up.

Tips: No one will ever know that there is zucchini in these delicious cupcakes. Cocoa powder is high in many minerals, but should be used sparingly because of the caffeine content. Cocoa is high in magnesium, phosphorus, zinc, manganese, and sulfur. Chocolate contains theobromine and small amounts of caffeine, which are both stimulants. Theobromine has antioxidant properties as well as flavonoids and polyphenols. In milk chocolate, the fat and sugar contents are higher and nutritional benefits are significantly reduced.

Selection: Look for unsweetened cocoa (70 percent cocoa content), raw cacao, or fair trade organic cocoa from a high-quality company.

Storage: Store cocoa in a cool, dry place.

See page 262 for information on Sucanat.

> 8 tablespoons unsalted butter, softened at room temperature
> ¾ cup unsweetened cocoa powder
> 1 cup hot water or hot milk**
> 1½ teaspoons baking powder
> 1½ cups Sucanat or turbinado sugar
> 1½ teaspoons baking soda
> 1¾ cups whole-wheat pastry flour
> ½ teaspoon salt
> 2 eggs
> 2¼ teaspoons vanilla extract
> 2 small zucchinis** or 1 cup pureed zucchini (see Zucchini Puree recipe on page 195)

Preheat oven to 350° F.

Place paper muffin cups in muffin pan or grease and flour 2 9-inch baking pans.

In electric mixing bowl, add softened butter and all dry ingredients.

Mix for 1 to 2 minutes, until blended.

Add eggs, vanilla, and zucchini and mix for 2 minutes.

Whisk cocoa into the hot liquid and slowly mix it into mixer bowl until batter is quite thin.

Pour in hot liquid and stir until batter is quite thin.

Fill each muffin cup about ⅔ full.

Bake for 25 minutes, until a toothpick comes out of cupcake clean.

Cool before icing. Cupcakes are great plain or with Mascarpone Icing (recipe following).

Batch and freeze in a sealed container.

*Heating the liquid makes the chocolate slightly richer, but is not required.

**If using whole zucchinis, scrub stem, and quarter them. Place cut zucchini pieces in food processor and process for 1 to 2 minutes, scraping down the sides occasionally, until zucchini is consistency of wet applesauce. Measure one cup for use in recipe.

Nutrition Facts

Amount Per Serving (1 cupcake)
Calories 117   Calories from Fat 57

Total Fat   6 g
Saturated Fat   3.7 g
Trans Fat   0 g
Poly Fat   0.4 g
Mono Fat   1.7 g
Cholesterol   37 mg
Sodium   215 mg
Total Carbohydrate   14 g
Dietary Fiber   3 g
Sugars   3 g
Protein   3 g

Mascarpone Icing

Makes 16 servings (1 tablespoon)
Age: Appropriate for age 18 months and up.
Tips: This is a creamy frosting for the Celebration Cupcakes (see page 308 for recipe). Mascarpone cheese is made from the milk of cows that have been fed special grasses filled with herbs and flowers, which create a unique flavor that is fresh and delicious.
Selection: Available in specialty stores such as Trader Joe's.
Storage: Store in the least cool place in the refrigerator.

5 tablespoons agave nectar or maple syrup
½ cup mascarpone cheese
1 teaspoon vanilla extract

In a small bowl, mix cocoa and hot water.

Add agave nectar, mascarpone cheese, and vanilla extract and mix until well blended.

Using a spreading knife, spread about 1 tablespoon on each cupcake.

Nutrition Facts

Amount Per Serving (1 tablespoon)
Calories 48   Calories from Fat 29

Total Fat   3 g
Saturated Fat   1.9 g
Trans Fat   0 g
Poly Fat   0 g
Mono Fat   0.1 g
Cholesterol   10 mg
Sodium   7 mg
Total Carbohydrate   5 g
Dietary Fiber   0 g
Sugars   4 g
Protein   1 g

Protein Entrée Recipes

KRAZY FOR KABOBS

There's no doubt about it: Lay a chunk of meat on his plate and your toddler might easily turn his nose up at it. Put that same chunk on a stick, however, and presto: That boring old meat magically transforms into a special and appealing dipping kabob your toddler can't wait to get his hands on. Both stainless and bamboo skewers typically have sharp points on at least one side, which could be harmful to your toddler. We recommend using bamboo skewers. If you can't find a double-blunted variety, blunt the sharp end yourself by snipping off the point with a good pair of kitchen scissors. Take the food off the skewers completely before serving to a younger toddler.

Use the skewer method to entice your finicky toddler to eat more protein, vegetables, or fruit. Make "sticks and dips" a regular offering at this age. Here are four recipes to get you started.

Shrimp Kabobs

Makes 8 toddler servings (½ skewer); or 4 adult servings (1 skewer)

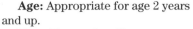

Age: Appropriate for age 2 years and up.

Tips: Pineapple adds sweetness to the shrimp, fennel, and tomatoes. Fennel is crunchy and slightly sweet with a tinge of licorice flavor. The bulb, stalk, and seeds are edible, but the bulb is the most versatile and great eaten fresh: Chop it and chill it in ice water for a quick crunchy snack. Fennel is high in vitamin C, fiber, folic acid, potassium, and many phytonutrients, including flavonoids, which are helpful for good digestion. When threading ingredients on to skewers, one alternative is to put shrimp and pineapple on half and tomatoes and fennel on the others.

Season: Peak for fennel is October through April.

Selection: Look for fennel that has a light green top and slightly greenish bulb. It should not have any marks, and the top should be feathery without budding flowers, which would indicate aging. It should have a slight licorice scent.

Storage: Store fennel in a plastic bag in the crisper drawer for up to 4 days. It is best to use as soon as possible, since it loses its flavor quickly. Fennel seeds, which are dried, are best stored in an airtight container in a cool dry area for about 6 months, or longer in a refrigerator.

    1 pound shrimp, peeled and
        deveined
    2 cups pineapple, fresh,
        thawed frozen, or canned
        with no added sugar
    1 cup fresh cherry tomatoes
    1 fennel bulb, cut into kabob
        pieces

    4 12-inch bamboo or stainless
        steel skewers

For Marinade
    ¼ cup tamari or soy sauce
    ¼ cup balsamic vinegar
    ¼ cup unsweetened pineapple
        juice
    1 clove garlic, minced

In a shallow dish, add marinade ingredients and whisk together.

If using wooden skewers, soak in water for 1 hour so they don't burn during grilling process.

Thread the shrimp, pineapple, tomatoes, and fennel onto skewers in a pattern.

Place in shallow dish and marinate for 1 to 2 hours.

Heat grill or grill pan over medium heat and grill skewers for 1 to 2 minutes on each side.

Continue to grill covered for an additional 3 to 4 minutes, until shrimp is pink and vegetables are soft.

Be careful not to overcook.

Suggestion: Serve over brown rice, quinoa, couscous, or millet.

Nutrition Facts

Amount Per Serving (½ skewer)
Calories 123   Calories from Fat 13

Total Fat   1 g
Saturated Fat   0.3 g
Trans Fat   0 g
Poly Fat   0.6 g
Mono Fat   0.2 g
Cholesterol   115 mg
Sodium   708 mg
Total Carbohydrate   11 g
Dietary Fiber   1 g
Sugars   7 g
Protein   17 g

Chicken Kabobs

*Makes 8 toddler servings
(½ skewer); or 4 adult servings
(1 skewer)*

Age: Appropriate for age 18 months and up.

Tips: Be sure to cut chicken and vegetables into smaller pieces for younger children. Serve over a whole grain, such as quinoa, millet, or brown rice. This recipe can be prepared with any marinade. Try a prepared teriyaki or even a simple Italian dressing.

- 1 pound boneless and skinless chicken or turkey breast
- 1 large zucchini, cut into kabob pieces
- 1 large yellow squash, cut into kabob pieces
- 1 medium mango (fresh or frozen), peeled cut into kabob pieces
- 1 cup Orange Ginger Marinade (see page 268 for recipe)
- 4 12-inch bamboo or stainless steel skewers

Soak bamboo skewers in water for at least 1 hour to prevent burning.

In a bowl (or gallon-sized zip-closure bag) combine chicken and ⅔ cup marinade. Mix well to coat.

In a second bowl (or zip-closure bag), combine remaining marinade and vegetables.

Marinate covered in refrigerator for about 30 minutes or overnight.

Heat grill to low-medium heat.

Thread the chicken and vegetables on to the skewers, leaving a little space between each piece to allow even cooking.

Grill for 8 to 10 minutes, until vegetables are browned and crisp and chicken is opaque in the center. Temperature of chicken or turkey should read 170° F for white meat and 180° F for dark meat.

Nutrition Facts

Amount Per Serving (½ skewer)
Calories 68   Calories from Fat 21

Total Fat   2 g
Saturated Fat   0.4 g
Trans Fat   0 g
Poly Fat   0.9 g
Mono Fat   0.8 g
Cholesterol   9 mg
Sodium   456 mg
Total Carbohydrate   7 g
Dietary Fiber   2 g
Sugars   5 g
Protein   5 g

Balsamic Steak Kabobs

Makes 8 toddler servings (1 kabob); or 4 adult servings (2 kabobs)

Age: Appropriate for age 18 months and up.

Tips: This marinade is also great on a flank steak. Portobello mushrooms are a fungi, but prepared like a vegetable. They have anticancer properties and contain L-ergothioneine, an antioxidant found in the largest amounts in shitake, oyster, king oyster, and maitake mushrooms. Portobellos are also a good source of riboflavin, pantothenic acid, copper, niacin, potassium, phosphorus, and fiber. Do not feed raw mushrooms to children less than twelve months of age; raw mushrooms can harbor bacteria. Use a brush or cloth to remove any dirt from mushrooms, as rinsing them with water makes them slimy.

Selection: Look for portobello mushrooms that are creamy brown in color, dry and clean without any marks.

Storage: Store mushrooms in refrigerator in original container for 1 week or in a glass dish, wrapped in moist paper towel and sealed in a plastic bag.

1½ pounds lean London broil beef (round steak)
2 large colored bell peppers (red, orange, or yellow), cut into kabob pieces
16 stemmed baby portobello mushrooms
2 medium Vidalia onions, cut into kabob pieces
8 12-inch bamboo or stainless steel skewers

For Marinade
⅓ cup balsamic vinegar
⅓ cup molasses
1 teaspoon thyme
¼ teaspoon nutmeg
¼ teaspoon salt
1 clove garlic, minced

In a large bowl or plastic bag, combine marinade ingredients.

Marinate London broil in refrigerator for 2 hours or overnight; the longer it's marinated, the more flavorful it will be.

Preheat barbeque on medium heat or broiler.

If broiling, position broiler pan 3 to 4 inches from heating element and spray with a high-temperature cooking spray like grapeseed or sunflower oil.

Carve meat into kabob pieces.

Thread meat and vegetables on to skewers, making a pattern.

Broil or grill skewers for 8 to 10 minutes, turning occasionally.

Check meat by making a small cut in the center of one piece. Meat should be slightly less done than preferred, because it will continue to cook once removed from heat.

Suggestion: Serve over brown rice, quinoa, couscous, or millet.

Nutrition Facts

Amount Per Serving (1 kabob)
Calories 152   Calories from Fat 63

Total Fat   7 g
Saturated Fat   1.7 g
Trans Fat   0 g
Poly Fat   1.6 g
Mono Fat   2.9 g
Cholesterol   41 mg
Sodium   405 mg
Total Carbohydrate   7 g
Dietary Fiber   1 g
Sugars   4 g
Protein   15 g

Fruit Kabobs

Makes 5 toddler servings (1 skewer); or 2 to 3 adult servings (1½ skewers)

Age: Appropriate for age 18 months and up.

Tips: These fruit kabobs make a nice presentation at a birthday celebration served with Yogurt Dip (see page 314 for recipe). Any fruit combinations can work for these kabobs. In the winter, use banana, pears, and apples sprinkled with a little lemon juice to prevent browning.

Season: Peak for fruit is spring and summer.

See page 295 for information on strawberries; page 226 for information on pineapple; page 200 for information on cantaloupe.

½ cup fresh strawberries, halved

1 ½ cups fresh pineapple, cubed, or cut into decorative shapes

¾ cup fresh cantaloupe, cubed, scooped into balls, or cut into decorative shape

¾ cup fresh honeydew melon, cubed, scooped into balls, or cut into decorative shape

5 12-inch bamboo or stainless steel skewers

Thread fruit in a pattern on skewers. Serve with Yogurt Dip.

Nutrition Facts

Amount Per Serving (3 ounces)
Calories 35   Calories from Fat 1

Total Fat   0 g
Saturated Fat   0 g
Trans Fat   0 g
Poly Fat   0.1 g
Mono Fat   0 g
Cholesterol   0 mg
Sodium   4 mg
Total Carbohydrate   9 g
Dietary Fiber   1 g
Sugars   7 g
Protein   1 g

Yogurt Dip

Makes 16 toddler servings (1 tablespoon); or 4 adult servings (¼ cup)

Age: Appropriate for age 18 months and up.

Tips: This dip is meant to be served with the preceding Fruit Kabobs recipe. However, if serving with something else, appropriate age may change. In addition to the Fruit Kabobs, this dip works

well tossed with any fresh fruit or granola mix.

1 cup plain Greek yogurt
2 teaspoons honey or blackstrap molasses
2 tablespoons pineapple or orange juice
½ teaspoon ground cinnamon
¼ teaspoon ground ginger

In a small bowl or yogurt container, combine all ingredients and mix well. Serve with Fruit Kabobs.

Refrigerate in a sealed container until yogurt's expiration date.

Nutrition Facts

Amount Per Serving (1 tablespoon)
Calories 21   Calories from Fat 13

Total Fat   1 g
Saturated Fat   1.1 g
Trans Fat   0 g
Poly Fat   0.4 g
Mono Fat   0.1 g
Cholesterol   2 mg
Sodium   5 mg
Total Carbohydrate   1 g
Dietary Fiber   0 g
Sugars   0 g
Protein   1 g

Tangy Tempeh Finger Sandwich

Makes 6 toddler servings (½ sandwich); or 3 adult servings (1 sandwich)

Age: Appropriate for age 2 years and up.

Tips: Tempeh is a meat alternative made from fermented soybeans. Though not a typical toddler food, tempeh does provide another digestible form of nonmeat protein, great for vegetarian toddlers. It is high in riboflavin, magnesium, manganese, and copper.

Variation: You can also try this recipe substituting about 8 ounces of extra-firm tofu. If using tofu, press the block firmly with a spatula to drain and then cut into strips. Marinate for at least 15 to 20 minutes (to overnight), then sauté in a small amount of olive oil over low medium heat for 2 to 3 minutes on each side until browned. Or, alternately, bake tofu in the oven at 350° F for about 20 to 25 minutes until brown.

Selection: Look for tempeh that has a whitish color with tinges of pink, yellow, and a few gray spots. Different varieties include grain and vegetable.

Storage: Refrigerate for up to 10 days (check the expiration date), or freeze for up to 3 months.

> 1 8-ounce package tempeh
> ½ cup organic ketchup
> 1 tablespoon soy sauce
> 2 tablespoons apple cider vinegar
> ½ teaspoon garlic powder
> 1 tablespoon olive oil
> ¼ cup water
> ¼ cup shredded four cheese Mexican blend
> 6 slices whole-wheat, sprouted grain, rye, or pumpernickel bread
> Avocado, lettuce, and tomato for sandwich fixins (optional)

Cut tempeh in half lengthwise then cut each half into thirds.

In a small bowl, mix ketchup, soy sauce, apple cider vinegar, and garlic powder.

In a medium pan, add sunflower oil and tempeh and sauté over low-medium heat.

Cook tempeh for 2 minutes on each side, until browned.

Add marinade mixture to tempeh and heat for 2 minutes.

Add water and simmer for 20 minutes.

Sprinkle cheese over tempeh and cover for 2 minutes.

Toast bread.

Place the tempeh slices on a paper towel-covered plate to absorb any excess marinade, then place 1 piece of tempeh on a slice of bread.

Top with a thin slice of avocado, tomato, and/or lettuce, if using.

Place another slice of bread on top and cut sandwich into halves, quarters or strips.

Nutrition Facts

Amount Per Serving (½ sandwich)
Calories 174   Calories from Fat 64

Total Fat   7 g
Saturated Fat   1.5 g
Trans Fat   0 g
Poly Fat   1.6 g
Mono Fat   3.3 g
Cholesterol   4 mg
Sodium   414 mg
Total Carbohydrate   20 g
Dietary Fiber   2 g
Sugars   8 g
Protein   9 g

Chicken Salad

Makes 5 toddler servings (3 ounces); or 4 adult servings (4 to 6 ounces)

Age: Appropriate for age 18 months and up.

Tips: Tailor this recipe to your

toddler's tastes. Try serving it on a bed of cabbage, over salad, or in a whole-grain pita or wrap. Yogurt is a healthier alternative to traditional mayonnaise and goes well with a variety of sweet or savory flavors. If your toddler loves the taste of mayonnaise, you can make a mixture of half mayo, half yogurt.

See page 237 for information on poached chicken.

⅓ cup Greek yogurt
1 teaspoon fresh-squeezed lemon juice
½ teaspoon Dijon mustard
12 ounces cooked chicken breast, shredded or cut into ½-inch pieces
¼ cup grated carrots
1 small pear or apple, diced or grated
1 medium celery stalk, finely diced and stringy pieces removed
1 tablespoon chopped cilantro or ¼ teaspoon ground coriander or ¼ teaspoon tarragon
Sprinkle ground ginger (optional)

In a small bowl, add yogurt, lemon juice, Dijon mustard and mix together.

Add diced chicken, carrots, pear, celery, and spice choice and mix well.

Nutrition Facts

Amount Per Serving (3 ounces)
Calories 194   Calories from Fat 64

Total Fat   7 g
Saturated Fat   4.3 g

Trans Fat   0 g
Poly Fat   0.5 g
Mono Fat   0.9 g
Cholesterol   66 mg
Sodium   98 mg
Total Carbohydrate   7 g
Dietary Fiber   1 g
Sugars   5 g
Protein   24 g

Fish Fingers

Makes 8 toddler servings (3 ounces; 1 fish finger); or 4 adult servings (6 ounces; 2 fish fingers)

Age: Appropriate for age 18 months and up.

Tips: Sole, haddock are good alternatives, if cod is not available.

¾ cup roughly chopped shallot or yellow onion
½ cup tomato juice
1 tablespoon olive oil
1 pound Pacific cod fillet, skinned, rinsed, and patted dry
1 cup whole-wheat spelt or oat flour
¼ cup ground flaxseeds
1 egg
1½ cups crushed cereal flakes (bran, corn, or heirloom whole-grain cereal)
1 tablespoon butter

Combine chopped shallot or onion, tomato juice, and olive oil in a shallow baking dish.

Add the fish fillet to the dish, cover with plastic wrap and marinate in the refrigerator for 15 to 30 minutes.

Combine whole-wheat flour and flaxseeds in a gallon-sized zip-closure bag.

In a shallow bowl, beat egg.

Pour the crushed cereal onto a plate.

Remove the filet from marinade and cut into 6 diagonal strips.

Place fish strips into bag and shake gently to coat fish.

Remove and dip fish strips into the egg, then roll in crushed cereal flakes to coat evenly.

In a large skillet over medium heat, melt butter.

Add the fish strips and cook for about 2 to 3 minutes on each side, until slightly brown and flaky.

Serve with organic ketchup or tomato sauce for dipping.

Refrigerate for up to 3 days, or batch and freeze for up to 2 months.

Nutrition Facts

Amount Per Serving (3 ounces)
Calories 197   Calories from Fat 45

Total Fat   5 g
Saturated Fat   0.8 g
Trans Fat   0 g
Poly Fat   2.5 g
Mono Fat   1.0 g
Cholesterol   12 mg
Sodium   153 mg
Total Carbohydrate   21 g
Dietary Fiber   5 g
Sugars   2 g
Protein   18 g

Faux Fried Chicken

Makes 9 toddler servings (1 piece); or 4½ adult servings (2 pieces)

Age: Appropriate for age 18 months and up.

Tips: Faux Fried Chicken is a delicious baked chicken with fried chicken taste. It also provides an opportunity to sneak some invisible dairy (calcium) into a meat dish.

Drumsticks travel well—great for a picnic! They also make terrific snacks.

Sunflower oil spray or grapeseed oil spray
1 cup plain yogurt
2 teaspoons fresh-squeezed lemon juice
1 teaspoon onion powder
1 teaspoon garlic powder
1½ teaspoon dried oregano
1½ teaspoon dried basil
1½ cup whole-wheat panko breadcrumbs, whole-wheat breadcrumbs, or whole-wheat Wasa crackers ground up in a blender
1⅓ pounds skinless chicken thighs, very cold
1¼ pounds skinless chicken legs, very cold

Chill your chicken well (in a bowl over ice or in the freezer for 5 minutes). This is not necessary, but it will help the yogurt coating to stick to the skinless meat.

Preheat oven to 400°F.

Lightly spray cookie sheet with vegetable oil.

In a small bowl, combine yogurt, lemon juice, onion powder, and garlic powder and mix well.

In another small bowl, combine oregano, basil, and breadcrumbs.

Dip chilled chicken pieces first in yogurt mixture to coat, then roll in breadcrumb mixture—making sure chicken is evenly coated.

Place chicken pieces on cookie sheet.

Bake for 45 minutes, or until meat thermometer reads 165° F.

Once chicken is cool, refrigerate for up to 4 days, or freeze for up to 3 months.

Nutrition Facts

Amount Per Serving (1 piece)
Calories 156   Calories from Fat 66

Total Fat   7 g
Saturated Fat   2.3 g
Trans Fat   0 g
Poly Fat   1.5 g
Mono Fat   2.6 g
Cholesterol   63 mg
Sodium   69 mg
Total Carbohydrate   4 g
Dietary Fiber   0 g
Sugars   1 g
Protein   18 g

Creamy Salmon Casserole

Makes 16 toddler servings (2½-inch by 2½-inch piece); or 9 adult servings (2½-inch by 3½-inch piece)

Age: Appropriate age is 18 months and up.

Tips: This recipe is a healthier spin on the classic tuna casserole. Using tofu in place of the more traditional white sauce made with wheat and cream dramatically increases the protein content, while reducing cook time. While you can easily replace the salmon in this recipe with tuna, wild caught salmon has a higher concentration of omega-3 fatty acids and a lower concentration of mercury. See page 267 for more information on salmon.

9 ounces whole-wheat egg noodles
1 tablespoon olive oil
1 small sweet onion, diced fine
½ teaspoon salt
½ cup dry white wine
1 cup silken tofu

1½ cups milk (cow's or unsweetened almond milk)
½ teaspoon white pepper
½ teaspoon tarragon
1 7.5-ounce can boneless, skinless, wild Alaskan salmon, drained (or chunk light tuna)
1½ cup thawed frozen peas
1⅓ cup shredded Parmesan cheese, divided
⅓ cup whole-wheat panko breadcrumbs
¼ cup ground flaxseed

Preheat oven to 375° F.
Bring large pot of water to a boil.
Cook noodles until tender according to package directions.
Drain, rinse and place into a 9 inch by 13 inch baking pan or Dutch oven.
Heat oil in large ovenproof skillet over medium high heat. Add onion and salt and cook just until onion is soft, about 5 minutes.
Add wine and cook until evaporated, 4 to 5 minutes.
Combine silken tofu and milk in food processor or blender and process for 20 seconds or until smooth and creamy.
Pour tofu/milk mixture over onions in pan.
Stir in pepper, tarragon, salmon, peas, and 1 cup of the parmesan until well combined.
Pour mixture over noodles (in baking dish) and gently fold together.
Sprinkle casserole with panko crumbs, ground flax, and remaining ⅓ cup Parmesan.
Bake in oven until bubbly and lightly crispy on top, about 15 minutes.

Braising

Braising is a method of slow cooking hard vegetables (such as turnips or beets) and tougher cuts of meat (such as brisket or flank steak) to tender doneness. Braising can be done on the stove top in a covered sauté pan or soup pan, or in the oven in a covered baking dish, roasting pan, casserole, or Dutch oven. For toddler safety, stove top cooking is the preferred method—recommended oven temperature may be too low. Season your meat all over with herbs or spices, and a small amount of salt. Add enough healthy cooking oil (canola oil, sunflower oil, grapeseed oil, or coconut oil) to lightly coat the bottom of the braising pan and warm over medium-high heat for about a minute. Add your meat and brown it lightly, turning it periodically until all sides have been seared. Remove the meat and drain fat from the pan.

Following your recipe, you will add about 2 cups of cooking liquid (low-sodium beef or chicken broth work well), an acid-containing ingredient (tomatoes, tomato paste, a small amount of orange juice, etc. to help break down the tough meat fibers), and any herb and/ or spice combination. Deglaze the pan by scraping off any little brown bits of meat that are stuck to the bottom. Bring your liquid mixture to a low simmer and return the roast, plus any chopped (hard) vegetables, to the pan. Cover and reduce the heat, keeping a low simmer. Cook for prescribed amount of time, until meat is cooked to a safe temperature and all vegetables are soft.

Nutrition Facts

Serving size is 2½-inch by 2½-inch piece
Calories 192   Calories from Fat 86

Total Fat   10 g
Saturated Fat   4.6 g
Trans Fat   0 g
Poly Fat   1.2 g
Mono Fat   2.8 g
Cholesterol   36 mg
Sodium   477mg
Total Carbohydrate   13 g
Dietary Fiber   3 g
Sugars   4 g
Protein   15 g

Grilled Mozzarella, Tomato, and Avocado Sandwich

Makes 4 toddler servings (¼ to ½ sandwich); or 1 adult serving (1 sandwich)

Age: Appropriate for age 18 months and up.

Tips: This sandwich offers a healthier take on the classic, oily grilled American cheese. Try adding pesto or a basil leaf with a splash of balsamic vinegar for a tangier taste. You can also puree edamame (baby soy beans) with a few drops of oil and lemon squeeze for a high-protein, low-fat paste.

See page 282 for information on tomatoes; page 198 for information on avocados.

2 teaspoons butter or ghee
2 slices whole-wheat, cracked
   wheat, pumpernickel,
   sprouted grain, or rye bread
1 tablespoon fresh avocado
1 large slice tomato
1 ounce sliced fresh
   mozzarella
½ teaspoon balsamic vinegar
In a skillet, melt ghee over
   medium heat.

Spread avocado on one slice of
bread. Top with tomato, mozzarella,
vinegar, and second slice of bread.

Place sandwich in skillet and
press with a small saucepan to
flatten.

Remove saucepan, cover the
skillet, and toast sandwich for about
2 minutes.

Flip the sandwich and repeat.

Remove from heat when the
toast is lightly browned.

Cut sandwich into quarters and
serve.

Nutrition Facts

Amount Per Serving (¼ to ½ sandwich)
Calories 94   Calories from Fat 51

Total Fat   6 g
Saturated Fat   3.2 g
Trans Fat   0 g
Poly Fat   0.4 g
Mono Fat   1.7 g
Cholesterol   13 mg
Sodium   147 mg
Total Carbohydrate   7 g
Dietary Fiber   2 g
Sugars   1 g
Protein   5 g

Sweet Bean Burgers

*Makes 10 toddler servings (1½ to 2
burgers); or 8 to 9 adult servings
(2 to 3 burgers)*

Age: Appropriate for age 18
months and up.

Tips: Patties or burgers provide
another way to present beans to
your toddler. Although the taste is
the same, the texture and shape are
different. Some toddlers prefer to
eat all their beans in paste or patty
form.

See page 190 for information on
sweet potatoes.

   2 15-ounce cans black beans,
      rinsed and drained, or 3
      cups cooked beans
   1 large sweet potato
   ½ cup rolled oats
   2 tablespoons onion powder
   1 tablespoon Dijon mustard
   1 teaspoon ground cumin
   1 teaspoon ground ginger
   ½ teaspoon salt
   Sunflower oil cooking spray

Preheat oven to 400° F.

Scrub potatoes under running
water.

Pierce potatoes and spread on
baking sheet.

Bake for 45 to 60 minutes, until
tender.

Allow potatoes to cool slightly.
Cut a slit on the top of each potato,
scoop out the insides, and put in a
large bowl.

Mash black beans into sweet
potatoes.

Add all other ingredients and mix
well.

Form into 10 burgers, using ⅓
cup of the mix for each patty.

Adjust heat to 350° F.

Place burgers on lightly sprayed baking sheet.

Cook for 8 to 10 minutes, until brown. Flip burgers and bake for an additional 8 to 10 minutes.

Serve over salad or on a whole-wheat bun.

Nutrition Facts

Amount Per Serving (1½ to 2 burgers)
Calories 75   Calories from Fat 4

Total Fat   0 g
Saturated Fat   0.1 g
Trans Fat   0 g
Poly Fat   0.2 g
Mono Fat   0.2 g
Cholesterol   0 mg
Sodium   220 mg
Total Carbohydrate   15 g
Dietary Fiber   3 g
Sugars   3 g
Protein   3 g

Broccoli Egg Casserole

Makes 12 toddler servings (about 2-inch piece); or 9 adult servings (about 3-inch piece)

Age: Appropriate for age 18 months and up.

Tips: Eggs are an excellent source of protein. They are high in choline, which is helpful in brain development. This yummy, soft egg casserole is a great way to offer veggies to toddlers who aren't keen on the crunchier textures. Some alternate preparation suggestions include replacing broccoli with another vegetable, such as cauliflower, asparagus, or spinach; replacing Monterey Jack cheese with cheddar, a cheddar blend, or ricotta; or leaving out cheese altogether. Two percent cow's, rice, or almond milk can be used instead of whole milk if child is over 2 years old.

Selection: Eggs are classified according to interior and exterior quality and designated by letters in descending order: AA is the highest quality, A is just slightly lower, and B is the lowest, rarely sold in grocery stores. Eggs are also graded according to size: small, medium, large, and extra-large. Medium, large, and extra-large are the sizes most commonly available. Look for cage-free, organic eggs supplemented with omega-3.

Storage: Store eggs unwashed in original carton, pointy ends facedown, in refrigerator for up to 1 month.

See page 213 for information on broccoli.

1 teaspoon olive oil or butter
1 cup fresh broccoli, cut into bite-sized pieces
½ cup diced fresh tomatoes
½ cup shredded Monterey Jack cheese
5 extra-large eggs
½ cup whole milk
1 teaspoon paprika
½ teaspoon salt

Preheat oven to 375° F.

Lightly grease an 8-inch-by-8-inch casserole dish with olive oil or butter.

Spread broccoli pieces, tomatoes, and cheese evenly throughout casserole dish.

In a small bowl, beat eggs and milk with a whisk. Pour mixture over broccoli and cheese.

Sprinkle with paprika and salt.

Bake for 30 to 40 minutes, until broccoli is cooked and golden brown.

Refrigerate in a sealed container for up to 3 days.

Nutrition Facts

Amount Per Serving (2-inch piece)
Calories 124   Calories from Fat 54

Total Fat   6 g
Saturated Fat   2.8 g
Trans Fat   0 g
Poly Fat   0.5 g
Mono Fat   1.9 g
Cholesterol   112 mg
Sodium   130 mg
Total Carbohydrate   11 g
Dietary Fiber   2 g
Sugars   3 g
Protein   6 g

Egg in a Hole

Makes 2 toddler servings (1 slice); or 1 adult serving (2 slices)

Age: Appropriate for age 18 months and up.

Tips: This classic meal has been pleasing toddlers for decades. Use a cookie cutter to create fun cutouts. Offer your child a selection of toppings to sprinkle: cooked beans, shredded zucchini, shredded cheese, or avocado slices.

For more egg information see page 321.

1 teaspoon butter or ghee
2 extra-large eggs
2 slices whole-wheat, cracked wheat, pumpernickel, or rye bread
¼ cup chopped tomatoes
¼ cup shredded carrots

In a skillet, melt ghee over medium heat.

Using the top of a glass or a cookie cutter, cut a hole in the center of each slice of bread and place in skillet.

Crack eggs and drop into holes of each slice of bread and cook for 3 to 5 minutes.

Carefully flip bread and egg with a spatula, bursting yolk if necessary to cook through.

Top with veggies.

Nutrition Facts

Amount Per Serving (1 slice)
Calories 203   Calories from Fat 88

Total Fat   10 g
Saturated Fat   3 g
Trans Fat   0 g
Poly Fat   1.3 g
Mono Fat   3.6 g
Cholesterol   250 mg
Sodium   231 mg
Total Carbohydrate   21 g
Dietary Fiber   4 g
Sugars   5 g
Protein   11 g

Jazzy Shrimp Stir-Fry

Makes 8 toddler servings (½ cup); or 4 adult servings (1 cup)

Age: Appropriate for age 18 months and up.

Tips: This is a terrific quick meal that is delicious served over a whole grain, such as brown rice or udon noodles. Shrimp is high in protein, vitamins D and B_{12}, tryptophan, and selenium. It also has a fair amount of omega-3 fatty acids and niacin. It is low in fat and high in cholesterol, but studies show that shrimp raises HDL (good) cholesterol ratios and lowers LDL (bad) cholesterol ratios. U.S. farmed shrimp are very high in quality and produced sustainably. Many veggies are also delicious stir-fried with shrimp: Try bok choy, broccoli, water chestnuts, or snow peas.

Selection: There are over 300 types of shrimp. Black tiger shrimp from Asia is one of the most common varieties found in grocery stores. They have a gray shell with yellow, red, or black feelers and are typically not as flavorful as other varieties. Gulf brown and pink shrimp usually have a slight iodine flavor. Gulf white shrimp are very flavorful, with pale shells. Check that the shells don't have spots or marks, indicating that they may not be fresh. The shell should not look gritty or yellowish in color, which could indicate that a chemical such as sodium bisulfate was used to bleach it.

Storage: Place fresh shrimp on a bed of ice, cover, store in refrigerator, and use within 2 days, or freeze for later use. Defrost frozen shrimp in a bowl of cold water in the refrigerator.

> 1 tablespoon sesame, peanut, or vegetable oil
> 2 cloves garlic, minced
> 1 tablespoon peeled and finely chopped ginger
> 1 pound shrimp, cleaned and deveined
> 1 large red pepper, sliced
> 2½ cups bok choy, rinsed
> 5 scallion bottoms, chopped

Sauce
> 2 tablespoons soy sauce or low-sodium tamari
> 2 tablespoons rice wine vinegar

> 1 tablespoon orange juice
> 1 tablespoon sesame oil
> 1 tablespoon kudzu root (dissolved in 2 tablespoons water)

In a small bowl, add all sauce ingredients and mix well. Set aside.

Heat wok or skillet over medium-high heat for 30 to 60 seconds.

Add half the oil and spread to coat the wok.

Add garlic and sauté for 30 to 60 seconds.

Add ginger and shrimp and stir-fry for 2 minutes.

Remove shrimp from wok and put in a small bowl.

Add remaining oil and red pepper to the wok and stir-fry for 2 minutes.

Add bok choy and cook until wilted, about 1 to 3 minutes.

Add scallions and shrimp mixture and stir-fry for 2 to 3 minutes, until shrimp is pink and center is opaque.

Add sauce, stir, and cook until mixture thickens, about 1 to 3 minutes.

Suggestion: Serve over brown rice or noodles.

Nutrition Facts

Amount Per Serving (½ cup)
Calories 343   Calories from Fat 46

Total Fat   5 g
Saturated Fat   0.7 g
Trans Fat   0 g
Poly Fat   1.4 g
Mono Fat   2.3 g
Cholesterol   115 mg
Sodium   562 mg
Total Carbohydrate 55 g
Dietary Fiber   8 g
Sugars   3 g
Protein   19 g

Mini Turkey Burgers

Makes 12 toddler servings (one 3-ounce burger); or 6 adult servings (two 3-ounce burgers)

Age: Appropriate for age 2 years and up.

Tips: Black sesame seeds provide a great source of manganese, copper, calcium, iron, magnesium, zinc, phosphorous, vitamin B_1, and fiber.

Serve burgers as is, over a bed of lettuce and tomatoes, or on a whole-wheat wrap or bun.

Selection: Purchase prepackaged black sesame seeds.

Storage: Refrigerate sesame seeds.

> 12 ounces lean ground turkey
> ½ cup quick-cooking oats
> 2 tablespoons hoisin sauce
> 2 scallions, trimmed and chopped
> 2 teaspoons minced ginger
> ¼ teaspoon garlic salt
> 1 egg, beaten
> 1 tablespoon Dijon mustard
> ½ cup black or white sesame seeds (optional)
> Cooking oil spray

Preheat grill or grill pan on medium heat.

In a large bowl, combine ground turkey, oats, hoisin sauce, scallions, ginger, garlic salt, egg, mustard, and ¼ cup black sesame seeds, if using, (or may mix in full half cup and omit coating the outside with second portion). Mix well.

Using an ice cream scoop, portion out the mixture to make burgers.

Use remaining ¼ cup black sesame seeds to coat both sides of burgers.

Spray grill or grill pan with oil and cook burgers until browned, about 5 minutes each side, or until meat thermometer reads 170° F.

Freeze uncooked burgers for up to 3 months.

Nutrition Facts

Amount Per Serving (1 3-ounce burger)
Calories 146   Calories from Fat 79

Total Fat   9 g
Saturated Fat   2.1 g
Trans Fat   0 g
Poly Fat   1.3 g
Mono Fat   2.6 g
Cholesterol   117 mg
Sodium   190 mg
Total Carbohydrate   5 g
Dietary Fiber   1 g
Sugars   1 g
Protein   12 g

Tacos

Makes 12 toddler servings (1 taco); or 4 to 6 adult servings (2 to 3 tacos)

Age: Appropriate for age 18 months and up.

Tips: Tacos are an easy family meal. The fixins allow everyone to customize their own. The simplest version of this recipe is to combine the ground meat with a mild jarred salsa (omitting tomato, chili powder, and garlic), and load into tacos (see instructions below)—use whatever salad veggie you have in the fridge to dress them up.

> 1 tablespoon olive oil
> ½ cup diced onions
> 1 pound ground turkey or ground beef*
> ½ teaspoon salt

½ teaspoon black pepper

1 teaspoon chili powder (adds heat)

1 clove garlic, minced

1 14.5-ounce can diced tomatoes

½ cup diced mushrooms (optional)

Toppings

1 cup diced tomatoes

1 diced Hass avocado

1 cup shredded lettuce, Boston or romaine

¼ cup chopped black olives

¼ cup chopped green olives

1 ½ cups shredded cheddar cheese

2 cups Pinto Bean Puree (see page 242) or Easy Mexi-Beans (see page 273) or 1 can vegetarian refried beans

½ cup sour cream

12 miniature taco shells (3-inch wide)

In a medium pan over low-medium heat, add olive oil and onions and sauté for 3 to 5 minutes, until onions are translucent.

Add ground meat. Using the back of a spoon break the meat apart.

Add chili powder, salt, pepper, and garlic, and stir to combine. Continue browning meat for about 3 minutes.

Add tomatoes and mushrooms, if using, stir and let cook for about 10 minutes until meat is cooked through, no pink remaining.

While meat is cooking, prepare toppings.

Taco shells can be warmed in a conventional or toaster oven at 325° F for 3 to 5 minutes.

*For quickest tacos, simply brown meat with salt and pepper for about 8 minutes. Then stir in ⅔ cup to 1 cup mild salsa (to taste) and add mushrooms. Cook for 8 minutes more and serve.

Nutrition Facts

Amount Per Serving (1 taco)

Calories 362   Calories from Fat 152

Total Fat   17 g

Saturated Fat   4.6 g

Trans Fat   0 g

Poly Fat   2 g

Mono Fat   5.8 g

Cholesterol   43 mg

Sodium   669 mg

Total Carbohydrate   33 g

Dietary Fiber   9 g

Sugars   4 g

Protein   20 g

Slow Cooker Split Pea Soup

Makes 16 toddler servings (½ cup); or 8 adult servings (1 cup)

Age: Appropriate for age 18 months and up.

Tips: Split pea soup is high in vitamin B, protein, and fiber and has a high concentration of molybdenum. Add ham hock and/or cubed cooked ham for a more traditional split pea soup.

1 tablespoon olive oil (if cooking in stockpot)

1 diced onion or 1 tablespoon onion powder

1 pound split peas, sorted and drained (no presoaking required)

1 large sweet potato, peeled and cut into ½-inch cubes

4 medium carrots, peeled and cut into thin rounds

1 medium celery stalk, diced
8 cups vegetable broth
1 bay leaf
1 teaspoon dried tarragon
¾ teaspoon salt (omit if adding
ham)
1 teaspoon smoked or regular
paprika
1 teaspoon ume plum vinegar
or red wine vinegar
1 10-ounce bag frozen green
peas
2 tablespoons cooking sherry
1 ham hock (optional)
1 cup diced ham (optional)
Chopped parsley to garnish
(optional)

Slow Cooker
Combine onion, split peas, sweet
potatoes, carrots, celery, broth, bay
leaf, tarragon, paprika, vinegar and
ham hock, if using.

Cover and cook on low for 7 to 8
hours or on high for 4 to 5 hours.

Add green peas, sherry, and
diced ham, if using, during last 10
minutes of cooking and stir well.

Add more water or stock if soup
is too thick.

Remove ham hock and bay leaf
before serving.

Stove Top
In a large stockpot or Dutch oven
over medium heat, add olive oil and
onion and cook for 3 to 5 minutes,
until translucent (skip this step if
using onion powder and add with
sweet potatoes).

Add sweet potatoes, carrots,
tarragon, and paprika and cook for 2
to 3 minutes.

Add vinegar, celery, broth, and
bay leaf.

Add drained split peas and ham
hock, if using, and, stir, and bring to

a simmer. Reduce heat and cook for
about 50 minutes.

Add green peas, sherry, and
diced ham, if using, and stir well.
Continue cooking for about 10
minutes, until peas are dissolved
into the soup. If soup is too thick,
add more water or broth.

Remove ham hock and bay leaf
before serving.

Nutrition Facts

Amount Per Serving (½ cup)
Calories 155   Calories from Fat 16

Total Fat   2 g
Saturated Fat   0.3 g
Trans Fat   0 g
Poly Fat   0.4 g
Mono Fat   0.9 g
Cholesterol   0 mg
Sodium   467 mg
Total Carbohydrate   28 g
Dietary Fiber   9 g
Sugars   7 g
Protein   8 g

Easy One-Pot Beef Stew

*Makes 12 toddler servings (½ cup);
or 6 adult servings (1 cup)*

Age: Appropriate for age 18
months and up.

Tips: This can be made in a
Dutch oven or a slow cooker.
Complete the meal by serving dish
over a whole grain, such as brown
rice, quinoa, millet, or whole-grain
noodles. The alcohol from the
liquor, wine, or beer cooks out and
the flavor remains. If desired, puree
for children under 18 months.

Storage: Store in a sealed
container in the refrigerator for
up to 4 days, or freeze in a sealed

537

freezer-safe container for up to 3 months.

½ teaspoon salt
½ teaspoon pepper
1 teaspoon dried basil
1 teaspoon dried thyme
1 teaspoon dried oregano
1 medium onion, sliced
3 carrots, cooked and sliced into thin rounds
1½ cups butternut squash, peeled and cubed
2 cloves garlic, minced
1½ pounds beef stew meat, cubed
½ cup low-sodium beef broth
¾ cup burgundy wine, beer, or water
1 14.5-ounce can diced tomatoes
1 bay leaf
1 10-ounce package frozen green beans
1 tablespoon olive oil (if cooking in Dutch oven)

Slow Cooker

Turn on slow cooker. See below for timing.

In a small dish combine salt, pepper, basil, thyme, and oregano.

Divide in half and separate. Use half to season beef.

Add onion, carrots, butternut squash, garlic, beef, broth, wine, tomatoes, and remaining half of herb mixture to slow cooker, and mix gently to combine.

Add seasoned beef last and do not stir in.

Cook for 7 to 8 hours on low or 3 to 4 hours on high (slow cooker temperatures may vary). Add green beans during the last 10 to 15 minutes of cooking.

Serve over a whole grain.

Stove Top

In a small dish combine salt, pepper, basil, thyme, and oregano.

Divide in half and separate. Use half to season beef.

In a Dutch oven over medium high heat, add olive oil and beef, searing until beef is brown on all sides.

Remove browned beef to plate and set aside.

Add onion to Dutch oven and sauté for 3 to 5 minutes, until translucent.

Add garlic and sauté for about 1 minute, until lightly browned.

Add seared beef, tomatoes, remaining half of herb mixture, squash, carrots, wine, and bay leaf. Cover and simmer for 60 to 90 minutes, until meat and squash are tender.

Add green beans for last ten minutes of cook time.

Suggestion: Serve over whole grain.

Nutrition Facts

Amount Per Serving (½ cup)
Calories 132   Calories from Fat 40

Total Fat   4 g
Saturated Fat   1.5 g
Trans Fat   0 g
Poly Fat   0.4 g
Mono Fat   1.9 g
Cholesterol   34 mg
Sodium   420 mg
Total Carbohydrate   10 g
Dietary Fiber   2 g
Sugars   5 g
Protein   12 g

Grilled or Baked Pork Loin

Makes 10 toddler servings (3 ounces); or 7 adult servings (4 ounces)

Age: Appropriate for age 18 months and up.

Tips: Make this tender pork loin for dinner, and then slice up the meat for easy sandwiches or dippers later. You may also use the Hoisin Marinade (see page 285 for recipe) in place of this cilantro marinade, or simply roast the pork with a little salt and pepper and serve it plain, in pieces, with a dipping sauce (see page 281 for Creamy Peanut Sauce recipe).

Marinade

2 tablespoons tamari or soy sauce
1 tablespoon chopped fresh ginger
2 cloves garlic, minced or sliced
1 bunch fresh cilantro, cleaned and chopped
1 tablespoon lime juice
½ cup olive oil
¼ cup water

Pork Loin

2 pounds lean, fresh pork loin
Cooking oil spray (for grilling) or 2 tablespoons olive oil (for baking)
½ teaspoon salt

In a small bowl, whisk all marinade ingredients together.

Place pork in a BPA-free gallon-sized zip-closure bag or bowl and pour marinade over the top.

Marinate pork, covered, in the refrigerator for at least 30 minutes to overnight (best).

After marinating, remove pork and any cilantro leaves before cooking.

For Grilling

Spray grill with cooking oil and heat on high.

Cook with cover down and middle burner turned off for 40 to 45 minutes, until instant meat thermometer reads 160° F.

The meat will continue cooking for 5 to 10 minutes once off the grill.

Cover with tinfoil and let sit for 5 to 10 minutes before slicing.

For Baking

Preheat oven to 350° F.

Heat oil in a large ovenproof skillet or grill pan.

Add pork loin and brown on each side for about 3 minutes.

Place skillet in oven and cook for 25 minutes, until instant meat thermometer reads 160° F.

Cover with tinfoil and let sit for 5 to 10 minutes before slicing.

Nutrition Facts

Amount Per Serving (3 ounces)
Calories 125   Calories from Fat 51

Total Fat   6 g
Saturated Fat   1.4 g
Trans Fat   0 g
Poly Fat   0.6 g
Mono Fat   3.2 g
Cholesterol   37 mg
Sodium   394 mg
Total Carbohydrate   4 g
Dietary Fiber   0 g
Sugars   3 g
Protein   14 g

Drink Recipes

Strawberry Mango Smoothie

Makes 8 servings (½ cup); or 4 adult servings (1 cup)

Age: Appropriate for age 18 months and up.

Tips: This is a great breakfast or snack on the go. This smoothie can also be made into frozen ice pops, using an ice pop mold or an ice cube tray and wooden sticks.

See page 295 for information on strawberries; page 197 for information on bananas.

> 1 cup frozen strawberries
> ½ cup frozen mango chunks
> ½ cup sliced fresh or 1 small frozen banana
> 1 cup whole milk
> 1 cup plain Greek yogurt
> 1 tablespoon ground flaxseed
> 1 tablespoon maple syrup or honey
> 1 cup of ice (optional for slushier smoothie)

Combine all ingredients in a blender pitcher and blend on high until smooth.

Nutrition Facts

Amount Per Serving (½ cup)
Calories 75   Calories from Fat 24

Total Fat   3 g
Saturated Fat   1.3 g
Trans Fat   0 g
Poly Fat   0.5 g
Mono Fat   073 g
Cholesterol   7 mg
Sodium   28 mg
Total Carbohydrate   11 g
Dietary Fiber   1 g
Sugars   8 g
Protein   3 g

Fruit Pops

Most commercial frozen novelties are loaded with artificial flavors, colors, and lots of sugar. It's easy to make much healthier versions at home. Steep 3 strong cups of herbal raspberry, peach, or mint tea (to avoid caffeine, choose a true herbal tisane made without any tea leaves). Puree 2 cups of fruit (strawberries, raspberries, peaches, banana, blueberries, etc.) in a blender and add the tea. Process on low until well mixed. Try it unsweetened first, and if it needs a little sweetener, add a teaspoon of honey or maple syrup (for one year and up only) and reblend gently. Pour into ice pop holders or 3-ounce Dixie cups with a wooden stick in each cup (makes approximately twelve). Freeze for 3 to 4 hours and peel away paper cup to serve.

Tropical Smoothie

Makes 8 servings (½ cup); or 4 adult servings (1 cup)

Age: Appropriate for age 18 months and up.

Tips: Mangos are not only a delicious tropical fruit but also a great source of fiber, vitamins B_6, A, and C, and beta-carotene.

This smoothie can also be made into frozen ice pops, using an ice pop mold or an ice cube tray and wooden sticks.

Season: Peak for mango is spring and fall.

Selection: Look for mangos that are green or orange in color, with a slight give to the flesh when pressed.

Storage: Store whole mango on countertop to ripen. Once ripened, the mango can be refrigerated for a few days, but should be used shortly thereafter.

See page 295 for information on strawberries; page 226 for information on pineapples.

> 1 cup frozen strawberries
> ½ cup frozen pineapples
> ½ cup frozen mangos
> 1 cup apple juice or pomegranate juice
> ½ cup water
> 1½ cups ice
> 2 tablespoons ground flaxseed

Combine all ingredients in a blender pitcher and blend on high until smooth.

Nutrition Facts

Amount Per Serving (½ cup)
Calories 52   Calories from Fat 8

Total Fat   1 g
Saturated Fat   0.1 g
Trans Fat   0 g
Poly Fat   0.5 g
Mono Fat   0.2 g
Cholesterol   0 mg
Sodium   4 mg
Total Carbohydrate   11 g
Dietary Fiber   1 g

Sugars   9 g
Protein   1 g

Creamy Choco-Banana Smoothie

Makes 8 servings (½ cup); or 4 adult servings (1 cup)

Age: Appropriate for age 18 months and up.

Tips: This chocolate "shake" works as a snack or satisfying dessert. To make coconut milk ice cubes, pour a can of low-fat coconut milk into an ice tray, cover, and freeze for at least 4 hours, until frozen solid. Cubes can be popped out and stored in a freezer-safe bag. This is a great way to use leftover coconut milk if you've opened a can for a recipe.

See page 197 for information on bananas.

> 1 cup sliced fresh bananas or 2 small frozen bananas
> 1½ cups ice
> 2 cups cow's, almond, or rice milk
> 1 coconut milk ice cube or 2 tablespoons coconut milk
> ¼ teaspoon vanilla or almond extract
> 2 tablespoons honey or maple syrup
> 2 tablespoons unsweetened cocoa powder
> ½ teaspoon cinnamon

Combine all ingredients in a blender pitcher and blend on high until smooth.

Nutrition Facts

Amount Per Serving (½ cup)
Calories 62   Calories from Fat 7

Total Fat   1 g
Saturated Fat   0.8 g
Trans Fat   0 g
Poly Fat   0.2 g
Mono Fat   0.3 g
Cholesterol   0 mg
Sodium   22 mg
Total Carbohydrate   13 g
Dietary Fiber   1 g
Sugars   9 g
Protein   1 g

Fizzy Cran-Orange Spritzer

Makes 2 toddler servings (½ cup); or 1 adult serving (1 cup)

Age: Appropriate for age 18 months and up.

Tips: This is a refreshing drink that is low in sugar and may actually decrease sugar cravings because of the cranberry and lime combination. Fresh cranberries are a highly nutritious fruit. They are especially high in the antioxidant phenol, fiber, vitamin C, and manganese.

Fresh cranberries are more nutritious than all other forms: dried cranberries, unsweetened cranberry juice, or cranberry cocktails. Most cranberry juices are a blend of juices because pure cranberry juice is quite tart. Cranberry juice has been proven effective against urinary tract infections.

Pure cranberry juice is very sour and pure orange juice is very sweet. The combination, cut with seltzer and lime, offers a quenching alternative to soda or other classic juices during the hotter months.

Season: Peak for cranberries is October through December.

Selection: Look for round, crimson red cranberries that are hard to the touch. The darker red cranberries have higher amounts of healthy anthocyanin compounds.

> ¼ cup unsweetened 100
>   percent cranberry juice
> ¼ cup 100 percent orange juice
> ½ cup plain carbonated or
>   seltzer water
> 1 lime wedge
> ½ teaspoon honey (optional)

In a glass, combine cranberry and orange juices, carbonated water, and juice from lime wedge and mix with a stirrer. Taste and add honey, if using.

Nutrition Facts

Amount Per Serving (½ cup)
Calories 65   Calories from Fat 1

Total Fat   1 g
Saturated Fat   0 g
Trans Fat   0 g
Poly Fat   0 g
Mono Fat   0 g
Cholesterol   0 mg
Sodium   15 mg
Total Carbohydrate   16 g
Dietary Fiber   0 g
Sugars   15 g
Protein   0 g

Minty Lemonade with Honey

Makes 11 toddler servings (½ cup); or about 5 adult servings (1 cup)

Age: Appropriate for age 18 months and up.

Tips: This is a refreshing and cooling drink on hot days. Spearmint tends to grow easily, and makes a fun plant for your toddler to raise and harvest himself. It does spread, however, so plant in a separated area of your yard or in a pot. Spearmint can help neutralize stomach acid and soothe an upset stomach.

Season: Peak season for spearmint is summer.

Selection: Look for fresh spearmint that is bright green, pointed at the end, and exudes a wonderful minty flavor.

Storage: Store fresh spearmint in a moist paper towel for up to 3 days in the refrigerator.

1 cup water
½ to 1 cup fresh spearmint or 4 mint tea bags
5 lemons
4 cups cold water
¼ cup honey

Boil 1 cup of water and pour into a small bowl or glass measuring cup.

Add fresh mint or tea bags to the hot water, and steep for 15 minutes. Strain mint from water using sieve or cheesecloth and discard.

Add honey to the warm water and whisk to dissolve.

While tea is steeping, juice lemons into a glass measuring cup using a reamer or squeeze with your hands.

Combine mint tea and lemon in a pitcher. Add ice as desired.

Nutrition Facts

Amount Per Serving (½ cup)
Calories 31   Calories from Fat 0

Total Fat   0 g
Saturated Fat   0 g
Trans Fat   0 g
Poly Fat   0 g
Mono Fat   0.2 g
Cholesterol   0 mg
Sodium   4 mg
Total Carbohydrate   9 g
Dietary Fiber   0 g
Sugars   7 g
Protein   0 g

After a Day of Poor-Quality Eating . . .

If your toddler has had a big, exciting day and eaten a lot of less-than-healthy fare, as at a holiday celebration or at an amusement park, his system may be thrown off from too much salt and sugar. To gently help him get back into balance, encourage him to drink some extra water with a small amount of fresh-squeezed lemon juice the next morning to help flush some of the excess salt from his system. Offer him some grounding, balancing foods to eat that evening or the next morning: healthy, appealing protein choices such as thawed Meat Loaf Muffins (recipe page 280) or a bowl of chunky chicken soup (recipe page 276). This will help calm jangled nerves and balance out his blood sugar. Another relaxing, soothing food is warm grains, such as a nice bowl of oatmeal with ground nuts, or some simple rice with warmed greens. A simple vegetable miso soup is also nourishing and balancing (see page 292 for recipe). A good sleep and a balancing nourishing meal is probably all he'll need to calm the crankies and return to his regular, cheerful self.

Quick Snacks or Mini-Meals, 18 Months and Up

Need a quick, satisfying mini-meal to perk up your busy toddler? Try one of the suggestions below.

English muffin pizza: Lightly toast an open-face English muffin (organic whole grain is best). Spread a little prepared tomato or pizza sauce across each face and top it with a sprinkle of shredded mozzarella cheese. Bake it on a broiler pan in the toaster oven at 350º F for about 5 minutes, until the cheese is melted. If you aren't in a big hurry, you can dice some toppings and let your toddler decorate his own: Try chopped black or green olives, diced ham, or cooked ground beef.

Hummus or baba ghanoush with raw veggie sticks: Try cucumbers, colored bell peppers, carrots, celery sticks, endive, fennel, broccoli, cauliflower, or tomato wedges.

Wraps (organic whole grain, veggie): Hummus and sliced cucumbers or pickles; baba ghanoush and tomatoes; turkey, lettuce, and roasted muenster cheese; rice and beans; refried beans and shredded cheddar or Monterey Jack cheese.

Stuffed celery: Fill with hummus, seed or nut butter (if no allergy), and top with raisins, dried cranberries, diced apple, pear, banana, chopped nuts, wheat germ, or granola.

Avocado boat: Halve, pit, and peel an avocado. Stuff one half with diced turkey, diced tomato, and a drizzle of Italian dressing.

Turkey and crackers: Dice turkey breast, mix with a small amount of fruit-sweetened cranberry sauce or apricot jam, and serve on toast or whole-grain crackers.

Tuna and lettuce or crackers: Mix canned light tuna with a little bit of mayonnaise or lemon juice and chopped celery and roll into a lettuce leaf or serve on whole-grain crackers with chopped tomatoes.

Salmon and salsa: Take skinless, boneless canned salmon, mix with a bit of salsa, and press into a fish shape using a cookie cutter, or free-hand it with a flat knife by making a large oval with a triangle tail. Serve with celery stick or toast-strip scoops.

Eggs and veggies: Slice one or two hardboiled eggs or make an egg salad mashing them with 1 tablespoon of mayonnaise and 1 tablespoon of diced onion, celery, shredded carrot, parsley, or cilantro, or a combination. Serve with lettuce leaves and a couple of slices of avocado and tomato.

Spread sandwiches: These can be open-faced, two-slice, on a wrap, or on crackers. For the first layer, try mashed avocado; mashed egg yolk; vegetarian or regular refried beans; cheese (cream, cottage, ricotta, or shredded); or nut or seed butter (peanut, almond, cashew, sunflower, soy, or tahini). Add a second layer of flavor with apple, prune, or lemon butter; mashed banana; pureed or shredded fruit; applesauce; juice-sweetened jam or jelly; mashed sweet potatoes; juice-sweetened cranberry sauce; shredded carrots or lettuce; or cucumber or pickle slices.

continued on following page

Edamame (fresh baby soy beans): Buy them precooked and frozen. Thaw them quickly in a bowl of cold water and serve them with a pinch of salt (unless pre-salted) or with a peanut (if no allergy) or yogurt dipping sauce. The unshelled beans are especially fun for toddlers: Open the hulls at one end and show him how to squeeze out the beans through the tops.

Whole-grain toasties: For a sweet version, lightly toast bread, spread with nut or seed butter (if no allergy concerns), and offer your child a plate of thinly sliced fruit: banana, apple, pear, raisins, etc. to place on top. You can add a sprinkle of cinnamon or cardamom, if desired.

For a savory treat, spread with a thin layer of beans (refried or black beans) and top with shredded or sliced cheese (cheddar, Monterey Jack, etc.). Bake in toaster oven at 350º F until cheese is melted. Top with avocado or tomato slices, if desired.

Toddler tortilla: Using a soft, 6-inch corn tortilla as a base, add vegetarian refried beans or canned and rinsed black, pinto, or kidney beans; mild salsa; and shredded Mexican cheese. Bake in toaster oven at 350º F for about 5 minutes to melt cheese and warm beans. Top with avocado slices, chopped olives, shredded lettuce, or chopped tomatoes, if desired.

Looking Forward

By the time your toddler reaches his third birthday, much of the foundation for his future tastes and eating habits has been set. This does not mean, however, that you can stop attending to his eating behaviors now. It's a classic pattern in this country to be very diligent about feeding our babies, but then abandon those great feeding habits once the child nears school age. According to FITS 2008 (see more information about the FITS study on page 11), parents are listening and responding well to feeding guidelines for their babies, but they're not continuing to reinforce those healthy eating habits as children grow older.

It's true that as your child becomes older and more independent, he will likely be exposed to more food advertising, more restaurants, and more poor-quality playdate fare. But this increased exposure means that more, not less, care and attention should follow. Your school-aged child will be very vulnerable to exactly the types of foods and behaviors that have led us into the obesity crisis that we now face.

Your support of his healthy habits will change somewhat at every age, but it is possible to offer some protective strategies now, while he is still quite young.

Protective Practices

One of the most efficient ways of protecting your child's natural eating habits is to instill in him the inherent connection between his food and the natural world. Right now, one of the primary challenges we are facing is a fundamental disconnect between nature and our food sources. If a child has no idea where his food comes from or what it looks like in its natural form, how can he be expected to differentiate between a blueberry and a blue bubble gum lollipop? And once he is older, why would he be motivated to protect our natural food resources if he has never been made aware of the vital link between real food and our personal and environmental well-being?

Teach your toddler where food comes from, how it is stored, and how it can be prepared and eaten in healthy ways. Continue to involve him in all aspects of food preparation, shopping, setting the table, cooking, and clean up throughout his entire childhood.

THE 80 PERCENT RULE

Over the years, your child will be spending more and more of his time away from home. Although you can definitively encourage good eating while he is gone (by packing nutritious lunches for school, for instance), you won't be able to keep him from being exposed to the wide world of junk food. Occasionally eating poor-quality food is not a problem for a natural eater. It is the foods we eat consistently, over time, that give us our true foundation. If you are feeding him well at home, he will be healthy and balanced, even if he has doughnuts at school. Think of it as the 80 percent rule: If he continues to eat well at least 80 percent of the time, chances are he'll be able to continue his natural eating habits for a lifetime.

MAKE THE CONNECTION

Toddlers learn by doing. Take them into nature and the world of natural food production for some fun adventures in the sunshine.

Food Field Trips

If you are lucky enough to live near any farms, look for some that offer petting zoos or hayrides. Today, because large-scale farming has become so industrialized, these classic types of child-friendly learning experiences, typically offered by smaller family-owned farms, are becoming scarce.

In the face of this dwindling resource, however, one thing that is definitely on the rise all over the country, even in large urban settings, is the farmers' market. New ones are sprouting up all the time, and they typically provide higher quality fresh foods than your supermarket—often organic and/or locally grown. Look for one in your area and take your child with you to peruse the stalls. Encourage her to notice how the vegetables and the fruits change as the seasons change. Use this USDA Web site to find a list of farmer's markets in your area: www.ams.usda.gov/farmersmarkets/map.htm.

You can also visit an orchard or a berry farm to pick your own seasonal fruit. If you create seasonal family rituals, your child will learn to link the fall with all things apple, for instance.

Seasonal Activities

There are so many seasonal activities you can do to instill a connection with the natural realm in your growing child. Here are some ideas.

Autumn theme: apples. Pick a large bushel of apples at your local orchard and play apple games (hang them on strings by their stems and have your toddler and his friends try to bite them off with no hands!). Use them in creative ways and get your toddler to help you with apple projects in the kitchen: applesauce, dried apples, apple pie, baked apples, apple pancakes, apple pizza, apple compote, apple-stuffed chicken, etc.

Other autumn theme ideas: harvest, cornucopias, pumpkin carving.

Winter theme: roasting. Haul out the roasting pan. Teach your child the basic technique of roasting and make a list of things you will prepare and roast together to stay toasty in the winter months: chestnuts, winter squashes, root vegetables, green vegetables, meats, etc.

Other winter theme ideas: preserves, root vegetables, stewing.

Spring theme: new shoots. With a package of vegetable seeds and a small bag of seedling soil mix, you can grow little seedlings with your toddler. Choose a plant that you can replant outside later in a small garden or a deck pot. Explain to her how new seedlings are "baby plants," and they need protection from the cold weather outside. Use recycled containers, if you can. They should be able to hold soil and drain water without disintegrating. They need to be only about 3 inches deep. Yogurt, sour cream, and cottage cheese containers are good choices, although square containers, such as juice or milk cartons cut in half, take up less space than round ones. Punch a few holes in the bottoms for drainage, and follow the directions on the package for planting.

Other spring theme ideas: seedlings, leafy greens, first fruits.

Summer theme: berry madness. Seek out a berry farm and pick your own strawberries, blueberries, or raspberries. If you don't have a nearby farm, consider planting a couple of berry bushes in your yard. You can also go on nature walks to hunt down wild-growing berries. But be sure to train your child never to eat anything growing in the wild without first showing it to you. Strawberry treats to make could include strawberry shortcake, strawberry jam, strawberry banana bread, cold strawberry soup, etc.

Other summer theme ideas: planting, watering, weeding.

The Magic of Seeds

If you are able to keep a food garden, even a small one, this will do more than probably anything else to instill a true understanding and appreciation for the link between nature and what we eat. It does not have to be a large garden: A window box of herbs is all you need to share the magic of seeds with your toddler. If you don't have any land or even a deck (for a potted garden), see if there is a community garden or growing co-op that you and your child could visit or join. Consult online resources, such as www.kidsgardening.org, for tips on home and school gardening.

Supporting Natural Eaters

Keeping your children connected with the origins of food and encouraging them to help with its preparation throughout their childhood are two key protective strategies.

Don't forget these additional core practices as your child continues to grow.

Keep a high-quality pantry. Remember, the very best way to get your children to eat healthy foods is to serve them nothing but healthy foods! As he grows, continue to keep your pantry and home stocked with a variety of healthy selections and free of anything you don't want your child to eat.

Don't set up food restrictions at home. Studies have shown us time and time again that forbidding foods makes children crave them more. Keep all offerings healthy and make them available.

Beat the dessert and sweets trap. Make any sweet treats part of their regular meal. Treats shouldn't be a premium. This will encourage naturally balanced behaviors around eating them. If their sweet treats are high-quality, nutritious options, it's fine to include them as a regular part of the meal, right on the dinnertime plate.

Eat your veggies. Your eating behaviors matter. Ultimately, your children will eat what you eat. Show them, consistently over time, that you eat a healthy balance of all foods, especially vegetables. To encourage this for both of you, keep your fruit and veggie offerings creative and tasty. As they grow up, those toddler shakers, dips, and spreads will continue to make grains, meat, and veggies more appealing to older kids: Consider keeping a regular stock on a lazy Susan that stays on your table.

Continue to offer new foods. Even 13- and 14-year-olds should be regularly encouraged to try new foods. Remember that it can take ten to fifteen offerings of something new before it actually gets tasted. Be persistent with your offerings, even when they are older. But never force the tasting. Bribing, demanding, or wheedling kids into eating something good for them is the surest way to get them to avoid it in the future!

Keep it unemotional. Presenting a neutral attitude toward food at the table may seem like an impossibility when you know the importance of healthy eating habits. But that is by far the best approach. Overemphasis on the food, either positive or negative, leads to imbalanced eating behaviors. Make healthy meals and snacks that your family can enjoy, and allow the food to be a regular integrated part of your daily lives together.

Less Screen, More Play

Today's children spend far too much time in front of television, computer, and gaming screens. Put some limits on the amount of time you allow him to sit and watch. This will both reduce the number of junk food ads he sees, and also stimulate him to play in other, more active ways. Encourage him to get outside as much as possible. Children who play outdoors in all seasons tend to be hardier, healthier kids than those who are glued to the tube for most of the day.

Favorite Activity for Toddler Chefs

We polled a group of toddler moms to discover what cooking activity they most enjoyed doing with their child. The number one answer was: making pizza! Homemade pizza is a perfect meal for family fun. The recipe is simple and versatile, and kids love to knead, punch, and roll out the dough. Everyone can top it any way they like, and it makes a very healthy and satisfying meal for the whole family—a far cry from take out! Following is a compilation of the best pizza-making tips we collected.

Preparation. It's a nice idea to get your child an apron for kitchen work—aprons are useful for cuing when the activity begins and when it is over, as well as keeping little pants and shirts flour- and smear-free. You can also find toddler-sized measuring spoons, wooden spoons, whisks, bowls, etc., but these aren't necessary: Even a 2-year-old can handle standard measuring cups and spoons.

Wash your hands thoroughly and lay out everything you will need beforehand: measuring and mixing tools, and all of the ingredients. The chef's phrase for this is mise en place—everything put in its place. Doing this first helps organize the cooking, and also prevents the discovery of missing a key ingredient halfway through the recipe—something you definitely want to avoid with an eager toddler chef! Create a little working station at a low table or a countertop with a sturdy stool for your toddler to stand on. You can lay out some newspaper on the counter or the floor to catch stray flour, if you wish.

Kitchen tools for pizza dough.
• Small mixing bowl
• Large mixing bowl
• Measuring spoons
• Liquid cup measure
• Solids cup measures
• One or two small wooden spoons
• Dough cutter or large fork
• Medium-sized mixing bowl (glass works well for dough to rise)
• Clean dish towel
• Baking sheets

Basic Pizza Crust

1 package dry yeast (about 2 teaspoons)
1½ cups warm water
3½ cups white whole-wheat flour (King Arthur makes a good one) or 2 cups whole wheat flour and 1½ cups white flour—plus more to flour surface and incorporate into dough while kneading
1 teaspoon salt
Olive oil
Avocado, sunflower, or (if no allergy) almond oil

Invite your toddler to join you, and the two of you can put on your aprons and wash your hands (again!) at the same time.

Have your toddler help you measure out the water and pour it into a small bowl. Snip the corner off the yeast packet and allow him to pour it into the water and stir gently with a wooden spoon until it dissolves. While he is stirring, you can spread a thin layer of flour over a smooth surface for kneading: A clean countertop or large cutting board works well.

Help your toddler measure out the flour and salt into the large mixing bowl. Have him mix them together well with a dry wooden spoon. Ask him to scoop out a well in the middle to make a place for the yeast water.

Together, gently pour the water into the well, making a little pool. Measure out about 2 tablespoons of olive oil and add them to the mix. Notice how it sits on top of the water's surface.

Working together, you and your toddler can slowly work the flour into the liquid. Use a dough cutter or a fork at first, switching to your hands if the mixture becomes too sticky. As the flour and liquid combine, it will become a dough.

Once the dough is formed, roll it out of the bowl and onto your floured surface. Begin the kneading process yourself, showing your child how to do it: pushing it down, rolling it over on itself, working all the edges, etc. When it gets too sticky, add more flour. Let your toddler give it a try. Alternate the kneading between the two of you for 10 to 15 minutes, adding extra flour when necessary, until the dough becomes very smooth and elastic, no longer sticky.

While your toddler is kneading, lightly coat the surface of the medium bowl with oil. When the dough is ready, roll it into a ball and place it in the bowl, rolling it around to coat the whole surface with oil. Lay the dish towel over the top and place the bowl in a warm area for it to rise.

It should take about an hour for it to double in size. Let your toddler take periodic peeks to check on the progress. Clean up your working area together—remind him that the clean up is an important part of cooking.

You may choose to bake your pizza in the oven, or grill it on an outside barbecue. In either case, you will need to preheat. One of the keys to great pizzas is a very hot oven. Set your oven temp to 500° F and preheat for at least 30 minutes; or set your grill to high and preheat thoroughly.

Topping Assembly
While the dough is rising, you can prepare the ingredients you will use for toppings. Just about anything can go on a pizza: Be creative with your choices! A tomato sauce base is definitely a favorite, but tomato sauce may still be a little too acidic for some toddlers. You can also try a pesto, peanut sauce (if no allergy concerns), or barbecue base. Vegetable purees can make good bases, too. Add any vegetables or meats you like—just make sure they are toddler friendly: bite-sized and precooked or softened (leave the jalapeños off theirs!). Grated mozzarella or other pizza cheese

is the classic topping, but again, it is not necessary. If you are using cheese, try feta, Gouda, or chevre for a new taste. You can also make a sweet pizza with sauces like honey or molasses, and fruits.

Work with your toddler to choose some toppings. You will need to do all the pre-cooking, chopping, or grating, but he can help you lay things out in little bowls.

Combo Ideas to Get You Started

- Tomato sauce, precooked mini-meatballs, chopped broccoli, and mixed cheese
- Pesto, thawed frozen corn (or cut raw from the fresh cob), and tomato slices
- Peanut sauce, shredded carrots, shredded zucchini, and shredded precooked chicken breast
- Honey, apple or pear slices, and goat cheese
- Barbecue sauce, cubed precooked chicken breast, caramelized onions, and Jack cheese

Making the Pizza

Once the dough has risen, flour your surface again and roll it out. Let your toddler punch down the dough to deflate it. Knead it for a couple more minutes and then divide it into four parts to make four medium thin-crust pizzas, or into six to make six smaller individual pizzas.

To make your pizza, gently stretch and pull one ball of dough with your hands. Before it begins to tear, lay it on the floured surface and show your toddler how to roll it out into a flat oval or a circle (depending on the pan you're using) with a floured rolling pin. Keep rolling it out, coming from different directions, until you have a nice thin crust, ½ to ¼-inch thick. Try to keep the dough from breaking apart or sprouting holes.

To Refrigerate or Freeze

You can store any dough you won't use right away in the refrigerator or the freezer. Roll it into balls for individual crusts, lightly oil the surfaces, and wrap them tightly in BPA-free plastic wrap for refrigerator storage. Most sources advise using refrigerated dough within 24 hours, but others say the yeast will hold for up to three days. To freeze, follow the same process, but double-wrap in freezer-safe plastic and store for up to 1 month. Thaw frozen pizza dough in the fridge overnight, then allow refrigerated pizza dough to rest on the counter at room temperature for 1 hour to lose its chill (it's much harder to roll out cold dough).

To Bake

Oil a baking sheet with a high-heat oil (such as avocado or sunflower) and gently lay the crust onto the pan. Show your toddler how to prick the surface in several places with a fork. Help him spread a small amount of sauce (enough to lightly cover the surface, leaving about ½ inch around the edge). Let him arrange any fruits, vegetables, meats, or nuts (if no allergy) you are using and sprinkle cheese on top, if desired.

Cook the pizza in the preheated oven for 12 to 15 minutes, or until toppings are cooked and the dough is crisp and lightly browned.

To Grill

Oil a flat cookie sheet (no edges) with a high-heat oil (such as avocado or sunflower) and gently lay the crust onto the pan. Lift or slide the pizza crust gently from the pan and lay it directly on your preheated grill. Grill crust for only 1 to 2 minutes, watching carefully to prevent scorching. Remove the crust using a spatula and flip it over back onto the cookie sheet so the grill marks are visible on top.

Place the toppings on the grilled side as directed for baking, and return the pizza to the grill. Cook for another 1 to 2 minutes or so, until the toppings are warmed and the crust is lightly browned and crisp.

After cooking, allow the pizzas to cool to desired temperature and then cut them into quarters or eighths like a pie. Serve and enjoy!

Resources

Baby Bottles

Baby Life: We Go
www.gobabylife.com/products/
weegobottle.html
Glass bottles protected with a silicone
sleeve to prevent breaking

Born Free Natural Baby Products
www.newbornfree.com
Glass and BPA-free plastic bottles,
built-in air vent to reduce colic,
pacifiers, and stainless steel sippy
cups

Dr. Brown's Natural Flow Bottles
www.handi-craft.com/products/
bottles.htm
Glass and polypropylene bottles with
unique internal vent to reduce air colic

Evenflo Classic Bottles
www.babyearth.com/evenflo-classic-
clear-glass-nursers-3pk-8oz-silicone.
html
Glass bottles with Micro Air Vents
to keep air out and prevent gas, and
EvenPace nipple system based on age

Green to Grow
www.greentogrow.com
Bisphenol-A-, phthalates-, lead-, and
PVC-free bottles made with PES
plastics. Can recycle bottles to help
others in need: bottlestobabies@
greentogrow.com

Phillips Avent Baby Bottles
www.avent.com
Patented anti-vacuum skirt valve that
prevents baby from swallowing air;
BPA-free feeding systems and bag
liners

**Think Baby: Safer Products for
Healthier Babies**
www.thinkbabybottles.com/team.htm
Bottles free of bisphenol-A,
nitrosamine, lead, PVS, and
phthalates; vented nipples

Baby Food

Bella Baby
www.bellababyfood.com
Convenient 1.5 ounce packets

Earth's Best Organic Baby and Toddler Foods
www.earthsbest.com
Organic jarred baby food first, second, third, baby cereals, biscuits formula, baby body care products

Gerber Organics Baby Foods
www.gerber.com
Organic jarred baby food, baby cereals

Happy Baby
www.happybabyfood.com
Available at Amazon.com, Whole Foods markets, and many national grocery stores

Homemade Baby Organic Baby Foods
www.homemadebaby.com
Refrigerated baby food, tracked from the field to where it was cooked; in three stages: So Smooth, Good Mushy, and Kinda Chunky

Jack's Harvest
www.jacksharvest.com
Frozen in 1- or 3-ounce heart-shaped cubes, available online and in Whole Foods Markets and various stores in the South

Nice Cubes
www.nicecubes.com
Frozen baby food cubes available in Oregon

Petite Palate Gourmet Organic Baby Food
www.petitepalate.com/pp/index.html
Frozen organic baby food—available at Amazon.com and metropolitan area markets

Plum Organics
www.plumorganics.com
Frozen organic kids meals—available at Whole Foods markets and Super Target nationwide

Tasty Baby
www.tastybaby.com
Prepared and frozen organic baby foods—available at Amazon.com, Whole Foods Markets, and some national grocery stores

Baby Food Cube Containers
My Precious Kid Child Safety Products
www.mypreciouskid.com/baby-food-cubes.html
PVC- and PABA-free baby food cubes with covers

KidCo Inc.
www.kidco.com
Kidco baby cube storage trays, food grinders, gates, etc.

One Step Ahead
www.onestepahead.com
Baby food cubes, insulated feeding pots, bottles, etc.

Organically Hatched
www.organicallyhatched.com
Baby cube trays, snack traps, snack container balls; BPA-, PVC-, and phthalate-free

Baby Food Mills
Beaba: Baby Cook
www.beabausa.com
Four-in-one steam cooker, blender

Dexbaby
www.dexproducts.com
Baby food processor, Milk Bank storage system, bottle warmers, grab-n-go hot pack

Fante's Kitchen Wares Shop
www.fantes.com/food-mills.html
A variety of food mills

Green Sprouts
www.greensproutsbaby.com
Food mills, plates and accessories,
bibs, sun protective clothing and
glasses

KidCo Inc.
www.kidco.com
Food mill, food storage containers,
and feeding dishes with sections that
match the food storage containers

The Wean Machine
www.theweanmachine.com
Food puree machine

Baby and Toddler Tooth Care

Baby Buddy
www.babybuddy.com
Pediatrician-recommended first infant
toothbrush

Nature's Gate
www.natures-gate.com/
Fluoride and fluoride-free toothpaste
(ages 2 years and up)

Safety First
www.safety1st.com/product/detail.
asp?ID=2565
Toothbrush with soft bristles for
sensitive teeth and gums, and soft
and ergonomically designed head and
handle

Things for Kids: The Angel Brush Toothbrush
www.firstbrush.com
Three uses in one: toothbrush, teether,
and gum massager

Tom's of Maine
www.tomsofmaine.com
Anti-cavity fluoride and fluoride-free
toothpaste

Blenders

Oster
www.oster.com
A variety of blenders, including food
processing blades and high-speed ice
crushing models

Vita-Mix
www.vitamix.com
High-powered blender in a variety
of models with BPA-free container
purees fruits and vegetables quickly,
prepares nut butters, soups, and more.

Bread

Food for Life
www.foodforlife.com
Ezekiel sprouted-grain breads and
tortillas

King Arthur Flour
www.kingarthurflour.com/shop/detail.
jsp?select=C74&byCategory=C396&i
d=3544
Whole-grain pizza crust mix

Rudi's Organic Bakery
www.rudisorganicbakery.com
High-fructose-corn syrup-and
trans fat–free multigrain oat bread,
cinnamon raisin bread, and spelt
ancient grain bread

Breast Pumps

Ameda
www.ameda.com
Breast pumps, parts, and soothing
pads

Medela
www.medelabreastfeedingus.com/
products/breast-pumps

Breast pumps, storage bags, freezing and storage products, and breastfeeding information

Breastfeeding

La Leche League International (LLLI)
www.llli.org
International organization offering comprehensive resources to support the breastfeeding mom

U.S. Department of Health and Human Services
www.womenshealth.gov/breastfeeding/index.cfm?page=home
Breastfeeding support and resources

Dairy and Soy

8th Continent
www.8thcontinent.com
Soy milk

Alden's Ice Cream
www.aldensicecream.com
Organic ice cream, lower in sugar than many other brands

Bufala di Vermont
www.bufaladivermont.com
Water buffalo's milk yogurt and buffalo mozzarella

Fage USA
www.fageusa.com
Authentic Greek yogurt and feta cheese

Lightlife
www.lightlife.com
Organic tempeh

Natural by Nature
www.natural-by-nature.com
Grass-fed, organic ricotta cheese, butter, milk, and sour cream

Organic Valley
www.organicvalley.coop
Stringles (string cheese), cream cheese, and milk

Redwood Hill Farm
www.redwoodhill.com
Goat's milk yogurt and cheeses (most organic, not 100 percent)

Rice Dream
www.tastethedream.com
Nondairy frozen desserts

Seven Stars Farm
www.sevenstarsfarm.com
Yogurt

Silk
http://silksoymilk.com
Soy milk and soy creamer

Stonyfield Farm
www.stonyfieldfarm.com
Organic yogurts, all-natural yogurts, smoothies, ice cream, frozen yogurt, and milk

Vitasoy
www.vitasoy-usa.com
Nasoya organic tofu

Wallaby Organic
www.wallabyyogurt.com
Flavored yogurt

Dried and Canned Beans

Eden Organic
www.edenfoods.com
Canned beans (BPA-free can liners, cooked with kombu for digestibility)

Shiloh Farms
www.shilohfarms.net
Beans, lentils, and peas

Fish

Aaron's Gourmet Emporium
www.aaronsgourmet.com
Wild salmon

Vital Choice Wild Seafood and Organics
www.vitalchoice.com
Wild salmon, salmon, burgers, canned wild fish, organic teas, seasoning, berries, nuts, and dried fruits

Food Allergies and Sensitivities

Allergic Child
www.allergicchild.com
Supporting for families and communities for working with severe food allergies

American College of Allergy, Asthma and Immunology
www.acaai.org
An information and news service for patients, parents of patients, members, media, and purchasers of health-care programs

Food Allergy and Anaphylaxis Network
www.foodallergy.org
Education information, advocacy, and advance research for people affected by food allergies and anaphylaxis

The Food Allergy Project: Saving Children's Lives
www.foodallergyproject.org
Researching for a cure, important surveys for affected families

Kids with Food Allergies: A World of Support
www.kidswithfoodallergies.org
Food allergy support community

Food Processors

Cuisinart
www.cuisinart.com
Food processors, mini-prep processors, blenders, and mixers

Food Safety

USDA Food Safety and Inspection Service
www.fsis.usda.gov/factsheets/
Resource information on food safety for child caregivers

Formulas

Baby's Only Organic Formula
www.naturesone.com/index.php
Dairy-, soy-, and lactose-free formula with Life's DHA trademark Martek Biosciences, oral electrolyte formulas, PediaVance, and toddler formulas

Earth's Best Organic Formula
http://www.earthsbest.com/products/infant-formula.php
Soy and infant formula contain DHA and ARA

Enfamil
www.enfamil.com
Carry formulas for babies with special needs and feeding problems. Enfamil Lipil contains DHA and ARA

Parents Choice Baby Formula
www.parentschoiceformula.com
Gentle, organic, sensitive, milk, soy, lactose-free, and Stage 2 toddler formula, available at Wal-mart

Similac
www.similac.com
Formulas for babies with feeding issues, premature babies; Early Shield formula for immune support

Freezer-Safe Wraps

Glad: Food Storage Solutions
www.glad.com
Look for #4 Glad Cling Wrap, food
storage bags, freezer bags, and
sandwich bags; and #5 GladWare
containers and GladWare Store'N Eat
Microwave safe

**Green Feet: The Planet's Home
Store**
www.greenfeet.com
PVC- and BPA-free plastic wrap and
bags, wax paper bags, unbleached
wax paper cups, lunch-on-the-go food
containers, mesh produce bags, salad
bags, bento boxes, and more

Hefty Brand Products
http://heftybrands.pactiv.com
Look for #4 Hefty Baggies and Hefty
OneZip slider bags

Saran Simple Solutions
www.saranbrands.com/plastic-wrap/
Look for #4 Saran Cling Plus wrap

**Ziploc Food Storage Bags and
Containers**
www.ziploc.com
Look for #4 Ziploc bags and Ziploc
Double Guard Freezer bags; and #5
Ziploc Snap 'n Seal and Ziploc Table
Tops bowls

Freezing

**USDA Food Safety and Inspection
Service**
www.fsis.usda.gov/FactSheets/Focus_
On_Freezing/index.asp
Fact sheets on freezing and food
safety

Frozen Fruits and Vegetables

Alexia Foods
www.alexiafoods.com
Sweet potato fries and oven crinkles

Cascadian Farm
www.cascadianfarm.com
Frozen fruits and vegetables

Woodstock Farms
www.woodstock-farms.com
Organic frozen fruit, vegetables,
canned tomatoes, dried fruits

Frozen Toddler Dinners

Amy's Kitchen
www.amys.com
Pizza, rice bowls, enchiladas, and
burritos

Boca
www.bocaburger.com
Vegetarian burgers and breakfast
patties

Dr. Praeger's
www.drpraegers.com
Breaded fish fillets

Happy Bites
www.happybitesfood.com
Various frozen meals, such as fish
bites, salmon stix, breakfast pockets,
etc.

Health Is Wealth
www.healthiswealthfoods.com
Antibiotic-free chicken nuggets with
whole wheat breading

Morningstar Farms
www.morningstarfarms.com
Soy crumbles, meatless grillers, and
other meat alternatives

Wellshire Farms
www.wellshirefarms.com
Gluten-free chicken bites

Gardening with Children
Ed Hume Seeds
www.humeseeds.com/kids.htm
Children's indoor gardening activities

National Gardening Association
www.kidsgardening.com
Information on the benefits of youth
gardening and resources and activities
for parents and schools

Nature Moms
www.naturemoms.com/seed-
suppliers-list.html
List of many organic seed companies

Organicasm
www.organiccoupons.org/
blog/2008/07/greener-thumb-100-
resources-to-grow-your-own-organic-
fruits-and-vegetables/
One hundred resources to grow your
own organic fruits and vegetables

Gluten-Free
Amy's Kitchen
www.amys.com
Gluten-free rice pizza crust and
prepared foods

Bionaturae
www.bionaturae.com
Gluten-free pasta

Bob's Red Mill
www.bobsredmill.com
Gluten-free flour

Dr. Schar
www.schar.com
Crackers, cookies, pasta, mixes, and
coatings

Gluten Free.com
www.glutenfree.com
Partnered with Glutino and Gluten
Free pantry, Web site offers various
gluten-free baked goods, mixes,
pastas, cereals, soups

Ian's Natural Foods
www.iansnaturalfoods.com
Ian's allergen-free (WF/GF Recipe)
food products designed for kids
with special dietary needs including
breakfasts, entrees, snacks and fries.

Pamela's Products
www.pamelasproducts.com
Wheat- and gluten-free baking and
pancake mixes

Tinkyada
www.tinkyada.com
Wheat- and gluten-free pasta

Wellshire Farms
www.wellshirefarms.com
Gluten-free chicken bites

Grains, Rice, Pasta, Flour, and Cereals
Annie's Homegrown
www.annies.com
Whole wheat pasta and whole-grain
macaroni and cheese

Arrowhead Mills
www.arrowheadmills.com
Ancient grains, beans, pancake mix,
and nut butters

Back to Nature
www.backtonaturefoods.com
Cereals and granola

Barbara's Bakery
www.barbarasbakery.com
Whole-grain, low-sugar sweet cereals
(also low-sugar animal crackers,
granola, and cereal bars)

Barilla
www.barillaus.com
Barilla Plus Penne (enriched
multigrain pasta)

Bob's Red Mill
www.bobsredmill.com
Organic steel-cut oats, 10-grain hot
cereal, and whole grains

Country Choice Organic
www.countrychoiceorganic.com
Steel-cut and quick old-fashioned oats

Eden Organic
www.edenfoods.com
Organic grains

Health Valley
www.healthvalley.com
Cereals and cereal bars

Hodgson Mill
www.hodgsonmill.com
All-natural flours, cornmeal, baking
mixes, pancake mix, whole wheat
pastas, and veggie pastas

Kashi
www.kashi.com
Kashi Mighty Bites cereal and TLC
crackers and bars

Lundberg
www.lundberg.com
Assorted whole-grain rice, rice cakes,
and rice chips

Mr. Krispers
www.mr.krispers.com
Baked Rice Krisps, certified gluten-free

Nature's Path Organic
www.naturespath.com
Pasta and granola bars

Rice Select
www.riceselect.com
Organic and nonorganic rice products,
including Texmati

Infant and Toddler Nutrition

American Academy of Pediatrics
www.aap.org/healthtopics/nutrition.
cfm
Family and community information on
nutrition

American Dietetic Association
www.eatright.org/cps/rde/xchg/ada/
hs.xsl/nutrition_12541_ENU_HTML.htm
Book references and resources on
childhood nutrition

Integrative Pediatrics Council
www.holisticmedicine.org
Covers all aspects of well-being,
with national listing of integrative
pediatricians who provide
comprehensive holistic care to
children and families

MyPyramid
www.nal.usda.gov/fnic/pubs/bibs/gen/
toddler.pdf
Resources for child nutrition and
health through the life cycle

**Produce for Better Health
Foundation**
www.fruitsandveggiesmorematters.
org; www.5aday.org
Education, recipes, and resources
for families in support of increased
vegetable consumption
www.foodchamps.org
Children's education site with fruit
and veggie activities and recipes

U.S. Department of Agriculture
www.fns.usda.gov/tn/Resources/
feeding_infants.pdf
Guide to making baby food at home

USDA Nutrient Data Laboratory
www.nal.usda.gov/fnic/foodcomp/
search/
A comprehensive search engine that
provides reliable nutrient information
on almost any food

WholesomeBabyFood.com
www.wholesomebabyfood.com
Excellent resource for making quality
baby foods at home

Kids' Aprons and Cooking Tools
All Heart Chefs
www.allheartchefs.com
Kids' aprons (embroidery available)
and table setting supplies

Chocolate Cake Club
www.chocolatecakeclub.com
Kids' cooking kits, placemats, and tea
sets

Growing Cooks
www.growingcooks.com
Kids' cookware and cooking supplies,
tea party sets and cooking party kits

Meal Kits
The Healthy Pantry
www.thehealthypantry.com
Homemade recipe kits for the family
with primarily organic and non-
genetically-modified ingredients, can
be prepared with an item or two from
your fridge, all chopping, measuring,
and seasoning done for you

Seeds of Change
www.seedsofchange.com
Quinoa seed mixes

Shiloh Farms
www.shilohfarms.net
Grains, cereals, spelt pretzels, and rice

Mealtime Grace
About.com
www.entertaining.about.com/cs/
etiquette/a/sayinggrace.htm
Nonsectarian information about
mealtime grace

100 Graces: Mealtime Blessings
by Marcia M. Kelly and Jack Kelly
Book with 100 different ways to take a
pause before eating to give thanks

Meat and Poultry
Aaron's Gourmet Emporium
www.aaronsgourmet.com
Chicken, turkey, duck, and other
grass-fed meat

Applegate Farms
www.applegatefarms.com
Cold cuts, bacon, hot dogs, and
chicken nuggets without nitrates,
antibiotics, or chemical preservatives

Bell and Evans
www.bellandevans.com
Free-range, antibiotic and hormone
free organic chicken and turkey;
gluten-free nuggets, air chilled

Coleman Natural
www.colemannatural.com
Antibiotic-, hormone-, and
preservative-free, vegetarian-fed beef
and chicken, and pork sausage

Eberly Poultry
www.eberlypoultry.com
Free-range chicken and turkey

Grateful Harvest
www.albertsorganics.com
Grass-fed beef

Laura's Lean Beef
www.laurasleanbeef.com
Cattle never given antibiotics or added
growth hormones

Murray's Chicken
www.murrayschicken.com
Antibiotic- and hormone-free chicken,
turkey, and sausage

Niman Ranch
www.nimanranch.com
Humanely raised meats on sustainable
farms; no antibiotics or hormones
used

Plainville Farms
www.plainvillefarms.com
All-natural, hormone-free, antibiotic-
free ground turkey and full line of deli
products

Shelton's Premium Poultry
www.sheltons.com
Free-range chicken and turkey,
antibotic and hormone-free; canned
chicken, ground turkey and chicken,
gluten-free broth, burgers

Wholesome Harvest
www.wholesomeharvest.com
Organic chicken, turkey, beef, pork

Natural Food Coloring, Candy, and Decorations
Edward and Sons
www.edwardandsons.com/let_do_
organic.html
Let's Do…Sprinkelz: organic, colorful
sprinkle decorations with all natural
ingredients

India Tree
www.indiatree.com
Nature's Colors decorating sugars and
products using natural colorants and
no trans fats

Naturesflavors.com
www.naturesflavors.com/product_
info.php?cPath=72&products_id=4313
Nature's Rainbow Natural Color Pack
all-natural food colorings

Sunspire
www.sunspire.com
Chocolate bars, grain-sweetened
chocolate chips, and baking SunDrops

Vita Muffin
Low-fat, high-fiber, and high-nutrient
baked goods using natural ingredients
www.vitalicious.com

Online Grocery Delivery Services
A&P Online and Delivery Service
shop.apsupermarket.
com/#1+0+H+N+N
Online grocery shopping and delivery
service

Net Grocer.com
www.netgrocer.com
Groceries delivered to your door

Pea Pod Delivery Service
www.peapod.com
Grocery delivery service with Stop &
Shop and Giant

Ziplist
www.ziplist.com
Online grocery list: categorizes your
list, prioritizes items, and creates
recipe section. Use through smart
phones.

Plastics
The Green Guide
www.thegreenguide.com/products/
Kitchen/Plastic_Containers
A comprehensive listing of safe and
unsafe plastic products by brand

Premade Whole-Grain Pizza Dough and Crusts

Amy's Kitchen
www.amys.com
Frozen rice-crust pizza (gluten-free)

King Arthur Flour
www.kingarthurflour.com/shop/detail.
jsp?select=C74&byCategory=C396&i
d=3544
Whole-grain pizza crust mix

Trader Joe's
www.traderjoes.com
Range of healthy, organic ingredients
reasonably priced.

Rice Cookers

Kimchi
www.kimchius.com
Rice cookers

Sanyo
us.sanyo.com
Basic rice cookers, including Sanyo
model ECJ-N55W (highly rated and
reasonably priced)

Zojurishi
www.zojirushi.com/ourproducts/
ricecookers/ns_zcc.html
A variety of rice cookers, steamers,
warmers, most with timers, bento
boxes, and thermal lunch jars

Safe Food Storage Containers

Anchor Hocking
www.anchorhocking.com
Glass storage containers

Pyrex
www.pyrex.com
Pyrex food storage containers

Safe Vegetable Washes

Beaumont Products, Inc.
www.veggie-wash.com
Fruit and vegetable organic citrus
wash, 100 percent natural

Mom's Veggie Wash
www.veggiewash.com
Safe, nontoxic, inert liquid surfactants
that contain no animal products,
perfumes, preservatives, or colorants

Vegetarian/Veganism

American Dietetic Association
www.eatright.org/cps/rde/xchg/ada/
hs.xsl/advocacy_933_ENU_HTML.htm
American Dietetic Association
position on vegetarian diets, nutrient
information, and food sources

USDA Vegetarian Nutrition Resource List
www.nal.usda.gov/fnic/pubs/bibs/gen/
vegetarian.pdf
Multiple listings for reliable vegetarian
resources

The Vegetarian Resource Group
www.vrg.org
Nutrition information and vegetarian
recipes

Glossary

5-A-Day campaign A public message developed by the government to encourage Americans to eat at least 5 portions of fruits and vegetables per person per day to help reduce the risk of cancer, heart disease, and other chronic illnesses.

Acetic acid The ingredient found in vinegar that acts as a cleaning agent. Vinegar can be used to clean molds and pesticides off of foods, as a fabric softener for clothes, and as a natural substitute for window cleaners like Windex.

Alpha-carotene A precursor to vitamin A and part of the family of carotenoids. Found in red vegetables and dark leafy greens.

American Dietetic Association (ADA) The United States' largest organization of food and nutrition professionals. While a majority of ADA's members are registered dietitians, other members include researchers, educators, students, clinical and community dietetics professionals, consultants, and food service managers.

Amino acids The building blocks of proteins and intermediates in metabolism. There are ten essential amino acids, which humans can produce in their bodies. The other ten are called non-essential amino acids.

Amniotic fluid The liquid within the uterus of a pregnant woman in which the fetus lives until birth. Amniotic fluid consists mostly of water and serves as a protective shock absorber for the fetus while it is developing.

Anaphylaxis An extreme allergic reaction that can be fatal. Symptoms present within a few hours of eating a food and may include hives, wheezing, difficulty breathing, swelling of the lips, tongue, or mouth area, diarrhea, vomiting, belly pain, or unconsciousness.

Anodized aluminum A sealed form of aluminum used in pans that is safer than Teflon nonstick pans. The aluminum is oxidized to form a strong coating as it replaces the original aluminum on the surface, and the result is an extremely hard substance. The aluminum in non-stick Teflon pans have been shown to break down in high heat, resulting in the emission of harmful toxic particles.

Anti-vacuum or vented nipples Nipples that contain a tube or vent to remove any excess air. Aid in preventing colic and regurgitation.

Apgar scoring A method of scoring immediately after birth that can determine whether or not an infant requires additional medical care. APGAR is an acronym for **A**ctivity (including muscle tone), **P**ulse (heart rate), **G**rimace (a reflex response of irritability), **A**ppearance (skin color), and **R**espiration (breathing rate and effort to breathe). The test is given 1 minute after birth, and then again 5 minutes after birth. Sometimes if there is a concern about the baby's condition and the first two scores are low, a third test may be performed 10 minutes after birth. A baby who scores 7 or above on the first test is considered to be in good health.

ARA (arachidonic acid) An omega-6 fatty acid that, in small amounts, is essential for bodily functions, including brain, eye, and nervous system. Research suggests that increasing amounts in infancy may reduce the risk of developmental problems later in life. It is important to note that too much ARA (omega-6) without the balance of DHA and EPA (omega-3) can create a pro-inflammatory state. Corn oils and meats are examples of arachidonic acid.

Asthma A chronic condition involving the lungs and respiratory system in which the airways will sometimes constrict, become inflamed, and be lined with excessive amounts of mucus. This is usually in response to one or more triggers by such things as cold, warm or moist air, exposure to an environmental stimulant such as an allergen, cigarette smoke, perfume, pet dander, exercise, extreme exertion, or even emotional stress. This airway narrowing causes symptoms such as wheezing, shortness of breath, chest tightness, and coughing. The symptoms of asthma can be mild, moderate, or even life threatening, and are usually controlled with environmental changes, nutritional supplements, drugs, or a combination of these. In children, some of the more common triggers are viral illnesses such as those that cause the common cold.

Baby fat The extra fat that an infant or young child may carry before a growth spurt in the toddler years.

Baby food cube A cube of food (usually the size of an ice cube) that is frozen and stored for future use. Baby food cubes allow you to cook extra batches of food and save them for future meal preparation. They are also convenient and helpful when planning a child's meals.

Bacteria Microscopic organisms that are largely responsible for foodborne illnesses. A type of bacteria called *pathogenic bacteria* grows rapidly on foods in temperatures between 40° F and 140° F, making the food dangerous to eat, although it may smell and look fine. When foods are left out too long or removed from the freezer to thaw outside of the refrigerator, they may develop this type of bacteria. *E. coli* O157:H7, *Campylobacter*, and *Salmonella* are examples of pathogenic bacteria.

Batching Cooking large amounts of food, and then freezing or storing extra portions of it for use at a later date.

Beta-carotene A precursor to vitamin A and part of the family of carotenoids.

Blood sugar The body's primary source of fuel. Also called blood glucose.

BMI or body mass index A measure of body fat based on height and weight. It is a useful tool in assessing a healthy weight for an individual based on their height and is defined as the individual's body weight divided by the square of their height. BMI has become a widely used tool in the identification of obesity, although it does have a major shortcoming in that it does not take into consideration the muscle-to-fat ratio of an individual. Thus, someone with a high amount of lean body mass (e.g., athletes) may wrongly be classified as overweight, while others with subnormal amounts of lean body mass (e.g., elderly) may be wrongly classified as being at a healthy weight. For children and teens, BMI is age- and sex-specific and is often referred to as BMI-for-age, due to the fact that the amount of body fat changes with age and differs between boys and girls.

Bottle brush Cleaning instrument specifically designed to clean the inside of bottles.

Bottle drying rack Additional rack in the dishwasher for placing baby bottles. Avoids loss of various bottle parts.

Botulism Foodborne illness caused from eating canned foods containing the toxin produced by an anaerobic bacterium known as *Clostridium botulinum*. This organism is usually associated with improperly canned foods.

BPA-free plastic Plastic that is free of the chemical bisphenol-A (BPA), widely in plastic containers, water bottles, toys, and baby bottles (to name a few). This chemical has been shown to leach potentially harmful levels into foods and cause developmental, neural, and reproductive problems. BPA mimics the action of the human hormone estrogen, and its exposure to humans is widespread. Many companies are now working toward removing BPA from their products.

Breast pads Round absorbent pads placed over the nipple to prevent leakage.

Breast pump A manual or electric device that helps extract milk from the breasts during periods in which the baby is not nursing.

Breastfeeding The act of a baby extracting milk through suckling from the mother's breasts for nourishment.

Breastmilk The milk produced by a female, which is fed to infants through breastfeeding. It is considered the best source of nutrition for babies as its nutrients help protect the child against infections and reduce the rates of future health problems, such as diabetes, obesity, and asthma.

Calorie A unit of energy-producing potential contained in food. A Nutrition Facts label lists the measurement or amount of energy in a serving of food. For example, there are about 110 calories in 1 cup (8 fluid ounces) of orange juice. The average recommended intake of calories for a healthy adult is 2,000 to 2,400 calories per day. Calories for children between birth and 1 year of age are estimated by calculating 90 to 120 calories per kilogram of weight per day. One- to 3-year-old children should eat an average of 1,300 calories per day, and children 4 and older should eat about 1,800 calories per day.

Carbohydrates Macronutrients that provide the primary source of fuel. Also called glucose or blood sugar. Found in milk sugar (lactose), complex carbohydrates like whole grains, legumes, and vegetables.

Childhood cancer Cancers in children originate primarily from noninherited mutations in the genes of growing cells. These types of cancers affect approximately 14 out of every 100,000 children in the United States each year, and the most common cancers are leukemia, lymphoma, and brain cancer. Teens are also more susceptible to bone cancer. Symptoms can vary widely and resemble other childhood illnesses: fever, swollen glands, frequent infections, anemia, or bruises. The good news is that, according to the Nemours Foundation, approximately 70 percent of childhood cancers can be cured today because of medical advances.

Childhood cardiovascular disease A condition that has been increasing over the past two decades due to the increase in childhood **body mass index** (BMI). Presently, 17 percent of children have a BMI of 95 percent and higher, and approximately one-third of all youth have a BMI of 85 percent and higher. Cardiovascular disease includes high blood pressure and atherosclerosis (high cholesterol). According to a recent study, children ages 7 through 13 had a greater risk of cardiovascular disease as adults if they were overweight. The goal is to prevent childhood obesity as young as possible, by teaching good nutrition and healthy eating habits, while also encouraging children to exercise.

Childhood overweight and obesity According to the Centers for Disease Control and Prevention (CDC), overweight is defined as having a BMI of between the eighty-fifth and ninety-fifth percentile, with obese is defined as having a BMI equal to or greater than the ninety-fifth percentile for children of the same age and sex.

Colic Regular extended bouts of crying in a young baby. This is attributed to an immature nervous system or being highly sensitive.

Colostrum Early milk, produced in the breast immediately after birth of the infant. Colostrum quantities last for a few days. Very rich in protein and antibodies to help boost the baby's immune system.

CPR (cardiopulmonary resuscitation) An emergency procedure that is performed to maintain the circulation of oxygen to the brain. This is usually performed if someone is experiencing a heart attack.

DHA (docosahexaenoic acid) An omega-3 essential fatty acid most noted for brain development and retinal development in infants. DHA is considered an anti-inflammatory essential fatty acid.

Diabetes, type 1 Also known as insulin-dependent diabetes; a chronic (lifelong) disease that occurs when the pancreas does not produce enough of the hormone insulin to properly control blood-sugar levels.

Diabetes, type 2 Also known as noninsulin-dependent diabetes; a chronic disease marked by high levels of sugar in the blood. It occurs when the body does not respond correctly to insulin, a hormone released by the pancreas that controls the amount of sugar in the blood.

Dietary Guidelines for Americans Developed by the Department of Health and Human Services and the Department of Agriculture, the Dietary Guidelines for Americans is a comprehensive and authoritative collection of advice for humans, 2 years and older, about the benefits of good dietary habits. These guidelines also provide the foundation for the Federal food and nutrition education programs. The guidelines are published every 5 years. For more information, you can visit the Web site at www.health.gov/DietaryGuidelines/dga2005.

Divided plates Breakfast, lunch, or dinnerware made specifically for children. The plates divide food into different food categories. Plates are usually divided into thirds and parents usually use each third for a meat or protein, vegetable or fruit, and a starch. Children who are picky eaters or who do not like their foods to touch enjoy these plates. A wide variety of plates are available at www.kidsplates.com.

Electrolytes Minerals that help to keep bodily fluids in balance, for optimal nerve function and muscle movement.

Engorgement A condition that develops when the breast is too full of milk. This creates an uncomfortable feeling, but can be relieved with more frequent nursings.

Extended nursing Breastfeeding an infant beyond 12 months of age.

Extrusion reflex (also called tongue-thrust reflex) The natural process by which infants push food out with their tongues. This reflex prevents them from choking.

Factory farmed If a meat or fish does not carry a label saying "organic," "natural," or "wild caught," it is most likely farmed in the conventional manner known as factory farmed. Factory farming is the raising of fish and livestock (including cows, laying hens, broiler chickens, pigs, veal calves, etc.) indoors throughout most of their lives. Animals are fed grains such as genetically modified corn, with no restrictions on pesticides, herbicides, fungicides, and fertilizers. Their living conditions allow for very limited movement, and they may be fed growth hormones, sprayed with fungicides, and fed antibiotics in an attempt to avoid potential diseases that may arise from crowded living conditions. From a nutritional viewpoint, farmed fish provide lower amounts of beneficial omega-3 fats than wild caught fish.

Fats or fatty acids Macronutrients that help maintain healthy immune function, hair, and skin health are vital for energy and normal development; support the digestive tract, blood, nerves, and arteries; and protect against heart disease. Fats also lubricate and protect the organs.

Feeding readiness The point at which a child is ready to begin eating solid foods, usually between 4 and 6 months of age. A baby who is ready to eat will offer physical cues to communicate readiness.

Fiber Carbohydrates that the body does not digest, which help with elimination. Also helps prevent blood-sugar spikes and bind up toxins for elimination. There are two forms of fiber: soluble and insoluble. Soluble fiber (present in legumes, fruits, etc.) dissolves in water. Insoluble fiber (present in whole grains, vegetables, fruit skins, etc.) does not dissolve in water.

Finicky eater A child who has a limited palate and will eat only a restricted amount of foods because of issues with taste or texture.

Fluorosis A condition that causes discoloration and pitting of the teeth due to an intake of excessive fluorides. Whitish spots on the teeth may appear as a result of ingesting too much fluoride toothpaste, drinking tap water that is fluorinated, or ingesting fluoride tablets.

Food and Drug Administration (FDA) An agency of the United States Department of Health and Human Services that is responsible for the safety regulation of most types of foods, dietary supplements, drugs, vaccines, and other areas related to human health.

Food allergies An overreaction of the body's immune system, brought on by a food that the body views as an irritant. Food allergies can bring on immediate reactions like hives and anaphylactic shock.

Foodborne illness A sickness caused by eating food or drinking liquids contaminated with bacteria, viruses, or parasites. Foodborne illnesses can cause symptoms that range from an upset stomach to more serious symptoms, including diarrhea, fever, vomiting, abdominal cramps, and dehydration. Most foodborne infections are undiagnosed and unreported, though the Centers for Disease Control and Prevention estimates that every year about 76 million people in the United States become ill from pathogens or disease-causing substances in food—about 5,000 people.

Food hypersensitivities An overreaction of the body's immune system to a particular food, but with a 24- to 72-hour delay in symptoms. Food hypersensitivities are difficult to pinpoint, and a food elimination diet is often recommended in order to determine the trigger food(s).

Formula A substitute for human breastmilk, designed for infant consumption. There are many different infant formulas on the market, and the one you choose will most likely depend on its ingredients, and how well your baby responds to them. Finding the right formula will take some investigative work (compare expensive brands as well as store brands), but the best way to choose is through trial and error: A baby may react differently to each type of formula, as some are formulated to help with digestion, some are soy based, and many are cow's-milk based. A baby who seems uncomfortable, gassy, or fussy after feeding may have a lactose sensitivity, or may not be able to digest that particular formula well.

Fruitarians Vegetarians who choose to eat only fruit, seeds, and nuts.

Gastroesophageal reflux (or reflux) The process by which milk is regurgitated after a feeding. This is normal for infants and usually declines as the baby grows and develops.

Glucose Also called blood sugar; it is the body's primary source of fuel.

Grazing Eating small portions of food in place of a full-sized meal, or to snack during the course of the day in place of regular meals.

Heimlich maneuver An action that pushes air from the lungs in an effort to release a blocked object.

Heme A type of iron present in flesh foods such as beef, poultry, fish, and shellfish.

High blood pressure (or hypertension) Blood pressure that is chronically elevated; in an adult, it is defined as blood pressure greater than or equal to 140 mmHg systolic pressure (the force in the arteries when the heart beats) or greater than or equal to 90 mmHg diastolic pressure (when the heart is at rest).

High cholesterol A condition of too much cholesterol (a waxy, fatlike substance), which deposits in the walls of the arteries that supply oxygen to the heart. Also called atherosclerosis, this can lead to heart attack and other forms of heart disease. A desirable cholesterol is 200mg/dl or lower.

Hind milk The milk toward the end of the feeding, rich in fat, which provides satiety and fullness.

Homocysteine An amino acid that, in a healthy balance in the body, helps with metabolism and building proteins. High levels of homocysteine, however, may contribute to heart disease risk by damaging blood vessel linings and increasing clotting action of the blood.

Honey A sweet fluid produced by bees. Raw, organic honey is full of vitamins and antioxidants, and has been used for centuries to alleviate some symptoms of the common cold. In fact, it has been shown—as early as the ninth century BC—to have wonderful medicinal properties, especially for children. However, raw honey—or any honey, for that matter—should not be given to children under 1 year of age because it may contain *Chlorstridium botulinum*, a deadly bacterium more commonly known as botulism. If this bacterium enters the digestive tract of a young child, it can produce a toxin that causes botulism, which is rare, but sometimes deadly.

Hydrogenation The process of solidifying an oil by adding a hydrogen atom. Hydrogenation makes foods more shelf stable.

Infant rice cereal The first type of cereal introduced for infants around 4 months of age. Recommended first food by the American Academy of Pediatrics.

Invisible nutrition Adding healthy foods into a child's meal without the child realizing it in order to boost certain nutrients.

Iron-deficiency anemia The most common type of anemia. Occurs when either the dietary intake or the absorption of iron is insufficient. When this happens, hemoglobin in the blood cannot be formed. Twenty percent of all women of childbearing age have iron deficiency anemia.

Junk food Foods that have a high number of calories and a low concentration of nutrients. Also called empty calories. They may also contain many chemicals, additives, artificial ingredients, sugar, and salt.

Kangaroo care Covering a baby or holding a baby close to the mother. Often called pouching. This gives the baby a sense of comfort and peace. Often used with preemies.

Lacto-vegetarians Vegetarians who will not eat animal products but will eat dairy.

Lacto-ovo vegetarians Vegetarians who will not eat animal products but will eat both eggs and dairy products.

Latex nipples Light brown, softer than silicone. They wear out faster than silicone.

Letdown A reflex by which the mother's milk is released or let down so that the baby may be nourished by it. Upon placing an infant at the breast, the infant will begin to suckle, and this sucking action stimulates the nerve endings at the mother's nipple, which in turn causes a gland in the breast to produce a hormone called prolactin. This hormone then signals the breast to produce milk.

Macronutrients Nutrients that are needed in large quantities by humans. Carbohydrates, proteins, and fats are considered categories of macronutrients.

Mastitis Infection of the breast, usually due to a blocked breast duct, long-term engorgement, or yeast or thrush infection.

Meat thermometer A tool for measuring internal temperatures of all types of meat. The meat thermometer ensures that meat is heated to a degree that will destroy potentially harmful bacteria, like *E. coli* O157:H7 and *Salmonella*. It also helps prevent overcooking.

Micronutrients Nutrients, such as vitamins, minerals, and trace minerals, that are needed in small quantities by humans.

Minerals The chemical elements, such as chromium, potassium, and chromium, required by humans. Many minerals play a role in the structure and function of each cell.

Modeling Offering up a good example to children (or others) so that they might be influenced to act in the same way. Parents are often the best role models for children, and their actions will affect how children eat, play, and socialize in a variety of situations. Children naturally pick up on their parents' behavior and mimic it, so parents must lead by example. This is especially true in terms of healthy eating behavior.

MyPyramid An eating and exercise guide developed by the U.S. Department of Agriculture. MyPyramid offers general guides for optimal nutrition by food categories.

Natural According to the Food Safety and Inspection Service's (division of the USDA) guidelines, the word *natural* on meat and poultry products means that the products cannot contain artificial flavor, coloring, or preservatives and cannot be more than minimally processed. In addition, the "natural" label also must explain why the term was used, stating, for example, that a product was minimally processed. This definition refers only to how the meat is processed, not to the way the animals were raised.

Natural eating Eating according to our human genetic programming, as in how our Paleolithic ancestors ate. Healthy eating is based on internal cues for hunger, satiety, and certain foods.

Nipple and ring cage Additional rack in the dishwasher, used to contain small bottle parts, including nipples.

Nonheme A type of iron present in plant foods. It is more absorbable than heme, but intake requirements are higher.

Nursing bra A bra that is specially designed for nursing mothers, which detaches over each breast so that the whole bra does not have to be removed or lifted up.

Omega-3 An essential fatty acid that is critical for infant brain and retina development. Babies whose diet includes omega-3 fats have been shown in studies to have better attention spans by age 2 than those babies who did not get adequate omega-3s. Omega-3—specifically DHA—is naturally found in breastmilk. Omega-3s—both DHA and EPA—are found in fish.

Omega-6 An important essential fatty acid, also known as GLA. It is found in evening primrose oil, borage oil, black currant oil, and hemp seed oil. Breastmilk also naturally contains GLA. Most infants who are not breastfed are deficient in the enzyme that helps to metabolize GLA, that may lead to such conditions as eczema and neural membrane issues.

Organic Foods labeled "organic" are produced according to standardized guidelines without the use of conventional fungicides, pesticides, and artificial fertilizers; livestock and fish are not treated with growth hormones or excessive antibiotics. In addition, organic foods may not be genetically modified or processed with radiation or chemical additives.

Outlet covers Plastic covers that fit over electrical wall outlets to protect children from electrical shock.

Overstimulating Providing an excessive amount of stimulation and excitement.

Ovo-vegetarians Vegetarians who will not eat most animal products but will eat eggs.

Oxalic acid A substance in some calcium-rich plant foods that inhibits the absorption of calcium. Found in high concentrations in spinach, beet greens, Swiss chard, and parsley.

Oxytocin Immediately following childbirth (within the first few hours), this hormone is produced to help stimulate the uterus to contract and return to its original size. Oxytocin causes the cells around the nipple (called the alveoli) to contract and eject milk down into the milk ducts, preparing the breasts for feeding. This hormone is also secreted when a baby and mother come together, in skin-to-skin contact, making mothers feel relaxed, contented, and less anxious. For this reason it is often called the love hormone.

Partially hydrogenated oils Man-made oils that are hardened (saturated) using a manufacturing process and that contain unhealthy trans fats.

Pasteurization The process of heating liquids for the purpose of destroying bacteria, molds, and yeasts. This process destroys all disease-producing organisms, including *E. coli* O157:H7.

Pasteurized Food that has a reduced and safe level of pathogens, due to the heating of the liquid by the **pasteurization** process.

Pedialyte A drink, specifically designed for children, to help restore electrolyte balance after a bout of diarrhea or vomiting.

Perishable items Food items that, if not refrigerated, will develop bacteria and pathogens that may be harmful for human consumption. Examples of perishable items are meats, poultry, fish, cooked vegetables, dairy products, and eggs. Most of these foods are naturally contaminated with pathogens, so the general rule is to heat them to temperatures high enough to kill off pathogens. It is best to discard cooked vegetables and meats after 4 days, to avoid contamination.

Peristalsis The coordinated muscle action required to move food physically through the digestive system. This action allows a child to pass a stool. It is critically important for babies and children to have normal, healthy bowel movements; this function can have profound effects on his overall health. The longer a stool sits in the colon and doesn't pass, the more water from the stool is drawn back into the body, which makes the stool hard and painful to pass. For babies and infants, breastmilk or formula aid in regular elimination. But when solid foods are introduced, and typically toward the end of the first year, a child's system must readjust to different foods, consistencies, and fiber. Children must drink plenty of water and eat a variety of fiber-rich fruits and vegetables. Exercise is also important.

Phytic acid A substance found in the tough outer hull of most grains, beans, seeds, and nuts that inhibits the absorption of calcium, iron, and other important nutrients. Much of the phytic acid content of grains and beans can be eliminated by pre-soaking before cooking.

Positive peer pressure Surrounding a picky eater with other children who are not picky, so as to entice the child to try a new, healthy foods that the other children like.

Preformed vitamin A Vitamin A obtained from animal sources, such as chicken liver, whole milk, and eggs.

Protein A macronutrient that is made up of amino acids. Protein is important for supporting the structural and functional operations of the body. They help build cells, especially muscles and bones, and support the body's communication system.

Provitamin A carotenoids Plant sources of vitamin A, which are converted into retinol by the body. Good sources are carrots, sweet potatoes, pumpkin, and spinach.

Pyloric stenosis A condition that affects the gastrointestinal tract of an infant (or adult). Technically, it is a narrowing of the pylorus, the lower part of the stomach through which food and other stomach contents pass to enter the small intestine. Food then is prevented from emptying out of the stomach, and as a reflex, food comes back up. Symptoms to note are vomiting (with the baby being hungry again soon after), fewer stools, failure to gain weight, and lethargy. Pyloric stenosis is common—it affects 3 out of 1,000 infants in the United States, and is more likely to occur in male babies. It usually occurs between 2 weeks and 2 months of age. Surgery is often recommended to relieve the obstruction (called a pylormoyotomy). Before this, however, you may want to eliminate cow-based milk products, which have been shown to be the cause of 40 percent of acid reflux problems in infants (acid reflux also causes food to rebound).

Real food Food that comes from plants and animals in their natural state, without a lot of added sugar, salt, or chemicals. Real foods are packed with healthy nutrients, and are also sometimes referred to as nutrient dense.

Retinol The form in which vitamin A from animal sources is absorbed into the body.

Rooting reflex Also called the search reflex, it causes the baby to naturally open his mouth wide when he is hungry. If a baby's cheek is lightly brushed with a finger or any soft object, the baby will turn toward the object and attempt to suck. It allows the baby to get a good latch on the nipple to aid breastfeeding. This reflex disappears around 4 months of age.

Safety latches Latches that secure cabinet doors and drawers to help prevent children from gaining access to potentially harmful household items, such as medicines, household cleaners, and sharp objects. The Center for Science in the Public Interest recommends latches that are easy to install, but are sturdy enough to withstand pulls and tugs from children. While the latches are not a guarantee of protection, they can make it more difficult for a child to reach dangerous substances.

Satiety The feeling of fullness or satisfaction that is experienced after the consumption of food.

Silicone nipples Firmer than latex and hold their shape longer.

Sleep apnea A common disorder where one or more pauses in breathing or shallow breaths occur during sleep. This is usually a chronic condition that often goes undiagnosed since it occurs only during sleep. It results in a poor quality of sleep, which, in turn, can lead to excessive daytime sleepiness. Sleep apnea can increase the risk for high blood pressure, heart attacks, stroke, diabetes, and obesity.

Slow-flow nipple A nipple that limits the flow of formula to an amount that is manageable by the infant. The hole at the tip of the nipple is smaller than on other nipples.

Sodium nitrite or nitrate A preservative used in bacon, ham, hot dogs, lunch meats, smoked fish, and other processed meats. These additives are used to preserve shelf life and prevent bacterial growth, but they may also lead to the formation of cancer-causing chemicals called nitrosamines.

Solid foods Any dietary sustenance that is not in liquid form.

Standard American Diet (S.A.D.) A diet in which too few nutrient-rich foods and too many high-calorie and low nutrient foods are consumed.

Sudden infant death syndrome (SIDS) The sudden death of an infant under one year of age that remains unexplained after investigation. According to the American Sudden Infant Death Institute, about 2,500 infant deaths each year are classified as SIDS.

Teflon A chemical manufactured by DuPont used as a nonstick coating on pans. At high temperatures (500° F), this chemical has been shown to deteriorate. That means that at high heat, the fumes are released from the nonstick surface. In 2005, the Environmental Protection Agency found that the chemical used to make Teflon (PFOA) is potentially carcinogenic to humans, and it has also been shown to cause tumors and infertility in lab rats. Teflon can be found not only in pans, but also on clothes, in stain repellents, in food packaging, and in cosmetics.

Tempered glass Glass that absorbs heat well. This means that when you cook with a baking dish made of tempered glass, it will take longer for the glass to reach oven temperature, and retain that temperature longer when you remove it from the oven. "Tempered" means that the glass is oven safe and can withstand temperatures over 500° F.

Tongue-thrust reflex (extrusion reflex) The natural process by which an infant's tongue automatically moves forward in the mouth. This reflex exists in infancy because it helps a baby feed from a bottle or the breast. It usually fades around 3 or 4 months of age. If you begin to feed the baby solid foods at this time and it appears as if she is pushing the food out of her mouth, it may just be because of this reflex, and not a dislike of food. In this case, a tongue thrust is a sign that your baby may not be ready to eat solid foods.

Trans fats Fats that are chemically altered to become more shelf stable. Trans fats are created during the food-manufacturing process when vegetable oils undergo hydrogenation. These fats are also bleached and deodorized to make them more palatable.

Unpasteurized Food that has not been pasteurized. Raw milk is an example of an unpasteurized food.

U.S. Department of Agriculture (USDA) The government agency responsible for regulating the safety and development of food, agriculture, and natural resources.

Vegans Vegetarians who choose not to eat animal products of any kind, including honey. Not recommended for children by the American Academy of Pediatrics.

Vegetarian version of Standard American Diet A vegetarian diet that includes sugar and junk food with lots of nutrient-dense proteins and healthy fats.

Vegetarianism A diet that excludes animal meats, poultry, or fish, and is primarily plant based.

Vitamin A A fat-soluble vitamin that is critical for infant vision, bone, tissue, and immune system development. Most infants are low in vitamin A.

Vitamins Substances that occur in many foods that are essential to the nutrition and normal metabolic functioning of the body. Vitamins are either fat-soluble (vitamins A, D, E, and K) or water-soluble (vitamin C and the B vitamins).

Wild caught As the name implies, this label is used for fish caught in the wild, thus no antibiotics are used and the fish cannot be processed with additives of any kind. Wild caught fish, however, are subject to ocean toxins, such as mercury and PCBs, and wide scale fishing of this type is contributing to depletion of some natural fish populations.

Index

Acetic acid, 166–167, 355

Agar agar, 243

Agave nectar, 91, 101, 109, 120, 165, 180, 243

Alpha-carotene, 126, 355

American Dietetic Association (ADA), 40, 42, 350, 355

Amino acids, 24, 25, 355. *See also* Proteins

Amniotic fluid, 23, 355

Anaphylaxis, 97–98, 347, 356

Anemia, 33, 45, 114, 121, 128, 363

Anodized aluminum, 156, 356

Anti-vacuum or vented nipples, 86–87, 356

Apgar scoring, 57, 356

Appetite. *See* Hunger/fullness cues

ARA (arachidonic acid), 82, 356

Artificial additives, 16–17

Asthma and asthma medications, 3, 5, 75, 185, 188, 189, 201, 227, 356

Baby fat, 125, 357

Baby food cube concept, 137, 357

Bacteria, 109, 155; beneficial, 99, 244; cutting boards and, 155; defined, 357; mastitis and, 64; mushrooms and, 312; preventing/killing, 14, 17, 83, 160–162, 166–167, 170, 173, 176; soft cheeses and, 109

Baking, 171–172

Batching, 166, 173, 182, 357

Beans. *See* Grains and beans

Beta-carotene, 126, 357

Bibs, 106

Birthday cakes, 307

Blanching, 170–171

Blood sugar, 13. *See also* Carbohydrates; 2- to 3-year-olds and, 137, 138; balancing, 25, 28–29, 137, 215, 332; defined, 357; high/low, 17; protein and, 25; roller coaster, 17–18, 22, 28, 40; S.A.D. and, 17–18; snacks and, 138; vegetarian diets and, 40

BMI (Body Mass Index), 357

Book overview, IX

Boosters. *See* Invisible nutrition

Bottle brush, 87, 357

Bottle drying rack, 87, 357

Bottle-feeding. *See* Formula

Bottles. *See* Nipples and bottles

Botulism, 91, 180

Boundaries, setting, 134–136

BPA-free plastic, 84–86, 159, 358

Bragg liquid aminos, 243

Breads. *See* Muffin, bread, cookie, and cake recipes

Breast care, 69

Breastfeeding, 55–81; at 12- to 18-months, 122; after C-section, 57–58; assessing proper intake, 67. *See also* hunger/fullness signs; baby gas and, 78–79; baby weight loss and, 67; benefits of, 4–6, 55; as best choice, 55; burping baby after, 64–65, 80; challenge and success, 58; childhood weight problems and, 4–5, 10; colic and, 5, 79, 98, 222, 245–246, 359; colostrum and, 56, 58, 59, 61, 69, 359; defined, 358; drugs, alcohol, cigarettes and, 73; early weeks of, 61–62; eating enough and, 67; engorgement and, 61, 62–63, 64, 106–107, 360; extended nursing, 122, 360; first session and days of, 56–59; flat nipples and, 60–61; frequency of, 65; full feedings, 64; getting good latch, 57, 59–61; hind milk and, 64, 362; hunger/fullness signs, 65–67, 68; letdown, 68, 78, 363; mastitis and, 64, 364; medications and, 74–76; nipple discomfort and, 63; not giving up, 77–78; nutrition for moms, 69–73; others wanting to feed baby when, 79–80; positions, 76–77; preparing for, 56; resources, 346; rooting reflex, 59, 68, 367; spitting up after, 68–69; support and resources, 77–78; 100-step success summary, 68; training taste buds and, 6–7; vegans and vegetarians, 33; weaning from, 106–107; work and, 100

Breastmilk. *See also* Breastfeeding: as best choice, 55; exclusive use of, 4; foods affecting taste of, 5; formula milk and, 88; nutritional value of, 24–25, 26, 27, 29, 33, 43, 44, 45, 55, 93; nutrition guidelines for moms producing, 69–73; pumping. *See* Breast pumps; storing, thawing, serving, 80–81, 175

Breast pads, 63, 69, 100, 358

Breast pumps, 60–62, 80, 345–346, 358

Broiling, 171

Burping baby, 64–65, 80

Cake, cookie, bread and muffin recipes, 257–265, 304–310

Calcium, 30, 31, 44, 46, 121, 122, 127, 130, 135, 141

Calories: by age, 35; boosters, 288; defined, 36, 358

Cancer, childhood, 3, 17, 358

Carbohydrates: for baby and toddler, 26–29; categories of, 29; defined, 358; functions and characteristics, 26–29, 34

Cardiovascular disease, childhood, 3, 359
Celiac disease, 113–114
Choking, 111–113, 131–132
Cholesterol: carbohydrates, fiber and, 27; essential fatty acids and, 26; foods improving levels, 49; high, defined, 362; obesity and, 3; reading labels and, 36, 38; soy products and, 49; vegetarian diets and, 49
Colic, 5, 79, 98, 222, 245–246, 359
Colostrum, 56, 58, 59, 61, 69, 359
Constipation, 18, 27, 33, 70, 134
Cookie, cake, bread, and muffin recipes, 257–265, 304–310
Cooking equipment, 154–159, 347, 350
Cooking techniques, 165–177
CPR (cardiopulmonary resuscitation), 113, 131, 359
C-section, breastfeeding after, 57–58
Cube concept (baby food), 137, 357
Cups, starting, 108, 117, 123
Dehydration, 7, 133, 134, 149
Developmental indicators/actions: 4- to 6-month-olds, 91–93; 6- to 9-month-olds, 101–102; 9- to12-month-olds, 110–113; 12- to 18-month-olds, 124–128; 18-month- to three-year-olds, 136–140
DHA (docosahexaenoic acid), 82, 359
Diabetes, 3, 5, 15, 359
Diarrhea, 5, 97, 98, 99, 114, 133–134
Dietary Guidelines for Americans, 91, 359–360
Distractions, minimizing, 108, 146
Divided plates, 145, 360
Drink recipes, 329–332
80 Percent rule, 336
Electrolytes, 133, 360
Energy: eating for, 258; need, fiber and, 42–43
Engorgement, 61, 62–63, 64, 106–107, 360
Epazote, 243
Extended nursing, 122, 360
Extrusion reflex (tongue-thrust reflex), 92, 360, 368–369
Factory farming, 41, 360
Fats or fatty acids: for baby and toddler, 25–26; defined, 360; functions and characteristics, 25–26, 34; shopping guide, 165
Feeding child (birth to 4 months). *See* Breastfeeding; Breastmilk; Formula
Feeding child (4 to 6 months), 89–100; allergic reactions and. *See* Food allergies; best foods, 89–90; breast- or bottle feeding, 89–90; comforting without food, 99; developmental indicators/actions and, 91–93; foods to avoid, 90–91; healthy strategies for raising natural eaters, 99–100;

introducing solid foods, 90, 93–95; preparing meals, 168
Feeding child (6 to 9 months), 100–108; best foods, 100–101, 102–103; developmental indicators/actions and, 101–102, 107–108; foods to avoid, 101; gear for (chairs, bibs, mats), 104–106; healthy strategies for raising natural eaters, 107–108; portion guides and meal planning, 102–104; weaning from breast, 106–107
Feeding child (9 to 12 months), 108–118; best foods, 108–109, 114–116; breast- or bottle feeding, 109; developmental indicators/actions and, 110–113; foods to avoid, 109–110; getting enough food, 111; portion guides and meal planning, 114–116; preparing meals, 168–169
Feeding child (12 to 18 months), 119–136; about: becoming toddler and, 119; appetite and, 124–125; best drinks, 121–123; best foods, 119–120, 129; developmental indicators/actions and, 124–128; foods to avoid, 120–121; key nutrients, 125–128; portion guides and meal planning, 129–130; setting boundaries and, 134–136; strategies for raising natural eaters, 132–136
Feeding child (18 months to 3 years), 136–149; balancing act, 137; best foods, 140–142; daily nutrition guide, 141; developmental indicators/actions and, 136–140; eating enough and, 138–139; eating out and traveling, 148–149; engaging their interest, 137–138; finicky eaters, 144–148; mealtime rhythm and routine, 142–144; our food beliefs and, 140; overweight children, 139–140; portion guides and meal planning, 140–142; preparing meals, 168–169; role model for, 142; snacks, 136–137; strategies for raising natural eaters, 142–149; underweight children, 139; unemotional approach to, 136
Feeding readiness, 89, 93, 360–361
Fiber: benefits of, 18–19; boosters, 288; carbohydrates and, 26, 27–28; constipation and, 18, 27, 134; defined, 361; energy needs and, 42–43; higher-quality foods and, 163; junk foods and, 13; lack of, 18; protein and, 25; reading labels and, 36, 37, 38; recommendations for 1- to 3-year-olds, 28
Finger foods, 211–212
Finicky eaters, 138, 144–148, 310, 361
5-A-Day Campaign, 142, 355
Flaxseed and oil, 243
Floor mats, 106
Fluorosis, 31, 361